WORKBOOK AND LAB MANUAL
by Eric Figueras and Lisa Nalbone to Accompany

¡ARRIBA!
Comunicación y cultura
Fourth Edition

Eduardo Zayas-Bazán and Susan M. Bacon

Taken from:
Workbook and Lab Manual by Eric Figueras and Lisa Nalbone to Accompany ¡Arriba!: Comunicación y cultura, Fourth Edition
by Eduardo Zayas-Bazán and Susan M. Bacon

Taken from:

Workbook and Lab Manual by Eric Figueras and Lisa Nalbone to Accompany ¡Arriba!: Comunicación y cultura, Fourth Edition
by Eduardo Zayas-Bazán and Susan M. Bacon

Published by Pearson Prentice Hall
Upper Saddle River, New Jersey 07458

This special edition published in cooperation with Pearson Custom Publishing.

Printed in the United States of America

10 9 8 7 6 5 4 3 2 1

ISBN 0-536-91308-0

2005320003

EH

Please visit our web site at *www.pearsoncustom.com*

PEARSON CUSTOM PUBLISHING
75 Arlington Street, Suite 300, Boston, MA 02116
A Pearson Education Company

CONTENTS

NOTE TO THE STUDENT

This ***Workbook/Lab Manual*** was created to accompany ***¡Arriba! Comunicación y cultura, Fourth Edition*** and ***Brief Edition.***

The ***Workbook*** activities are designed to help you further develop your reading and writing skills while practicing the vocabulary and grammar points featured in your textbook. Each lesson in the ***Workbook*** segments corresponds to the topics presented in your textbook and is divided into three sections: **Primera parte, Segunda parte,** and **Nuestro mundo.** Each **parte** focuses on the particular vocabulary and grammar points of the textbook and is divided into three subsections: **¡Así es la vida!, ¡Así lo decimos! Vocabulario,** and **¡Así lo hacemos! Estructuras.** The **Nuestro mundo** section is divided into two subsections: **Panoramas** and **Taller.** The **Panoramas** section provides an opportunity to further explore the cultural aspects presented in the textbook. The **Taller** section allows you to enhance your reading and writing skills through a variety of practical approaches, including Internet searches and open-ended writing exercises. Finally, the **¿Cuánto sabes tú?** section provides additional opportunities to review the main grammatical points studied in each lesson.

The purpose of the ***Lab Manual*** segments is to serve as a rewarding experience that will enhance your proficiency in Spanish. Take full advantage of all that the ***Lab Manual*** segments have to offer. When you have completed the ***Lab Manual*** activities, take the time to work on your pronunciation to improve your oral proficiency in Spanish. Each of the activities blends grammar and vocabulary topics from the textbook to provide optimum learning to you, the student. The ***Lab Manual*** segments were designed, in part, based on comments from students who have enjoyed using the text since its first edition. They also reflect improvements based on years of experience in using ***¡Arriba! Comunicación y cultura.*** If you feel that the speakers on the audio go too fast, you are not alone. There are several ways that you can improve your understanding:

- Listen to the audio a while longer to pinpoint the trouble spots and to pick up the gist of the exercise.
- After you have determined the trouble spots, listen to the audio again, with your textbook open to the corresponding pages.
- If needed, ask your professor to show you the Audioscript.

Although this method might take a little extra time, your efforts will start to pay off quickly. By listening to the audio and repeating what you hear, you will gain valuable skills in speaking Spanish. Because the activities in the ***Lab Manual*** segments carefully match the content of the textbook, you are very likely to fill in any comprehension gaps.

¡Bienvenidos!

Nombre: ______________________ Fecha: ______________

1 Hola, ¿qué tal?

Workbook

Primera parte

¡Así es la vida!

1-1 Saludos y despedidas. Reread the conversations in **¡Así es la vida!** on page 4 of your textbook and indicate whether each statement is true (**C: cierto**) or false (**F: falso**).

En la cola

C F 1. El chico se llama Jorge Hernández.

C F 2. La chica se llama Elena Acosta.

En clase

C F 3. La estudiante se llama María Luisa Gómez.

C F 4. La profesora se llama profesora Gómez.

En el pasillo

C F 5. Jorge está muy bien.

C F 6. Rosa está muy mal.

En la biblioteca

C F 7. José Manuel no está muy bien.

C F 8. La señora Peñalver está bastante bien.

Nombre: ______________________ Fecha: ______________________

¡Así lo decimos! Vocabulario

1-2 ¿Saludo o despedida? Decide if each expression should be used as a **saludo** or **despedida**, and choose the correct answer.

1. Adiós.

   a. saludo b. despedida

2. Hasta pronto.

   a. saludo b. despedida

3. Hasta mañana.

   a. saludo b. despedida

4. Hasta luego.

   a. saludo b. despedida

5. Buenos días.

   a. saludo b. despedida

6. Buenas noches.

   a. saludo b. despedida

7. ¿Qué hay?

   a. saludo b. despedida

8. ¡Hola!

   a. saludo b. despedida

1-3 ¿Formal o informal? Imagine that you are at a party in which you talk to friends as well as older people you don't know. How would you ask a friend and then a stranger the following questions? Match the question in English with the correct question in Spanish.

1. How are you? (*friend*)
2. How are you? (*stranger*)
3. And you? (*friend*)
4. And you? (*stranger*)
5. How's it going? (*friend*)
6. How's it going? (*stranger*)
7. What's your name? (*friend*)
8. What's your name? (*stranger*)

a. ¿Y usted?
b. ¿Cómo te llamas?
c. ¿Cómo estás?
d. ¿Cómo se llama usted?
e. ¿Cómo te va?
f. ¿Cómo está usted?
g. ¿Y tú?
h. ¿Cómo le va?

Nombre: ______________________________ Fecha: ______________________

1-4 Respuestas. Imagine that you are speaking with several friends and strangers at the party. How would you respond to the following questions or statements? Choose the most appropriate answer.

1. ¿Qué tal?

   a. ¡Buenos días! b. Más o menos. c. ¿Cómo te llamas?

2. ¡Buenos días!

   a. ¡Buenos días! b. Hasta luego. c. Mucho gusto.

3. ¡Hasta mañana!

   a. ¿Y usted? b. Adiós. c. ¿Cómo te va?

4. ¿Cómo te va?

   a. Hola. b. Hasta pronto. c. Bastante bien.

5. ¡Buenas noches!

   a. ¡Buenos días! b. No muy bien. c. ¡Buenas noches!

6. ¡Mucho gusto!

   a. Más o menos. b. Igualmente. c. Gracias.

7. ¿Cómo estás?

   a. ¿Qué tal? b. No muy bien. c. Hasta pronto.

1-5 Conversaciones. Complete each conversation logically by writing in the appropriate words or phrases. Select from the list provided for each set.

1. adiós cómo estás gracias tú usted

Sr. Morales: Hola, Felipe! ¿______________________?

Felipe: Muy bien, ______________________. ¿Y ______________________, señor Morales?

Sr. Morales: No muy bien.

Felipe: ______________________, señor.

Nombre: ______________________ Fecha: ______________________

2. buenas tardes   el gusto es   gusto   me llamo

Enrique: Buenas tardes.

Carlos: ¡______________________! ¿Cómo se llama usted?

Enrique: ______________________ Enrique Fernández.

Carlos: Mucho ______________________.

Enrique: ______________________ mío.

3. adiós   buenos días   cómo está usted   muy bien

Felipe: Buenos días, profesor Rodríguez.

Prof. Rodríguez: ______________________, Felipe.

Felipe: ¿______________________?

Prof. Rodríguez: ______________________, gracias.

Felipe: Hasta luego.

Prof. Rodríguez: ______________________.

4. bien   cómo estás   tú

Juana: Hola, Jorge, ¿______________________?

Jorge: Más o menos, Juana, ¿y ______________________?

Juana: ______________________, gracias.

¡Así lo hacemos! Estructuras

1. The Spanish alphabet

1-6 Emparejar. Match the Spanish letter with the correct explanation.

____ 1. Spanish **g**

____ 2. Spanish **k**

____ 3. Spanish **b**

____ 4. Spanish **y**

____ 5. Spanish **z**

a. letter that can be a semivowel or a consonant

b. letter that is pronounced like the English *th* in much of Spain

c. letter that is pronounced like the hard English *h* before *e* or *i*

d. letter that appears in words borrowed from other languages

e. one of two letters that are pronounced exactly alike

Nombre: ______________________ Fecha: ______________________

2. The numbers 0–100

1-7 Más números. Complete the following sequences in a logical manner.

1. ______________, catorce, quince, dieciséis, ______________
2. ______________, diez, doce, catorce, ______________
3. ______________, veinte, veintiuno, veintidós, ______________
4. ______________, treinta y seis, cuarenta y siete, cincuenta y ocho, ______________
5. ______________, sesenta, setenta, ochenta, ______________
6. ______________, treinta, veintinueve, veintiocho, ______________
7. ______________, ochenta, ochenta y cinco, noventa, ______________
8. ______________, sesenta y seis, setenta y siete, ochenta y ocho, ______________
9. ______________, siete, cinco, tres, ______________
10. ______________, treinta, cuarenta y cinco, sesenta y uno, ______________

1-8 Las matemáticas. Imagine that Pedro is practicing his math facts. How would he complete each of the following equations? Write the missing number in Spanish.

1. Once menos ______________ son dos.
2. Treinta más ______________ son noventa.
3. Ochenta menos ______________ son diez.
4. Tres por ______________ son cuarenta y ocho.
5. Quince entre ______________ son cinco.
6. Dos por ______________ son cuarenta.
7. Cien menos ______________ son cuarenta y nueve.
8. Doce entre ______________ son dos.
9. Once más ______________ son treinta y dos.
10. Ocho entre ______________ son dos.

Nombre: ______________________ Fecha: ______________________

1-9 Números de teléfonos. Write the telephone number in each advertisement in Spanish.

1. Número Uno Taxi ______________________

2. Plazas de Garaje ______________________

3. The days of the week, the months, and the seasons

1-10 Los días de la semana. Write, in Spanish, the day of the week that completes the sequence.

1. martes, ______________________, jueves
2. domingo, ______________________, martes
3. miércoles, ______________________, viernes
4. lunes, ______________________, miércoles
5. jueves, ______________________, sábado
6. sábado, ______________________, lunes
7. viernes, ______________________, domingo

Nombre: ______________________ Fecha: ______________________

1-11 Los meses del año. Complete by writing in Spanish the missing month in sequence.

1. enero, febrero, ______________________
2. ______________________, julio, agosto
3. noviembre, diciembre, ______________________
4. mayo, ______________________, julio
5. ______________________, octubre, noviembre
6. marzo, ______________________, mayo
7. ______________________, septiembre, octubre
8. ______________________, mayo, junio

1-12 Los días, los meses y las estaciones. Circle all the days of the week, the months, and the seasons in the puzzle.

C	O	D	I	C	I	E	M	B	R	E	V	O	S
E	P	S	S	E	T	R	A	M	U	I	A	S	A
A	B	R	I	L	T	E	D	A	E	U	G	E	B
J	A	N	I	N	V	I	E	R	N	O	O	P	A
U	U	O	V	M	A	E	N	Z	A	T	S	T	D
E	J	L	A	A	A	E	R	O	M	O	T	I	O
V	U	E	I	Y	S	V	C	A	O	Ñ	O	E	G
E	N	E	R	O	R	A	E	T	N	O	L	M	N
S	I	T	F	E	B	R	E	R	O	O	O	B	I
T	O	O	C	T	U	B	R	E	A	O	M	R	M
N	O	V	I	E	M	B	R	E	A	S	R	E	O
L	U	N	E	S	E	L	O	C	R	E	I	M	D

Nombre: ______________________ Fecha: ______________________

1-13 ¿Cierto o falso? Read the following statements and indicate whether the statement is **cierto (C)** or **falso (F).**

C F 1. El invierno es en enero.

C F 2. Abril tiene treinta días.

C F 3. Hay (*there are*) once meses en un año.

C F 4. El verano tiene un mes.

C F 5. La Navidad es en la primavera.

C F 6. El día de los enamorados es en agosto.

C F 7. Agosto tiene treinta y un días.

C F 8. Hay dos estaciones en un año.

SEGUNDA PARTE

¡Así es la vida!

1-14 Fuera de lugar. Choose the letter corresponding to the word that does not fit in each group.

1. a. papel
   b. libros
   c. cuaderno
   d. puerta

2. a. silla
   b. lápiz
   c. mesa
   d. puerta

3. a. el estudiante
   b. el mapa
   c. la estudiante
   d. la profesora

4. a. bolígrafo
   b. reloj
   c. lápiz
   d. papel

Nombre: ______________________ Fecha: ______________________

¡Así lo decimos! Vocabulario

1-15 En la clase. Imagine that you are a Spanish instructor. How would you tell your students to do the following?

MODELO: Tell a student to write in Spanish.
Escriba (Escribe) en español.

1. Tell a student to answer in Spanish.

   ____

2. Tell students to listen.

   ____

3. Tell a student to go to the board.

   ____

4. Tell students to study the lesson.

   ____

5. Tell a student to read the lesson.

   ____

6. Tell a student to close the book.

   ____

1-16 ¿Qué hay en la mochila? Imagine that a classmate has invited you to have lunch with him and his family. His little brother is very curious about what you have in your book bag. Answer his questions based on the model.

MODELO: ¿Qué hay en la mochila? (books)
Hay unos libros.

¿Qué hay en la mochila?

1. (*pencils*) Hay ______________________.
2. (*pens*) Hay ______________________.
3. (*a notebook*) Hay ______________________.
4. (*a map*) Hay ______________________.
5. (*papers*) Hay ______________________.

Nombre: ______________________ Fecha: ______________________

1-17 ¿Qué hay en la clase? Write at least seven items that are in your classroom.

MODELO: *Hay una pizarra.*

1. ______________________
2. ______________________
3. ______________________
4. ______________________
5. ______________________
6. ______________________
7. ______________________

1-18 En la librería. Imagine that you are taking inventory in a bookstore warehouse. Write out, in Spanish, the number of each item you have in stock. Make the necessary changes to keep gender agreement between the number and the item.

1. 21 ______________________ mesas
2. 31 ______________________ bolígrafos
3. 66 ______________________ lápices
4. 16 ______________________ relojes
5. 1 ______________________ mapa
6. 30 ______________________ diccionarios
7. 71 ______________________ cuadernos
8. 100 ______________________ libros
9. 10 ______________________ sillas
10. 18 ______________________ mochilas

Nombre: ______________________ Fecha: ______________________

1-19 Los colores. Find and circle the names of ten colors in the puzzle.

E	D	M	A	L	B	M	H	J	F	Y
S	A	Z	U	L	O	D	A	S	O	R
T	D	M	A	R	R	O	N	E	E	C
R	A	N	A	R	A	N	J	A	D	O
A	C	D	L	R	S	H	O	R	R	A
O	O	P	M	C	I	I	D	G	E	E
W	S	O	J	O	R	L	E	S	V	N
P	U	E	N	D	G	N	L	S	T	E
Ñ	D	P	O	Q	U	R	I	O	R	B

1-20 Los antónimos. Match the opposite adjectives in the following lists.

_____ 1. simpático	a. inteligente
_____ 2. interesante	b. caro
_____ 3. grande	c. mala
_____ 4. tonto	d. pequeña
_____ 5. buena	e. perezoso (*lazy*)
_____ 6. trabajador	f. aburrido
_____ 7. barato	g. antipático
_____ 8. tímida	h. extrovertida

Nombre: ______________________ Fecha: ______________________

¡Así lo hacemos! Estructuras

4. Nouns and articles

1-21 El artículo definido. Write the correct form of the definite article for each noun.

1. ____________ sillas
2. ____________ pupitres (*student desks*)
3. ____________ relojes
4. ____________ mesa
5. ____________ pizarras
6. ____________ borrador (*eraser*)
7. ____________ papel
8. ____________ mapa
9. ____________ mochila
10. ____________ bolígrafo

1-22 El artículo indefinido. Write the correct form of the indefinite article for each noun.

1. ____________ lápiz
2. ____________ relojes
3. ____________ mochila
4. ____________ silla
5. ____________ mapas
6. ____________ tiza
7. ____________ pupitres
8. ____________ escritorio (*desk*)
9. ____________ pizarras
10. ____________ mesa

1-23 ¡A cambiar! Change the gender of each noun.

Modelo: el profesor
la profesora

1. el señor ____________
2. el hombre ____________
3. el alumno ____________
4. la estudiante ____________
5. el chico ____________
6. la niña ____________
7. la mujer ____________
8. la muchacha ____________

Nombre: ______________________ Fecha: ______________

1-24 ¿Masculino o femenino? Indicate whether the following nouns are masculine or feminine by placing an **M** or **F** before each noun.

1. ________ libro
2. ________ microscopio
3. ________ clase
4. ________ mapa
5. ________ pupitre
6. ________ tiza
7. ________ lápiz
8. ________ universidad
9. ________ pizarra
10. ________ borrador

1-25 Del plural al singular. Change each phrase from plural to singular.

MODELO: los libros grandes
el libro grande

1. las clases interesantes ______________________
2. unos diccionarios pequeños ______________________
3. los papeles blancos ______________________
4. unos cuadernos anaranjados ______________________
5. las sillas azules ______________________
6. los relojes redondos ______________________
7. los pupitres caros ______________________
8. unas mesas cuadradas ______________________

1-26 En la librería. Imagine that you work at a bookstore. A customer calls and asks if you carry certain items. Complete his questions and the affirmative answers.

MODELO: ¿Hay una mochila?
Sí, hay unas mochilas.

1. a. ¿Hay ________ bolígrafo?
   b. Sí, hay ______________________.
2. a. ¿Hay ________ libros?
   b. Sí, hay ______________________.
3. a. ¿Hay ________ mapa?
   b. Sí, hay ______________________.

Nombre: ______________________ Fecha: ______________________

4. a. ¿Hay __________ lápices?

   b. Sí, hay ______________________________.

5. a. ¿Hay __________ computadora?

   b. Sí, hay ______________________________.

6. a. ¿Hay __________ cuaderno?

   b. Sí, hay ______________________________.

7. a. ¿Hay __________ papeles?

   b. Sí, hay ______________________________.

8. a. ¿Hay __________ pizarra?

   b. Sí, hay ______________________________.

5. Adjective form, position, and agreement

1-27 ¡A completar! Fill in the blanks with the correct forms of the words in parentheses.

MODELO: *la* pizarra *negra* (el / negro)

1. __________ relojes ______________________ (un / caro)
2. __________ señoritas ______________________ (el / antipático)
3. __________ señora ______________________ (el / trabajador)
4. __________ profesores ______________________ (un / aburrido)
5. __________ profesora ______________________ (un / interesante)
6. __________ clase ______________________ (el / grande)
7. __________ luces ______________________ (el / amarilla)
8. __________ libros ______________________ (el / azul)

Nombre: ______________________ Fecha: ______________________

1-28 No... Tony likes to practice Spanish with his friend Isabel, but he sometimes uses the wrong gender. How would Isabel correct the following questions? Fill in the blanks following the model.

MODELO: ¿Es una estudiante mala?
No, es un estudiante malo.

1. ¿Son unos señores extrovertidos?

   No, son ______________________.

2. ¿Son unos profesores simpáticos?

   No, son ______________________.

3. ¿Es un estudiante tímido?

   No, es ______________________.

4. ¿Es una señorita fascinante?

   No, es ______________________.

5. ¿Es una estudiante inteligente?

   No, es ______________________.

6. ¿Son unos profesores aburridos?

   No, son ______________________.

7. ¿Es una señora buena?

   No, es ______________________.

8. ¿Son unas señoritas trabajadoras?

   No, son ______________________.

1-29 En general. Imagine that a friend is making observations about things at the university or in your class. Complete the sentence with the the correct answer.

MODELO: Los libros negros son...
baratos.

1. Los escritorios marrones son...

   a. caro. b. caros. c. caras. d. cara.

2. Las mochilas grises son...

   a. caro. b. caros. c. caras. d. cara.

3. Los relojes grandes son...
   a. barata. b. baratas. c. baratos. d. barato.
4. Las mesas son...
   a. blancos. b. blanca. c. blancas. d. blanco.
5. Los cuadernos son...
   a. amarillo. b. amarillos. c. amarilla. d. amarillas.
6. Los estudiantes son...
   a. trabajadoras. b. trabajador. c. trabajadores. d. trabajadora.
7. Las clases son...
   a. aburrida. b. aburridos. c. aburrido. d. aburridas.
8. Los libros en la mesa son...
   a. pequeño. b. pequeños. c. pequeñas. d. pequeña.

1-30 En clase. Complete the following descriptions of people and objects you know. Use colors, adjectives of nationality, or descriptive adjectives.

1. El libro de español es ______________________.
2. El cuaderno es ______________________.
3. El/La profesor/a es ______________________.
4. Las sillas son ______________________.
5. Los estudiantes son ______________________.
6. La pizarra es ______________________.

Nombre: ______________________ Fecha: ______________

6. Subject pronouns and the present tense of *ser* (to be)

1-31 Los sujetos. Choose the corresponding subject pronoun for each person or group of people.

1. Charo
   a. yo b. usted c. ella
2. Susana y yo
   a. ellos/as b. nosotros/as c. yo
3. Quique y Paco
   a. ellos b. nosotros c. vosotros
4. Las profesoras
   a. ellas b. ustedes c. ellos
5. Tú y yo
   a. nosotros/as b. ellos/as c. vosotros
6. Ustedes y yo
   a. ustedes b. nosotros/as c. vosotros
7. Francisco
   a. él b. ella c. tú
8. Anita, Carmen y Pepe
   a. yo b. ellos c. ellas
9. Lucia, Mercedes y Lola
   a. tú b. ellos c. ellas
10. Beto y las estudiantes
    a. nosotros b. ellos c. ustedes
11. Mongo y ellas
    a. ellas b. ellos c. ustedes
12. Toño y tú
    a. nosotros/as b. ustedes c. usted

1-32 Francisco Figueres Rivera. Complete Francisco's description with the correct form of the verb **ser.**

¡Hola! Me llamo Francisco Figueres Rivera y mi apodo (1) __________ Paco. (2) __________ de Sevilla, (3) __________ español. Mi papá (4) __________ colombiano y mi mamá (5) __________ española. Mis padres (6)__________ muy trabajadores. Mis padres y yo (7) __________ muy simpáticos. ¿De dónde (8) __________ tú? ¿Cómo (9) __________ tú, y cómo (10) __________ tu clase de español?

Nombre: ______________________ Fecha: ______________________

1-33 Identidades. Use the words provided and the correct form of the verb **ser** to form complete sentences or questions. Remember to change the forms of articles and adjectives as necessary.

Modelo: yo / ser / un / alumna / puertorriqueño
Yo soy una alumna puertorriqueña.

1. nosotros / ser / el / profesores / estadounidense

____

2. Ana y Felipe / ser / el / estudiantes / perezoso

____

3. ¿ser / tú / el / estudiante (*female*) / argentino?

____

4. Marisol / ser / un / señora / delgada

____

5. ¿ser / ustedes / el / estudiantes / francés?

____

6. ¿ser / usted / el / señor / mexicano?

____

7. María Eugenia / ser / un / señorita / dominicano

____

8. Mongo y Guille / ser / un / chico / delgado y simpático

____

9. ustedes y yo / ser / español

____

10. Cheo y yo / ser / un / estudiante / inteligente

____

Nombre: ______________________________ Fecha: ____________________

1-34 Combinación. Write at least six sentences in Spanish by combining the appropriate items from each column. Remember to change adjectives when necessary.

yo		venezolano
Pepe y Chayo		argentino
tú		puertorriqueño
Mongo y yo	ser	dominicano
tú y él		trabajador
ella		paciente

1. ____
2. ____
3. ____
4. ____
5. ____
6. ____

1-35 Ramón y Rosario. Complete the conversation between Ramón and Rosario with the correct form of the verb **ser.**

Mongo: Hola, me llamo Ramón Larrea Arias y mi apodo (1) __________ Mongo.

Rosario: Mucho gusto, Mongo. (2) __________ Rosario Vélez Cuadra.

Mongo: ¿De dónde (3) __________?

Rosario: (4) __________ puertorriqueña, ¿y tú?

Mongo: (5) __________ panameño, pero mis padres (6) __________ colombianos.

Rosario: ¿Cómo (7) __________ tu clase de inglés?

Mongo: Mi clase (8) __________ muy interesante y todos nosotros (9) __________ muy trabajadores.

Rosario: Y, ¿cómo (10) __________ la profesora?

Mongo: La profesora (11) __________ muy simpática. Ella (12) __________ canadiense. (13) __________ de la ciudad de Vancouver.

Rosario: ¡Ay! (14) __________ las doce en punto. Mucho gusto, Mongo. Hasta luego.

Mongo: Mucho gusto. Adiós, Rosario.

NUESTRO MUNDO

Panoramas

1-36 ¡A informarse! Based on the information from **Nuestro mundo** on pages 32–33 of your textbook, decide if the following statements are **cierto (C)** or **falso (F).**

1. Hay muchos hispanos en el suroeste de los EE.UU.
2. En las capitales suramericanas no hay rascacielos (*skyscrapers*).
3. Las capitales suramericanas son pequeñas.
4. En muchas capitales hay contaminación (*pollution*).
5. Santa Fe de Bogotá es la capital de Venezuela.
6. El nombre de Santa Fe de Bogotá es de origen indígena y español.
7. Cristóbal Colón llegó (*arrived*) a América en 1492.
8. No hay comunicación entre (*between*) España y las Américas.
9. En la cordillera de los Andes no hace mucho frío.
10. En el Amazonas hay mucha vegetación.

1-37 Tu propia experiencia. Make a list of all the Spanish-speaking countries in the world. Then choose one that you would like to visit and explain why.

Taller

1-38 La comunidad: Una entrevista

Primera fase. Identify a native Spanish speaker at your university or in your community whom you can interview. Write four or five things you might tell or ask him/her.

Segunda fase. Interview the person you identified using the expressions and questions from the **Primera fase.** If no native speakers are available, interview a classmate or your professor.

Nombre: ______________________ Fecha: ______________________

Tercera fase. Summarize the information you learned about the person you interviewed. Include one or two sentences describing his/her personality.

____

____

____

____

1-39 Cultura: Geografía. The geography of the Spanish-speaking world is amazingly varied and beautiful. Select a city or region in the Spanish-speaking world and list the geographical features of that area. How have these features influenced the culture, cuisine, language, and so forth of the Hispanic community? You may write in English, if you wish.

____

____

____

____

1-40 Más allá de las páginas. Identify all the words you know from the poem found on page 36 of your textbook. Replace the adjectives with other adjectives you know, the nouns with other nouns you know, and so forth, and rewrite the poem with all the new words.

____

____

____

____

1-41 La clase. Write a brief paragraph describing your classroom. Name as many objects as you can, including information about number and color. Describe your classmates' nationalities. End with a description of your professor.

____

____

____

____

____

Nombre: ______________________ Fecha: ______________

¿Cuánto sabes tú?

1-42 ¿Sabes saludar y despedirte? Choose the most logical response to each **saludo** or **despedida.**

1. Buenos días.
   a. ¿Y tú?
   b. Buenos días.
   c. Adiós.
   d. Encantado/a.

2. ¿Cómo estás?
   a. Muchas gracias.
   b. Bien, gracias.
   c. Hasta mañana.
   d. Lo siento.

3. Mucho gusto.
   a. ¿Cómo te llamas?
   b. Bien, gracias.
   c. Regular.
   d. El gusto es mío.

4. Hasta mañana.
   a. Hola.
   b. Adiós.
   c. ¿Qué hay?
   d. ¿Y usted?

1-43 ¿Sabes matemáticas? Solve the following calculations. Write out the answer in Spanish.

1. $53 + 14 =$ ______________________.
2. $66 - 33 =$ ______________________.
3. $33 \times 3 =$ ______________________.
4. $10 + 14 =$ ______________________.
5. $20 \times 5 =$ ______________________.

1-44 ¿Sabes los días, meses y estaciones? Fill in the blanks with the corresponding name of the day of the week, the month, or the season.

1. El día de la Independencia es el cuatro de ______________.
2. Navidad es el veinticinco de ______________.
3. El día de San Valentín es el catorce de ______________.
4. Halloween es el treinta y uno de ______________.
5. Los días del fin de semana (*weekend*) son el ______________ y el ______________.

6. En ____________ hace mucho frío (*it's cold*).

7. En ____________ hace mucho calor (*it's hot*).

8. Entre (*between*) el martes y el jueves, hay el ____________.

9. Septiembre, octubre y ____________ son los meses de ____________.

10. Marzo, ____________ y mayo son los meses de ____________.

1-45 ¿Sabes sobre mi escuela? Fill in the blanks with the appropriate form of the verb **ser.**

Hola. (1) ____________ Roberto. Yo (2) ____________ un estudiante trabajador. Mi hermana Julia no (3) ____________ perezosa, ella (4) ____________ trabajadora. En la escuela, las clases (5) ____________ un poco aburridas, pero los profesores (6) ____________ muy inteligentes. Hay veinticuatro estudiantes en mi clase. ¡Ellos (7) ____________ muy simpáticos! Nosotros (8) ____________ muy buenos estudiantes. Mi clase (9) ____________ grande y las paredes (*walls*) (10) ____________ blancas.

Nombre: ______________________ Fecha: ______________________

Lab Manual

PRIMERA PARTE

¡Así es la vida!

1-46 ¿Formal o informal? Listen to the following conversations. After hearing each conversation, indicate with a check mark whether the relationship between the people is formal or informal.

	1	2	3	4	5	6	7	8
Formal								
Informal								

¡Así lo decimos! Vocabulario

1-47 ¡Hola! ¿Qué tal? Listen to the following speakers as they initiate a conversation. Then select the letter that corresponds to the most appropriate response. Finally, listen and repeat as the speaker gives the correct answer.

1. a. Mucho gusto. Yo soy Pablo Santos.
   b. El gusto es mío.
   c. Estoy regular.
2. a. Buenos días.
   b. El gusto es mío.
   c. Bastante bien, gracias.
3. a. Encantada.
   b. El gusto es mío.
   c. Muy bien, ¿y usted?
4. a. Muchas gracias, soy Felipe.
   b. Es Felipe.
   c. Me llamo Felipe.
5. a. Adiós, buenas tardes.
   b. Muy bien, adiós.
   c. Bastante bien, gracias.

Nombre: ______________________ Fecha: ______________________

Pronunciación

The Spanish vowels

Each Spanish vowel consists of one clear, short sound that varies little in pronunciation. The crisp sound contrasts with English where often a vowel consists of two sounds, or diphthonged glides,[1] as in the words *note, mine,* and *made.*

Las vocales. The Spanish vowels are pronounced as follows.

1. The **a** is like *a* in *father.*

   casa **mañana** **papá** **Marta**

2. The **e** is like the sound in the English word *eighty.*

   Pepe **mes** **té** **mete**

3. The **i** is like *e* in the English word *me.*

   ti **sí** **mi** **libro**

4. The **o** is like a shortened *o* in the English word *so.*

   poco **tono** **rosa** **caso**

5. The **u** is like the *oo* sound in the English word *moon.*

   luna **usted** **uno** **Susana**

[1]Pronounce the words given (*note, mine,* and *made*) out loud, listening to the sound of the vowels in each word. You should note a slight change in the sound as you pronounce the vowel's sound. This is a diphthonged glide.

1-48 Las vocales. You will hear a series of Spanish words. Select all letters corresponding to the words that contain the **a** sound.

1. a b c d 2. a b c d 3. a b c d

You will now hear a different series of Spanish words. Select all letters corresponding to the words that contain the **e** sound.

4. a b c d 5. a b c d 6. a b c d

Now listen to a series of Spanish words. Select all letters corresponding to the words that contain the **i** sound.

7. a b c d 8. a b c d 9. a b c d

You will hear another series of words. Select all letters corresponding to those that contain the **o** sound.

10. a b c d 11. a b c d 12. a b c d

For this final series, select all letters corresponding to the words that contain the **u** sound.

13. a b c d 14. a b c d 15. a b c d

Nombre: ______________________ Fecha: ______________

1-49 Imitar. Repeat the following phrases, imitating as closely as possible the speaker's pronunciation.

1. la clase de español
2. ¿Cómo se llama usted?
3. ¿Qué tal, Lola?
4. los siete días de la semana
5. la luz azul

¡Así lo hacemos! Estructuras

1. The Spanish alphabet

1-50 ¿Cuál es la letra? Write down the letters as you hear the speaker spell several phrases aloud. The speaker will confirm your responses.

1. ___ ___ ___ ___ ___ / ___ ___ ___ ___ ___.

2. ___ ___ ___ ___ ___ / ___ ___ ___ ___ ___.

3. ___ ___ ___ / ___ ___ ___ ___.

1-51 ¿Cómo se escribe? Read aloud and spell the following words in Spanish. Then listen and repeat as the speaker gives the correct answer.

Modelo: You see: Marta
You say: *eme-a-ere-te-a*

1. español
2. gracias
3. Jorge
4. Víctor
5. Ricardo
6. regular
7. llama
8. Gutiérrez

2. The numbers 0–100

1-52 Las matemáticas. Write out the correct answers to the following math problems in Spanish. Then listen and repeat as the speaker gives the correct answer.

1. quince más diez

____

2. cincuenta y cuatro menos cuarenta y tres

____

3. ocho por siete

____

4. cuarenta y cinco entre nueve

____

5. sesenta y seis entre tres

____

6. ochenta y tres menos doce

____

7. quince por cuatro

____

8. noventa y nueve entre nueve

____

3. The days of the week, the months, and the seasons

1-53 ¿Qué día es? Complete each statement with the appropriate day of the week. Then listen and repeat as the speaker gives the correct answer.

1. Hoy es lunes, mañana es...
2. Hoy es jueves, mañana es...
3. Hoy es martes, mañana es...
4. Hoy es viernes, mañana es...
5. Hoy es miércoles, mañana es...
6. Hoy es domingo, mañana es...
7. Hoy es sábado, mañana es...

1-54 ¿Cuándo es? Name the date on which the following events occur each year. Then listen and repeat as the speaker gives the correct answer.

1. el primer (*first*) día de primavera
2. el primer día de invierno
3. el primer día de verano
4. el día de la independencia de los EE.UU.
5. el día de San Valentín
6. el día de Navidad (*Christmas*)

1-55 ¿Cuál es la fecha? Give the following dates in Spanish. Then listen and repeat as the speaker gives the correct answer.

1. 15/10
2. 12/2
3. 5/8
4. 16/1
5. 2/11
6. 20/5
7. 7/4
8. 13/3
9. 9/6

Nombre: ______________________ Fecha: ______________________

1-56 Conversaciones. Listen to the following conversations and then write their numbers next to the corresponding picture. You may need to listen to the conversations more than once.

a. ____

c. ____

b. ____

d. ____

SEGUNDA PARTE

¡Así es la vida!

1-57 En la clase. You will hear a conversation that takes place in a classroom. As you listen, check off all the items mentioned in the list. You may need to listen more than once.

____bolígrafo	____libros	____profesor	____sillas
____mapa	____profesora	____cuadernos	____mesa
____puerta	____estudiantes	____mochila	____diccionario
____lápiz	____pizarra	____reloj	____tiza

Nombre: ______________________ Fecha: ______________________

¡Así lo decimos! Vocabulario

1-58 ¡Muchos mandatos! You will hear a teacher giving various commands. In each case, number the picture that corresponds to the command.

a. ___ b. ___ c. ___ d. ___ e. ___ f. ___

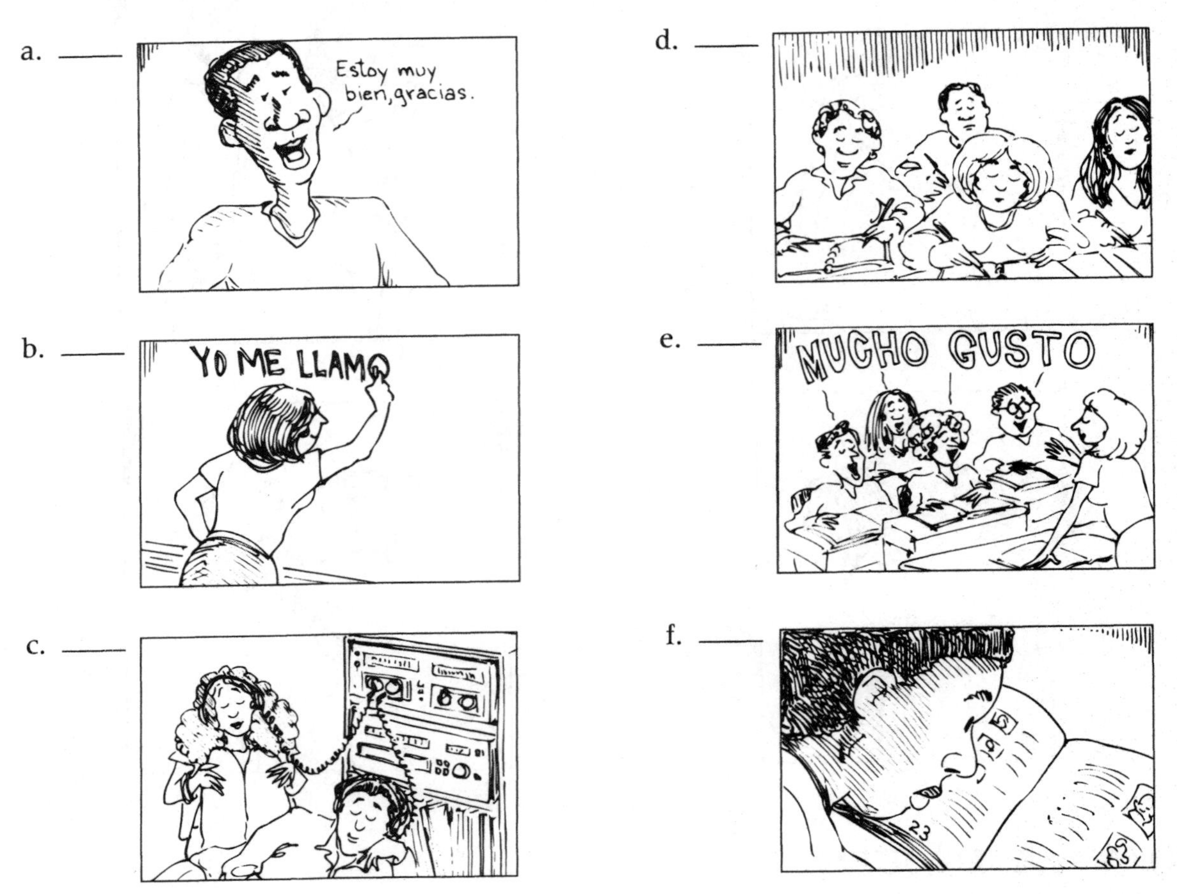

1-59 ¿Pregunta o respuesta? You will hear five sentences. Two of the sentences are questions and three are answers. Your task is to complete the following chart with the sentences you hear on the recording.

PREGUNTA	RESPUESTA
¿Cuántos estudiantes hay?	
	Dos pesos.
	Es una mochila.
¿De qué color es?	
¿Qué hay en la mochila?	

Nombre: ______________________ Fecha: ______________________

Pronunciación

El silabeo (*Syllabification*)

Spanish words are divided into syllables, as follows.

1. Single consonants (including **ch, ll, rr**) are attached to the vowel that follows.

   si-lla **ro-jo** **me-sa** **bo-rra-dor**

2. Two consonants are usually separated.

   tar-des **ver-de** **i-gual-men-te**

3. When a consonant is followed by **l** or **r**, both consonants are attached to the following vowel.

   Pa-blo **Pe-dro**

   However, the combinations **nl, rl, sl, nr,** and **sr** are separated.

   Car-los **is-la** **En-ri-que**

4. In groups of three or more consonants, only the last consonant or the consonant followed by **l** or **r** (with the exceptions listed previously) begins a syllable.

   ins-ta-lar **in-glés** **es-cri-to-rio**

5. Adjacent strong vowels (**a, e,** or **o**) form separate syllables.

   ma-es-tro **le-an**

6. Generally, when there is a combination of a strong vowel (**a, e,** or **o**) with a weak vowel (**i** or **u**) with no accent mark, they form one sound called a *diphthong* and the stress falls on the strong vowel.

   E-duar-do **puer-ta**

   However, the diphthong is broken when the stress falls on either of the weak vowels, **i** or **u.** In these cases, the weak vowel carries a written accent.

   Ma-rí-a **dí-as**

7. When two weak vowels are together, the second of the two is stressed.

   viu-da **bui-tre** **fui**

La acentuación (*Word stress*)

1. Words that end in a vowel or the consonants **n** or **s** are stressed on the next to the last syllable.

   mo-chi-la **Car-los** **re-pi-tan**

2. Words that end in a consonant other than **n** or **s** are stressed on the last syllable.

   us-ted **to-tal** **pro-fe-sor**

3. Words that do not follow the regular stress patterns mentioned require a written accent on the stressed syllable.

   lá-piz **Víc-tor** **lec-ción**

Nombre: ____________________ Fecha: ____________________

4. A written accent is used to differentiate between words that are spelled the same but have different meanings.

   él (*he*) **el** (*the*)

   sí (*yes*) **si** (*if*)

   tú (*you*) **tu** (*your*)

5. A written accent is also used on the stressed syllable of all interrogative (question) words and in exclamatory expressions.

   ¿Cuánto? (*How much?*) **¿Qué?** (*What?*) **¡Qué sorpresa!** (*What a surprise!*)

1-60 Muchas sílabas. You will hear a series of Spanish words. Indicate the correct number of syllables in each word by placing a check mark beside the appropriate number. You will hear the correct answer on the recording.

a. 1 ____ 2 ____ 3 ____ 4 ____

b. 1 ____ 2 ____ 3 ____ 4 ____

c. 1 ____ 2 ____ 3 ____ 4 ____

d. 1 ____ 2 ____ 3 ____ 4 ____

e. 1 ____ 2 ____ 3 ____ 4 ____

f. 1 ____ 2 ____ 3 ____ 4 ____

g. 1 ____ 2 ____ 3 ____ 4 ____

h. 1 ____ 2 ____ 3 ____ 4 ____

i. 1 ____ 2 ____ 3 ____ 4 ____

j. 1 ____ 2 ____ 3 ____ 4 ____

1-61 ¿Dónde está el énfasis? Listen as the speaker pronounces the following listed words and circle the syllable that is stressed.

1. r e l o j
2. p r o f e s o r
3. l á p i z
4. p a p e l
5. b o l í g r a f o
6. e s t u d i a n t e
7. d i c c i o n a r i o
8. L u i s
9. E d u a r d o
10. m o c h i l a

Nombre: ______________________________ Fecha: ____________________

¡Así lo hacemos! Estructuras

4. Nouns and articles

1-62 ¿El, la, los o las? Read each of the following sentences, adding the appropriate form of the definite article when necessary. Then listen and repeat as the speaker gives the correct answer.

1. Es ____ profesora García.
2. Buenas noches, ____ señorita Guzmán.
3. Soy ____ doctora Méndez.
4. Estudien bien ____ mapa.
5. Cierre ____ puerta, por favor.
6. Abran ____ libro en ____ página 29.
7. Son ____ señores Pardo.
8. Pongan ____ lápices en ____ mesa.
9. Escuchen ____ la conversación.
10. Adiós, ____ señorita Peña.

1-63 ¿Qué hay en la clase? Using the cues provided and the appropriate forms of the indefinite articles, answer the question **¿Qué hay en la clase?** Then listen and repeat as the speaker gives the correct answer.

MODELO: You see: puerta
You say: *En la clase hay una puerta.*

1. ventanas
2. reloj
3. diccionarios
4. mapa
5. estudiantes
6. profesora
7. cuadernos
8. lápices
9. sillas
10. libros

Nombre: ______________________ Fecha: ______________________

1-64 ¿Qué hay en la clase? Answer the question **¿Qué hay en la clase?** using the cues provided. Then listen and repeat as the speaker gives the correct answer.

MODELO: You see: papeles / blanco
You say: *En la clase hay papeles blancos.*

1. estudiante / trabajador
2. veinte / silla / negra
3. cuadernos / gris
4. bolígrafos / rojo y verde
5. un / profesora / extrovertido

1-65 Más de uno. Change the following sentences from singular to plural. Then listen and repeat as the speaker gives the correct answer.

1. ¿La pizarra es negra o verde? ______________________
2. El profesor es colombiano. ______________________
3. La estudiante mexicana es inteligente. ______________________
4. El estudiante chileno es trabajador. ______________________
5. La mochila azul es francesa. ______________________

Now change these sentences from plural to singular. Then listen and repeat as the speaker gives the correct answer.

6. Los libros franceses son interesantes. ______________________
7. Los estudiantes españoles son inteligentes. ______________________
8. ¿Las mochilas son verdes, amarillas o azules? ______________________
9. Las pizarras son blancas y las puertas son azules. ______________________
10. Los profesores panameños son trabajadores. ______________________

Nombre: ______________________ Fecha: ______________________

5. Adjective form, position, and agreement

1-66 ¿Cómo es tu clase? Describe your class using the cues provided. Then listen and repeat as the speaker gives the correct answer.

Modelo: You see: un / pizarra / grande / negra
You say: *En mi clase hay una pizarra grande y negra.*

1. 18 / silla / rojo / 9 / computadora / moderna
2. tres / ventana / grande / un / rejoj / pequeño
3. dos / estudiante / chileno / un / profesora / colombiano
4. 15 / cuaderno / rojo / 14 / libro / interesante
5. mesa / rojo / 15 / silla / marrón

6. Subject pronouns and the present tense of *ser* (to be)

1-67 Mis amigos. Ana, a student at the Universidad de Salamanca, is describing a picture of three of her friends, Andrea, Pablo, and Felipe. Listen to her description and complete the following sentences with the appropriate subject pronouns, as well as forms of the verb **ser.**

Hola, (1) __________ (yo) Ana. Las tres personas en la foto (2) __________ mis amigos, Andrea, Pablo y Felipe. Nosotros (3) __________ de diferentes países. (4) __________ soy de Sevilla, una ciudad al sur (*south*) de España. La chica en la foto (5) __________ Andrea. (6) __________ somos inseparables. (7) __________ es baja y delgada. Andrea (8) __________ de Madrid, pero los padres de Andrea (9) __________ de Toledo. Andrea y yo (10) __________ estudiantes de medicina. El muchacho del centro (11) __________ Pablo. (12) __________ es de Barcelona y también (13) __________ estudiante en la universidad. Pablo (14) __________ muy simpático y trabajador. El otro chico (15) __________ Felipe. (16) __________ es también simpático y muy trabajador. Felipe (17) __________ alto y un poco gordito. Pablo (18) __________ delgado y un poco bajo. (19) __________ son muy inteligentes. (20) __________ somos muy buenos amigos.

Nombre: ______________________ Fecha: ______________________

1-68 ¡Claro que sí! Answer the following questions affirmatively, using the appropriate subject pronouns, as well as forms of the verb **ser.** Then listen and repeat as the speaker gives the correct answer.

MODELO: You hear: ¿Somos Elvira y yo inteligentes?
You say: *Sí, ustedes son inteligentes.*

1. Sí, ______________________.
2. Sí, ______________________.
3. Sí, ______________________.
4. Sí, ______________________.
5. Sí, ______________________.
6. Sí, ______________________.
7. Sí, ______________________.
8. Sí, ______________________.
9. Sí, ______________________.
10. Sí, ______________________.
11. Sí, ______________________.
12. Sí, ______________________.

1-69 Nacionalidades. Give the nationality of the following people and ask where the second person is from. Then listen and repeat as the speaker gives the correct answer.

MODELO: You see: Marta / Argentina / tú
You say: *Marta es argentina. ¿De dónde eres tú?*

1. Marcos y Eric / Puerto Rico / Ana

____

2. Ana / Bolivia / ustedes

____

3. nosotros / República Dominicana / usted

____

4. yo / Panamá / Lucía y Roberto

____

5. Lucía y Roberto / Colombia / tú

____

Nombre: ______________________ Fecha: ______________________

¿Cuánto sabes tú?

1-70 El primer día de clases. Write an appropriate response to the following questions or statements. Because answers will vary, compare your answer to the answer that is provided. Then read your response to practice communication and pronunciation.

1. ______________________
2. ______________________
3. ______________________
4. ______________________
5. ______________________

1-71 ¿Cómo se dice? How would you accomplish the following communication tasks in Spanish? After completing each item, listen and repeat as the speaker gives the correct answer.

1. Request politely that someone open the door.

   ____

2. Tell Professor Martín that you are pleased to meet her.

   ____

3. Ask if there are some papers on the desk.

   ____

4. Tell someone that the classroom is big.

   ____

5. Ask how much the pencils and notebooks cost.

   ____

6. Say that the books are expensive.

   ____

7. Ask your instructor to please repeat the question.

   ____

8. Tell two other students to write the exercises with a pen.

   ____

Nombre: ______________________ Fecha: ______________________

2 ¿De dónde eres?

Workbook

PRIMERA PARTE

¡Así es la vida!

2-1 ¿Cierto o falso? Reread the conversations in **¡Así es la vida!** on page 40 of your textbook and indicate whether each statement is **cierto (C)** or **falso (F).**

C F 1. José es español.

C F 2. Isabel es dominicana.

C F 3. Daniel es de la capital de España.

C F 4. María es de Barcelona.

C F 5. Paco es del sur de España.

C F 6. Los padres de María son de Barcelona.

C F 7. Las clases de Paco son por la mañana.

C F 8. La clase de álgebra es a las diez.

¡Así lo decimos! Vocabulario

2-2 Nacionalidades. Terry explains where some of her friends and acquaintances are from. Complete each of her explanations with the correct form of the corresponding adjective of nationality.

MODELO: Luisa y Ramón son de Puerto Rico.
Son puertorriqueños.

1. Ana es de Colombia. Es ______________________.
2. Federico es de La Habana, Cuba. Es ______________________.
3. Nosotras somos de Buenos Aires, Argentina. Somos ______________________.
4. Alicia es de la República Dominicana. Es ______________________.

Nombre: ______________________ Fecha: ______________________

5. Los profesores son de México. Son ______________________.

6. La señora Prieto es de Caracas, Venezuela. Es ______________________.

7. Eva y Claire son de Toronto, Canadá. Son ______________________.

8. Anita y Lucía son de Panamá. Son ______________________.

2-3 También. For each person or group of people that Diego describes, a person or group of people can be described in the same way. How would you tell him this? Write your response to each of these statements, changing the gender of the people from masculine to feminine or vice versa.

Modelo: El señor pelirrojo es mexicano.
La señora pelirroja es mexicana también.

1. El profesor argentino es delgado.

____

2. Los jóvenes morenos son norteamericanos.

____

3. Las chicas simpáticas son panameñas.

____

4. La señora guapa es chilena.

____

5. El novio español es alto.

____

6. El padre es puertorriqueño y rubio.

____

7. Los muchachos son inteligentes y trabajadores.

____

8. La chica es delgada y joven.

____

Nombre: ______________________ Fecha: ______________________

2-4 Muchas preguntas. Imagine that you've just met Susana and you are trying to get to know her. Taking Susana's answers into consideration, complete each question with the most appropriate interrogative words from the word bank. You will have to use one of the interrogative words twice.

Cómo	De dónde	De qué	Dónde	Qué	Quién	Quiénes

1. ¿______________ te llamas?

   Me llamo Susana.

2. ¿______________ eres?

   Soy de los EE.UU.

3. ¿______________ estudias?

   En la universidad.

4. ¿______________ estudias?

   Historia y matemáticas.

5. ¿______________ ciudad eres?

   Soy de Houston.

6. ¿______________ son estos (*these*) en la foto?

   Son mis padres y Antonio.

7. ¿______________ es Antonio?

   Es un amigo.

8. ¿______________ es?

   Es alto, delgado y muy simpático.

2-5 Los contrarios. Some people are contradictive and seem to oppose everything you say. How would they respond to each of the following statements? Match each statement with the opposing adjective.

1. Las estudiantes son pobres. No, son ____.
2. El libro es bonito. No, es ____.
3. Es una clase buena. No, es una clase ____.
4. Adela es muy trabajadora. No, es muy ____.
5. Los estudiantes son antipáticos. No, son ____.
6. La mochila es nueva. No, es ____.
7. El profesor es joven. No, es ____.
8. El cuaderno es barato. No, es ____.
9. Las sillas son grandes. No, son ____.
10. La profesora es rubia. No, es ____.

a. perezosa
b. morena
c. viejo
d. ricas
e. mala
f. pequeñas
g. feo
h. caro
i. vieja
j. simpáticos

Nombre: ______________________ Fecha: ______________________

2-6 En la cafetería. Imagine that you have just met someone in the cafeteria. He asks you the following questions. How would you answer? Use complete sentences.

1. ¿Cómo te llamas? ______________________
2. ¿De qué país eres? ______________________
3. ¿De qué ciudad eres? ______________________
4. ¿Cómo eres? ______________________
5. ¿Cómo es tu clase de español? ______________________
6. ¿De dónde es el/la profesor/a de español? ______________________

2-7 Nombres, apodos y direcciones. Reread the **Comparaciones** section about names on page 56 of your textbook. Then answer the following questions about the business cards.

Eduardo Soto España
Director Ejecutivo
Comisión de Intercambio Educativo Entre Estados Unidos y Venezuela (Fullbright Commission)
Palomo 305 - 3º
Tel. 392-4971/3855
2013 - 6047
Caracas

José Sigüenza Escudero
Tomasa Miranda de Sigüenza
C/ El Molino, 11
Teléfono 39 21 37
QUEL (Logroño)

José Bernardo Fernández

Aníbal Ruiz Pérez
Departamento de Matemáticas
Universidad de Puerto Rico,
Río Piedras

SERVICIO DE VIAJES RODRÍGUEZ TRAVEL SERVICE
Antonio Rodríguez
DIRECTOR GENERAL
PASEO DE CABALLOS 371
58300 MONTERREY,
MÉXICO
TELS. 21-14-75 Y 21-14-93
TELEX 4902384 HOTME

1. ¿De dónde es Aníbal Ruiz Pérez?

   a. Departamento de matemáticas b. Puerto Rico c. España

2. ¿De qué país es Eduardo Soto España?

   a. España b. Estados Unidos c. Venezuela

3. ¿De dónde es Antonio Rodríguez?

   a. director general b. México c. en su oficina

4. ¿Cuál es el apodo de José?

   a. Pancho b. Tony c. Pepe

5. ¿Quién es Tomasa Miranda de Sigüenza?

   a. esposa de José b. hija de José c. madre de José

6. ¿Quién se llama Pérez?

   a. la madre de Antonio b. la madre de Aníbal c. la madre de Eduardo

Nombre: ______________________ Fecha: ______________________

¡Así lo hacemos! Estructuras

1. Telling time

2-8 Horario (*schedule*) de clases. Read Carolina's schedule and match each activity with the correct time.

1. _____ Tiene clase de biología a la una en punto de la tarde. — a. 11:15 A.M.
2. _____ Tiene clase de español a las diez y cuarto de la mañana. — b. 9:05 A.M.
3. _____ Tiene clase de arte a las siete y media de la noche. — c. 1:00 P.M.
4. _____ Tiene clase de francés a las once y cuarto de la mañana. — d. 7:30 P.M.
5. _____ Tiene clase de matemáticas a las cinco menos cuarto de la tarde. — e. 4:45 P.M.
6. _____ Tiene clase de historia a las nueve y cinco de la mañana. — f. 10:15 A.M.

2-9 Los horarios de vuelo. Read the timetable of AEROMEDitariano flights and answer the following questions.

(Horarios sujetos a posibles variaciones)

España - Italia (IDA) — AEROMEDitariano

RUTA	VUELO	DÍAS	SALIDA	LLEGADA
MADRID-ROMA*	AZ1373	DIARIO	07:55	10:20
MADRID-ROMA*	AZ367	DIARIO	12:50	15:15
MADRID-ROMA*	AZ365	DIARIO	17:55	20:20
MADRID-MILÁN	AZ1377	DIARIO	08:15	10:20
MADRID-MILÁN	AZ1355	DIARIO	12:20	14:25
MADRID-MILÁN	AZ355	DIARIO	18:25	20:30

Teléfonos de Información y Reservas:
- Madrid-Ciudad: 559 95 00 (De lunes a viernes, de 9 a 19h.)
- Aeropuerto de Barajas: 305 43 35 (Todos los días, de 7 a 19h.)
- AEROMED Premium Program: 900 210 599 (De lunes a viernes, de 9 a 17h.)

*Más de 150 conexiones a 40 ciudades de todo el mundo.

1. ¿A qué hora es la salida (*departure*) del vuelo AZ 1373?

   a. 18:25　b. 07:55　c. 10:20　d. 14:25

2. ¿Cuántos vuelos (*flights*) diarios hay de Madrid a Milán?

   a. tres　b. uno　c. seis　d. dos

Nombre: ______________________ Fecha: ______________________

3. ¿A qué hora es la llegada (*arrival*) del vuelo AZ 1377?

   a. 12:50 b. 20:30 c. 10:20 d. 15:15

4. ¿A cuántas ciudades hay conexiones?

   a. cuarenta b. ciento cincuenta c. tres d. dos

5. ¿Cuál es el número del teléfono de información en Madrid?

   a. 555 95 00 b. 305 43 35 c. 900 210 599 d. 367 13 73

2. Formation of yes/no questions and negation

2-10 ¿No? Unscramble each group of words to form statements with tag questions.

MODELO: ¿verdad? es Mariberta de Colombia
Mariberta es de Colombia, ¿verdad?

1. ¿no? / son / muy delgados / Arturo y David

   ____

2. es / inteligente / la estudiante / ¿cierto? / cubana

   ____

3. Verónica / ¿verdad? / se llama / la señora

   ____

4. gordo / ¿no? / es / Toño / bajo y

   ____

5. es / ¿sí? / Gregorio / simpático

   ____

Nombre: ______________________________ Fecha: ______________________

2-11 De mal humor. Your friend is in a bad mood and says no to everything you say. Fill in the blanks to form affirmative and negative sentences.

MODELO: Luisa / ser / trabajador
Luisa es trabajadora.
Luisa no es trabajadora.

1. Pepe / ser /venezolano

   Pepe ____________ venezolano.

   Pepe ____________ venezolano.

2. Arturo y Miguel / ser / inteligente

   Arturo y Miguel ____________ inteligentes.

   Arturo y Miguel ____________ inteligentes.

3. Beto y Mongo / ser / pobre

   Beto y Mongo ____________ pobres.

   Beto y Mongo ____________ pobres.

4. Tú y yo / ser / canadiense

   Tú y yo ____________ canadienses.

   Tú y yo ____________ canadienses.

2-12 Preguntas y respuestas. A new friend has many questions to ask you. First, fill in the blanks to make yes/no questions. Then fill in the blanks to answer the questions.

MODELO: Tú eres de Bilbao.
¿Eres de Bilbao?
No, no soy de Bilbao, soy de Barcelona.

1. Tú eres de Salamanca.

   ¿__________ de Salamanca?

   No, no __________ de Salamanca, soy __________ Madrid.

2. Los estudiantes son de Valencia.

   ¿__________ de Valencia?

   No, __________ son de Valencia, son de Alicante.

3. Rosa y Chayo son de Santander.

   ¿__________ de Santander?

   No, no __________ de Santander, son __________ Oviedo.

4. Tú eres de Madrid.

   ¿__________ de Madrid?

   No, no __________ de Madrid, soy de Sevilla.

5. El profesor de matemáticas es aburrido.

   ¿__________ aburrido?

   No, no __________ aburrido, es interesante.

Nombre: ______________________ Fecha: ______________________

3. Interrogative words

2-13 ¿Cuáles son las preguntas? You heard the answers in an interview but you didn't catch the questions. Choose the questions that prompted each response.

Modelo: Soy Antonio Ramírez.
¿Quién es usted?

1. Soy de Santiago de Compostela.

   a. ¿Quién eres?
   b. ¿De dónde eres?
   c. ¿Cómo eres?
   d. ¿Qué eres?

2. El profesor es muy simpático.

   a. ¿Quién es el profesor?
   b. ¿De dónde es el profesor?
   c. ¿Cómo es el profesor?
   d. ¿Qué es el profesor?

3. Los estudiantes de la clase son inteligentes.

   a. ¿Cómo se llaman los estudiantes?
   b. ¿Qué son los estudiantes?
   c. ¿De dónde son los estudiantes?
   d. ¿Cómo son los estudiantes?

4. La mochila es de Raúl.

   a. ¿Cómo es la mochila?
   b. ¿De dónde es Raúl?
   c. ¿Cómo es Raúl?
   d. ¿De quién es la mochila?

5. Los estudiantes venezolanos son Carlos, Andrés y Rafael.

   a. ¿De dónde son los estudiantes?
   b. ¿Quiénes son los estudiantes venezolanos?
   c. ¿Cómo son los estudiantes venezolanos?
   d. ¿Qué son los estudiantes venezolanos?

6. El examen es a las dos de la tarde.

   a. ¿Cómo es el examen?
   b. ¿Cuándo es el examen?
   c. ¿Por qué hay examen?
   d. ¿Dónde es el examen?

Nombre: ______________________ Fecha: ______________________

2-14 Las decisiones. You have entered a contest and must decide between the use of **qué** or **cuál(es),** based on the context, in order to be the winner.

MODELO: *¿Qué hora es?*

1. ¿__________ de los estudiantes es Cheo?
2. ¿__________ son tus clases interesantes?
3. ¿__________ hay en la clase de español?
4. ¿__________ hora es?
5. ¿__________ día es hoy?
6. ¿__________ es el libro de español?

2-15 En la clase. The new student has many questions about the class. Complete her questions with the correct interrogative word from the word bank.

Cuál(es)	Cuándo	Cuántas	De dónde	De qué	Por qué	Qué	Quiénes

1. ¿__________ no hay un escritorio en la clase?
2. ¿__________ es el examen de español?
3. ¿__________ es la mochila de Raúl?
4. ¿__________ mesas hay en la clase?
5. ¿__________ días hay tarea?
6. ¿__________ son los estudiantes españoles?
7. ¿__________ es la profesora Diéguez?
8. ¿__________ ciudad es la profesora?

SEGUNDA PARTE

¡Así es la vida!

2-16 Nuevos amigos. Look again at the photos on page 57 of your textbook and reread the descriptions. Then answer the questions in complete sentences in Spanish. You may want to review the interrogative words on page 52 of your textbook before you begin.

Celia Cifuentes Bernal

1. ¿De dónde es ella?

   a. León b. Toledo c. Málaga d. Bilbao

2. ¿Cuántos idiomas habla?

   a. dos b. tres c. cuatro d. uno

3. ¿Cuáles son?

   a. inglés b. inglés y español c. inglés, español y francés d. francés y español

Nombre: ______________________ Fecha: ______________________

4. ¿Qué estudia?

   a. matemáticas b. biología c. medicina d. derecho

5. ¿Cuándo es el examen de biología?

   a. hoy b. esta tarde c. mañana por la mañana d. mañana por la tarde

6. Son fáciles los exámenes de la profesora, ¿verdad?

   a. sí b. no

Alberto López Silvero

1. ¿Cuántos años tiene?

   a. veintidós b. doce c. treinta y dos d. cuarenta y dos

2. ¿Cuál es su (*his*) nacionalidad?

   a. mexicana b. americana c. europea d. española

3. ¿Qué habla?

   a. español b. español y un poco de inglés c. inglés y un poco de español d. inglés

4. ¿Qué estudia?

   a. matemáticas b. inglés c. derecho d. medicina

5. ¿Cuándo trabaja?

   a. muy tarde b. esta noche c. por la mañana d. por la tarde

6. ¿Dónde trabaja?

   a. en la universidad b. en una librería c. en casa d. en un concierto

Nombre: ______________________ Fecha: ______________________

Adela María de la Torre Jiménez

1. ¿Es rubia o morena?

   a. rubia b. morena

2. ¿De dónde es?

   a. Granada b. Bilbao c. Málaga d. Pamplona

3. ¿Qué estudia?

   a. derecho b. ingeniería c. biología d. matemáticas

4. ¿Cuándo baila con sus amigos?

   a. los domingos b. tarde c. sábados por la mañana d. sábados por la noche

5. ¿Dónde baila?

   a. en una discoteca b. en la universidad c. en casa d. en Málaga

Rogelio Miranda Suárez

1. ¿Qué estudia?

   a. biología b. matemáticas c. derecho d. ingeniería

2. ¿Cómo son las clases?

   a. interesantes b. difíciles c. interesantes y difíciles d. fáciles

3. ¿Cuándo estudia con los amigos?

   a. los lunes b. los lunes y miércoles c. mañana d. los lunes, miércoles y viernes

4. ¿Cuándo practica tenis él?

   a. por la noche b. esta tarde c. mañana d. los lunes, miércoles y viernes

Nombre: ______________________ Fecha: ______________________

¡Así lo decimos! Vocabulario

2-17 Actividades

Primera fase. Match each activity with the most logical expression.

1. ____ escuchar
2. ____ bailar
3. ____ hablar
4. ____ nadar
5. ____ leer
6. ____ mirar
7. ____ trabajar
8. ____ estudiar
9. ____ practicar
10. ____ escribir

a. en el cuaderno
b. en una discoteca
c. mucho béisbol
d. historia en la universidad
e. español, italiano, francés y un poco de inglés
f. en una librería
g. música clásica
h. la televisión
i. en el mar
j. un libro muy interesante

Segunda fase. Now write a complete sentence using each pair from the **Primera fase** and the following personal pronoun(s) as the subject. The first sentence is done for you.

1. Tú *escuchas música clásica* ______________________.
2. Nosotras ______________________.
3. Yo ______________________.
4. Ella y yo ______________________.
5. Tú y él ______________________.
6. Yo ______________________.
7. Tú y yo ______________________.
8. Ella y él ______________________.
9. Él ______________________.
10. Yo ______________________.

Nombre: ____________________ Fecha: ____________________

2-18 Fuera de lugar. Choose the letter corresponding to the word that does not fit in each group.

1. a. baloncesto b. francés c. italiano d. vietnamita
2. a. tenis b. reloj c. natación d. fútbol
3. a. ingeniería b. derecho c. mañana d. historia
4. a. trabajar b. practicar c. estudiar d. mucho
5. a. portugués b. coreano c. examen d. español
6. a. arte b. derecho c. geografía d. béisbol

¡Así lo hacemos! Estructuras

4. The present tense of regular *-ar, -er,* and *-ir* verbs

2-19 ¿Qué hacen? Complete each sentence with the correct form of the verb in parentheses.

1. Nosotros (caminar) ____________________ por las tardes.
2. Los estudiantes (preparar) ____________________ la lección.
3. ¿(Trabajar) ____________________ tú mucho?
4. Las señoritas (nadar) ____________________ bien.
5. Alejandro y yo (practicar) ____________________ mucho el fútbol.
6. ¿Qué (mirar) ____________________ ellos?
7. Ana y Federico (bailar) ____________________ muy mal.
8. Los amigos (conversar) ____________________ en el café.
9. Amalia y Laura (estudiar) ____________________ historia.
10. Yo (escuchar) ____________________ música popular.

2-20 Mis amigas. Complete the description of friends with the correct form of the verb in parentheses.

Mis amigas Bárbara, Isabel y Victoria (1. vivir) ______________ en la residencia estudiantil. Ellas (2. aprender) ______________ inglés en la universidad y (3. asistir) ______________ a clase por la mañana. Isabel y Bárbara (4. escribir) ______________ inglés muy bien, pero Victoria no (5. leer) ______________ inglés muy bien. Yo (6. creer) ______________ que ella (7. deber) ______________ estudiar más. Al mediodía, cuando (8. abrir) ______________ la cafetería, ellas (9. comer) ______________ allí. Yo también (10. comer) ______________ con ellas en la cafetería. Victoria y yo solamente (11. comer) ______________ ensalada y (12. beber) ______________ jugo. Isabel y Bárbara (13. comer) ______________ hamburguesas y (14. beber) ______________ agua mineral. Mis amigas (15. creer) ______________ que es bueno ir al gimnasio después del almuerzo, pero yo (16. creer) ______________ que es mejor tomar una siesta. Y tú, ¿dónde (17. vivir) ______________?

2-21 Actividades. Everyone is busy today. Describe what each person is doing with the correct form of the verb in parentheses.

1. Adela (asistir) ______________________ a la clase de francés mientras yo (escribir) ______________________ una composición.
2. Mis padres (leer) ______________________ un libro mientras mi hermanita (aprender) ______________________ a bailar.
3. Yo (comer) ______________________ una ensalada mientras tú (beber) ______________________ un refresco.
4. Mi novio (abrir) ______________________ la puerta de la biblioteca mientras nosotros (leer) ______________________ un libro.

Nombre: ______________________ Fecha: ______________________

2-22 Preguntas y respuestas. Here are some questions a new friend asks you. Complete each question with the correct form of the verb in parentheses. Then answer the question.

1. ¿Qué (aprender) ______________________ en la universidad?

   ____

2. ¿A qué hora (abrir) ______________________ el centro estudiantil?

   ____

3. ¿Qué (beber) ______________________ con el almuerzo?

   ____

4. ¿Qué (deber) ______________________ hacer por la tarde?

   ____

5. ¿Qué (leer) ______________________ en la clase de inglés?

   ____

6. ¿(creer) ______________________ que es bueno dar un paseo después del almuerzo?

   ____

7. ¿Qué (hacer)______________________ hoy por la noche?

   ____

8. ¿A qué clases (asistir) ______________________ hoy?

   ____

5. The present tense of *tener* (to have) and the expression *tener que* (to have to)

2-23 Tener. Complete each statement with the correct form of **tener.**

1. Tú ______________________ clase todos los días.
2. Él y yo ______________________ que estudiar esta noche.
3. Carlos y Adela ______________________ dos clases esta tarde.
4. Usted ______________________ novio/a, ¿no?
5. Nosotras ______________________ que hablar con María.
6. Yo ______________________ muchos amigos en la universidad.

Nombre: ________________________ Fecha: ________________

2-24 Responsabilidades. List three things you have to do tomorrow and three things other people have to do.

MODELO: *Yo tengo que estudiar.*

1. Yo ________________________.
2. Yo ________________________.
3. Yo ________________________.
4. Mis padres ________________________.
5. Mi amigo ________________________.
6. El/La profesor/a ________________________.

2-25 Montserrat. Complete the following descriptions with the correct form of the verb in parentheses.

Yo (1) ______________ (ser) amigo de Montserrat Pons Roy. Ella (2) ______________ (ser) de Barcelona. Ella (3) ______________ (tener) un trabajo y (4) ______________ (estudiar) en la Universidad de Barcelona. Montserrat (5) ______________ (tener) novio. Él se llama Juan Berenguer Castells. Juan (6) ______________ (ser) de Barcelona también. Juan y Montserrat (7) ______________ (estudiar) derecho. Ellos (8) ______________ (practicar) el tenis cuando Juan no (9) ______________ (tener) que trabajar. ¿(10) ______________ (Tener) tú que trabajar hoy?

Nombre: ______________________________ Fecha: ______________________

NUESTRO MUNDO

Panoramas

2-26 ¡A informarse! Based on the information from **Nuestro mundo** on pages 70–71 of your textbook, decide if the following statements are **cierto (C)** or **falso (F).**

1. La pesca (*fishing*) en España es muy mala.
2. Las aceitunas (*olives*) se cultivan en Andalucía.
3. En España no se producen (*manufacture*) automóviles.
4. SEAT es un coche (*car*) caro.
5. El museo Guggenheim está en Bilbao.
6. El museo es diseño de un arquitecto español.
7. La Costa del Sol está en el norte de España.
8. Millones de turistas visitan España.
9. Pedro Almodóvar es un director de cine.
10. Pedro Almodóvar nunca (*never*) recibió un Óscar.

Nombre: ______________________ Fecha: ______________

2-27 Tu propia experiencia. Think of two Spanish personalities, cities, or monuments that you know and describe them.

____

____

____

____

____

____

____

____

Taller

2-28 La vida de Marisol.

Primera fase. Read the following description of Marisol. Then answer the questions.

Marisol es una estudiante muy buena en la Universidad de Navarra. Marisol es dominicana. Tiene veinte años y es inteligente y muy trabajadora. Habla tres idiomas—español, inglés y francés. Estudia derecho en la universidad y participa en muchas otras actividades. Nada por las tardes y también practica el fútbol. Hoy tiene que estudiar mucho porque tiene un examen de derecho mañana. Ella también tiene una clase de francés. No hay muchos estudiantes en la clase, solamente nueve—tres españoles, dos chilenos, un italiano, dos portugueses y ella. La profesora es española y es muy simpática. Siempre prepara bien la lección para la clase.

1. ¿Quién es Marisol? ______________________
2. ¿Dónde estudia? ¿Qué estudia? ______________________
3. ¿En qué actividades participa Marisol? ______________________
4. ¿Cuántos estudiantes hay en la clase de francés? ______________________
5. ¿Cuáles son las nacionalidades de los estudiantes y de Marisol? ______________________

   ____
6. ¿Cómo es la profesora de francés? ______________________
7. ¿Cuántos años tiene Marisol? ______________________
8. ¿Qué tiene que hacer Marisol hoy? ______________________

Segunda fase. Use the questions from the **Primera fase** as models for questions to interview a classmate. Write at least five questions that you can ask. Interview a classmate. Try to complete the student information card for him/her with the information you obtain.

1. ______________________
2. ______________________
3. ______________________
4. ______________________
5. ______________________

Nombre: ______________ Apellido: ______________
Nacionalidad: ______________ Edad (*age*): ______________
Ciudad: ______________ País: ______________
Concentración (*major*): ______________
Clases: ______________ ______________
______________ ______________
______________ ______________
______________ ______________

2-29 Tu vida universitaria. Using the description in activity **2-28** as a model, write a brief paragraph about yourself and your life in school. Be sure to include your age, physical description, activities, and responsibilities. First, fill in the necessary information for your student identification card.

Nombre: ______________ Apellido: ______________
Nacionalidad: ______________ Edad (*age*): ______________
Ciudad: ______________ País: ______________
Descripción física: ______________

____

____

Nombre: ______________________ Fecha: ______________

2-30 La Universidad de Salamanca. Use the Internet or library resources to find information about the University of Salamanca or another university in Spain. Look for and jot down the information in the following categories. What aspects of the university interest you?

LA HISTORIA

The founders and the year established ______________

Famous students and professors ______________

LOS EDIFICIOS Y LA ARQUITECTURA

Historical buildings/architecture ______________

New facilities ______________

CURSOS Y PROGRAMAS

Nombre: ______________________ Fecha: ______________________

2-31 Más allá de las páginas. Using the Internet, look for photos of two famous designers and describe them. State their age and nationality as well.

____

____

____

____

____

____

____

____

____

¿Cuánto sabes tú?

2-32 ¿Sabes qué hora es? Match the times given in Spanish with with the correct numerical time.

1. ____ mediodía	a. 7:40
2. ____ las tres y diez	b. 12:00 P.M.
3. ____ las ocho menos cuarto	c. 3:15
4. ____ las ocho y media	d. 7:45
5. ____ las tres y cuarto	e. 12:00 A.M.
6. ____ las ocho menos veinte	f. 8:30
7. ____ medianoche	g. 3:10

Nombre: ______________________________ Fecha: ______________________

2-33 ¿Sabes preguntar? Fill in the blanks with the most logical interrogative word from the word bank.

Cómo Cuántos Dónde Por qué Qué Quién

1. ¿__________ se llama tu amigo?
2. ¿__________ años tiene él?
3. ¿__________ es tu amigo?
4. ¿__________ estudia él?
5. ¿__________ es la novia de tu amigo?
6. ¿__________ vive tu amigo?

2-34 ¿Sabes de mi vida en la universidad? Fill in the blanks with the appropriate form of the verbs from the word bank. You will have to use one of the verbs twice.

aprender asistir comer enseñar estudiar nadar regresar trabajar vivir

Yo (1) __________ en la universidad. Todos los días, yo (2) __________ a mis clases. (Yo) (3) __________ mucho en mis clases porque los profesores (4) __________ muy bien. Mis amigos y yo (5) __________ en la cafetería al mediodía. Después, nosotros (6) __________ en el supermercado para ganar un poco de dinero. A las cinco de la tarde, nosotros (7) __________ en la piscina (*swimming pool*) de la universidad y (8) __________ (nosotros) a casa. Yo (9) __________ con mis padres, pero ellos (10) __________ en un apartamento cerca del campus universitario.

2-35 ¿Sabes de obligaciones y posesiones? Fill in the blanks with the appropriate form of the verb **tener.**

1. Lucía y Marisol __________ que trabajar esta tarde.
2. Lucía __________ muchas clases en la universidad.
3. Marisol __________ mucha tarea.
4. Yo __________ que ayudar a Marisol con su tarea.
5. Nosotros __________ un examen mañana.

Nombre: ______________________ Fecha: ______________

Lab Manual

Primera parte

¡Así es la vida!

2-36 Tres amigos. Listen to the following conversation. Then indicate whether each of the following statements is **cierto (C)** or **falso (F)** based on what you hear. You may need to listen to the conversation more than once.

C F 1. Marta es argentina.

C F 2. Mateo es mexicano.

C F 3. Clara es colombiana.

C F 4. Marta es inteligente.

C F 5. Mateo es simpático.

C F 6. Clara es trabajadora.

C F 7. Clara es de la capital.

C F 8. Mateo es alto.

C F 9. Mateo es inteligente.

C F 10. Marta es de Bogotá.

¡Así lo decimos! Vocabulario

2-37 ¿Lógico o ilógico? Listen to the following questions. Then select all letters corresponding to logical answers. There may be more than one logical answer for each question.

1. a. José Blanco.
   b. Se llama José.
   c. Me llamo José.

2. a. Están muy bien, gracias.
   b. Inteligentes y trabajadores.
   c. Buenos y gordos.

3. a. Sí. ¿Tú también?
   b. Sí, de Caracas, la capital.
   c. Sí, colombianos, de Cali.
4. a. En México. Paco es de Cancún.
   b. No, soy mexicano. ¿Y tú?
   c. En México. ¿Verdad?
5. a. No, la capital es Washington, D.C.
   b. No, pero es una ciudad importante.
   c. No, es la capital.
6. a. Es de un estudiante panameño.
   b. Es de Panamá, de la capital.
   c. Son de mis padres.

Pronunciación

Linking

In Spanish, as in English, speakers group words into units that are separated by pauses. Each unit, called a *breath group*, is pronounced as if it were one long word. In Spanish, the words are linked together within the breath group, depending on whether the first word ends in a consonant or a vowel.

1. In a breath group, if a word ends in a vowel and the following word begins with a vowel, the vowels are linked.

   Tú eres de la capital. **Túe-res-de-la-ca-pi-tal.**

   ¿Cómo estás tú? **¿Có-moes-tás-tú?**

2. When the vowel ending one word and the vowel beginning the next word are identical, they are pronounced as one sound.

   una amiga **u-na-mi-ga.**

3. If a word ends in a consonant and the following word begins with a vowel, the consonant and vowel become part of the same syllable.

   ¿Él es de Puerto Rico? **¿É-les-de-Puer-to-Ri-co?**

2-38 Imitar. Listen to and repeat the following sentences, paying close attention to Spanish linking patterns.

1. Tú eres española.
2. Laura Esquivel es una autora famosa.
3. Hay una fiesta en mi apartamento ahora.
4. ¿De dónde es tu amigo?

Nombre: ______________________ Fecha: ______________

¡Así lo hacemos! Estructuras

1. Telling time

2-39 ¿A qué hora...? Answer the questions you hear, using the times given in this activity. Then listen and repeat the correct answer after the speaker. You may need to listen to each question more than once.

MODELO: You hear: ¿A qué hora tomas el autobús?
You see: 07:45
You say: *Tomo el autobús a las ocho menos cuarto de la mañana.*

1. 20:45
2. 07:15
3. 09:30
4. 08:00
5. 13:10
6. 24:00

2. Formation of yes/no questions and negation

2-40 ¿Sí o no? Change the following statements to questions by inverting the subject and the verb. Then listen and repeat as the speaker gives the correct answer.

MODELO: You see: Usted es puertorriqueño.
You say: *¿Es usted puertorriqueño?*

1. Andrea y Felipe son amigos.
2. Tú eres nicaragüense.
3. Nosotros somos novios.
4. Clara es dominicana.
5. Yo soy muy baja.
6. Ustedes son muy inteligentes.

Nombre: ______________________ Fecha: ______________________

2-41 ¡Absolutamente no! Answer the following questions negatively. Then listen and repeat as the speaker gives the correct answer.

MODELO: You see: ¿Es usted puertorriqueño?
You say: *No, no soy puertorriqueño.*

1. ¿Son Andrea y Felipe amigos?
2. ¿Eres tú nicaragüense?
3. ¿Somos nosotros novios?
4. ¿Es Clara dominicana?
5. ¿Soy yo muy baja?

3. Interrogative words

2-42 Más preguntas. Answer the questions you hear, using the cues given in this activity. Then listen and repeat the correct answer after the speaker. You may need to listen to each question more than once.

MODELO: You hear: ¿Cuándo es tu cumpleaños?
You see: 13/8
You say: *Es el trece de agosto.*

1. joven y rubia
2. 23/2
3. Pamplona
4. gordito y moreno
5. martes

Nombre: ______________________ Fecha: ______________________

Segunda parte

¡Así es la vida!

2-43 En la cafetería. Listen to the following conversation among three students at the university cafeteria. Then select all letters corresponding to statements that are correct, according to what you hear. Listen to the recording as many times as necessary to find all the correct statements.

1. Ana está...

   a. bastante mal.

   b. bastante bien.

   c. más o menos.

2. Manuel...

   a. está más o menos.

   b. está bastante bien.

   c. tiene que trabajar.

3. Pedro y Ana son...

   a. amigos.

   b. simpáticos.

   c. estudiantes.

4. Manuel y Pedro son...

   a. amigos.

   b. estudiantes.

   c. mexicanos.

5. Ana...

   a. estudia administración de empresas.

   b. estudia ingeniería.

   c. trabaja en una empresa.

6. Pedro...

   a. estudia y trabaja.

   b. tiene una fiesta.

   c. practica tenis.

7. Manuel...

   a. estudia y trabaja.

   b. practica fútbol.

   c. practica tenis.

8. Ana...

   a. practica tenis.

   b. camina.

   c. tiene un examen de inglés.

Nombre: ______________________ Fecha: ______________________

¡Así lo decimos! Vocabulario

2-44 ¿Lógico o ilógico? Select the letter corresponding to the most logical answer to each question you hear. Then listen and repeat as the speaker gives the correct answer.

1. a. Sí, hablo francés.
   b. No, hablo francés.
   c. Sí, hablas alemán.
2. a. No, trabajamos por las tardes.
   b. Sí, practicas fútbol.
   c. Sí, vamos a nadar por las tardes.
3. a. Sí, estudia ciencias políticas.
   b. Sí, tiene un examen.
   c. Sí, estudia historia.
4. a. Esta noche camino con él.
   b. Converso con él en español.
   c. Vas a mirar los libros y conversar un poco.
5. a. Estudio esta noche y mañana.
   b. Estudian con amigos.
   c. Yo estudio derecho y Pedro estudia matemáticas.
6. a. Estudiamos por la tarde.
   b. Estudian en la cafetería.
   c. Estudiamos y practicamos tenis.
7. a. Estudio historia con Raúl.
   b. ¡Hombre, es interesante!
   c. ¡Bailo con mis amigas!

Pronunciación

Spanish intonation in questions

Intonation is the sequence of voice pitch (rising or falling) in normal speech, in accordance with the type of message intended and the context in which it is communicated. Intonation patterns in Spanish are very useful when posing questions. With yes/no questions, the pattern is somewhat different. The voice rises to an above normal pitch at the end of the question. Note the following examples.

¿Ellos son de los Estados Unidos?

¿Tú eres de la capital?

In questions that use interrogative words, the pitch level at the beginning is high and gradually falls toward the end of the question. Note the following examples.

¿De dónde es Jaime?

¿Quién es el profesor?

Nombre: ____________________ Fecha: ____________________

2-45 Unas preguntas. Practice asking questions based on the following phrases. Then listen and repeat after the speaker.

1. hay un examen mañana
2. necesitamos un lápiz para el examen
3. el libro de español es viejo
4. el profesor habla japonés

2-46 ¿Pregunta o respuesta? Listen carefully to the intonation patterns in the following sentences. Check the appropriate column to indicate whether the sentence is a question or a statement.

MODELO: You hear: ¿Juan es alto?
You mark: *Question*

	QUESTION	STATEMENT
1.	____	____
2.	____	____
3.	____	____
4.	____	____
5.	____	____
6.	____	____

¡Así lo hacemos! Estructuras

4. The present tense of regular *-ar, -er,* and *-ir* verbs

2-47 Más actividades. Answer the following questions, using the words provided and the correct form of the verb. Then listen and repeat as the speaker gives the correct answer.

MODELO: You hear: ¿Miramos televisión o preparamos el examen?
You see: Nosotros (mirar) __________ televisión.
You write and say: *Nosotros miramos televisión.*

1. Sí, yo (bailar) __________ salsa.
2. Sí, nosotros (practicar) __________ fútbol.
3. Ana (escuchar) __________ la radio y yo (mirar) __________ la televisión.
4. Sí, Débora (caminar) __________ por el parque.
5. Sí, Paola y Manuel (conversar) __________ con Juan.
6. No, yo (regresar) __________ en dos días.

Nombre: ______________________ Fecha: ______________________

2-48 Muchas actividades. Complete each sentence with the correct form of the verb you hear. Then listen and repeat as the speaker gives the correct answer.

MODELO: You see: Nosotros __________ un examen mañana.
You hear: tener
You write and say: *Nosotros tenemos un examen mañana.*

1. Yo __________ fútbol por las tardes.
2. ¿Tú __________ con Elena?
3. Ella __________ por las mañanas.
4. Usted __________ en la librería, ¿cierto?
5. Nosotros __________ con el profesor Vargas.
6. Ángela y Rita __________ mucho la television.

2-49 Otras actividades. Listen for the subject and write the corresponding form of the verb in parentheses. Then listen and repeat as the speaker gives the correct answer.

MODELO: You see: (Caminar) __________ en el parque.
You hear: nosotros
You write and say: *Caminamos en el parque.*

1. (Creer) __________ que son las tres.
2. (Comprender) __________ muy bien la lección.
3. (Escribir) __________ muy bien.
4. ¿(Vender) __________ tus libros al final del semestre?
5. (Abrir) __________ el laboratorio a las 8:00.
6. (Decidir) __________ regresar pronto.

2-50 Actividades adicionales. Complete each sentence with the correct form of the verb you hear. Then listen and repeat as the speaker gives the correct answer.

1. Mis amigos __________ en la residencia estudiantil.
2. Yo __________ la lección.
3. La profesora __________ las instrucciones en la pizarra.
4. Tú __________ a la universidad.
5. Nosotros __________ la información en la clase.

Nombre: ______________________ Fecha: ______________________

2-51 Nosotros... Answer the questions you hear, using the **nosotros** form of the verb and the cues provided. Then listen and repeat as the speaker gives the correct answer.

Modelo: You hear: ¿A qué hora abren ustedes por la mañana? (9:00)
You say: *Abrimos a las nueve.*

1. Sí, ______________________.
2. ______________________ dónde estudiar esta tarde.
3. ______________________ ir a estudiar en casa esta tarde.
4. ______________________ mucho en la clase de música.
5. ______________________ un trabajo para la clase de historia.
6. ______________________ que la biblioteca está enfrente de la Facultad de Derecho.

5. The present tense of *tener* (to have) and the expression *tener que* (to have to)

2-52 ¿Qué tienen? Using the appropriate form of the verb **tener,** tell what the following people have. Then listen and repeat as the speaker gives the correct answer.

1. yo / el disco compacto
2. Manuel y Federico / mucho tiempo
3. usted / muchas clases, ¿verdad?
4. nosotros / una clase interesante
5. Ana / profesores exigentes
6. tú / tres libros en la mochila
7. Javier y yo / la clase de inglés esta tarde

Nombre: ______________________ Fecha: ______________________

2-53 ¿Qué tienes? Answer the questions you hear affirmatively, using the appropriate form of the verb **tener.** Then listen and repeat as the speaker gives the correct answer.

Modelo: You hear: ¿Tienes un lápiz?
You say: *Sí, tengo un lápiz.*

1. Sí, ______________________.
2. Sí, ______________________.
3. Sí, ______________________.
4. Sí, ______________________.
5. Sí, ______________________.

¿Cuánto sabes tú?

2-54 Preguntas personales. Answer the personal questions you hear, using complete Spanish sentences. Answers will vary.

1. ______________________
2. ______________________
3. ______________________
4. ______________________
5. ______________________
6. ______________________
7. ______________________
8. ______________________
9. ______________________
10. ______________________
11. ______________________

Nombre: ______________________________ Fecha: ____________________

3 ¿Qué estudias?

Workbook

PRIMERA PARTE

¡Así es la vida!

3-1 ¿Recuerdas? Reread the conversations in **¡Así es la vida!** on page 78 of your textbook and answer the questions with complete sentences in Spanish.

1. ¿Qué tiene Pedro ya?

   ____

2. ¿Cuáles son las materias que va a tomar Eduardo?

   ____

3. ¿Cuántas materias tiene que tomar Pedro?

   ____

4. ¿Qué quiere Luisa de Carmen?

   ____

5. ¿Por qué le pide (*to ask for*) Luisa dinero a Carmen?

   ____

6. ¿Qué tiene que hacer Carmen ahora?

   ____

7. ¿A qué hora es la clase de biología?

   ____

8. ¿Cómo está Roberto?

   ____

9. ¿Qué tiene que hacer Roberto?

____

10. ¿Qué idiomas estudia Roberto?

____

¡Así lo decimos! Vocabulario

3-2 Mis clases. Tonya always talks about her classes. Complete each of the statements she makes with the corresponding word from the word bank. Make any changes that are necessary.

biblioteca	curso	gimnasio	tarea
computadora	diccionario	materia	todo

1. ______________________ mis clases son por la mañana.
2. Compré tres ______________________ para mi clase de inglés.
3. El ______________________ de álgebra es fácil.
4. Necesito una ______________________ para mi clase de informática.
5. Siempre tengo mucha ______________________ de cálculo.
6. Tengo que sacar unos libros de la ______________________.
7. Economía es una ______________________ difícil para mí.
8. Voy al ______________________ a hacer ejercicio después de clase.

Nombre: ______________________ Fecha: ______________

3-3 El horario de Pedro Arturo. Complete the following passage with the appropriate words from the word bank. Make any changes that are necessary.

bailar	exigente	gimnasio	materias	solamente	todo
complicado	generalmente	inteligente	nadar	tarea	tomar

Pedro Arturo Ruiseño es un estudiante muy (1) ____________, pero tiene un horario muy (2) ____________, porque (3) ____________ muchas (4) ____________.

(5) ____________ tiene clases los lunes, miércoles y viernes. El martes (6) ____________ tiene una clase. (7) ____________ los días, Pedro Arturo tiene que hacer muchas (8) ____________ porque sus profesores son muy (9) ____________. Los fines de semana no tiene clases. Va al (10) ____________ a hacer ejercicio y también (11) ____________ en el mar y (12) ____________ en la discoteca con su novia Rebeca.

3-4 Tu horario. Complete the chart to show your class schedule for this semester.

NOMBRE: ______________________ FECHA: ______________

	9 A.M.	10 A.M.	11 A.M.	12 A.M.	1 P.M.	2 P.M.	3 P.M.	4 P.M.	5 P.M.	6 P.M.
lun.										
mar.										
miér.										
jue.										
vier.										

3-5 ¿Qué clases tienen? Use the cues in parentheses and follow the model to tell what classes these people have. Fill in the blanks to give the complete information.

MODELO: A las diez y cinco, Andrés estudia la relación entre Cortés y Moctezuma y los conflictos entre los españoles y los aztecas.
Andrés tiene una clase de historia.

1. A la una y cuarto, estudiamos fórmulas y ecuaciones como $2a + b = x - y/z$.

   Nosotros __________ una clase de __________.

2. A las siete y veinticinco de la noche, estudias programas e idiomas de la computadora, como Java.

   Tú __________ una clase de __________.

Nombre: ______________________ Fecha: ______________________

3. A las tres y cuarto, estudio la construcción de un puente (*bridge*).

   Yo ______________ una clase de ______________.

4. A las nueve menos cinco, Paco estudia instrumentos musicales y ritmos de varias culturas.

   Paco ______________ una clase de ______________.

5. A las doce y media, Sofía estudia carbonos óxidos, dióxidos (*carbon monoxides, dioxides*), etcétera.

   Sofía ______________ una clase de ______________.

6. A las once y cuarto, mis amigos estudian el dinero, los precios (*prices*) de productos nacionales y el mercado (*market*) del país.

   Ellos ______________ una clase de ______________.

7. A las cuatro y cuarto, yo estudio las novelas de Carlos Fuentes y otros novelistas mexicanos.

   Yo ______________ una clase de ______________.

8. A las siete menos diez, Andrés estudia la clasificación de animales y plantas.

   Andrés ______________ una clase de ______________.

¡Así lo hacemos! Estructuras

1. Los números 101–3.000.000

3-6 La benefactora. One of the richest ladies in the world has given a number of items to the university. Spell out the numbers for each item in Spanish. Remember to watch for agreement.

1. 601 ______________________________ calculadoras
2. 202 ______________________________ escritorios
3. 101 ______________________________ mapas
4. 124 ______________________________ relojes
5. 10.212 ______________________________ diccionarios
6. 1.500.000 ______________________________ libros
7. 1.216 ______________________________ pupitres
8. 799 ______________________________ computadoras
9. 10.001 ______________________________ pizarras
10. 1.000 ______________________________ luces

Nombre: ______________________ Fecha: ______________

3-7 Los viajes. Read the following advertisement. Then answer the questions by choosing the most appropriate answer.

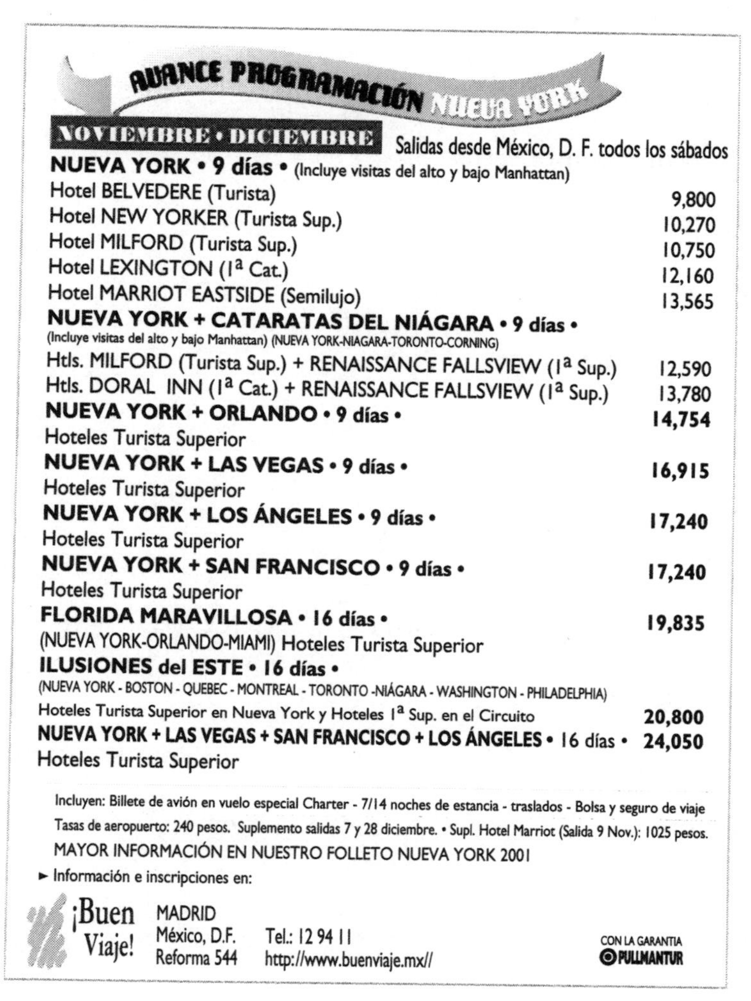

1. ¿Cuándo son las salidas (*departures*)?

   a. todos los días b. jueves c. todos los sábados d. en verano

2. ¿De dónde son las salidas?

   a. Nueva York b. Las Vegas c. San Francisco d. México, D.F.

3. ¿Cuánto cuesta el viaje a Nueva York y a Orlando?

   a. cuarenta mil setecientos cincuenta y cuatro pesos

   b. cuatro mil setecientos cincuenta y cuatro pesos

   c. catorce mil setecientos cincuenta y cuatro pesos

   d. mil cuatrocientos setenta y cuatro pesos

Nombre: ______________________ Fecha: ______________________

4. ¿Cuánto cuesta el viaje a Nueva York y a San Francisco?

   a. diecisiete mil doscientos cuarenta pesos

   b. mil setecientos cuarenta pesos

   c. siete mil cuatrocientos veinte pesos

   d. setenta mil doscientos cuarenta pesos

5. ¿Cuántas ciudades hay en el viaje de Florida Maravillosa?

   a. dieciséis   b. diecinueve mil   c. una   d. tres

6. ¿De cuántos días es el viaje de Ilusiones del Este?

   a. dieciséis   b. ocho   c. veinte   d. catorce

7. ¿Cuál es el viaje más caro?

   a. Nueva York   b. Florida Maravillosa   c. NY + LV + SF + LA   d. NY + LA

8. ¿En qué meses son los viajes?

   a. noviembre y diciembre   c. diciembre y enero

   b. octubre y noviembre   d. enero y febrero

Nombre: ______________________ Fecha: ______________

3-8 La Loto. Select the most appropriate answer for the following questions.

LA LOTO		Escrutinio	
28 de mayo		Acertantes	Pesos
Combinación ganadora:	6	1	4.256.090
2 17 25 35 37 48	5+c	4	447.056
	5	101	7.082
Complementario: 31 Reintegro 7	4	6.775	167
	3	123.439	22

1. ¿Cuál es la fecha del sorteo (*drawing*)?

   a. la loto b. escrutinio c. veintiocho de mayo d. seis

2. ¿Cuál es la combinación ganadora (*winning*)?

   a. 31-7 b. 4.256.090 c. 447.056 d. 2-17-25-35-37-48

3. ¿Cuántos pesos gana (*wins*) el único acertante (*winner*)?

   a. siete mil ochenta y dos pesos

   b. cuatro millones doscientos cincuenta y seis mil noventa pesos

   c. ciento sesenta y siete pesos

   d. cuatrocientos cuarenta y siete mil cincuenta y seis pesos

4. ¿Cuántos acertantes tienen todos los números?

   a. todos b. cuatro c. ciento uno d. uno

5. ¿Cuántos acertantes hay con cuatro números?

   a. cuatro b. seis mil setecientos setenta y cinco c. uno d. ciento uno

6. ¿Cuántos pesos gana cada uno (*each one*) de los acertantes que tiene tres números?

   a. siete mil ochenta y dos pesos

   b. veintidós pesos

   c. ciento sesenta y siete pesos

   d. ciento veintitrés mil cuatrocientos treinta y nueve pesos

Nombre: ______________________ Fecha: ______________________

2. Possessive adjectives

3-9 ¿De quién son estos objetos? Identify to whom these objects belong so that they can be returned to their owners.

MODELO: ¿De quién es la mochila? (Sara)
La mochila es de Sara.
Es su mochila.

1. ¿De quién es el bolígrafo verde? (el profesor)

   El bolígrafo verde es del profesor.

   ______________________ bolígrafo verde.

2. ¿De quién es el libro grande? (Ana y Sofía)

   El libro grande es de Ana y Sofía.

   ______________________ libro grande.

3. ¿De quién es la mochila? (Evangelina)

   La mochila es de Evangelina.

   ______________________ mochila.

4. ¿De quién son los lápices morados? (Alberto)

   Los lápices morados son de Alberto.

   ______________________ lápices morados.

5. ¿De quién es el cuaderno? (el chico)

   El cuaderno es del chico.

   ______________________ cuaderno.

6. ¿De quién son los diccionarios? (él)

   Los diccionarios son de él.

   ______________________ diccionarios.

7. ¿De quién es la calculadora? (usted)

   La calculadora es mía.

   ______________________ calculadora.

8. ¿De quién es el horario de clases? (ustedes)

   El horario de clases es nuestro.

   ______________________ horario de clases.

9. ¿De quiénes son los microscopios? (las estudiantes de biología)

   Los microscopios son de los estudiantes de biología.

   ______________________ microscopios.

10. ¿De quién son los papeles? (la profesora)

    Los papeles son de la profesora.

    ______________________ papeles.

Nombre: ______________________ Fecha: ______________

3-10 ¿Es tu...? Roberto is trying to return several objects to their owners, but he never gets it quite right. Write the answer to each of his questions negatively, then give him the correct answer.

MODELO: ¿Son tus libros? (Esteban)
No, no son mis libros. Son los libros de Esteban.

1. ¿Es tu diccionario? (el estudiante de francés)

   ____

2. ¿Son de ustedes los bolígrafos? (tu amigo)

   ____

3. ¿Son sus libros, señor? (José Antonio)

   ____

4. ¿Es de ustedes la clase? (los estudiantes argentinos)

   ____

5. ¿Es tu calculadora? (Paco)

   ____

6. ¿Son tus lápices? (mis padres)

   ____

7. ¿Es su profesora, Juan y Ana? (María Cristina)

   ____

8. ¿Es tu borrador? (la chica dominicana)

   ____

Nombre: ______________________ Fecha: ______________________

3-11 Mis amigos. Complete David's description of his friends with the correct form in Spanish of the possessive adjective in parentheses.

(1. Our) __________ amigos José y María asisten a (2. our) __________ universidad. (3. Their) __________ horarios son diferentes. María tiene cuatro clases. (4. Her) __________ clases son matemáticas, informática, biología y química. (5. Her) __________ clases favoritas son química y biología, porque (6. her) __________ profesores no son muy exigentes. José tiene cuatro materias también. (7. His) __________ materias son literatura, francés, música y psicología. (8. His) __________ materia favorita es música. José y María tienen muchos amigos. (9. Their) __________ amigos son (10. my) __________ amigos también. ¿Cómo son (11. your) __________ amigos? Vas a ser (12. my) __________ amigo/a, ¿verdad?

3. Other expressions with *tener*

3-12 Asociaciones. Complete each sentence with the corresponding **tener** expression from page 88 of your textbook, based on the clues in parentheses.

MODELO: *Yo tengo miedo.* (un programa de horror)

1. Yo ______________________________. (un refresco)
2. Nosotros ______________________________. (un suéter [*sweater*])
3. Los chicos ______________________________. (un fantasma [*ghost*])
4. Tú ______________________________. (una hamburguesa)
5. La señora ______________________________. (mucho tráfico)
6. La bebé ______________________________. (una siesta)

Nombre: ______________________ Fecha: ______________________

SEGUNDA PARTE

¡Así es la vida!

3-13 ¿Cierto o falso? Reread the conversations in **¡Así es la vida¡** on page 92 of your textbook, and indicate if each statement is **cierto (C)** or **falso (F).**

C F 1. Son las once y media de la noche.

C F 2. Ana Rosa y Luis hablan en clase.

C F 3. La librería está detrás de la Facultad de Ingeniería.

C F 4. Ana Rosa necesita terminar una novela para la clase de literatura.

C F 5. Luis está escribiendo una biografía de Frida Kahlo.

C F 6. La vida de Frida Kahlo es muy fácil.

C F 7. Luis está tranquilo.

C F 8. La especialidad de Marisa es el arte mexicano.

C F 9. Marisa vive cerca de la universidad.

C F 10. Marisa sólo va a la universidad los martes y jueves.

Nombre: ______________________ Fecha: ______________________

¡Así lo decimos! Vocabulario

3-14 La universidad. Some new students on campus need help finding their classes. Answer their questions, based on the campus map and following the model.

MODELO: ¿Dónde es la clase de anatomía?
Es en la Facultad de Medicina que (that) *está en frente de la cafetería.*

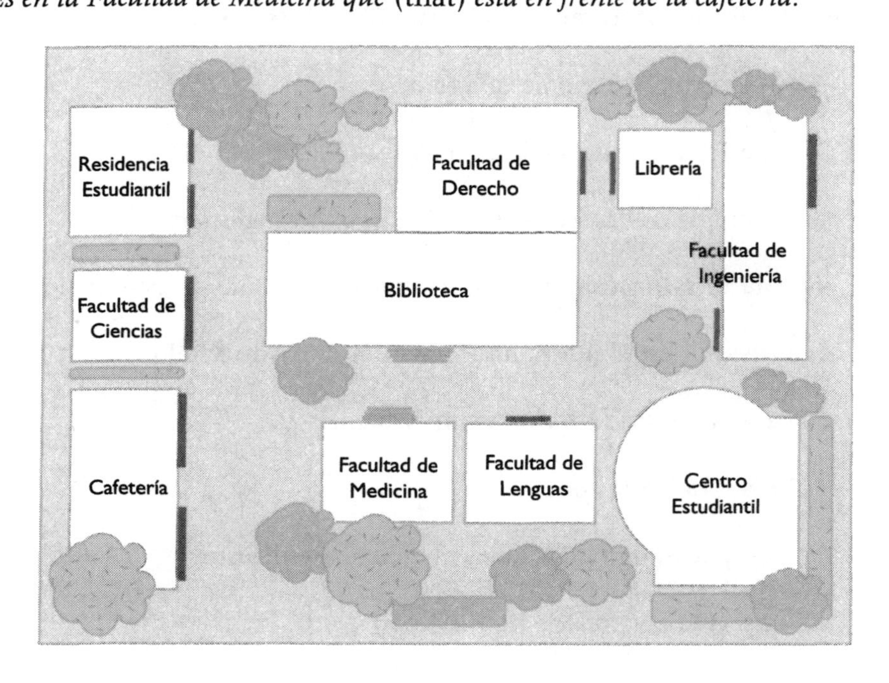

1. ¿Dónde es la clase de derecho?

____

____

2. ¿Dónde es la clase de ingeniería?

____

____

3. ¿Dónde es la clase de alemán?

____

____

4. ¿Dónde es la clase de química?

____

____

Nombre: ______________________ Fecha: ______________________

3-15 ¡Fuera de lugar! Select the letter corresponding to the word or expression that does not fit in each group.

1. a. biblioteca
   b. agua mineral
   c. café
   d. refresco
2. a. ensalada
   b. hamburguesa
   c. sándwich
   d. librería
3. a. Facultad de Arte
   b. almuerzo
   c. Rectoría
   d. residencia estudiantil
4. a. enfrente
   b. mientras
   c. al lado
   d. delante

3-16 Consejos. Imagine that your friends have a tendency to bring their problems to you. Match their problems with the appropriate advice for each problem.

1. ____ Creo que estoy enfermo. Tengo calor y mucha sed.
2. ____ Tengo un examen difícil en la clase de literatura.
3. ____ Mis amigos tienen mucha hambre.
4. ____ Tenemos que hablar con la profesora de química.
5. ____ Tenemos interés en hablar otra lengua.
6. ____ Tenemos que escribir una composición para la clase de español.

a. Es necesario preparar un almuerzo magnífico.
b. Hay que asistir a una clase de francés.
c. Hay que comprar un diccionario de español.
d. Es necesario beber mucha agua.
e. Es necesario leer muy bien la novela.
f. Hay que ir a la Facultad de Ciencias.

¡Así lo hacemos! Estructuras

4. The present indicative tense of *ir* (to go) and *hacer* (to do; to make)

3-17 ¿Adónde van? Complete each sentence with the correct form of the verb **ir** to show where each person is going.

1. Beto ______________________ a la universidad.
2. Susana y yo ______________________ a la librería.

3. Yo ______________________ a la biblioteca.

4. Los estudiantes ______________________ a la cafetería.

5. La profesora ______________________ al gimnasio.

6. Beto y Maribel ______________________ a la Facultad de Idiomas.

7. ¿Tú ______________________ a una fiesta?

8. María Amalia y tú ______________________ a la discoteca el sábado.

3-18 Mañana. Ana thinks these activities are happening today, but you know they will all take place tomorrow. Correct each of her statements, using the appropriate form of **ir a** and the infinitive.

MODELO: Estrella estudia hoy.
No, ella va a estudiar mañana.

1. Bernardo practica el béisbol hoy.

____

2. Necesito mi calculadora hoy.

____

3. Vamos al concierto esta noche.

____

4. Elena conversa con sus amigos esta tarde.

____

5. Nuestros padres llegan tarde esta noche.

____

6. Cheo y tú van al gimnasio.

____

Nombre: ______________________ Fecha: ______________

3-19 ¿Qué va a hacer? Match each of the following sentences with a logical related statement.

Modelo: Tenemos mucha hambre.
Vamos a comer a la cafetería.

1. ____ Pepe tiene mucha sed.
2. ____ Carlos y Juan están muy cansados.
3. ____ Laura y Virgilio están muy aburridos.
4. ____ Yo tengo un examen mañana.
5. ____ Tú tienes que hacer ejercicio.

a. Vas a ir al gimnasio.
b. Van a ir a una fiesta.
c. Van a dormir la siesta.
d. Voy a estudiar a la biblioteca.
e. Va a beber agua mineral.

3-20 En la residencia estudiantil. Complete the following description of what the students do at their dorm with the correct form of the verb **hacer.**

Mis amigas y yo vivimos en la residencia estudiantil de nuestra universidad y nosotras (1) __________ muchas cosas todo el día. Por la mañana, yo (2) __________ ejercicio en el gimnasio y mi amiga Elisa (3) __________ su tarea. Por la tarde, mis otras amigas Marta y Mirta (4) __________ su trabajo. Por la noche, ellas (5) __________ la comida y siempre (6) __________ hamburguesas. ¿Qué (7) __________ tú en la residencia estudiantil? ¿Qué vas a (8) __________ este fin de semana?

5. The present tense of *estar* (to be) and the present progressive

3-21 ¿Cómo están? Describe the probable feelings or conditions of each person, using the appropriate form of the verb **estar** and one of the adjectives from the word bank. Remember to watch for agreement.

aburrido	cansado	enfermo	perdido
apurado	enfadado	ocupado	triste

1. ¡Son las dos y diez y mi clase es a las dos y cuarto!

   Yo ______________________________________.

2. Tienen que leer una novela, escribir una composición y estudiar para un examen.

   Ellos ______________________________________.

Nombre: ______________________ Fecha: ______________________

3. No estudiamos más. Es medianoche.

   Nosotros ____.

4. El profesor de historia habla y habla y habla. No es interesante.

   Nosotros ____.

5. El perro (*dog*) de Benito está muerto (*dead*).

   Benito ____.

6. Tú llegas muy tarde a casa sin (*without*) telefonear.

   Tus padres ____.

7. Mi novia no está bien. Va al hospital.

   Ella ____.

8. Victor no sabe (*know*) dónde está la biblioteca.

   Él ____.

Nombre: ______________________ Fecha: ______________

3-22 ¡Apenas puedes estudiar! You've tried to study in your house, but there's too much noise. Describe what each person in the picture is doing, using the following expressions in the present progressive.

aprender a cantar	hablar por teléfono	tocar la guitarra
comer hamburguesas	hacer ejercicio	ver la televisión
escribir una carta	preparar el almuerzo	
escuchar música	servir unos refrescos	

1. Ana ______________________________.
2. Margarita ______________________________.
3. Pepe ______________________________.
4. Clara ______________________________.
5. Felipe ______________________________.
6. Marta ______________________________.
7. Chonín ______________________________.
8. Olga ______________________________.
9. Alfredo ______________________________.
10. Esteban ______________________________.

Nombre: ______________________________ Fecha: ______________________

3-23 En el teléfono. Complete the telephone conversation between Alfredo and Teresa with the correct form of the verb **estar.**

Alfredo: ¡Hola, Teresa! ¿Cómo (1) __________?

Teresa: (2) __________ bien, gracias, ¿y tú?

Alfredo: (3) __________ bien también. Oye, ¿dónde (4) __________ Eduardo?

Teresa: Él (5) __________ en su casa, porque (6) __________ muy ocupado.

Alfredo: Y, ¿dónde (7) __________ Rafaela y Sandra?

Teresa: Ellas (8) __________ enfermas. Pero, ahora yo (9) __________ preocupada. No sé (*know*) dónde (10) __________ mi novio.

Alfredo: ¿Tu novio? ¿Pedro? Ay, Teresa... Pues, él (11) __________ en un concierto en un teatro que (12) __________ cerca de aquí. Él (13) __________ con Viviana Benavides.

Teresa: ¡Con Viviana Benavides! ¡Mañana va a (14) __________ muerto!

3-24 Una conversación por teléfono. Felipe is thinking about his family and calls to see what everyone is doing. His mother picks up the telephone and answers all of Felipe's questions. Using the present progressive of the verbs in parentheses, fill in the blanks to complete the conversation. The first one has been done for you.

Felipe: ¡Hola, mamá! *¿Qué estás haciendo?* (hacer)

Mamá: (1) ______________________ (preparar) la comida.

Felipe: ¿Y Alberto?

Mamá: (2) ______________________ (jugar) al fútbol.

Felipe: ¿Y Belinda y Felo?

Mamá: (3) ______________________ (dormir) la siesta.

Felipe: ¿Y Érica?

Mamá: (4) ______________________ (servir) los refrescos.

Felipe: ¿Y mi perro?

Mamá: (5) ______________________ (comer).

Felipe: Bueno, hasta pronto, mamá.

Mamá: Adiós, hijo.

Nombre: ______________________ Fecha: ______________________

6. Summary of uses of *ser* and *estar*

3-25 Mi pequeño mundo. Complete the descriptions of the following people with the correct forms of the verbs **ser** or **estar.**

1. Mi novio __________ alto y delgado. __________ ecuatoriano, pero ahora __________ en los EE.UU. __________ un chico muy trabajador. __________ trabajando en una librería esta tarde. Él __________ contento aquí porque toda la familia __________ aquí también.
2. Mis primas __________ bonitas, pero esta noche __________ más bonitas porque van a una fiesta con sus novios. La fiesta __________ a las nueve. __________ las ocho ahora y ellas __________ muy contentas. La fiesta __________ en casa de una amiga.
3. Mis padres __________ fantásticos. Ellos __________ amables y aún (*still*) __________ enamorados. Su aniversario __________ mañana. Ellos __________ muy trabajadores. Mi madre __________ abogada y mi padre __________ profesor. Yo __________ muy contenta con mis padres.

3-26 Vicente. Complete Vicente's description with the correct forms of the verbs **ser** or **estar.**

—¡Hola! ¿Cómo te llamas? ¿De dónde (1) __________?

—Me llamo Vicente Bernardo Balvuena Estévez. (2) __________ mexicano, pero mis padres (3) __________ venezolanos. Ellos (4) __________ de Mérida, Venezuela, pero ahora todos nosotros (5) __________ en la Ciudad de México, que (6) __________ la capital del país y una ciudad muy bonita. La Ciudad de México (7) __________ muy grande. En la capital voy a muchos conciertos que (8) __________ divertidos. Esta noche voy a ir al concierto de Mongo Clipper. El concierto (9) __________ a las diez de la noche. (10) __________ en el teatro que (11) __________ cerca de mi casa. Voy con un amigo porque mi novia (12) __________ enferma.

3-27 Entrevista. Answer the following questions about yourself and your family by using the correct form of the verbs **ser** or **estar.**

Modelo: tú
¿enfermo/a?
Sí, estoy enfermo/a. (or) *No, no estoy enfermo/a.*

tu papá / mamá / hijo/a

1. ¿de los EE.UU.? ____

2. ¿en la universidad ahora? _______________

3. ¿joven? _______________

4. ¿trabajando? _______________

tú

5. ¿una buena persona? _______________

6. ¿listo/a? _______________

7. ¿listo/a para ir al cine? _______________

8. ¿estudiando? _______________

9. ¿alto/a? _______________

ustedes (tú y tus padres / hijos)

10. ¿españoles? _______________

11. ¿en casa? _______________

12. ¿enfermos? _______________

3-28 ¡A escribir! Write complete questions, using the words in parentheses and the correct form of the verbs **ser** or **estar.** Follow the model.

MODELO: ¿tu familia? (española)
¿Es española tu familia?

1. ¿tu amiga Viviana? (vieja) _______________

2. ¿tus amigos Pedro y Pablo? (enfermos) _______________

3. ¿tú? (contento) _______________

4. ¿tus amigos? (listos para ir a la biblioteca) _______________

5. ¿tu profesora de francés? (alta) _______________

6. ¿tu madre? (abogada) _______________

7. ¿tu perro (*dog*)? (alegre) _______________

Nombre: ______________________ Fecha: ______________________

Nuestro mundo

Panoramas

3-29 ¡A informarse! Based on the information from **Nuestro mundo** on pages 108–109 of your textbook, decide if the following statements are **cierto (C)** or **falso (F).**

1. Taxco es famosa por la artesanía de plata.
2. En Oaxaco se puede encontrar artesanía de madera.
3. Las maquiladoras no son importantes para la economía de EE.UU.
4. Los trabajadores de las maquiladoras ganan (*earn*) mucho dinero.
5. En las maquiladoras se producen principalmente aparatos electrónicos y componentes de automóviles.
6. Los mariachis tienen su origen en el siglo XVII.
7. "Las mañanitas" es una serenata para celebrar la Navidad.
8. Los estudiantes del Tec de Monterrey no van a estudiar a otros países.
9. Los estudiantes principiantes toman clases de ingeniería.
10. La isla de Cozumel es un lugar muy turístico.

3-30 Tu propia experiencia. Make a list of cultural facts that you know about México (festivities, traditions, old civilizations, cities, etc.). Then choose two of the facts and describe what you know about them in Spanish.

____

____

____

____

____

____

____

____

Nombre: ______________________ Fecha: ______________________

Taller

3-31 Una conversación entre amigos

Primera fase. Alejandro and Tomás are at their favorite café. Read their conversation, and then answer the questions.

Alejandro: ¡Hola, Tomás! ¿Qué hay?

Tomás: Pues, estoy aquí porque estoy muerto de cansancio. ¡Hoy no estudio más!

Alejandro: Chico, ¿por qué estás cansado?

Tomás: ¡Ay! Tengo que trabajar en el centro estudiantil hoy y mañana, tengo que escribir una composición para la clase de literatura, necesito estudiar para un examen de química y el cumpleaños de mi novia es el jueves. Hay una fiesta para ella en mi apartamento el viernes y hay que preparar todo...

Alejandro: ¡Tranquilo, hombre! Soy tu amigo y no estoy ocupado esta semana. Voy a ayudarte (*help you*). ¿Qué necesitas?

Tomás: Hay que preparar comida y comprar refrescos para la fiesta.

Alejandro: Está bien. Yo hago eso.

Tomás: ¡Muchísimas gracias! ¡Tú sí eres mi amigo!

1. ¿Cómo está Tomás?

____

2. ¿Cuándo tiene que trabajar Tomás?

____

3. ¿Para qué clase tiene que escribir una composición?

____

4. ¿En qué clase tiene examen?

____

5. ¿Qué hay en el apartamento de Tomás el viernes? ¿Por qué?

____

6. ¿Cómo va a ayudar Alejandro a Tomás?

____

Nombre: ____________________ Fecha: ____________________

Segunda fase. Based on the conversation and the questions from the **Primera fase,** write at least four questions you can use to ask a classmate when you see him/her on campus. Then use the questions to guide a conversation in Spanish between you and a classmate from your Spanish class. Be sure to include the following points in your interview. If you cannot interview a classmate, write a conversation in Spanish that you might have with a classmate.

- Mood and feelings today
- Classes and class times today
- Schedule (today, this weekend, etc.)
- Homework and exams

1. ____________________

____

2. ____________________

____

3. ____________________

____

4. ____________________

____

3-32 México

Primera fase. Mexican culture and cuisine have been influential in many areas. Interview four U.S. or Canadian students to find out how much they know about Mexico. Use the following chart to guide and record your interviews.

	Estudiante 1	Estudiante 2	Estudiante 3	Estudiante 4
Platos (*dishes*) populares				
La capital				
El presidente				
Grupos políticos				
Geografía				
Grupos indígenas				
Artistas famosos				
Escritores (*writers*) famosos				
¿...?				
¿...?				
¿...?				

Segunda fase. Now, interview a Hispanic student or professor in your community. If possible, interview someone who is from Mexico. Form questions based on the kind of information you gathered in the **Primera fase.** Ask for information about schools and universities in Mexico, as well. Jot down the information he/she gives you, and compare it with the information from the **Primera fase.** How much do students at your university seem to know about Mexico?

MODELO: *¿Quién es el presidente de México?*
¿Cómo es la geografía de México?
¿Cómo son las universidades de México?

____

____

____

____

____

____

3-33 Más allá de las páginas. The Aztecs were a very advanced civilization. In Mexico it is still possible to visit different sites and admire the Aztec ruins. Using the Internet, explore one of these sites. Explain where the site is located, what can be found there, and the significance of the site.

____

____

____

____

____

Nombre: ______________________ Fecha: ______________________

¿Cuánto sabes tú?

3-34 ¿Sabes los números? Match the numbers with their written equivalent.

1. ____ cinco mil ciento cincuenta y cinco
2. ____ doscientos veintidós mil ochocientos veintitrés
3. ____ mil uno
4. ____ veintidós mil doscientos ochenta y tres
5. ____ quinientos quince

a. 1.001
b. 515
c. 222.823
d. 5.155
e. 22.283

3-35 ¿Sabes de posesiones? Match each possessive adjective with the item. Watch for gender and number agreement.

1. ____ nuestros
2. ____ vuestro
3. ____ nuestra
4. ____ su
5. ____ sus
6. ____ vuestros

a. la computadora de ella
b. la calculadora de nosotros
c. los horarios de ustedes
d. los microscopios de nosotros
e. el diccionario de vosotros
f. los mapas de vosotros

3-36 ¿Sabes usar el verbo *tener*? Match each **tener** expression with the most logical statement.

1. ____ La temperatura exterior es 110°F.
2. ____ Él tiene 95 años.
3. ____ Veo una película de terror.
4. ____ La temperatura exterior es −10°F.
5. ____ Hago ejercio por dos horas.
6. ____ Está lloviendo y voy en coche.

a. Tengo miedo.
b. Tengo sed.
c. Tengo frío.
d. Tengo calor.
e. Tengo cuidado.
f. Él es viejo.

Nombre: ______________________________ Fecha: ______________________

3-37 ¿Sabes hacer planes? Fill in the blanks with the appropriate form of the verbs **ir** or **hacer.**

Yo (1) __________ todos los días a la biblioteca y (2) __________ mi tarea allí. Mis amigos también (3) __________ a la biblioteca para estudiar. Después de estudiar, nosotros (4) __________ los planes para el fin de semana. Todos los viernes, nosotros (5) __________ a bailar a la discoteca. Los sábados, nosostros (6) __________ nuestra tarea del fin de semana y por la noche (7) __________ a ver una película a casa de un amigo. Los domingos, yo (8) __________ a trabajar al centro estudiantil y ellos (9) __________ a nadar a la piscina de la universidad. Nosotros (10) __________ lo mismo (*the same*) casi (*almost*) todos los fines de semana.

3-38 ¿Sabes la diferencia entre *ser* y *estar*? Fill in the blanks with the appropriate form of the verbs **ser** or **estar.**

Toño (1) __________ un estudiante mexicano. Él (2) __________ estudiando en los EE.UU. para (3) __________ ingeniero. Toño (4) __________ un buen estudiante, pero hoy (5) __________ preocupado (*worried*) porque tiene un examen de matemáticas. Los exámenes de matemáticas (6) __________ difíciles, pero Toño (7) __________ preparado (*ready*). La profesora de matemáticas (8) __________ muy amable y ella (9) __________ muy contenta porque los estudiantes (10) __________ estudiando mucho para los exámenes.

Nombre: ______________________ Fecha: ______________

Lab Manual

PRIMERA PARTE

¡Así es la vida!

3-39 Llega el autobús. Listen to the following conversation. Then select the letters for all statements that are correct, according to the dialog. You may need to listen to the conversation more than once.

1. Antonio y Silvia hablan...
   a. de las clases.
   b. en la universidad.
   c. con un amigo.
2. Silvia toma... este semestre.
   a. cuatro materias
   b. tres materias
   c. psicología
3. Antonio toma... este semestre.
   a. seis clases
   b. tres clases por la mañana
   c. tres clases por la noche
4. La profesora Corrales es...
   a. profesora de música.
   b. exigente.
   c. aburrida.
5. Antonio tiene que...
   a. estudiar en la biblioteca.
   b. comer en la cafetería.
   c. conversar con la profesora.

Nombre: ______________________ Fecha: ______________________

¡Así lo decimos! Vocabulario

3-40 ¿Lógico o ilógico? Listen to the questions and select the letter that corresponds to the most logical answer. Then listen and repeat as the speaker gives the correct answer.

1. a. En la biblioteca yo estudio álgebra.

   b. Álgebra, química, historia e inglés.

   c. Me gustan el álgebra y la química.

2. a. ¿Estás loco? ¡Él es muy exigente!

   b. No chico, me gusta la clase.

   c. Sí, conozco a la profesora.

3. a. Es a las nueve en punto.

   b. Mi reloj tiene las nueve en punto.

   c. Es a las nueve de la mañana.

4. a. En agosto.

   b. En enero y febrero.

   c. En junio y julio.

5. a. No, solamente 250.

   b. Sí, tengo 30 pesetas.

   c. No, solamente 330.

6. a. Inés estudia en la UBA (Universidad de Buenos Aires).

   b. En la Facultad de Filosofía.

   c. En la biblioteca de la facultad.

Nombre: ______________________ Fecha: ______________________

Pronunciación

Sounds of Spanish *b*, *v*, and *p*

1. In Spanish the letters **b** and **v** are pronounced in exactly the same manner. They have two different sounds.

   At the beginning of a breath group or after the letters **m** or **n**, the **b** and **v** are pronounced like the **b** in the English word *boy*, as in the following examples. This is an occlusive sound.

   buen **vaso** **bastante** **vino** **invierno**

   In any other position, the **b** and **v** are pronounced with the lips slightly open. These are called *fricatives*.

   una biblioteca **ellos van** **nosotros vivimos** **la ventana**

2. The **p** is pronounced like the English *p*, but without the strong puff of air.

   papa **papel** **poco** **política** **Pedro**

3-41 Pronunciemos. You will hear a series of words containing the letters **b** and **v (chica).** Repeat each word or phrase after the speaker. Be sure to pronounce them with your lips pressed together.

1. veces
2. biblioteca
3. vida
4. visitantes
5. buenos
6. también
7. un beso
8. bola
9. tambor
10. baile

3-42 Pronunciemos más. You will hear a series of words that contain the letters **b** and **v (chica)** within a breath group. Your lips should not be completely closed, letting air pass through them. Repeat each word or phrase after the speaker.

1. resolver
2. yo voy a hablar
3. no vamos
4. el banco
5. los labios
6. es buena persona
7. una visita
8. estoy bastante preocupado
9. muy bien
10. el viernes

Nombre: ______________________ Fecha: ______________________

3-43 Y pronunciemos más. You will hear a series of words that contain the letter **p.** When placing your hand in front of your mouth, you should not feel any puff of air. Repeat each word or phrase after the speaker.

1. Pinta
2. partir
3. pronto
4. Paco
5. pito
6. primero

¡Así lo hacemos! Estructuras

1. Los números 101–3.000.000

3-44 Más matemáticas. Solve the following addition problems out loud in Spanish. Then listen and repeat as the speaker gives the correct answer.

1. 100 + 21 = ______________
2. 233 + 117 = ______________
3. 3.104 + 436 = ______________
4. 180.000 + 1.000.000 = ______________
5. 2.129 + 811 = ______________
6. 1.000 + 3.484 = ______________

2. Possessive adjectives

3-45 ¿Es mío o tuyo? Complete each sentence with the appropriate possessive adjective. Then listen and repeat as the speaker gives the correct answer.

Modelo: You see: Yo miro ____ libros.
You say: *Yo miro mis libros.*

1. Nosotras estudiamos mucho en __________ clase.
2. Ellas escuchan a __________ profesora.
3. ¿Tú tienes __________ papeles?
4. Pablo habla con __________ amigo.
5. Yo escribo en __________ cuaderno.
6. ¿Ustedes están en __________ casa por la noche?

Nombre: ______________________ Fecha: ______________________

3-46 Preguntas en la clase. Using the appropriate possessive adjective, answer each question affirmatively. Then listen and repeat as the speaker gives the correct answer.

1. ¿Es la clase de la profesora Serrano?

   Sí, ______________________.

2. ¿Es el libro de nosotros?

   Sí, ______________________.

3. ¿Es el profesor de ustedes?

   Sí, ______________________.

4. ¿Son tus diccionarios?

   Sí, ______________________.

5. ¿Son los cuadernos de Inés?

   Sí, ______________________.

6. ¿Es mi profesora?

   Sí, ______________________.

3. Other expressions with *tener*

3-47 En situaciones diferentes. Listen to what the following people are experiencing in each situation. Then listen and repeat as the speaker gives the correct answer.

1. Yo ______________________.
2. El niño ______________________.
3. Usted ______________________.
4. Tú ______________________.
5. Julia y Tomás ______________________.

Nombre: ______________________________ Fecha: ______________________

SEGUNDA PARTE

¡Así es la vida!

3-48 Después de clase. Listen to the following conversation among three students. Then read the statements that follow. Each statement is followed by three items. Select all the items that apply to each statement. You may need to listen to the conversation more than once.

1. Estudia(n) biología.

   a. Pablo

   b. Inés

   c. Elena

2. Necesita(n) ir a la biblioteca de música hoy.

   a. Inés

   b. Pablo

   c. Elena

3. Está enfrente del laboratorio de lenguas.

   a. la librería

   b. la biblioteca de música

   c. la cafetería

4. Está al lado del centro estudiantil.

   a. la biblioteca de música

   b. la cafetería

   c. el laboratorio de lenguas

¡Así lo decimos! Vocabulario

3-49 ¿Lógico o ilógico? Complete the following sentences with the most logical choice. Then listen and repeat as the speaker gives the correct answer.

1. La cafetería...
   a. está cerca de la biblioteca.
   b. está en mi casa.
   c. vende libros.
2. Mi amigo chileno siempre...
   a. es cerca de la biblioteca.
   b. toma un bocadillo en el almuerzo.
   c. es necesario el refresco.
3. ¿Qué hora es?
   a. Está a la izquierda.
   b. Es la rectoría.
   c. Es la hora del almuerzo.
4. La rectoría está...
   a. enferma.
   b. al lado de la cafetería.
   c. después del café.
5. Usted está en la cafetería y desea un refresco. Usted dice:
   a. "Con permiso, un refresco".
   b. "Perdón, un refresco".
   c. "Por favor, un refresco".

Pronunciación

Sounds of Spanish *k*, *c*, and *z*

1. In Spanish, the **k** and the combinations **qu, ca, co,** and **cu** are pronounced like the English *c* in the word *cut*, but without the puff of air.

   kilómetro **Quito** **casa** **color** **cuna**

2. In Spanish America, the letters **c** (before **e** and **i**) and **z** are pronounced like the English *s* in the word *sense*. In most of Spain, these sounds are pronounced like the *th* in *think*.

   cena **ciudad** **zapato** **zona** **manzana**

Nombre: ______________________ Fecha: ______________________

3-50 Pronunciemos. You will hear a series of words that contain the **k** sound represented by the combinations **qu, ca, co, cu,** and the letter **k.** Listen and repeat each word after the speaker. Be sure to avoid the puff of air.

1. calculadora
2. kilo
3. queso
4. kiosco
5. Colón
6. que
7. casa
8. cosa
9. cura
10. caso

3-51 Pronunciemos más. You will now hear the **s** sound represented by the combinations **ce, ci,** and the letter **z.** Listen and repeat each word after the speaker.

1. zapato
2. cesto
3. cine
4. gracias
5. cerveza
6. ciudad
7. cemento
8. cita
9. taza
10. hace

¡Así lo hacemos! Estructuras

4. The present indicative tense of *ir* (to go) and *hacer* (to do; to make)

3-52 ¿A dónde vas? Using the words provided, tell where the following people are going. Then listen and repeat as the speaker gives the correct answer.

MODELO: You see: yo / a mi clase
You say: *Yo voy a mi clase.*

1. yo / a la Facultad de Medicina
2. tú / a tu casa
3. usted / a la biblioteca
4. ella / al laboratorio de lenguas
5. nosotras / a la Facultad de Filosofía y Letras
6. ellos / al centro estudiantil

Nombre: ________________________ Fecha: ____________________

3-53 ¿A dónde van? Answer the questions that you hear affirmatively. Then listen and repeat as the speaker gives the correct answer.

1. Sí, ______________________.
2. Sí, ______________________.
3. Sí, ______________________.
4. Sí, ______________________.
5. Sí, ______________________.
6. Sí, ______________________.
7. Sí, ______________________.

3-54 ¿Qué vamos a hacer? Say what the following people are going to do. Then listen and repeat as the speaker gives the correct answer.

1. Ustedes __________ a trabajar esta noche.
2. Tú __________ a tomar un café.
3. Eduardo y Fabián __________ a practicar béisbol.
4. Magdalena y yo __________ a preparar una ensalada.
5. Yo __________ a vivir en un apartamento.
6. David __________ a estar en la biblioteca.
7. Yo __________ a comer en la cafetería.

5. The present tense of *estar* (to be) and the present progressive

3-55 ¿Dónde están? Tell where the following people and places are, using the cues provided. Then listen and repeat as the speaker gives the correct answer.

1. mis amigos y yo / cerca de la biblioteca
2. tú / enfrente de la cafetería
3. la Facultad de Medicina / detrás de la biblioteca
4. yo / en el centro estudiantil
5. la Facultad de Arte y la Facultad de Ciencias / lejos

Nombre: ________________________________ Fecha: ______________________

3-56 ¿Cómo estás? Answer the questions you hear, using the appropriate form of the word or phrase provided. Then listen and repeat as the speaker gives the correct answer.

1. aburrido
2. enfermo
3. cansado
4. ocupado
5. muy enfadado

3-57 ¿Qué estás haciendo? Look at the following pictures and write, and then say, what the people are doing, using the cues provided. Then listen and repeat as the speaker gives the correct answer.

1. tú (dormir)

____

2. nosotros (hablar)

____

3. yo (pedir)

____

4. Pedro (comer)

____

5. Teresa (escribir)

____

6. nosotros (correr)

____

7. tú (leer)

____

8. Carlota y Lupe (cantar)

____

Nombre: ______________________ Fecha: ______________________

3-58 ¿Qué están haciendo? Tell what the following people are doing, using the cues provided. Then listen and repeat as the speaker gives the correct answer.

1. tú / escribir / tu nombre, ¿no?
2. Ana Florencia / leer / el mapa
3. nosotros / discutir / una novela
4. ustedes / repetir / el vocabulario
5. yo / hablar / con el profesor
6. Ana y Cecilia / pedir / un video en el laboratorio de lenguas

6. Summary of uses of *ser* and *estar*

3-59 ¿Ser o no ser? Make complete sentences using the appropriate form of **ser** or **estar** and the cues provided. Then listen and repeat as the speaker gives the correct answer.

Modelo: You see: mis padres / de España
You say: *Mis padres son de España.*

1. el padre de Armando / mexicano
2. el primer día de primavera / el 20 de marzo
3. Marcos / hablando por teléfono y Fernando / leyendo un libro
4. la biblioteca / allí, detrás de la Facultad de Medicina
5. mi padre / bajo y gordito y mi madre / baja pero delgada
6. el concierto / en el Teatro Cervantes

3-60 Descripciones. Complete each description with the correct form of **ser** or **estar** and the appropriate adjective. Then listen and repeat as the speaker gives the correct answer.

Modelo: You see: Los profesores (to be sick)
You write and say: *Los profesores están enfermos.*

1. Jaime y María (to be bad) ______________________.
2. José (to be ugly) ______________________.
3. Josefina (to look pretty) ______________________ esta noche.
4. Tus amigos (to be clever) ______________________.

Nombre: ______________________ Fecha: ______________________

5. Mis padres (to be ready) ______________________.

6. Tu profesora (to be funny) ______________________.

¿Cuánto sabes tú?

3-61 ¿Qué hacemos? Tell what you and your friends are doing, using the words provided. Then listen and repeat as the speaker gives the correct answer.

1. yo / ir / a la Facultad de Medicina
2. luego Susana y yo / ir / a la cafetería
3. Pablo / aprender / mucho / en la clase de historia
4. hoy / él y Pedro / ir / a casa a estudiar
5. tú / ir / a la biblioteca, ¿verdad?
6. perdón / ¿ustedes / comer / en casa?
7. yo / estar / aburrido / de la comida / de la cafetería
8. Inés / trabajar / estudiar / leer / en la biblioteca

3-62 Preguntas personales. Listen to the questions you hear. Then write, as well as say, your answers. Answers will vary.

1. ______________________
2. ______________________
3. ______________________
4. ______________________
5. ______________________
6. ______________________

Nombre: ______________________________ Fecha: ______________________

4 ¿Cómo es tu familia?

Workbook

PRIMERA PARTE

¡Así es la vida!

4-1 ¿Recuerdas? Answer the following questions in Spanish. Choose the correct option, according to the e-mail in **¡Así es la vida!** on page 116 of your textbook.

1. ¿De quién recibe un correo electrónico Juan Antonio?

   a. su padre b. su hermano c. su amiga Ana María d. su prima Ana María

2. ¿De dónde es Juan Antonio?

   a. Guatemala b. Honduras c. Puerto Rico d. Costa Rica

3. ¿Con quién está Ana María ahora?

   a. sus amigos b. su familia c. sus compañeros de clase d. sus profesores

4. ¿Qué es el padre de Ana María?

   a. abogado b. profesor c. dentista d. ingeniero

5. ¿Cuántos hermanos tiene Ana María?

   a. tres b. cuatro c. dos d. uno

6. ¿Cuántos años tiene el hermano menor?

   a. veintidós b. diecinueve c. quince d. nueve

7. ¿Quiénes son Gustavo y Elena?

   a. los padres de Ana María c. los abuelos de Ana María

   b. los tíos de Ana María d. los hermanos de Ana María

Nombre: ______________________ Fecha: ______________________

8. ¿Quién es Pablo?

   a. el hijo de Ana María   c. el primo de Ana María

   b. el hermano de Ana María   d. el abuelo de Ana María

9. ¿Cómo es él?

   a. pequeño   b. gracioso   c. tranquilo   d. simpático

10. ¿A dónde va la familia de Ana en julio?

   a. Tikal   b. Costa Rica   c. Guatemala   d. la universidad

¡Así lo decimos! Vocabulario

4-2 Tu familia. Describe your family relationships by completing each sentence with a vocabulary word from **¡Así lo decimos!** on page 117 of your textbook.

1. El padre de mi padre es mi ______________________.
2. La hermana de mi madre es mi ______________________.
3. El esposo de mi hermana es mi ______________________.
4. Los hijos de mi hermana son mis ______________________.
5. La madre de mi esposo es mi ______________________.
6. Las hijas de mi tío son mis ______________________.
7. La esposa de mi hijo es mi ______________________.
8. El hijo de mis padres es mi ______________________.
9. Los padres de mi madre son mis ______________________.
10. El esposo de mi hija es mi ______________________.

Nombre: ______________________ Fecha: ______________________

4-3 Preguntas personales. Your roommate wants to know more about your family. Answer your roomate's questions in Spanish.

1. ¿De dónde son tus abuelos?

   ____

2. ¿Viven tus abuelos cerca o lejos de tu casa?

   ____

3. ¿Tienes hermanos o hermanas? ¿Son mayores o menores?

   ____

4. ¿Tienes muchos primos?

   ____

5. ¿Cómo son ellos?

   ____

6. ¿Cuántas tías tienes?

   ____

7. ¿Quién es el miembro favorito de tu familia?

   ____

Nombre: ______________________________ Fecha: ______________________

¡Así lo hacemos! Estructuras

1. The present tense of stem-changing verbs: *e → ie, e → i, o → ue*

4-4 ¡A escoger! Explain what's going on at your home by choosing one of the verbs from the word bank and logically completing the sentences.

dormir   jugar   preferir hablar   querer   servir   soñar

1. Nosotros ____________________ la comida.
2. Nuestros abuelos ____________________ con ser jóvenes.
3. Mis tías ____________________ sobre (*about*) sus familias con sus cuñadas.
4. Mi prima ____________________ ir a una discoteca.
5. Yo ____________________ hasta (*until*) las once de la mañana.
6. Mi hermana y su novio ____________________ a fútbol con nuestros primos en el jardín.

4-5 Nuestra familia. Fill in the blanks with the correct form of the verbs in parentheses.

1. Cuando yo (almorzar) ____________________ en la cafetería, yo (pedir) ____________________ una hamburguesa y un refresco.
2. Mi hermana (poder) ____________________ jugar bien al tenis, pero mi hermano no (jugar) ____________________ bien.
3. Mi tío siempre (dormir) ____________________ una siesta por la tarde, pero mi tía no (entender) ____________________ por qué.
4. Mis primas (servir) ____________________ bocadillos cuando mis abuelos (venir) ____________________ a casa.
5. Yo (poder) ____________________ perder la paciencia cuando (pensar) ____________________ en mis problemas.

Nombre: ____________________ Fecha: ____________________

4-6 Tu familia. Answer these questions about your family with complete sentences in Spanish.

1. ¿Tienes muchos hermanos?

   ____

2. ¿Vienen ellos a la universidad?

   ____

3. ¿Riñes (*quarrel*) mucho con ellos?

   ____

4. ¿Piensas visitar a tu familia pronto? ¿Cuándo?

   ____

5. ¿Entienden tus padres español?

   ____

6. Generalmente, ¿donde almuerzan tus padres?

   ____

7. ¿Con qué sueñan ellos?

   ____

8. ¿Qué prefieres hacer con tu familia, tener una fiesta o conversar?

   ____

4-7 Un día en la vida de Tomás. What does Tomás do on a typical day? Complete the description with the correct form of each verb in parentheses.

Todos los días, Tomás (1. tener) ____________ que asistir a tres clases. La primera clase (2. empezar) ____________ a las ocho de la mañana y, a esa hora, Tomás está cansado. Cuando (3. poder) ____________, (4. preferir) ____________ dormir y (5. dormir) ____________ hasta muy tarde. A las once y media, (6. almorzar) ____________. Casi siempre (7. pedir) ____________ una hamburguesa en el centro estudiantil. Según Tomás, el centro (8. servir) ____________ las mejores hamburguesas del mundo. A las dos, (9. volver) ____________ a su

Nombre: ______________________ Fecha: ______________________

residencia y (10. comenzar) ______________ a estudiar. (11. Querer) ______________ salir, pero estudiar es muy importante. A las cuatro, (12. jugar) ______________ baloncesto con unos amigos. Él (13. pensar) ______________ que juega bien, pero sus amigos (14. decir) ______________ que no. Después, cena en la cafetería porque (15. pensar) ______________ que la comida es bastante buena ahí. Finalmente, a las ocho, termina su día.

2. Direct objects, the personal *a,* and direct object pronouns

4-8 El fin de semana. Complete the following descriptions of weekend plans with the personal **a,** when needed.

1. Esteban va a ver ______________ Jorge y ______________ Gustavo.
2. Llevo ______________ mis hermanos a dar un paseo.
3. Vemos ______________ la película en el cine.
4. Invito ______________ Daniel a pasear por el centro.
5. Edmundo tiene ______________ amigos peruanos y va a visitarlos.
6. Marta y tú llevan ______________ los refrescos a una fiesta.
7. Ana compra ______________ las entradas para asistir a un partido.
8. Vamos a invitar ______________ nuestros tíos a ir a la playa.
9. Eduardo y Mario llaman por teléfono ______________ sus amigos.
10. Mi mamá va a visitar ______________ un museo.

Nombre: ______________________ Fecha: ______________

4-9 ¡A completar! Complete each sentence with the direct object pronoun that corresponds to the subject in italics.

Modelo: *Nosotros* debemos esperar aquí, porque tu madre *nos* busca.

1. *Yo* no puedo ir al centro, porque mis padres ______________ necesitan.
2. *Tú* llamas a María, pero ella no ______________ llama.
3. *Marta y Gisela* viven lejos, pero yo siempre ______________ visito.
4. *Yo* hablo con mi hermano, pero él no ______________ escucha.
5. *Carlos y Adrián* miran a las chicas correr por el parque, pero ellas no ______________ ven.
6. *Ella* te quiere mucho, pero tú no ______________ quieres.
7. *Ana y Carmen* buscan a Marisa para conversar en un café, pero ella no ______________ busca.
8. *Él* quiere a su novia, pero ella no ______________ quiere a él.

4-10 Rolando redundante. Rolando tends to be redundant, repeating unnecessary information. Rephrase each of his second sentences, using a direct object pronoun.

1. Yo tengo tres primos. Yo llamo a mis primos todos los días.

   Yo ______________ llamo todos los días.

2. Tus abuelos son divertidos. Mi tía visita a tus abuelos mucho.

   Mi tía ______________ visita mucho.

3. Bebemos muchos refrescos en casa. Mi madrastra compra refrescos.

   Mi madrastra ______________ compra.

4. Los padres de mi padrastro viven cerca. Mi padrastro invita a sus padres a comer en casa todos los viernes.

   Mi padrastro ______________ invita a comer en casa todos los viernes.

5. Tu coche es muy grande. Tu cuñado necesita tu coche esta semana.

   Tu cuñado ______________ necesita esta semana.

6. Creo que éstos son el libro y la novela de sus sobrinos. Sus sobrinos buscan su libro y su novela.

   Sus sobrinos ______________ buscan.

7. Tu mapa tiene mucha información. Nuestra sobrina mira tu mapa.

   Nuestra sobrina ______________ mira.

8. Necesitan una hamburguesa y dos sándwiches para el almuerzo. Su madrina prepara una hamburguesa y dos sándwiches.

   Su madrina ______________ prepara.

9. Hay dos cámaras en la mesa. El esposo busca dos cámaras.

   El esposo ______________ busca.

10. Las nueras llegan mañana. Sus suegros invitan a sus nueras a la fiesta.

   Sus suegros ______________ invitan a la fiesta.

4-11 El vecino (*neighbor*). Your neighbor is a busybody and wants to know what everyone in your family is doing. Answer each question by using the progressive form of the verb and the pronoun of the direct object.

MODELO: ¿Prepara tu hermana el sándwich?
Sí, mi hermana está preparándolo.

1. ¿Miran la televisión tus padres?

   ____

2. ¿Lee la novela tu hermana?

   ____

3. ¿Beben refrescos tus hermanos?

   ____

4. ¿Come el sándwich tu abuelo?

   ____

5. ¿Escribe la carta tu prima?

   ____

6. ¿Toca la guitarra tu tío?

   ____

7. ¿Sirve los refrescos tu abuela?

   ____

8. ¿Escuchan música tus hermanas?

   ____

Nombre: ______________________________ Fecha: ______________________

3. The present tense of *poner, salir,* and *traer*

4-12 Varias situaciones. What do people do on different occasions? Fill in the blanks with the correct form of the indicated verb.

poner

1. Ana y Pepe siempre ________________ los libros en la mochila. Yo ________________ los libros en una bolsa grande. Y tú, ¿dónde ________________ los libros? Mi amigo Raúl no ________________ los libros en una mochila. ¡Los tiene en el coche!

salir

2. Sandra ________________ con Teodoro. Ellos ________________ a nadar todas las tardes y por la noche, ________________ a comer en un restaurante. Mi vida es más difícil. Yo ________________ de la casa a las ocho de la mañana y ________________ del trabajo a las cinco. Mis amigos y yo sólo ________________ a cenar a restaurantes los viernes, porque son muy caros. Los sábados, ________________ para las montañas para pasar el fin de semana.

traer

3. ¿Qué ________________ tú a la clase? Yo ________________ el libro y Teresa ________________ el cuaderno de actividades. Quique y Eduardo ________________ el diccionario.

4-13 Los planes. These friends have plans for the weekend. Fill in the blanks with the correct form (conjugated or infinitive) of the most logical verb: **poner, salir,** or **traer.**

Federico y Timoteo (1) ________________ hoy para la playa. Timoteo (2) ________________ los sándwiches. Federico (3) ________________ los refrescos. Federico (4) ________________ todas las cosas en su coche. Piensan (5) ________________ a las tres de la tarde. A las dos y media Timoteo llama a Federico.

Timoteo: ¡Hola, Federico! ¿A qué hora (6) ________________ (nosotros)?

Federico: En treinta minutos. Yo (7) ________________ mis cosas en el coche ahora.

Timoteo: Fede, no es posible (8) ________________ a las tres. Necesito ver a mi mamá antes de (9) ________________.

Nombre: ______________________ Fecha: ______________________

Federico: ¿A qué hora tienes que ver a tu mamá?

Timoteo: A las tres y cuarto. (10) ______________ (Yo) de mi casa ahora.

Federico: Chico, no hay problema. Tú y yo (11) ______________ a las cuatro.

SEGUNDA PARTE

¡Así es la vida!

4-14 Una invitación. Complete the sentences, according to the dialog in **¡Así es la vida!** on page 133 of your textbook.

1. Raúl llama a Laura para ver si...

   a. está bien   b. quiere ir al cine   c. quiere ir a cenar

2. El cine se llama...

   a. *Abre los ojos*   b. Rialto   c. *Vanilla Sky*

3. En el cine están presentando...

   a. *Abre los ojos*   b. Rialto   c. *Vanilla Sky*

4. Laura le pregunta a Raúl...

   a. quiénes son los actores   b. cuánto cuesta el cine   c. a qué hora es la película

5. La película comienza...

   a. a las siete   b. a las seis y media   c. esta noche

6. Raúl pasa por Laura...

   a. a las siete   b. a las seis y media   c. esta noche

Nombre: ______________________ Fecha: ______________________

¡Así lo decimos! Vocabulario

4-15 Más invitaciones. Laura and Raúl had a wonderful time at the movies and have decided to see each other again. Using the dialog in **¡Así es la vida!** on page 133 of your textbook as a model, write a brief conversation to suit the following situation.

Laura calls Raúl and invites him to go dancing at the new club La Bamba. He says he would love to and asks Laura what time she's coming by for him. She answers at 8:15, and then they say good-bye.

____

____

____

____

4-16 Unas preguntas. Match each question with a response from the list.

1. ____ ¿Puedes ir al cine esta noche?
2. ____ ¿A qué hora pasas por mí?
3. ____ ¡Qué bonita estás!
4. ____ ¿Vamos al concierto esta noche?
5. ____ ¿Cómo estás, cariño?
6. ____ ¿Donde estás, mi amor?

a. Sí, me encantaría.
b. En casa, mi vida.
c. A las seis.
d. Muchas gracias.
e. Muy bien, mi cielo.
f. Sí, claro.

¡Así lo hacemos! Estructuras

4. Demonstrative adjectives and pronouns

4-17 De compras. You are shopping at a store. Indicate your preferences by completing each of the following statements with the correct demonstrative adjective.

1. Quiero (these) ______________ camisas.
2. Prefiero (those) ______________ camisas.
3. No me gustan (those over there) ______________ suéteres.
4. Voy a comprar (that) ______________ suéter.
5. Deseo probarme (these) ______________ zapatos.

Nombre: ______________________ Fecha: ______________________

4-18 ¿Qué prefieres? At the university store, a clerk asks you which of the following items you would like to buy. Reply, following the model, and make changes when necessary.

MODELO: camisa (este/ése)
Prefiero estas camisas, no ésas.

1. cuaderno (este/ése)

   Prefiero ______________ cuadernos, no ______________.

2. mochila (ese/aquél)

   Prefiero ______________ mochilas, no ______________.

3. suéter (ese/aquél)

   Prefiero ______________ suéter, no ______________.

4. diccionario (este/ése)

   Prefiero ______________ diccionario, no ______________.

5. calculadora (ese/aquél)

   Prefiero ______________ calculadora, no ______________.

6. lápiz (ese/aquél)

   Prefiero ______________ lápiz, no ______________.

Nombre: ____________________ Fecha: ____________________

4-19 En la fiesta. Your family is attending a party at your friend's house. He approaches you and wants to know who, among the crowd, each member of your family is. Fill in the blanks with the appropriate demonstrative adjective or pronoun.

Amigo: Hola. Veo que toda tu familia está aquí.

Usted: Sí, gracias por invitarnos.

Amigo: ¿Quiénes son tus padres?

Usted: Mi padre es (1) ____________ señor alto y calvo (*bald*) que está allá (*over there*) lejos hablando con tu padre.

Amigo: ¿Es tu madre (2) ____________ señora que está aquí?

Usted: No, (3) ____________ es mi tía. Mi madre es (4) ____________ señora que está cerca de mi padre.

Amigo: ¿Están tus hermanos en la fiesta?

Usted: ¡Por supuesto! Mi hermano es (5) ____________ chico de allí, (6) ____________ que está cerca de la puerta.

Amigo: ¿Y tus hermanas?

Usted: Son (7) ____________ chicas con las que estoy hablando. Te las presento. (8) ____________ es Ángela y (9) ____________ es Carmen.

Amigo: Encantado. Mucho gusto en conocerlas.

Usted: Muchas gracias por invitarnos. ¡(10) ____________ fiesta es maravillosa!

5. *Saber* and *conocer*

4-20 Unas preguntas. Imagine that you and your friend are discussing your common acquaintances. Complete the questions with the correct forms of the verbs **saber** and **conocer.** Then answer the questions.

1. ¿____________ (tú) bien a mis primas?

____

2. ¿____________ (tú) dónde viven exactamente?

____

3. ¿________________________ (tú) también a mis tíos?

____

4. ¿________________________ mi tía que tú eres mi amigo/a?

____

5. ¿________________________ (ellas) cuándo es la reunión de toda la familia?

____

4-21 Más información. Your friend wants to know more about your cousins. Complete each question with the correct form of the verbs **saber** or **conocer.**

1. ¿________________________ ellas jugar al vólibol?
2. ¿________________________ ellas a toda tu familia también?
3. ¿________________________ bailar bien Marcela?
4. ¿________________________ (ellas) a tus padres también?
5. ¿________________________ (tú) si ellos visitan a sus padres en diciembre?
6. ¿________________________ (ellas) que yo estudio español?
7. ¿________________________ Anita que tu vives en la residencia estudiantil?
8. ¿________________________ (tú) al novio de Anita?
9. ¿________________________ Carmen hablar francés?
10. ¿________________________ (tú) a mis tíos?

Nombre: ______________________________ Fecha: ______________________

4-22 Una conversación. Complete the following conversation that two friends are having about a new student with the correct form of the verbs **saber** or **conocer.**

Juan: ¿(1) ______________ al estudiante nuevo? ¿(2) ______________ cómo se llama?

Pablo: No (3) ______________ cómo se llama, pero (4) ______________ que su apodo es Macho Camacho.

Juan: ¿(5) ______________ si Macho habla español?

Pablo: Sí, (6) ______________ que habla español.

Juan: ¿(7) ______________ dónde vive?

Pablo: Yo no (8) ______________ dónde vive, pero mi hermano Paco (9) ______________ que vive cerca de la universidad.

Juan: Y ¿Paco (10) ______________ a Macho?

Pablo: Sí, Paco (11) ______________ a Macho y también (12) ______________ a su novia. Yo no (13) ______________ a la novia de Macho, pero (14) ______________ que se llama Remedios.

Juan: ¿(15) ______________ tú a Remedios?

Pablo: No, yo no (16) ______________ a Remedios.

Juan: Bueno, hasta luego. Tengo que estudiar.

Pablo: Adiós.

NUESTRO MUNDO

Panoramas

4-23 ¡A informarse! Based on the information from **Nuestro mundo** on pages 144–145 of your textbook, decide if the following statements are **cierto (C)** or **falso (F).**

1. Hay muchas montañas y selvas en Centroamérica.
2. Los gobiernos centroamericanos no hacen nada para hacer llegar los avances de la medicina al pueblo.
3. La paz llegó (*arrived*) a El Salvador en 1992.

Nombre: ______________________ Fecha: ______________________

4. El Izalco es un volcán en El Salvador.
5. En El Salvador, no es posible hacer ecoturismo.
6. Tikal es una ciudad de ruinas aztecas.
7. Los mayas ya (*already*) utilizaban canales para el agua de la lluvia.
8. Los tejidos (*woven goods*) tradicionales indígenas no son populares entre los turistas.
9. La economía centroamericana se basa (*is based*) en la industria.
10. El café es un producto muy importante para la economía de Centroamérica.

4-24 Tu propia experiencia. Make a list of the common characteristics among the countries in Central America. Then, choose two, and describe what you know about them in Spanish.

____

____

____

____

____

Taller

4-25 La familia

Primera fase. Write at least eight questions in Spanish that you can use to find out about someone's family.

Modelo: ¿Estás casado/a?
¿Cuántos hijos/hermanos tienes?

____

____

____

____

____

____

____

____

Nombre: ______________________ Fecha: ______________________

Segunda fase. Interview a Spanish-speaking student, professor, or other community member about his/her family. Use the questions you wrote in the **Primera fase** and jot down the information you learn.

MODELO: Tú: *¿Estás casado?*
Entrevistado/a: *Sí, estoy casado y tengo hijos.*
Tú: *¿Cuántos hijos tienes?*

____

____

____

____

____

____

____

Tercera fase. Use the information from the **Segunda fase** to write a brief paragraph about the family of the person you interviewed.

MODELO: *Eduardo tiene una familia muy interesante y grande...*

____

____

____

____

____

____

____

4-26 Rigoberta Menchú. Select and research one of the following topics related to Rigoberta Menchú. Use the Internet or library resources, and prepare a brief presentation in English or Spanish to present to the class. The presentation can be artwork (a poster with images and captions), a report, a summary, and so forth.

- Rigoberta Menchú and her family have strong ties, some of which were formed through very difficult and sad years. Find out more about Rigoberta's childhood family, the problems they faced, and how they influenced her life and her current family.

- Rigoberta Menchú is almost always found wearing traditional woven goods from Guatemala. Find out more about this tradition, the dyeing and weaving processes, and the people who continue the tradition.
- Rigoberta Menchú worked with a writer to produce a very important book about the plight of many indigenous Guatemalans. Find out more about the book, how it was produced, the information and messages presented, and so forth.

4-27 Más allá de las páginas. Using the Internet, look up an organization, magazine, or community effort based on protecting the rights of women in Latin America. What do you think the current social status of women in Latin America is? Based on your investigation, do you think there is any social change taking place? Explain your answer.

____

____

____

____

____

¿Cuánto sabes tú?

4-28 ¿Sabes usar los verbos irregulares? Complete the following sentences with the appropriate form of the verbs in parentheses.

1. Mi madre me (querer) ______________ mucho.
2. Yo no (entender) ______________ las matemáticas.
3. Nosotros (pensar) ______________ estudiar ingeniería.
4. Mis tíos (preferir) ______________ pasar las fiestas en su casa.
5. Normalmente, yo (volver) ______________ tarde de la escuela.
6. ¿(Poder) ______________ ir (tú) al cine con nosotros?

Nombre: ______________________ Fecha: ______________________

4-29 ¿Sabes usar pronombres de objeto directo? Match the following sentences with the appropriate direct object pronoun.

1. Quiero mucho a mis abuelos y ________ visito todas las semanas. — a. me
2. Mi hermana ayuda mucho a mi madre; ________ quiere mucho. — b. la
3. Mi primo me pide ayuda y yo ________ ayudo. — c. los
4. Yo pido ayuda a mi primo y él ________ ayuda. — d. nos
5. Mis abuelos viven cerca de nuestra casa; ________ visitan frecuentemente. — e. lo

4-30 ¿Sabes usar los verbos *poner, salir* y *traer*? Fill in the blanks with the appropriate form of the verbs **poner, salir,** or **traer.**

1. Los estudiantes siempre ______________ sus libros a clase.
2. Yo nunca ______________ de casa sin mis libros.
3. Mis padres siempre ______________ a cenar los viernes por la noche.
4. Yo siempre ______________ los libros encima de la mesa.
5. Mis amigos y yo ______________ la comida a la fiesta.
6. Mi abuelo ______________ azúcar en el café.

4-31 ¿Sabes usar los adjetivos y pronombres demostrativos? Complete each sentence with the most appropriate demonstrative adjective or pronoun.

1. Esta casa es de mis abuelos, pero ______________ es de mis tíos.

   a. este b. aquella c. aquélla d. esos

2. Mi primo es ______________ chico que está aquí.

   a. aquel b. este c. aquél d. éste

3. Mi hermana no quiere esta silla, sino que quiere ______________ que está allí.

   a. ésa b. ese c. esa d. ése

4. Mis padres trabajan en ______________ edificio (*building*) allá lejos.

   a. esta b. ésta c. aquellos d. aquel

5. ______________ chico es mi amigo Ramón.

a. Estos b. Este c. Esos d. Aquellas

6. ¿Qué es ______________ que tienes en la mano?

a. estos b. este c. éste d. eso

4-32 ¿Sabes la diferencia entre *saber* y *conocer*? Fill in the blanks with the appropriate form of the verbs **saber** or **conocer.**

1. Yo no ______________ Nueva York. Me gustaría visitarla algún día.
2. Mi madre ______________ cocinar muy bien.
3. Todos ______________ quién es Antonio Banderas.
4. Mis padres ______________ a todos mis amigos.
5. Los estudiantes de español ______________ la diferencia entre *saber* y *conocer*.

Nombre: ______________________ Fecha: ______________________

Lab Manual

Primera parte

¡Así es la vida!

4-33 La familia de Éster. Listen to the following description. Then select all the letters corresponding to the statements that are correct, according to what you heard. Listen as many times as necessary to find all the correct statements.

1. ... de Éster celebran el aniversario.
   a. Los tíos
   b. Los padres
   c. Los abuelos
2. La familia de Éster...
   a. es unida.
   b. vive en México.
   c. es importante para ella.
3. Federico es...
   a. el esposo de Catalina.
   b. el padre de Éster.
   c. el primo de Samuel.
4. Samuel...
   a. es gracioso.
   b. está casado.
   c. está ahora en Puebla.
5. Griselda es...
   a. la hermana de Samuel.
   b. la hija de Catalina.
   c. la cuñada de Federico.
6. El hijo de Catalina...
   a. es menor que Éster.
   b. tiene primos en la capital.
   c. se llama Héctor.
7. ... de Juana viven en Puebla.
   a. El abuelo
   b. El tío
   c. El hermano
8. Éster visita a sus... en la capital.
   a. tíos
   b. primos
   c. abuelos

¡Así lo decimos! Vocabulario

4-34 El árbol genealógico. Look at the following family tree and answer the questions you hear logically, using expressions and vocabulary from **¡Así lo decimos!** on page 117 of your textbook. Then listen and repeat as the speaker gives the correct answer.

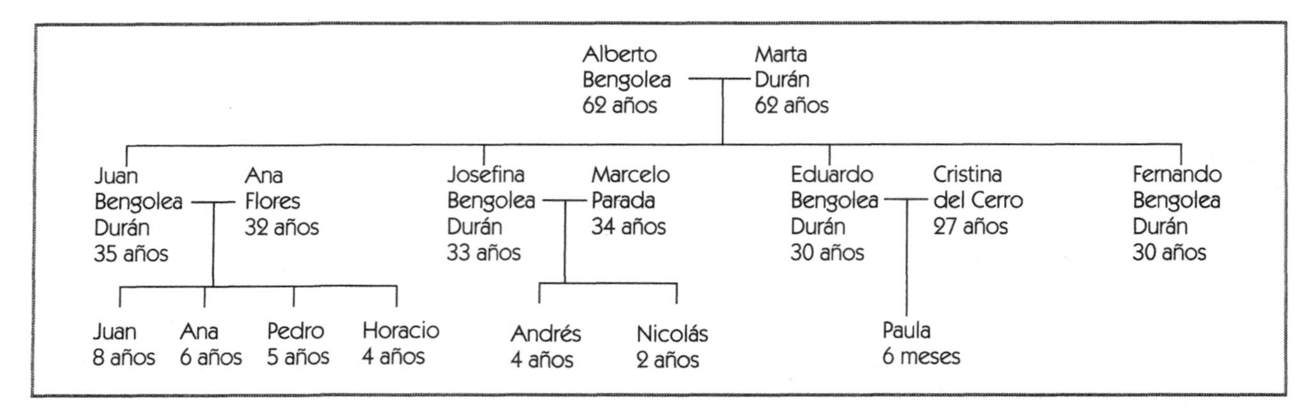

1. ...
2. ...
3. ...
4. ...
5. ...
6. ...
7. ...
8. ...

Pronunciación

Sounds of *d* and *t*

1. The Spanish **d** has two distinct sounds: dental and interdental. At the beginning of a breath group or after the letters **l** or **n,** the **d** is dental. Pronounce it with the tip of the tongue pressed against the back of the upper front teeth. In all other cases, the **d** is interdental. Place the tip of the tongue between the upper and lower teeth, like the weak English *th* in *that*. Note the following examples.

Dental:	**dar**	**andar**	**caldera**	**Daniel**	**falda**	**senda**
Interdental:	**modo**	**cada**	**verdad**	**edad**	**unida**	**cada**

2. The Spanish **t** is pronounced by pressing the tip of the tongue against the upper front teeth rather than against the ridge above the teeth, as in English. The Spanish **t** is also pronounced without the puff of air that normally follows the English *t*. Note the following examples.

torre	**meta**	**tú**
Tomás	**puerta**	**otoño**
tanto	**octubre**	**taco**

Nombre: ______________________________ Fecha: ______________________

4-35 Pronunciemos. You will hear a series of Spanish words that begin with the letter **d** or that have a **d** at the beginning of a breath group. Repeat each word after the speaker.

1. diaria
2. después
3. dónde
4. desgracia
5. dentro
6. aldea
7. andando
8. día
9. grande
10. dormir

4-36 Pronunciemos más. Now you will hear a series of Spanish words and phrases that contain the interdental **d.** Repeat the word or phrase after the speaker.

1. vida
2. sábado
3. estudiantil
4. ideal
5. nadar
6. idea
7. residencia de estudiantes
8. con usted
9. buenos días
10. tarde

4-37 Y pronunciemos más. Now you will hear a series of Spanish words that begin with the **t** sound. Repeat each word after the speaker.

1. Tomás
2. tienes
3. traer
4. Tejas
5. también
6. taco
7. tomamos
8. todos
9. té
10. trópico

Nombre: ______________________ Fecha: ______________________

¡Así lo hacemos! Estructuras

1. The present tense of stem-changing verbs: *e → ie, e → i, o → ue*

4-38 ¿Qué piensas tú? Read each item, filling in the blanks with the correct form of the verbs in parentheses. Then listen and repeat as the speaker gives the correct answer.

1. Yo (preferir) ______________________ las películas cómicas, pero Juan (preferir) ______________________ las de misterio.
2. Tú (almorzar) ______________________ todos los días con la familia, pero nosotros (almorzar) ______________________ con nuestros amigos.
3. Nosotros (pensar) ______________________ ir a la playa este fin de semana, pero ¿qué (pensar) ______________________ hacer tú?
4. ¿Cuántas horas (dormir) ______________________ tu hermana? Yo, en general, (dormir) ______________________ ocho horas.
5. ¿Tú (venir) ______________________ con Rodrigo a clase? Sí, yo (venir) ______________________ con él.
6. Nosotros (venir) ______________________ por ti a las ocho. (Preferir) ______________________ llegar al cine temprano.

4-39 Cosas de la vida. Form complete sentences, using the cues provided. Then listen and repeat as the speaker gives the correct answer.

1. mi / prima / soñar / con / visitar / Guatemala
2. nosotros / jugar al / tenis
3. tú / siempre / pedir / agua con limón
4. tu / yernos / no encontrar / nombre / mi tía
5. yo / poder / servir el almuerzo
6. mi / abuelo / no / venir / tarde / librería
7. su / cuñados / volver / temprano / gimnasio
8. la casa / prima / costar / mucho dinero.

Nombre: ______________________ Fecha: ______________________

4-40 ¡El preguntón! Answer each of the questions your hear in complete sentences. Then listen and repeat as the speaker gives the correct answer.

1. No, ______________________.
2. Sí, ______________________.
3. No, ______________________.
4. Sí, ______________________.
5. No, ______________________.
6. Sí, ______________________.

4-41 "No, pero..." Answer each question you hear negatively. Then using the following cues provided, give additional information in complete sentences. Follow the model. Finally, listen and repeat as the speaker gives the correct answer.

Modelo: You hear: ¿Quieres ir al cine?
You see: mis primos
You say: *No, no quiero ir al cine. Mis primos quieren ir al cine.*

1. tarde
2. jugar al básquetbol
3. mañana
4. yo
5. tú
6. mi sobrina

4-42 Preguntas personales. Answer the questions you hear based on your personal experience. Compare your responses with the sample answers in the Answer Key.

1. ______________________
2. ______________________
3. ______________________
4. ______________________
5. ______________________
6. ______________________

2. Direct objects, the personal *a,* and direct object pronouns

4-43 ¿Cuál es el complemento? Listen to the following sentences and write down the direct object in the space provided. Then listen and repeat as the speaker gives the correct answer.

1. ______________________
2. ______________________
3. ______________________
4. ______________________
5. ______________________

Nombre: ______________________ Fecha: ______________________

4-44 *A* personal. Complete the sentences with the personal **a,** when necessary. Then listen and repeat as the speaker gives the correct answer.

1. Llaman __________ su abuelo.
2. Llaman __________ un taxi.
3. Ven __________ el accidente.
4. Veo __________ José.
5. Invito __________ Laura, __________ Miguel y __________ Raúl a la fiesta.
6. Quiero __________ un amigo gracioso.
7. Quiero mucho __________ mis padres.
8. ¿__________ Q(q)uién visitas frecuentemente?
9. ¿__________ Q(q)uién te visita frecuentemente?

4-45 ¿Quién hace qué? Answer the following questions, replacing the direct objects with the appropriate pronouns. Then listen and repeat as the speaker gives the correct answer.

Modelo: You hear: ¿Quién llama a Susana?
You see: yo
You say: *Yo la llamo.*

1. nosotros
2. ustedes
3. yo
4. ella
5. Rodrigo y yo
6. tú
7. yo
8. mi prima

4-46 "No, pero..." Answer the following questions negatively, giving additional information with the cues provided. Then listen and repeat as the speaker gives the correct answer.

Modelo: You hear: ¿Ves a los García allí?
You see: los González
You say: *No, no los veo; veo a los González.*

1. profesora López
2. mochila
3. Cristina
4. los sándwiches
5. mis nietas
6. Susana

Nombre: ______________________________ Fecha: ______________________

4-47 ¿Quién hace qué? Answer the questions you hear using direct object pronouns. Then listen and repeat as the speaker gives the correct answer.

Modelo: You hear: ¿Quién va a comprar los refrescos?
You see: yo
You say: *Yo voy a comprarlos.*

1. nosotros
2. yo
3. tú
4. Santiago
5. Olivia y Juan

4-48 Al centro. Listen to the conversation and answer the following questions, using direct object pronouns whenever possible. Then listen and repeat as the speaker gives the correct answer. Listen to the conversation as many times as necessary.

1. ¿Quiénes van al centro?
2. ¿Quién visita a los amigos?
3. ¿Quiénes miran la película?
4. ¿Quién compra las entradas?

3. The present tense of *poner, salir,* and *traer*

4-49 Planes para la noche. Fill in the blanks with the correct form of the verbs in parentheses. Then listen and repeat as the speaker gives the correct answer.

1. Yo (poner) ____________________ los nombres de nuestros amigos al lado de cada plato.
2. Buena idea. Tú (traer) ____________________ pollo y papas fritas de la cafetería, y yo (traer) ____________________ los otros ingredientes.
3. ¡Fantástico! Ustedes (traer) ____________________ la comida, y yo (traer) ____________________ los refrescos. Yo los (poner) ____________________ en el refrigerador.
4. ¿Qué te parece si ella (salir) ____________________ de casa ahora?
5. Buena idea. ¿Por qué no (salir) ____________________ tú?
6. Está bien, yo (salir) ____________________ y (traer) ____________________ la comida.

Nombre: ______________________ Fecha: ______________________

4-50 Preferencias. Answer each question with a complete sentence, using the cues provided. Then listen and repeat as the speaker gives the correct answer.

Modelo: You hear: ¿Qué hacemos esta noche?
You see: las tareas domésticas
You say: *Hacemos las tareas domésticas esta noche.*

1. una película en DVD
2. yo / la mochila y tú / los refrescos
3. muchos ingredientes
4. yo / a las ocho y media, pero mi hermano a las nueve
5. las / en la mesa

4-51 ¿A qué salen? Complete the sentences with the correct form of the verb **salir** and the appropriate prepositions. Then listen and repeat as the speaker gives the correct answer.

Modelo: Yo *salgo a* (to go out) correr todos los días.

1. ¿Ustedes ______________ (to go out with) sus sobrinas?
2. Mis abuelos y yo ______________ (to leave on) viaje en el verano.
3. Elvira ______________ (to date) Ignacio.
4. Yo ______________ (to leave) casa con mi hermana a las nueve y cuarto.

Segunda parte

¡Así es la vida!

4-52 ¿Al cine? Listen to the following conversation. Then indicate whether the statements that follow are **cierto (C)** or **falso (F).**

C F 1. Jorge invita a Ana y a Santiago al cine.

C F 2. Jorge quiere ver una película del director Almodóvar.

C F 3. La película empieza a las siete y media.

C F 4. Santiago va al cine con sus amigos.

C F 5. Jorge pasa por Ana.

Nombre: ______________________ Fecha: ______________________

¡Así lo decimos! Vocabulario

4-53 ¿Lógico o ilógico? Complete the dialog that you hear by selecting the letter corresponding to the most logical expression given below. Then listen and repeat as the speaker gives the correct answer.

1. a. Sí, con Jorge, por favor.

   b. Bueno.

   c. Aló.

2. a. Bueno.

   b. Pues, llamo para ver si quieres ir al cine.

   c. Habla Pablo. ¿Quién habla?

3. a. Te llamo para ver si quieres ir a bailar esta noche.

   b. Esta noche, lo siento pero no puedo.

   c. Quiero ir al cine.

4. a. Lo siento, no puedo.

   b. Paso por ti a las diez y media.

   c. Claro, ¿quieres pasear por el centro?

5. a. No, gracias. Estoy ocupado.

   b. Me gusta la orquesta.

   c. Es un café al aire libre.

6. a. De acuerdo. Vamos al teatro el sábado.

   b. Sí, claro. ¡Me encantaría ver el partido!

   c. El parque es muy popular.

7. a. ¡Qué aburrido! Mejor vamos a bailar, mi vida.

   b. Me encantaría, mi cielo.

   c. De acuerdo, ¿qué están presentando?

8. a. ¡Qué divertido! ¿A qué hora es la función?

   b. Gracias, pero no puedo.

   c. ¿Puedes ir al cine?

Pronunciación

Sounds of *j* and *g*

1. The Spanish **j** is pronounced like a forceful English *h* in the word *hat*.

jamón	**Tajo**	**caja**
jugar	**Jaime**	**jarra**

2. The letter **g** has three distinct sounds. Before **e** and **i**, it is pronounced like a forceful English *h* in *hat*. Note these examples.

gitano	**Germán**	**agitar**	**coger**

At the start of a breath group or after **n**, the combinations **ga, go, gu, gue,** and **gui** are pronounced like a weak English *g*, as in *gate*. Note these examples.

guerra	**gol**	**mango**
ganar	**guitarra**	**un gato**

Everywhere else (except for the combinations **ge** and **gi**) the sound is weaker, with the breath continuing to pass between the palate and the back of the tongue. Note these examples.

algo	**agricultura**	**agua**
contigo	**ogro**	**negro**

4-54 Pronunciemos. Each of the following words contains the letter **j**. Repeat each word after the speaker.

1. jota
2. jamón
3. jugadores
4. jardinero
5. Alejandra
6. Luján
7. junio
8. jugar
9. jefe
10. julio

Nombre: ______________________ Fecha: ______________________

4-55 Pronunciemos más. You will hear a series of Spanish words that contain the combinations **ge** and **gi.** Repeat each word after the speaker.

1. gente
2. gimnasia
3. general
4. genial
5. dirigir
6. gitano
7. geología
8. geografía
9. Jorge
10. girar

4-56 Pronunciemos más. The following words contain the combinations **ga, go, gu, gue,** and **gui.** Repeat each word after the speaker.

1. gota
2. guante
3. gato
4. golf
5. aguantar
6. ganar
7. guerra
8. vengo
9. guía
10. tengo

4-57 Y pronunciemos más. You will hear a series of words and phrases that contain the combinations **ga, go, gu, gue,** and **gui** within a breath group. Repeat each word or phrase after the speaker.

1. me gustan
2. liga
3. algunos
4. mucho gusto
5. jugo
6. ¿Te gusta?
7. yo hago
8. agosto
9. gato
10. llego

¡Así lo hacemos! Estructuras

4. Demonstrative adjectives and pronouns

4-58 Identificaciones. Complete the following sentences with the correct form of the demonstrative adjectives in parentheses. Then listen and repeat as the speaker gives the correct answer.

1. ¡Qué interesante son ______________________ partidos de fútbol! (este)
2. ¿Cuánto cuestan ______________________ refrescos? (ese)

Nombre: ______________________ Fecha: ______________________

3. Escucho mi música favorita cuando toca ______________ orquesta. (aquel)

4. Marcos va a comprar ______________ entradas. (ese)

5. ______________ biblioteca es grande. (ese)

6. Vengo frecuentemente a ______________ cine. (este)

7. Me gusta correr en ______________ parque. (aquel)

8. Me gustan ______________ películas. (este)

9. Quiero hacer ejercicio en ______________ gimnasio. (ese)

10. Siempre hay muchos turistas en ______________ cafés al aire libre. (aquel)

11. Vamos a salir ______________ noche. (este)

12. No quiero hablar con ______________ chicas. (aquel)

4-59 ¿Éste, ése o aquél? Answer the following questions using the cues provided. Then listen and repeat as the speaker gives the correct answer.

Modelo: You hear: ¿Vas a comer en esta cafetería?
You see: aquél
You say: *No, voy a comer en aquélla.*

1. éste
2. aquél
3. ése
4. éste
5. ésos
6. aquéllas

5. *Saber* and *conocer*

4-60 ¿Saber o conocer? Give the Spanish equivalent of the following sentences. Then listen and repeat as the speaker gives the correct answer.

1. I know that they want to go to the movies.
2. You don't know my mother-in-law?
3. My daughter knows (how to speak) French.
4. Does your sister know Barcelona?
5. Does she know where the concert is?
6. I know my boyfriend's family well.

Nombre: ______________________ Fecha: ______________

4-61 "Mi familia sabe..." Use the cues provided to form complete sentences, in order to find out what or whom the following people know. Then listen and repeat as the speaker gives the correct answer.

1. mi suegra / hablar ruso
2. nuestros sobrinos / Puerto Rico
3. los niños / dónde viven
4. mis padres / las películas de Almodóvar
5. mi novio / a mis padres

¿Cuánto sabes tú?

4-62 Federico y Elena. Listen to the dialog and answer the following questions with a complete sentence. Listen as many times as necessary to determine all the correct answers.

1. ¿Cómo es Federico?

   ____

2. ¿Quién es trabajador, Federico o Elena?

   ____

3. ¿Cómo está Elena hoy?

   ____

4. ¿Qué tiene Federico hoy?

   ____

5. ¿Cuándo empieza la función?

   ____

6. ¿Qué piensa Elena? ¿Hay tiempo para ir al centro?

   ____

7. ¿Por qué sabe Federico ir al cine?

   ____

8. ¿Conoce Elena a los primos de Federico?

   ____

Nombre: ______________________ Fecha: ______________________

9. ¿De dónde son los primos de Federico?

____

10. ¿Qué están haciendo en San Juan?

____

4-63 Preguntas personales. Write an appropriate response to the following questions or statements. Because answers will vary, compare your answer to the answer that is provided. Then read your response to practice communication and pronunciation.

1. ¿Quieres ir al cine esta noche?

____

2. ¿A qué hora comienza la película?

____

3. ¿Cuándo vuelves a la universidad?

____

4. ¿Visitas a tus tíos frecuentemente?

____

5. ¿Tienes una familia grande o pequeña?

____

6. ¿Conoces una persona famosa?

____

7. ¿Sabes cuántos años tiene tu profesor(a) de español?

____

8. ¿Estas preguntas son fáciles o difíciles?

____

Nombre: ______________________ Fecha: ______________

5 ¿Cómo pasas el día?

Workbook

Primera parte

¡Así es la vida!

5-1 ¿Recuerdas? Reread the conversations in **¡Así es la vida!** on page 154 of your textbook. Then answer the following questions with complete sentences in Spanish.

1. ¿Cuántos hijos tiene la familia Pérez Zamora?

____

2. ¿Por qué la señora Pérez les pide ayuda a sus hijos?

____

3. ¿Por qué todos tienen que trabajar?

____

4. ¿A quién no le gusta limpiar?

____

5. ¿Qué tiene que hacer Cristina?

____

6. ¿Qué va a hacer Rosa?

____

7. ¿Qué va a comprar Rosa en el mercado?

____

8. ¿Quién va a sacudir el polvo de los muebles?

____

Nombre: ______________________________ Fecha: ______________________

¡Así lo decimos! Vocabulario

5-2 ¡A completar! Fill in the blanks with the appropriate vocabulary word from the word bank.

basura	cuadro	garaje	libreros	secadora
cama	escoba	lavaplatos	sala	sillón

1. Todos prefieren sentarse en el ______________ porque es más cómodo.
2. Hay un ______________ de ese pintor en la pared.
3. Mi carro está en el ______________.
4. Tengo que poner los platos en el ______________. Están sucios.
5. Tú tienes que barrer la ______________ hoy.
6. Las novelas están en esos ______________.
7. En mi casa, yo saco la ______________ los jueves.
8. Hago la ______________ todas las mañanas cuando me levanto.
9. La ropa está en la ______________. Tienes que doblarla.
10. Barro la terraza con una ______________.

Nombre: ______________________ Fecha: ______________________

5-3 Cómo ordenar tu apartamento. You have moved to a new apartment. Explain what you do to arrange the furniture. Follow the model.

Modelo: *Pongo el sillón contra la pared.*

En la sala

1. ______________________
2. ______________________
3. ______________________
4. ______________________
5. ______________________

En el dormitorio

6. ______________________
7. ______________________
8. ______________________
9. ______________________

En el comedor

10. ______________________
11. ______________________
12. ______________________
13. ______________________

Nombre: ______________________ Fecha: ______________________

5-4 ¿Con qué frecuencia haces estos quehaceres? Answer the following questions, using words that indicate time or using expressions from the Study Tips on page 156 of your textbook.

MODELO: ¿Con qué frecuencia cortas (*cut*) la hierba (*grass*)?
Corto la hierba una vez a la semana.

1. ¿Con qué frecuencia limpias tu cuarto?

____

2. ¿Cuándo haces la cama?

____

3. ¿Con qué frecuencia lavas la ropa?

____

4. ¿Con qué frecuencia pasas la aspiradora?

____

5. ¿Con qué frecuencia sacas la basura?

____

6. ¿Cuándo barres el pasillo?

____

Nombre: ______________________________ Fecha: ______________________

5-5 Casas y apartamentos. Read the following advertisement. Then answer the questions by choosing the correct response.

Los Arcos
Cariari
4 dormitorios, 3 baños, garaje, terraza.
Superficie: 1.025 m^2.
Precio venta: 45.000.980 colones.

Parritta
2 dormitorios, 1 baño, 1 aseo, 2 plantas, piscina, acceso directo a la playa, casa de huéspedes.
Superficie: 820 m^2.
Precio venta: 39.700.000 colones.

Palo Seco
(cerca de Parritta)
5 dormitorios, 5 baños, alojamiento de criadas, suite principal, 3 plantas, jacuzzi, piscina, garaje, jardines, acceso directo a la playa.
Superficie: 1.575 m^2.
Precio venta: 144.999.900 colones.

Santo Domingo de Heredia
(15 minutos de San José)
3 dormitorios, 2 baños, chimenea, sobre parcela de 15.000 m^2 con jardines, frutas, vista del valle.
Superficie: 900 m^2.
Precio venta: 39.265.000 colones.

Para su información llame al (506) 222-8989

OFERTA INMOBILIARIA • COSTAMAX OFERTA INMOBILIARIA • COSTAMAX

1. ¿Cuántas plantas (*floors*) tiene la casa que está en Palo Seco?

   a. 5

   b. 3

   c. 1.575

2. ¿Qué tiene la casa?

   a. 5 dormitorios, jacuzzi, garaje

   b. 5 dormitorios, terraza, piscina, jardines

   c. 4 dormitorios, alojamiento de criadas, chimenea, 5 baños

3. ¿Cuál es más grande, la casa que está en Los Arcos, la casa que está en Santo Domingo de Heredia o la casa que está en Parritta?

   a. Los Arcos

   b. Santo Domingo de Heredia

   c. Parritta

Nombre: ______________________________ Fecha: ______________________

4. ¿Cuál es la casa con más baños?

   a. Los Arcos

   b. Parritta

   c. Palo Seco

5. ¿Cuál de las casas tiene garaje?

   a. Los Arcos

   b. Santo Domingo de Heredia

   c. Parritta

6. ¿Cuál es la casa más cara de todas?

   a. Los Arcos

   b. Santo Domingo de Heredia

   c. Parritta

   d. Palo Seco

7. ¿Cuánto cuesta la casa más cara?

   a. 39.265.00 colones

   b. 1.575 m

   c. 144.999.900 colones

   d. 15.000 m

8. ¿Cuánto vale la casa que está en Paritta?

   a. 820

   b. 45.000.980

   c. 39.700.000

Nombre: ______________________ Fecha: ______________________

¡Así lo hacemos! Estructuras

1. The verbs *decir* and *dar*, indirect objects, and indirect object pronouns

5-6 Hoy. Find out what is happening today by using the present tense of the verb **dar.**

1. El profesor ______________ un examen a las nueve.
2. Yo ______________ un paseo por el parque.
3. ¿Tú les ______________ mucho dinero a tus hijos?
4. Sergio y Virginia ______________ una fiesta por la noche.
5. Paco y yo ______________ una fiesta por la tarde.

5-7 Los chismosos. Armando and Mario are always spreading rumors. Find out their latest rumor by completing the conversation between Amanda and Juana. Use the present tense of the verb **decir.**

Juana: Oye, Amanda, Mario y Armando (1) ______________ que tú eres la novia de Gerardo.

Amanda: ¿Qué (2) ______________ tú, Juana?

Juana: Yo solamente (*only*) (3) ______________ que Mario y Armando (4) ______________ que tú eres la novia de Gerardo.

Amanda: Y ¿qué (5) ______________ ustedes?

Juana: Nosotros (6) ______________ que no es verdad, pero Mario (7) ______________ que tú vas a la playa con Gerardo todos los sábados.

Amanda: Pues, yo (8) ______________ que él no dice la verdad y que es un mentiroso (*liar*).

5-8 ¡A completar! Fill in each blank with the appropriate pronoun to match the indirect object.

1. Mi hermana ______________ lava la ropa (a mí).
2. Ella ______________ plancha la ropa a sus hermanos.
3. Tú ______________ pones la mesa a tu tío y a tu primo.
4. Ella ______________ habla (a ti).

Nombre: ______________________ Fecha: ______________________

5. Mis amigos ____________ sacan la basura (a ella).

6. Yo ____________ preparo la cena a mi novia.

7. Él ____________ barre la terraza a mi hermana y a mí.

8. Ustedes ____________ hacen la cama a su madrastra.

9. Tú ____________ quitas la mesas a tus tíos.

10. Tú y tu hermano ____________ sacuden los muebles a su cuñada.

5-9 En la tienda. You are shopping at a store. Explain whom each gift is for, using the appropriate indirect object pronoun.

Modelo: a mi tío / un cubo
Le doy un cubo a mi tío.

1. a mis primos / una plancha

   ________ doy una plancha a mis primos.

2. a tu mamá / una alfombra

   ________ das una alfombra a tu mamá.

3. a tu papá / una lámpara

   ________ das una lampara a tu papá.

4. a mi primo y a su esposa / una secadora

   ________ doy una secadora a mi primo y a su esposa.

5. a nuestras hermanas / estéreo

   ________ doy un estéreo a nuestras hermanas.

6. a nuestra profesora / cuadro

   ________ doy un cuadro a nuestra profesora.

Nombre: ______________________ Fecha: ______________

2. *Gustar* and similar verbs

5-10 ¡A completar! Complete each statement with the correct form of the verbs in parentheses and the corresponding indirect object pronoun. Follow the model.

MODELO: A mí (gustar) *me gustan* los muebles.

1. A nosotros no (quedar) ______________ comida en el refrigerador.
2. A ti (fascinar) ______________ una sala grande.
3. A ellos no (gustar) ______________ limpiar la casa.
4. ¿(Interesar) ______________ a ti los muebles antiguos (*antiques*)?
5. ¿Qué (parecer) ______________ a ellas la nueva casa?
6. Al señor (encantar) ______________ el cuadro de la sala.
7. A mí (molestar) ______________ la cocina sucia (*dirty*).
8. A usted (faltar) ______________ una cómoda en el dormitorio.
9. ¿(Gustar) ______________ a usted el sofá nuevo?
10. A mí (caer bien) ______________ Julia y Cristina.

5-11 Mis opiniones. Complete the following paragraph with the correct form of the verbs in parentheses.

A mí me (1. gustar) ______________ la nueva casa, pero no me (2. gustar) ______________ hablar con los vecinos porque me (3. caer mal) ______________. ¿Te (4. gustar) ______________ la nueva casa? A mis amigos les (5. fascinar) ______________ los dormitorios de la casa y también les (6. encantar) ______________ el patio. ¿Te (7. gustar) ______________ comer en el patio? Si quieres, te invito porque tú me (8. caer) ______________ bien.

5-12 Los gustos. Write sentences describing how you feel about the following rooms, parts of a house, or pieces of furniture.

MODELO: la cocina
A mí me encanta la cocina grande, porque me gusta cocinar.

1. el comedor ____

____

2. los dormitorios ______________________________
____

3. el garaje ______________________________
____

4. el jardín ______________________________
____

5. el patio ______________________________
____

6. la sala ______________________________
____

7. el sofá ______________________________
____

8. el librero ______________________________
____

Nombre: ______________________ Fecha: ______________________

SEGUNDA PARTE

¡Así es la vida!

5-13 ¿Cierto o falso? Reread the descriptions in **¡Así es la vida!** on page 167 of your textbook and indicate whether each statement is **cierto (C)** or **falso (F).**

C F 1. Los hermanos Castillo son españoles.

C F 2. A Antonio le gusta mucho dormir.

C F 3. Todas las mañanas, Antonio se cepilla los dientes después de levantarse.

C F 4. Antonio les prepara el desayuno a sus hermanos.

C F 5. A Beatriz le gusta levantarse temprano.

C F 6. Ella sale de la casa hoy después de maquillarse.

C F 7. Beatriz se lava la cara por la mañana.

C F 8. Enrique es madrugador (*early riser*).

C F 9. Por las noches, se acuesta muy temprano.

C F 10. El jefe de Enrique siempre está contento con Enrique.

¡Así lo decimos! Vocabulario

5-14 ¡A completar! Complete each statement with an appropriate word or expression from the word bank.

cepillo de dientes	desayuno	espejo	maquillaje	pintalabios
crema de afeitar	despertador	jabón	peine	secadora

1. Para despertarme a tiempo, necesito un ______________.
2. Uso ______________ para bañarme.
3. Para cepillarme los dientes, necesito un ______________.
4. Para peinarme, uso el ______________.
5. Para pintarme los labios, uso un ______________.
6. Antes de salir, me miro en el ______________.

Nombre: ______________________ Fecha: ______________________

7. Para secarme el pelo, uso una ______________.

8. Antes de afeitarme, uso una ______________.

9. Para pintarme la cara, uso ______________.

10. Por la mañana como el ______________.

5-15 Un poco de lógica. For each group of sentences, match each sentence with a given ordinal numbers in a logical order.

1. a. Me seco con una toalla. ____ 1. primero
   b. Me preparo el desayuno. ____ 2. segundo
   c. Me levanto. ____ 3. tercero
   d. Me baño. ____ 4. cuarto
   e. Me despierto. ____ 5. quinto
2. a. Raúl se viste. ____ 1. primero
   b. Se afeita. ____ 2. segundo
   c. Raúl se ducha. ____ 3. tercero
   d. Se cepilla el pelo. ____ 4. cuarto
   e. Se mira en el espejo. ____ 5. quinto
3. a. Mis amigos se quitan la ropa. ____ 1. primero
   b. Se acuestan. ____ 2. segundo
   c. Se cepillan los dientes. ____ 3. tercero
   d. Se duermen. ____ 4. cuarto
4. a. Nos ponemos la ropa. ____ 1. primero
   b. Nosotros nos ponemos la crema de afeitar. ____ 2. segundo
   c. Nos lavamos la cara. ____ 3. tercero
   d. Nos afeitamos. ____ 4. cuarto

Nombre: ______________________ Fecha: ______________________

5-16 ¡Fuera de lugar! In each set of words, choose the word or expression that is out of place.

1. a. acostarse
   b. bañarse
   c. dormirse
   d. despertarse
2. a. la secadora
   b. el peine
   c. los dedos
   d. la máquina de afeitar
3. a. el maquillaje
   b. la pasta de dientes
   c. los dientes
   d. el cepillo
4. a. afeitarse
   b. ducharse
   c. ponerse contento
   d. peinarse
5. a. la secadora
   b. la cara
   c. el lápiz labial
   d. el jabón
6. a. la navaja de afeitar
   b. la nariz
   c. los labios
   d. los ojos

¡Así lo hacemos! Estructuras

3. Reflexive constructions: Pronouns and verbs

5-17 ¿Qué hacen estas personas por la mañana? Complete the following sentences with the appropriate present tense form of the reflexive verbs in parentheses.

1. Ana María (mirarse) ______________ en el espejo antes de salir.
2. Nosotros (levantarse) ______________ a las siete.
3. Carlos (secarse) ______________ con una toalla.
4. ¿Tú (lavarse) ______________ la cara?
5. Mamá (maquillarse) ______________.
6. Los niños (bañarse) ______________ a las siete.
7. Yo (ducharse) ______________ después de levantarme.
8. Ana (ponerse) ______________ maquillaje.

Nombre: ______________________ Fecha: ______________________

9. Papá (afeitarse) ______________ con una máquina de afeitar.

10. ¿Tú (pintarse) ______________ las uñas por la mañana?

5-18 Por la mañana. Complete the following paragraph with the correct form of the present tense of the verbs from the word bank. You will have to use one of the verbs twice.

afeitarse	cepillarse	despertarse	lavarse	maquillarse	reunirse
bañarse	desayunarse	ducharse	levantarse	pintarse	

Yo (1) ______________ a las siete de la mañana. Después de despertarme, (2) ______________, (3) ______________ los dientes y (4) ______________ con la máquina de afeitar. Yo no (5) ______________ la cara, pero frecuentemente (6) ______________ el pelo. Mis hermanas (7) ______________ más tarde, a las siete y media. Mientras, Petra (8) ______________, Paula (9) ______________ y (10) ______________ los labios. Luego, todos nosotros (11) ______________ en la mesa y (12) ______________ cereales con leche.

5-19 Nos preparamos para la fiesta. There is a party at your dorm. Just as the party is about to begin, the residents are getting ready. Use the appropriate form of the verbs in parentheses.

1. Alicia (ponerse) ______________ el vestido nuevo.
2. Patricio no (dormirse) ______________.
3. Magdalena no (ponerse) ______________ nerviosa. Todo está bien.
4. Julio (afeitarse) ______________ ahora mismo.
5. Juan Bruno (ponerse) ______________ los zapatos.
6. Camila (sentarse) ______________ y (prepararse) ______________ una taza de té.
7. Rosa (peinarse) ______________.
8. Teresa (enojarse) ______________ conmigo.
9. Gilberto (lavarse) ______________ las manos antes de cocinar.
10. Rosaura (quitarse) ______________ de en medio (*gets out of the way*).

Nombre: ______________________ Fecha: ______________

5-20 Preguntas personales. Answer the following questions with complete sentences in Spanish.

1. ¿Eres madrugador/a (*early riser*)? ¿A qué hora te despiertas?

____

2. ¿Prefieres bañarte o ducharte?

____

3. ¿Con qué te afeitas?

____

4. ¿Cuándo te pones perfume o loción?

____

5. ¿Cuándo te pones impaciente?

____

6. ¿Cuándo te alegras y cuándo te pones triste?

____

7. ¿Cuándo te pones nervioso/a?

____

8. Generalmente, ¿a qué hora te acuestas?

____

5-21 Celina y Santiago. Celina and Santiago are madly in love with each other. What does Celina say they do?

Modelo: llamarse por teléfono todos los días
Nosotros nos llamamos por teléfono todos los días.

1. quererse mucho

   Nosotros ______________ mucho.

2. escribirse poemas todos los días

   Nosotros ______________ poemas todos los días.

Nombre: ______________________ Fecha: ______________________

3. contarse los problemas

   Nosotros ______________ los problemas.

4. hablarse antes y después de clase

   Nosotros ______________ antes y después de clase.

5. ayudarse con la tarea

   Nosotros ______________ con la tarea.

6. decirse que se aman

   Nosotros ______________ que ______________.

7. besarse mucho

   Nosotros ______________ mucho.

8. tratarse muy bien

   Nosotros ______________ muy bien.

5-22 Mis amigos. Complete the narrative about a day you spend with some friends by filling in the blanks with the correct form of the present tense of the appropriate verb from the word bank. You will need to use one of the verbs twice.

bañarse	despertarse	dormirse	ponerse	reunirse
despedirse	divertirse	llamarse	prepararse	sentarse

Mis amigos y yo (1) ______________ por teléfono el sábado y (2) ______________ en el centro estudiantil para ir a la playa ese día. En la playa, nosotros (3) ______________ en la arena y (4) ______________ en el mar. Luego, (5) ______________, porque estamos cansados y cuando (6) ______________, (7) ______________ en el mar otra vez. Después de llegar a casa, (8) ______________ unos sándwiches y (9) ______________ ropa para ir a una fiesta. Nosotros (10) ______________ mucho y luego (11) ______________ a la una de la mañana.

Nombre: ______________________ Fecha: ______________________

5-23 ¡Qué romántico! Jorge and Susana are in love. Tell how they meet by filling in the blanks with reciprocal reflexive verb forms.

MODELO: Jorge conoce a Susana en la fiesta. Susana conoce a Jorge en la fiesta.
Jorge y Susana se conocen en la fiesta.

1. Jorge mira a Susana. Susana mira a Jorge.

   Jorge y Susana ______________________.

2. Jorge le sonríe a Susana. Susana le sonríe a Jorge.

   Jorge y Susana ______________________.

3. Susana le dice "hola" a Jorge y Jorge le dice "hola" a Susana.

   Susana y Jorge ______________________ "hola".

4. Jorge le pide el nombre a Susana. Susana le pide el nombre a Jorge también.

   Jorge y Susana ______________________ el nombre.

5. Susana le ofrece un refresco a Jorge. Jorge le ofrece un refresco a Susana.

   Susana y Jorge ______________________ un refresco.

6. Jorge le habla a Susana del trabajo. Ella también le habla del trabajo.

   Jorge y Susana ______________________ del trabajo.

7. Jorge decide llamar a Susana. Susana decide llamar a Jorge también.

   Jorge y Susana deciden ______________________.

8. Jorge invita a Susana al cine. Ella también lo invita al cine.

   Jorge y Susana ______________________ al cine.

5-24 El verano. It's summer, and you are no longer on campus. Answer the following questions about your relationship with your friends.

1. ¿Se escriben a menudo (*often*) tú y tus amigos?

   ____

2. ¿Se cuentan cosas muy personales?

   ____

3. ¿Se hablan por teléfono?

____

4. ¿Se ven a menudo?

____

5. ¿Se visitan durante el verano?

____

4. Comparisons of equality and inequality

5-25 Cristina y Rosa. Cristina and Rosa are identical twins. Compare the twins by turning each sentence into a comparative statement, using **tan... como, tanto/a(s)... como,** or **tanto como.**

MODELO: Cristina y Rosa son muy amables.
Cristina es tan amable como Rosa.

1. Cristina y Rosa tienen muchos amigos.

____

2. Cristina y Rosa hablan mucho.

____

3. Cristina y Rosa son muy responsables.

____

4. Cristina y Rosa tienen mucha paciencia.

____

5. Cristina y Rosa se enamoran mucho.

____

6. Cristina y Rosa son muy simpáticas.

____

7. Cristina y Rosa son muy bonitas.

____

8. Cristina y Rosa tienen muchos quehaceres.

____

Nombre: ______________________________ Fecha: ______________________

5-26 La casa ideal. Carlos and Juan, two of your friends, are arguing about who has a better house. Fill in the blanks to make equal comparisons.

1. La casa de Carlos tiene ______________ dormitorios como la casa de Juan.
2. La casa de Juan es ______________ grande como la casa de Carlos.
3. La casa de Carlos es ______________ cara ______________ la casa de Juan.
4. La casa de Juan tiene ______________ dormitorios ______________ la casa de Carlos.
5. La casa de Carlos cuesta ______________ ______________ la casa de Juan.
6. La casa de Juan es ______________ bonita como la casa de Carlos.
7. La casa de Carlos me gusta ______________ ______________ la casa de Juan.

5-27 Más comparaciones. Based on the information from the advertisement on page 147, decide if the following statements are **cierto (C)** or **falso (F).**

C F 1. La casa en Los Arcos es más grande que la casa en Parritta.

C F 2. La casa en Santo Domingo de Heredia tiene más dormitorios que la casa en Parritta.

C F 3. La casa en Palo Seco tiene menos baños que la casa en Los Arcos.

C F 4. La casa en Palo Seco es más pequeña que la casa en Santo Domingo de Heredia.

C F 5. La casa en Palo Seco es más cara que la casa en Parritta.

C F 6. La casa en Santo Domingo de Heredia es más barata que la casa en Los Arcos.

C F 7. La casa en Palo Seco está más cerca de la playa que la casa en Santo Domingo de Heredia.

C F 8. En general, la casa en Parrita es mejor que la casa en Palo Seco.

5-28 Más casas y apartamentos. Use the advertisement on page 147 to write five original unequal comparisons, following the model.

Modelo: *La casa en Los Arcos tiene más dormitorios que la casa en Parritta.*

1. ____
2. ____
3. ____
4. ____
5. ____

Nombre: ______________________________ Fecha: ______________________

NUESTRO MUNDO

Panoramas

5-29 ¡A informarse! Based on the information from **Nuestro mundo** on pages 180–181 of your textbook, decide if the following statements are **cierto (C)** or **falso (F)**.

1. El Canal de Panamá fue (*was*) construido entre 1903 y 1910.
2. Los EE.UU. controló el canal hasta 1999.
3. Desde su construcción, 14.000 barcos han navegado por el canal.
4. Los Kuna son una sociedad patriarcal.
5. Los Kuna son conocidos por sus creaciones textiles.
6. Las ranas de las selvas costarricenses no son peligrosas.
7. Las ranas en Centroamérica son de oro.
8. La iguana verde es una especie protegida en Costa Rica.
9. En Centroamérica ocurren muchos desastres naturales.
10. Violeta Chamorro es la presidenta de Nicaragua.

5-30 Tu propia experiencia. Based on the information that you have learned and your own opinion, answer the following questions.

1. ¿Crees que es posible tener un país sin (*without*) ejército (*army*)?

____

____

____

____

2. ¿Por qué es importante el Canal de Panamá?

____

____

____

____

Nombre: ______________________ Fecha: ______________________

Taller

5-31 Las rutinas diarias

Primera fase. Make a list of your typical weekday morning or evening routine. Try to order the activities in sequence numerically.

MODELO:	ORDEN	ACTIVIDAD	LA HORA
	1.	*me despierto*	*las seis*
	2.	*me levanto*	*las seis y cuarto*

	ORDEN	ACTIVIDAD	LA HORA
1.	______	______	______
2.	______	______	______
3.	______	______	______
4.	______	______	______
5.	______	______	______
6.	______	______	______
7.	______	______	______
8.	______	______	______
9.	______	______	______
10.	______	______	______

Segunda fase. Use the information you provided in the **Primera fase** to write a description of your typical morning or evening. Add other details whenever possible.

MODELO: *En general, me despierto a las seis de la mañana, porque mi primera clase es a las siete y media, pero muchos días no me levanto inmediatamente. Me levanto a las seis y cuarto. Después...*

____

____

____

____

____

Nombre: ______________________ Fecha: ______________________

5-32 Cantantes. Rubén Blades, Willie Colón, and Adrián Goizueta are Hispanic singers and songwriters whose music often includes sociopolitical commentary. Use the Internet, library sources, and possibly music stores to look up more information about these artists, their music, and their sociopolitical concerns. Clips from some of their songs can be found online. Find out the following information on each singer.

- País de origen
- Tipo de música
- Los nombres de canciones y álbumes populares
- Su activismo

RUBÉN BLADES

____

____

____

WILLIE COLÓN

____

____

____

ADRIÁN GOIZUETA

____

____

____

5-33 Costa Rica. In an area no larger than the state of West Virginia, Costa Rica is home to 5 percent of all species of plants and animals that inhabit the earth. That's somewhere between 500,000 and one million species of flora and fauna. One quarter of the country is set aside for national parks and biological reserves. Research an aspect of Costa Rica's natural resources and beauty, and organize the information you find in a chart or on a poster.

- Los pájaros (*birds*) de Costa Rica
- Las mariposas (*butterflies*) de Costa Rica
- Los parques y las reservas biológicas de Costa Rica
- Los programas de preservación y protección en Costa Rica
- Los bosques (*forests*) tropicales

5-34 Más allá de las páginas. Using the Internet, look for different resorts in Costa Rica where there are houses for sale. Imagine you are in the market to buy a house. Choose one of the houses you find on the Internet that you would buy and explain why.

____

____

____

____

____

¿Cuánto sabes tú?

5-35 ¿Sabes de pronombres de objeto indirecto? Match the following sentences with the appropriate indirect object pronoun.

1. Nosotros __________ damos una lámpara a mi madre. a. nos
2. Yo __________ plancho la ropa a ti. b. me
3. Mi madre __________ dice a mí que limpie mi habitación. c. le
4. Mi padre __________ prepara el desayuno a nosotros. d. les
5. Yo __________ limpio la habitación a mis hermanas. e. te

5-36 ¿Sabes usar los verbos como *gustar*? Fill in the blanks with the appropriate form of the verbs in parentheses.

1. Me (encantar) __________________ las casas cerca de la playa.
2. A mi hermano no le (gustar) __________________ afeitarse.
3. Nos (interesar) __________________ las clases de español.
4. Te (fascinar) __________________ los cuadros de Picasso.
5. A mí me (molestar) __________________ los vecinos ruidosos (*noisy*).
6. A ella no le (caer bien) __________________ sus compañeros de clase.

Nombre: ______________________ Fecha: ______________________

5-37 ¿Sabes de acciones reflexivas y recíprocas? Read the following paragraph, and pay attention to the pronouns in italics. Fill in the blanks with the correct pronoun. Make all the necessary corrections to give logical sense to the paragraph. If no change is necessary, fill in the blank with the same pronoun in italics.

Yo *me* (1) ______________ levanto a las seis y media. *Me* (2) ______________ gusta levantar*te* (3) ______________ temprano porque puedo duchar*se* (4) ______________ tranquilamente. Después de duchar*me* (5) ______________, *me* (6) ______________ cepillo los dientes y *nos* (7) ______________ afeito. Cuando termino, despierto a mi hermana Rosa. A ella no *me* (8) ______________ gusta levantar*te* (9) ______________ temprano. Ella *se* (10) ______________ maquilla todas las mañanas después de duchar*nos* (11) ______________. Adriana *se* (12) ______________ levanta más tarde que todos. Ella *se* (13) ______________ ducha por las noches y por las mañanas sólo tiene que cepillar*nos* (14) ______________ los dientes y peinar*se* (15) ______________. Durante el desayuno, mis hermanas y yo *nos* (16) ______________ hablamos y , a veces, *se* (17) ______________ enojamos, pero *se* (18) ______________ queremos mucho.

5-38 ¿Sabes comparar? Ramón thinks he is better than his friend Rafael, and he likes to compare himself with Rafael. Read the following paragraph and fill in the blanks to complete the comparisons, choosing a word from the word bank. You will have to use some words twice.

más mayor mejor menos

¡Yo soy (1) ______________ que Rafael! Para empezar (*To start with*), yo tengo veintidós años y Rafael tiene veinte. Yo soy (2) ______________ que Rafael. Yo estudio (3) ______________ que él y sus clases son (4) ______________ fáciles que mis clases. Rafael es (5) ______________ inteligente que yo. En deportes, yo juego (6) ______________ que él al tenis, al fútbol y al baloncesto.

Nombre: ______________________ Fecha: ______________________

Lab Manual

PRIMERA PARTE

¡Así es la vida!

5-39 ¡Los quehaceres! Marcos, Verónica, and Diego are students sharing a house. Listen to the following descriptions of the household chores for which each of them is responsible. Then indicate whether each statement below is **cierto (C)** or **falso (F).**

C F 1. Dos veces por semana, Marcos sacude el polvo de los muebles.

C F 2. Una vez a la semana, Marcos usa la lavadora y la secadora.

C F 3. Todas las semanas, Verónica tiene que limpiar los baños.

C F 4. Verónica usa la aspiradora y el lavaplatos.

C F 5. Verónica come las comidas que prepara Diego.

C F 6. Diego usa la escoba para limpiar la cocina.

C F 7. Diego nunca se olvida de su trabajo y se pone furioso cuando Marcos no limpia.

C F 8. Marcos y Diego usan la aspiradora.

Nombre: ______________________ Fecha: ______________________

5-40 Mi casa nueva. Leticia is describing her new house to her mother. Looking at the picture that follows, answer her mother's questions. Then listen and repeat as the speaker gives the correct answer.

Modelo: You hear: ¿Qué hay sobre la cómoda?
You say: *Sobre la cómoda hay una lámpara.*

1. ...
2. ...
3. ...
4. ...
5. ...

¡Así lo decimos! Vocabulario

5-41 ¿Cómo es mi casa? Listen as Magdalena describes what happens in her house. Select all the letters corresponding to the statements that are correct, according to what you hear. Listen to Magdalena's description as many times as necessary to find all the correct statements.

1. ¿A quiénes les gusta limpiar la casa?
   a. Magdalena
   b. Rosario
   c. Diego
2. ¿Quién le cae mal a Magdalena?
   a. Rosario
   b. Roberto
   c. Diego
3. ¿Qué no le molesta hacer a Magdalena?
   a. lavar la ropa
   b. sacudir el polvo de los muebles
   c. secar la ropa
4. ¿A quién le gusta barrer?
   a. Rosario
   b. Roberto
   c. Diego
5. En los restaurantes, ¿qué le encantan a Diego?
   a. los refrescos
   b. las hamburguesas
   c. las ensaladas
6. ¿Qué le falta a Diego?
   a. una hamburguesa
   b. el dinero para comer
   c. el tiempo para comer bien

Nombre: ______________________ Fecha: ______________________

Pronunciación

Los sonidos *r* y *rr*

The Spanish **r** has two distinct sounds. The **rr** represents a strong trilled sound, and it is produced by striking the tip of the tongue against the ridge behind the upper front teeth in a series of rapid vibrations. When a single **r** appears at the beginning of a word or after the consonants **l, n,** and **s,** it is pronounced like the **rr.**

Roberto	**repetir**	**correr**	**alrededor**	**barrer**
cerrar	**ratón**	**enredo**	**Israel**	**terraza**

In all other positions, the Spanish **r** is a tap, pronounced similarly to the *dd* in the English word *ladder.*

cero	**oro**	**arena**	**abrir**	**estéreo**
ladra	**mira**	**pero**	**cara**	**dentro**

5-42 Pronunciemos. You will hear a series of words containing the trilled **r.** Repeat each word after the speaker.

1. Ramón
2. cerro
3. Enrique
4. regular
5. morro
6. alrededor
7. arriba
8. Roberto
9. enredo
10. perro

5-43 Pronunciemos más. You will now hear a series of words containing the "flap" **r** in Spanish. Repeat each word after the speaker.

1. pero
2. amarillo
3. ahora
4. mirar
5. abrir
6. azúcar
7. colores
8. caro
9. pera
10. mujer

Nombre: ______________________ Fecha: ______________________

5-44 En frases completas. Now repeat the following sentences that have words containing both the flap **r** and the trilled **r.** Imitate the speaker's pronunciation as closely as you can.

1. Roberto y Laura regresan en carro.
2. Ahora tú quieres una pera amarilla.
3. Es un carro muy caro de color rojo.
4. Enrique mira el perro en el cerro.
5. Rosa practica los verbos irregulares.

¡Así lo hacemos! Estructuras

1. The verbs *decir* and *dar,* indirect objects, and indirect object pronouns

5-45 ¿Decir o dar? Complete the following sentences with the correct form of the verbs **decir** or **dar.** Then listen and repeat as the speaker gives the correct answer.

1. La profesora __________ un examen a las ocho.
2. Yo __________ dónde están la escoba y el basurero.
3. Ellos siempre le __________, ¿"Qué pasa, calabaza"? a Federica.
4. Nosotros les __________ nuestra aspiradora a Carlos.
5. Tú le __________ una lámpara para su escritorio.

5-46 ¿A quién? Complete the following sentences with the correct form of the indirect object pronoun. Then listen and repeat as the speaker gives the correct answer.

1. ¿__________ traemos la aspiradora? (a ti)
2. ¿__________ das los muebles? (a nosotros)
3. ¿__________ enseñas a barrer el piso? (a ellas)
4. ¿__________ dices dónde está el lavaplatos? (a él)
5. ¿__________ puedes comprar este librero? (a mí)

5-47 ¡Claro que sí! Answer the questions you hear affirmatively, changing the position of the indirect object pronouns. Then listen and repeat as the speaker gives the correct answer.

MODELO: You hear: ¿Están comprándonos los cuadros?
You say: *Sí, nos están comprando los cuadros.*

1. Sí, ______________________________.
2. Sí, ______________________________.
3. Sí, ______________________________.
4. Sí, ______________________________.

Nombre: ________________________ Fecha: ________________

5-48 Mis amigos y yo cooperamos en la casa. Complete the following sentences with the correct indirect object pronoun, based on the indirect object you hear. Then listen and repeat as the speaker gives the correct answer.

1. Yo ______________ plancho los pantalones.
2. Tú ______________ barres el piso de la cocina.
3. Julia ______________ lava la ropa.
4. Silvia ______________ hace las compras.
5. Ricardo y Julia ______________ lavan los platos.

2. *Gustar* and similar verbs

5-49 ¿Qué te gusta? Tell what the following people like using the cues provided. Then listen and repeat as the speaker gives the correct answer.

Modelo: You see: A nosotros ______________ mesas redondas
You write and say: *A nosotros nos gustan las mesas redondas.*

1. A ti ______________ las paredes blancas.
2. A mí ______________ los cuadros abstractos.
3. A ustedes ______________ comer en la terraza.
4. A ella ______________ sacudir el polvo de los muebles.
5. A nosotros ______________ esa taza de porcelana inglesa.
6. A usted ______________ los muebles caros.

5-50 ¿Qué opinas? Make complete sentences using the words provided. Then listen and repeat as the speaker gives the correct answer.

1. A mí ______________ las personas que no limpian. (molestar)
2. A ti ______________ ver las lámparas de halógeno. (interesar)
3. A nosotros ______________ quitar la mesa. (faltar)
4. A ustedes ______________ Julián. (caer bien)
5. A usted ______________ Javier y Anita. (caer mal)
6. A Enrique y a mí ______________ nuestra aspiradora. (encantar)
7. A Isabel y a Teodor ______________ la alfombra en el comedor. (fascinar)

Nombre: ______________________ Fecha: ______________________

SEGUNDA PARTE

¡Así es la vida!

5-51 Teresa y Manuel. Listen to the following conversation. Then select the letters for all statements that are correct, according to what you hear.

1. Teresa...

   a. se despierta a las ocho y media.

   b. se despierta a las ocho y cuarto.

   c. se baña.

2. Manuel...

   a. despierta a Teresa.

   b. se duerme.

   c. se enoja con Teresa.

3. Teresa tiene que ver al señor Vargas y...

   a. no se siente nerviosa.

   b. se siente nerviosa.

   c. se pone contenta.

4. El hotel...

   a. no está limpio.

   b. es bonito.

   c. tiene toallas grandes.

5. Teresa necesita usar... del hotel.

   a. la pasta de dientes

   b. la loción

   c. el jabón

6. Teresa se pone...

   a. el suéter verde.

   b. los pantalones negros.

   c. la blusa blanca.

7. Antes de salir del hotel, Teresa...

   a. se viste.

   b. se sienta a desayunar.

   c. se ducha, se seca el pelo y se maquilla.

¡Así lo decimos! Vocabulario

5-52 ¡Una casa ocupada! Match the number of each description you hear with the scenes depicted in the following illustration. Check your answers in the Answer Key.

Nombre: ______________________ Fecha: ______________________

Pronunciación

Los sonidos *s, n* y *l*

1. The Spanish **s** is pronounced like the English *s* in the word *set.*

casa	**soy**	**soñar**	**sábado**	**mesa**	**solo**

2. The Spanish **n** is pronounced like the English *n* in the word *never.*

nunca	**nadie**	**andar**	**nada**	**pan**	**lunes**

However, before the letters **b, v, m,** and **p,** the pronunciation of the letter **n** approximates that of the letter **m.**

un beso	**un padre**	**en vano**	**sin mamá**	**inmediato**	**con prisa**

3. To pronounce the **l,** place the tip of your tongue on the ridge behind your upper front teeth. Your tongue does not touch the upper front teeth as it does when pronouncing the English *l.*

Luis	**vela**	**Lola**	**lunes**	**sal**	**loro**

5-53 Pronunciemos. You will hear a series of words beginning with the letter **s.** Repeat each word after the speaker.

1. sala
2. semana
3. salir
4. siento
5. sesenta
6. solamente
7. semestre
8. sábado
9. setenta
10. ser

5-54 Pronunciemos más. You will hear a series of words beginning with the letter **n.** Repeat each word after the speaker.

1. nada
2. no
3. nunca
4. nieve
5. nena
6. nota
7. nadie
8. nueve
9. nación
10. nube

Nombre: ______________________ Fecha: ______________________

5-55 Pronunciemos más. You will now hear a series of words and phrases in which the Spanish letter **n** precedes **b, v, m,** and **p.** Repeat each word or phrase after the speaker.

1. un vaso
2. investigar
3. un peso
4. un baño
5. invertir
6. un paso
7. un mes
8. un bolígrafo

5-56 Y pronunciemos más. You will now hear a series of words beginning with the letter **l.** Repeat each word after the speaker.

1. lado
2. los
3. Luis
4. lunes
5. lengua
6. Leticia
7. Lola
8. lanzar
9. López
10. luz

¡Así lo hacemos! Estructuras

3. Reflexive constructions: Pronouns and verbs

5-57 ¿Cuándo haces...? Form complete sentences using the cues provided. Then listen and repeat as the speaker gives the correct answer.

Modelo: You see: Sofía / levantarse / temprano
You say: *Sofía se levanta temprano.*

1. yo / acostarse / a las diez
2. tú / dormirse / a la medianoche
3. ella / quitarse / la ropa
4. nosotros / afeitarse / todas las mañanas
5. los niños / bañarse / por la tarde
6. ¿Arturo / cepillarse / los dientes?
7. tú / secarse / el pelo con la secadora
8. nosotros / divertirnos / en la fiesta
9. yo / enamorarse / mucho
10. nuestros abuelos / enojarse / a veces

Nombre: ______________________ Fecha: ______________________

5-58 Actividades diarias. Answer the following questions you hear either positively or negatively, according to the cues. Then listen and repeat as the speaker gives the correct answer.

MODELO: You hear: ¿Te despiertas a las siete?
You say: *Sí, me despierto a las siete.*
or
You say: *No, no me despierto a las siete.*

1. Sí, ______________________.
2. No, ______________________.
3. Sí, ______________________.
4. No, ______________________.
5. Sí, ______________________.
6. No, ______________________.

5-59 ¿Qué está pasando? Using the cues provided, tell what the following people are doing now. Follow the model. Then listen and repeat as the speaker gives the correct answer.

MODELO: You see: Carlos / afeitarse
You say: *Carlos está afeitándose.*

1. Margarita y Soledad / despertarse
2. Gabriel / ponerse nervioso
3. tú / dormirse
4. yo / mirarse en el espejo
5. nosotros / vestirse
6. mi prima y yo / divertirse

Now repeat the exercise, using the same cues and the following model. Then listen and repeat as the speaker gives the correct answer.

MODELO: You hear: Carlos / afeitarse
You write and say: *Carlos se está afeitando.*

7. Margarita y Soledad ______________________.
8. Gabriel ______________________ nervioso.
9. Tú ______________________ en el espejo.
10. Yo ______________________.
11. Nosotros ______________________.
12. Mi prima y yo ______________________.

Nombre: ______________________ Fecha: ______________

5-60 El amor de Jorge y Silvia. Reconstruct the love story of Jorge and Silvia using the cues provided. Then listen and repeat as the speaker gives the correct answer.

Modelo: You see: conocerse / una larga noche de verano
You say: *Se conocen una larga noche de verano.*

1. conocerse / en una fiesta de la universidad
2. entenderse / perfectamente
3. enamorarse / rápidamente
4. llamarse / por teléfono todos los días
5. casarse / en la primavera
6. enojarse / a menudo
7. separarse / en el otoño
8. encontrarse / en el invierno
9. besarse / con pasión
10. juntarse / otra vez

4. Comparisons of equality and inequality

5-61 Comentarios en una panadería. Compare what the following people have using the words provided. Then listen and repeat as the speaker gives the correct answer.

Modelo: You see: Ana / primos / yo
You say: *Ana tiene tantos primos como yo.*

1. abuela Dora / nietas / abuelo Enrique
2. tía Clara / sobrinos / tío Ernesto
3. yo / primas / tú
4. Enrique / nueras / papá
5. tu nuera / años / mi yerno

Nombre: ______________________ Fecha: ______________________

5-62 Hacer comparaciones. Compare the following people using the cues provided. Then listen and repeat as the speaker gives the correct answer.

Modelo: You see: Ana / ser / amable / yo
You say: *Ana es tan amable como yo.*

1. mi sobrino / ser / inteligente / su padre
2. mi hijo / hacer compras / rápidamente / su tío
3. tu nieta / ser / simpática / tu hija
4. yo / levantarse / temprano / mi madre
5. tú / hablar / español / bien / tu abuelo

5-63 ¿Cómo son? Compare the following shopping situations using the cues provided. Then listen and repeat as the speaker gives the correct answer.

Modelo: You see: Ana / + / alta / Pablo
You say: *Ana es más alta que Pablo.*

1. el centro comercial nuevo / + / grande / el centro comercial viejo
2. este almacén / – / elegante / ese almacén
3. estos dependientes / + / amable / aquellos dependientes
4. estos precios / – / barato / esos precios
5. las rebajas aquí / + / grande / las rebajas en la otra tienda

5-64 Dos dependientes en una joyería. Listen to the descriptions of Elena and Mariana, and answer the questions that follow. Then listen and repeat as the speaker gives the correct answer.

1. ¿Quién tiene menos años?
2. ¿Quién es más alta?
3. ¿Quién es más inteligente?
4. ¿Quién tiene menos hermanos?
5. ¿Quién es más simpática?

Nombre: ______________________________ Fecha: ____________________

¿Cuánto sabes tú?

5-65 La casa de mis sueños. As you listen to the description of the speaker's dream house, check each room and the items in that room that are mentioned.

____ aspiradora	____ cuadro	____ jardín	____ sillas
____ baño	____ dormitorio	____ lámpara	____ sillón
____ cama	____ escoba	____ mesa	____ sofá
____ cocina	____ escritorio	____ patio	
____ comedor	____ estantes	____ sala	
____ cómoda	____ garaje	____ secadora	

5-66 Tarea y quehaceres. Answer the questions you hear using the cues provided. Then listen and repeat as the speaker gives the correct answer.

Modelo: You hear: ¿Qué haces tú cuándo yo me acuesto?
You see: barrer el cuarto
You say: *Yo barro el cuarto cuando tú te acuestas.*

1. lavar la ropa
2. poner la mesa
3. preparar el desayuno
4. pelearse
5. pasar la aspiradora
6. ponerse enojada

5-67 ¿Que haces en casa? Answer the questions you hear according to the cues provided. Then listen and repeat as the speaker gives the correct answer.

Modelo: You hear: ¿Ordenas el cuarto?
You say: *Sí, lo ordeno.*
or
You say: *No, no lo ordeno.*

1. Sí, ______________________________.
2. No, ______________________________.
3. Sí, ______________________________.
4. No, ______________________________.
5. Sí, ______________________________.
6. No, ______________________________.

Nombre: ______________________ Fecha: ______________________

5-68 "No, pero..." Answer the following questions negatively using the cues provided. Then listen and repeat as the speaker gives the correct answer.

Modelo: You hear: ¿Te lavas las manos?
You see: pelo
You say: *No, no me lavo las manos. Me lavo el pelo.*

1. crema de afeitar
2. la loción
3. la máquina de afeitar
4. un suéter
5. los ojos
6. la secadora de pelo

5-69 Preguntas personales. Write an appropriate response to the questions or statements that you hear. Then read your response to practice communication and pronunciation.

1. ____
2. ____
3. ____
4. ____
5. ____
6. ____
7. ____
8. ____
9. ____

Nombre: ______________________ Fecha: ______________________

6 ¡Buen provecho!

Workbook

Primera parte

¡Así es la vida!

6-1 ¡Buen provecho! Reread the conversations in **¡Así es la vida!** on page 190 of your textbook and indicate whether each statement is **cierto (C)** or **falso (F)**.

Escena 1

C F 1. Marta no tiene hambre.

C F 2. Marta no quiere beber nada.

C F 3. Arturo quiere beber una limonada.

C F 4. La especialidad de la casa son los camarones.

C F 5. Los camarones son a la parrilla.

C F 6. A Marta le gustan mucho los camarones.

C F 7. Arturo pide un bistec con arroz y una ensalada.

Escena 2

C F 8. A Arturo no le gustan mucho los camarones.

C F 9. La comida de Marta está muy buena.

C F 10. Marta va a recomendarles el restaurante a sus amigos.

Nombre: ______________________ Fecha: ______________________

¡Así lo decimos! Vocabulario

6-2 En el restaurante. How would you respond to the following questions in a restaurant? Match each question with the best response.

1. _____¡Hola, Ana! ¿Quieres almorzar conmigo?
2. _____¿Qué recomienda usted?
3. _____¿Qué tal está la comida?
4. _____¿Cómo están las chuletas de cerdo?
5. _____Camarero, ¿puede usted traernos más vino?
6. _____¿Puedo traerles algo más?

a. Enseguida.

b. ¡Están ricas!

c. La especialidad de la casa son los camarones a la parrilla.

d. ¡Magnífica!

e. Sí, me muero de hambre.

f. Solamente la cuenta, por favor.

6-3 En la mesa. Locate fourteen items you might find on your table at a restaurant.

C	L	A	M	E	Z	A	T	C	L	O	S	P	L	I	T	U
A	M	A	N	T	E	Q	U	I	L	L	A	Z	Ú	C	A	R
P	I	M	I	E	N	T	A	T	E	L	L	I	V	R	E	S
A	A	O	E	N	P	L	A	T	O	I	D	T	A	Z	A	E
I	P	N	L	E	T	N	A	M	A	H	D	H	S	X	E	R
T	H	A	F	D	Y	A	S	W	P	C	C	U	O	S	D	V
E	U	I	O	O	T	W	E	E	O	U	V	D	O	Q	O	A
S	E	K	C	R	E	M	A	R	C	C	J	G	I	E	L	P

Nombre: ______________________ Fecha: ______________________

6-4 Categorías. You are a dietician and an expert on food categories. Select the correct category for each of the following.

1. el bistec

   a. frutas b. pescados y mariscos c. carnes d. verduras

2. la lechuga

   a. frutas b. verduras c. carnes d. bebidas

3. el bacalao (*cod*)

   a. pescados y mariscos b. bebidas c. carnes d. postres

4. la limonada

   a. frutas b. bebidas c. pescados y mariscos d. verduras

5. los frijoles

   a. legumbres b. frutas c. carnes d. bebidas

6. la manzana

   a. carnes b. pescados y mariscos c. frutas d. verduras

7. los camarones

   a. pescados y mariscos b. bebidas c. verduras d. carnes

8. la uva

   a. frutas b. carnes c. bebidas d. verduras

Nombre: ______________________________ Fecha: ______________________

6-5 ¿Cómo está la comida? Comment on the quality of the food by matching each statement with the appropriate adjective to fit each situation.

1. Es un buen restaurante. Toda la comida está __________.
2. Es un restaurante muy malo. Toda la comida está __________.
3. Camarero, quisiera un bistec bien cocido. Este bistec está __________.
4. En este restaurante, las ensaladas son excelentes. Las verduras están __________.
5. A mí me gusta la sopa caliente. No me gusta esta sopa porque está __________.

a. frescas
b. rica
c. fría
d. crudo
e. mala

6-6 Cuestionario. Your new friend is curious about your eating habits. Answer her questions with complete sentences in Spanish.

1. ¿A qué hora almuerzas?

____

2. ¿Qué comes de almuerzo normalmente?

____

3. ¿Dónde cenas?

____

4. ¿Desayunas? ¿Qué comes de desayuno?

____

5. ¿Cuál es tu plato favorito? ¿Por qué?

____

Nombre: ______________________________ Fecha: ______________________

¡Así lo hacemos! Estructuras

1. Los superlativos

6-7 ¡A escoger! Choose the correct superlative statement for each case.

1. Este restaurante es __________ del mundo.

   a. la mejor b. el mejor c. los mejores d. las mejores

2. Estos camarones son __________ del restaurante.

   a. las más ricas b. la más rica c. los más ricos d. el más rico

3. Aquella comida es __________ de la cafetería.

   a. la mejor b. el mejor c. los mejores d. las mejores

4. Esta bebida es __________ de la cafetería.

   a. el mejor b. las mejores c. los mejores d. la mejor

5. Aquellas verduras son __________ del mercado.

   a. las más frescas b. el más fresco c. los más frescos d. la más fresca

6. Este restaurante es __________ del centro de la ciudad.

   a. la más popular b. los más populares c. las más populares d. el más popular

7. Esta langosta es __________ de la ciudad.

   a. las más deliciosas b. la más deliciosa c. los más deliciosos d. el más delicioso

8. Esas naranjas son __________ del país. (dulce = *sweet*)

   a. el más dulce b. los más dulces c. las más dulces d. la más dulce

Nombre: ________________________ Fecha: ____________________

6-8 Paco y Jorge. Paco likes to top whatever his friend Jorge says. Using superlative forms, fill in the blanks to complete their conversation in a logical manner.

de la del el las mejores rico

Jorge: Yo compro unos tomates muy buenos en el mercado.

Paco: Pues, yo compro los (1) ________________ tomates del mundo.

Jorge: Yo siempre como pescado fresco.

Paco: Eso no es nada. Yo como (2) ________________ más fresco del país.

Jorge: Yo voy a restaurantes caros con mi esposa.

Paco: Pues, yo siempre voy al restaurante más caro (3) ________________ ciudad.

Jorge: Yo cocino un bacalao muy rico.

Paco: Pero no mejor que el mío. Yo cocino el bacalao más (4) ________________ del mundo.

Jorge: Yo siempre bebo bebidas saludables.

Paco: Pero ya sabes que yo bebo (5) ________________ más saludables (6) ________________ mercado.

Nombre: ______________________ Fecha: ______________________

6-9 Preguntas personales. Answer the following questions in Spanish.

1. ¿Quiénes en tu familia son mayores que tú?

____

2. ¿Quiénes en tu familia son menores que tú?

____

3. ¿Quién es la persona mayor de tu familia?

____

4. ¿Cómo se llama el mejor de tus amigos?

____

5. ¿Quiénes son los mejores estudiantes de tu clase?

____

6. ¿Quién es el peor chico de la residencia estudiantil? ¿Por qué?

____

7. ¿Quién es la mejor profesora de la universidad?

____

8. ¿Quién es el chico o la chica más inteligente de la clase?

____

2. Double object pronouns

6-10 Una cena horrible. You can hardly believe what your friend is saying. Express your disbelief by repeating what you were told, using direct and indirect object pronouns. Follow the model.

MODELO: La camarera no les trae el menú.
¿Cómo? ¿No se lo trae?

1. La camarera no les repite las especialidades a mis padres.

   ¿Cómo? ¿No ________________ repite?

2. Ella no les trae las bebidas.

   ¿Cómo? ¿No ________________ trae?

3. Ella no les pone la copa de vino.

   ¿Cómo? ¿No ________________ pone?

4. Ella no les sirve camarones a mis padres.

   ¿Cómo? ¿No ________________ sirve?

5. Ellos no le piden camarones a la camarera.

   ¿Cómo? ¿No ________________ piden?

6. Ella no les prepara la cuenta.

   ¿Cómo? ¿No ________________ prepara?

7. Ellos no le dan la propina a ella.

   ¿Cómo? ¿No ________________ dan?

8. Mis padres no le piden la cuenta a la camarera ahora y no van más allí.

   ¿Cómo? ¿No ________________ piden?

Nombre: ______________________________ Fecha: ______________________

6-11 En el restaurante Los Hermanos. The restaurant Los Hermanos has just opened, and one of the waiters informs the owner of what he is doing. Replace the nouns in the following sentences with direct and indirect object pronouns.

MODELO: Sirvo la comida a la señora.
Se la sirvo.

1. Les traigo el menú a los turistas ahora.

   ____________________ traigo.

2. Le llevo un tenedor y una cuchara a la señora.

   ____________________ llevo.

3. Le sirvo el pan y la mantequilla al niño.

   ____________________ sirvo.

4. Les pongo sal a las judías.

   ____________________ pongo.

5. Le corto la carne y el pollo al señor y a su señora.

   ____________________ corto.

6. Les lavo los platos y las tazas al camarero.

   ____________________ lavo.

7. Les busco el azúcar y la crema al cliente.

   ____________________ busco.

8. Le muestro el menú a sus clientes.

   ____________________ muestro.

9. Le pido la ayuda a la camarera.

   ____________________ pido.

10. Les preparo el cereal a las niñas.

    ____________________ preparo.

6-12 Actividades en el restaurante. Following the model, answer each question affirmatively. Use the corresponding direct and indirect object pronouns.

Modelo: ¿El camarero le está trayendo el menú al señor?
Sí, se lo está trayendo (está trayéndoselo).

1. ¿La camarera les está llevando los platos a los clientes?

____

2. ¿Los clientes alemanes les están pidiendo el desayuno a los camareros?

____

3. ¿Le están preparando el desayuno a Miguel?

____

4. ¿El camarero te está sirviendo los huevos fritos?

____

5. ¿Nosotros le estamos pagando la cuenta a nuestro amigo?

____

6. ¿Nos está trayendo el vino el camarero?

____

7. ¿La camarera me está poniendo los utensilios en la mesa?

____

8. ¿El chef nos está haciendo una ensalada de lechuga y tomate?

____

Nombre: ______________________ Fecha: ______________________

SEGUNDA PARTE

¡Así es la vida!

6-13 En la cocina. Reread the transcript of Aunt Julia's cooking show in **¡Así es la vida!** on page 202 of your textbook. Then answer the following questions.

1. ¿Qué les enseñó la tía Julia a los televidentes?

   a. a hacer arroz con pollo b. a hacer paella c. a hacer un delicioso plato

2. ¿Qué va a cocinar la tía Julia hoy?

   a. una paella b. arroz con pollo c. bistec con arroz

3. ¿Qué hay que cortar?

   a. el jugo de limón b. el recipiente c. el pollo

4. ¿Qué se le añade al pollo?

   a. el recipiente b. los pedazos c. jugo de limón y ajo

5. ¿Qué calienta la tía Julia?

   a. el pollo b. aceite de oliva c. cebolla

6. ¿Cómo fríe el pollo?

   a. a fuego mediano b. a fuego lento c. a fuego alto

7. ¿Qué le añade al pollo en la cazuela?

   a. aceite de oliva b. pedazos de pollo c. cebolla y ají verde

8. ¿Cuántos minutos lo cocina a fuego lento?

   a. cinco minutos b. veinticinco minutos c. cincuenta minutos

Nombre: ______________________ Fecha: ______________________

¡Así lo decimos! Vocabulario

6-14 ¡A completar! How well do you know your way around the kitchen? Complete each of the following statements, choosing the appropriate word from the word bank.

cafetera	congelador	estufa	lavaplatos	microondas	recipiente
mezclar	pizca	receta	refrigerador	sartén	tostadora

1. Hay que lavar los platos en el ______________________.
2. Hay que poner el helado en el ______________________.
3. Si tienes mucha prisa y no puedes usar el horno, puedes usar el ______________________.
4. Para hacer el café, necesitas usar la ______________________.
5. Cuando regreso del supermercado, pongo la leche inmediatamente en el ______________________.
6. Para calentar el agua, pongo la cazuela en la ______________________.
7. Para freír algo, lo pongo en la ______________________.
8. La lista de ingredientes y las instrucciones para preparar una comida se llama la ______________________.
9. Mezclo los ingredientes de una torta en un ______________________.
10. Siempre le añado una ______________________ de sal al arroz.
11. Para preparar tostadas, hay que poner el pan en la ______________________.
12. Hay que ______________________ el café y el azúcar antes de beberlo.

Nombre: ______________________ Fecha: ______________________

6-15 Muchos cocineros. The Spanish Club is having a party, and everyone is helping in the kitchen. Complete each sentence, describing what people are doing, with the present tense of the correct verb from the word bank.

Modelo: *La señora Vidueñas derrite la mantequilla en la sartén.*

añadir calentar freír mezclar preparar

1. Ramón y Nico ______________ el aceite en la estufa.
2. La profesora ______________ los ingredientes con un tenedor grande.
3. Carlos le ______________ un poco de limón a la ensalada.
4. Julio y Estrella ______________ los sándwiches.
5. Julio y Yolanda ______________ los huevos en la sartén.

echar hervir hornear tapar tostar

6. Carmen ______________ las zanahorias a la sartén.
7. Yo ______________ el agua en la estufa.
8. Tú ______________ el pan en la tostadora.
9. Jorge y Gerardo ______________ la torta a 200°C.
10. Tu hermano y tú ______________ la sartén.

6-16 Una receta. Write instructions for preparing a simple dish you know.

Modelo: *Primero, batimos los huevos por cinco minutos...*

INGREDIENTES

____

____

____

____

INSTRUCCIONES

____

____

____

____

Nombre: ______________________ Fecha: ______________________

¡Así lo hacemos! Estructuras

3. The preterit of regular verbs

6-17 ¿Qué hicieron en la clase de cocina? Find out what everyone did during a cooking class. Complete each sentence with the correct preterit form of the verbs in parentheses.

1. Alfredo (calentar) ______________ el aceite.
2. Ana y Silvia (hornear) ______________ el pastel.
3. El chef le (echar) ______________ sal al pollo.
4. Yo (mezclar) ______________ los ingredientes.
5. José (añadir) ______________ una pizca de sal a la carne.
6. Mi hermano (tapar) ______________ la cazuela.
7. Carlos y yo (cocinar) ______________ la cena.
8. Pepito (preparar) ______________ la tortilla.
9. Isabel y Enrique (tostar) ______________ el pan.
10. Todos nosotros (comer) ______________ la torta.

6-18 ¿Qué pasó ayer? Find out what happened yesterday. Complete the following paragraph with the complete preterit form of the verbs in parentheses.

Ayer, yo (1. despertarse) ______________ tarde y (2. decidir) ______________ ir a almorzar a un restaurante. (3. llamar) ______________ a mi amiga Silvia, y la (4. invitar) ______________ a almorzar conmigo. Nosotros (5. llegar) ______________ al restaurante a la una. Cuando nosotros (6. entrar) ______________ al restaurante, Silvia le (7. preguntar) ______________ a la camarera por la especialidad de la casa. Ella le (8. responder) ______________ "bistec con papas fritas". Silvia y yo (9. pedir) ______________ la especialidad de la casa. El cocinero (10. preparar) ______________ mi bistec muy bien, y yo le (11. añadir) ______________ picante. Mi bistec me (12. gustar) ______________ mucho. Yo (13. beber) ______________ un refresco con la comida, y Silvia (14. tomar) ______________ una taza de café con leche. Nosotros le (15. dejar) ______________ una buena propina a la camarera.

Nombre: ______________________ Fecha: ______________________

6-19 ¡A completar! Complete the following paragraph with the correct preterit form of the verbs in parentheses.

Carlos y Esteban (1. buscar) ______________ un restaurante donde almorzar. Ellos (2. caminar) ______________ mucho y por fin (3. encontrar) ______________ un restaurante. El camarero los (4. atender) ______________ enseguida. Carlos (5. comer) ______________ arroz con pollo, y Esteban (6. comer) ______________ arroz con frijoles. Ellos (7. salir) ______________ del restaurante a las dos y (8. volver) ______________ a casa a las tres. ¡

Hola, mi amor! ¿Qué (9. almorzar) ______________ hoy?

¿(10. comer) ______________ un plato sabroso?... ¿(11. esperar) ______________ mucho tiempo? ¿(12. pagar) ______________ mucho por el plato?... ¿Cómo?

¿(13. salir) ______________ sin pagar las cuenta? ¡Ay, mi cielo!

Mi hermana y yo (14. llegar) ______________ a nuestra clase de cocina. Mi hermana (15. abrazar) ______________ a la tía Julia, y yo (16. comenzar) ______________ a preparar los ingredientes. Yo (17. buscar) ______________ muchos ingredientes, y la tía Julia nos (18. explicar) ______________ muy bien la receta. A nosotros nos (19. gustar) ______________ mucho la clase de la tía Julia, y le (20. regalar) ______________ una botella de vino.

4. Verbs with irregular forms in the preterit (I)

6-20 La primera cita. Juan invited Ana over for dinner at his apartment. He did all the cooking; however, he had a little help. Fill in the blanks with the appropriate preterit form of the verbs in parentheses to explain what Juan did.

1. No (dormir) ______________ la noche anterior.
2. (Leer) ______________ las instrucciones en la receta.
3. (Seguir) ______________ todas las instrucciones en la receta.
4. Le (pedir) ______________ ayuda a su madre.
5. (Repetir) ______________ el proceso que le dijo su madre.
6. (Oír) ______________ a Ana llegar.
7. (Servir) ______________ la cena en la mesa.

6-21 Una mala experiencia. Read the following paragraph and fill in the blanks with the appropriate preterit form of the verbs in parentheses.

El viernes pasado fuimos al nuevo restaurante de la ciudad. Yo quería ir al cine, pero mis amigos (1. preferir) ________________ ir a cenar. Cuando llegamos, ellos (2. oír) ________________ que el restaurante estaba lleno (*full*), pero pudimos cenar. Yo no (3. leer) ________________ la carta, pero ellos sí la (4. leer) ________________. Yo (5. pedir) ________________ pescado, y ellos (6. pedir) ________________ carne. El camarero no nos (7. servir) ________________ bien y Paco, uno de mis amigos, (8. pedir) ________________ hablar con el encargado (*person in charge*). El encargado (9. creer) ________________ que Paco estaba mintiendo (*lying*). ¡Fue (*It was*) un desastre! Por la noche, Paco no (10. dormir) ________________ bien, y el resto de mis amigos no (11. sentirse) ________________ bien durante todo el fin de semana.

NUESTRO MUNDO

Panoramas

6-22 ¡A informarse! Based on the information from **Nuestro mundo** on pages 214–215 of your textbook, decide if the following statements are **cierto (C)** or **falso (F).**

1. En Chile sólo se produce vino.
2. Los productos agrícolas chilenos se exportan a otros países.
3. Chile es uno de los países productores de vino más importantes del mundo.
4. El pescado chileno sólo (*only*) se come en Chile.
5. Chile tiene unos diez mil kilómetros de costas.
6. El desierto de Atacama es importante por la producción agrícola.
7. El desierto de Atacama es rico en minerales.
8. Punta Arenas es la ciudad que está más cerca del Polo Sur.
9. El invierno chileno es de junio hasta octubre.
10. En Chile no hay lugares (*places*) para esquiar.

Nombre: ______________________ Fecha: ______________________

6-23 Tu propia experiencia. Use the Internet and library sources to research one of the many political events that have occurred in Chile in the last century and, in your own words, briefly explain what happened.

____

____

____

____

____

____

____

Taller

6-24 Los anuncios

Primera fase. Read the following restaurant ads and answer the questions.

1. ¿En qué país y ciudad están estos restaurantes?

____

Nombre: ______________________ Fecha: ______________________

2. ¿Qué restaurantes anuncian las especialidades? ¿Cuáles son?

____

3. ¿Qué restaurante ofrece platos especiales del día?

____

Segunda fase. Now, create your own restaurant ad for a restaurant you know or for an imaginary restaurant you would like to visit. Use Spanish in your ads, and include phrases or ideas that would make people want to eat at this restaurant.

____

____

____

____

____

6-25 Una receta. Use the Internet and library sources to look up and write down a Chilean recipe or a recipe from another South American country. Try to choose a recipe that sounds interesting to you. If possible, look for the history of the recipe: Was it an indigenous dish? Were the ingredients originally found in the Americas or were they brought in by the Europeans?

INGREDIENTES

____

____

____

INSTRUCCIONES

____

____

____

HISTORIA

____

____

____

Nombre: ______________________________ Fecha: ____________________

6-26 Más allá de las páginas: Odas y manzanas. Pablo Neruda, who lived in an agriculturally rich country, wrote several **odas** to different fruits and vegetables. Try to find out additional information about Chilean agriculture. Are apples grown in great quantities in Chile? Where are other fruits and vegetables grown and harvested? How much is grown for national consumption, and how much is exported to other countries? Research general information on agriculture or select a specific topic that interests you. Organize the information in a chart in Spanish.

____

____

____

____

____

¿Cuánto sabes tú?

6-27 ¿Sabes usar los superlativos? Fill in the blanks to complete the superlative construction, using the adjectives in parentheses.

1. Mi madre es ________________ cocinera del mundo. (mejor)
2. Eduardo es el estudiante ________________ de la clase. (inteligente)
3. Las naranjas de Valencia son ________________ de España. (sabroso)
4. La comida del restaurante Dos Hermanos es ________________ de la ciudad. (picante)
5. El café de Centroamérica es ________________ de las Américas. (rico)

6-28 ¿Sabes usar el doble pronombre? Read the following sentences and decide what pronoun each sentence is missing, according to the context.

la las lo los me nos se te

1. Mi hermana y yo le pedimos ayuda a mi madre y mi madre ________________ ________________ dio.
2. Eduardo quería la receta del arroz con pollo y yo ________________ ________________ di.
3. Yo quería pedir un café y Juan ________________ ________________ pidió.
4. Tú querías papas y el camarero ________________ ________________ sirvió.
5. Queríamos bocadillos; Paco ________________ ________________ preparó.

Nombre: ______________________________ Fecha: ______________________

6-29 ¿Sabes usar el pretérito regular e irregular? Fill in the blanks with the appropriate preterit form of the verbs in parentheses.

El fin de semana pasado, mi familia y yo (1. salir) ________________ a cenar a un restaurante. Cuando nosotros (2. llegar) ________________ al restaurante, (nosotros) (3. buscar) ________________ una mesa para sentarnos. Mi padre (4. leer) ________________ la carta de vinos y (él) (5. pedir) ________________ vino tinto. Mi madre (6. preferir) ________________ beber una copa de vino blanco. Nosotros (7. pedir) ________________ la comida y el camarero nos (8. servir) ________________ rápidamente (*quickly*). Cuando (nosotros) (9. salir) ________________ del restaurante, yo (10. pagar) ________________ la cuenta. (Yo) le (11. explicar) ________________ a mi padre que (yo) (12. hablar) ________________ con mi jefe y él me (13. aumentar) ________________ el sueldo (*to give a salary raise*). Mi padre se (14. sentir) ________________ muy orgulloso (*proud*) de mí.

Nombre: ______________________________ Fecha: ______________________

Lab Manual

Primera parte

¡Así es la vida!

6-30 Graciela y Adriana van a comer. Listen to the following conversation. Then select the letters for all statements that are correct, according to what you hear. Listen to the conversation as many times as is necessary to find all the correct statements.

1. Graciela y Adriana van a...
   a. desayunar.
   b. almorzar.
   c. cenar.
2. Graciela...
   a. está muerta de hambre.
   b. quiere un café solo.
   c. quiere un café con leche.
3. El camarero les sirve...
   a. café con leche.
   b. té.
   c. jugo de naranja.
4. Adriana quiere...
   a. un café solo.
   b. un café con leche.
   c. un té.
5. Graciela pide...
   a. tostadas.
   b. jugo de naranja.
   c. huevos fritos.
6. Adriana quiere...
   a. papas fritas.
   b. huevos revueltos.
   c. cereal.
7. Adriana dice...
   a. "Los huevos revueltos están deliciosos".
   b. "El desayuno de Adriana está frío".
   c. "Las papas fritas están crudas".
8. El camarero...
   a. le trae otra comida a Graciela.
   b. es muy amable.
   c. dice que no hay cuenta.

Nombre: ______________________ Fecha: ______________________

¡Así lo decimos! Vocabulario

6-31 ¿Cuál es la comida? Look at the following pictures and answer the questions you hear, using expressions and vocabulary in **¡Así lo decimos!** on page 191 of your textbook. Then listen and repeat as the speaker gives the correct answer.

1. ______________________________
2. ______________________________
3. ______________________________

4. ______________________________
5. ______________________________
6. ______________________________

7. ______________________________
8. ______________________________
9. ______________________________

Nombre: ______________________________ Fecha: ____________________

Pronunciación

Sounds of *y, ll,* and *ñ*

The Spanish **y** has two distinct sounds. At the beginning of a word or within a word, it is pronounced like the *y* in the English word *yes,* but with slightly more force.

yo	**oye**	**Yolanda**
leyes	**ya**	**arroyo**

When **y** is used to mean *and,* or when it appears at the end of a word, it is pronounced like the Spanish vowel **i.**

Jorge y María	**hay**	**cantar y bailar**	**voy**

The Spanish **double l (ll)** is pronounced in many regions like the **y** in **yo.**

llamar	**brilla**	**llorar**	**sello**

The **ñ** is pronounced by pressing the middle part of the tongue against the roof of the mouth or palate. Its sound is similar to the *ny* sound in the English word *onion.*

mañana	**puño**	**niño**	**señal**

6-32 Pronunciemos. You will hear a series of Spanish words that contain the letter **y.** Repeat each word after the speaker.

1. yo
2. oye
3. arroyo
4. joya
5. ayer
6. ya
7. mayo
8. yerba
9. leyes
10. haya

6-33 Pronunciemos más. You will now hear a series of words that contain the letter **y** by itself or at the end of the word. In such cases, the **y** is pronounced like the vowel **i.** Repeat each word after the speaker.

1. hoy
2. y
3. rey
4. hay
5. ¡ay!
6. ley

6-34 Pronunciemos más. The following words and phrases contain the letter **ll.** Repeat each word or phrase after the speaker.

1. me llamo
2. lluvia
3. allí
4. talla pequeña
5. silla
6. llamar
7. la tablilla
8. amarillo
9. una vista bella
10. voy a llevar

6-35 Y pronunciemos más. You will now hear a series of words that contain the letter **ñ.** Repeat each word after the speaker.

1. niño
2. años
3. señorita
4. mañana
5. montaña
6. español
7. señor
8. baño
9. ñato
10. añadir

¡Así lo hacemos! Estructuras

1. Los superlativos

6-36 Los mejores. Describe the following people and things using the cues provided. Then listen and repeat as the speaker gives the correct answer.

MODELO: You see: Ana / + / inteligente / la familia
You say: *Ana es la más inteligente de la familia.*

1. esta fruta / + / exótica / supermercado
2. el desayuno / la comida / + / importante / día
3. ésta / la sopa / – / picante / menú
4. éste / el restaurante italiano / + / famoso / ciudad
5. estos mariscos / – / caros / restaurante

Nombre: ______________________ Fecha: ______________________

6-37 Lo mejor de los restaurantes. Listen to the questions and write your response using the cues provided. Then listen and repeat as the speaker gives the correct answer.

1. enfrente de la librería: ______________________
2. Carlos Vargas: ______________________
3. sí: ______________________
4. el helado de chocolate: ______________________

2. Double object pronouns

6-38 Un cumpleaños en el restaurante. Answer the following questions affirmatively using double object pronouns. Then listen and repeat as the speaker gives the correct answer.

Modelo: You hear: ¿Le están enseñando el restaurante a Irma?
You say: *Sí, se lo están enseñando.*

1. ¿El camarero le está dando el vino a Pedro?
2. ¿La camarera le está sirviendo la ensalada a Carmen?
3. ¿Todos quieren darle un regalo al cocinero?
4. ¿Rodrigo te va a dar el dinero para pagar la comida?
5. ¿Papá les va a comprar los helados?
6. ¿Tu novia te va a cocinar langosta?

6-39 El camarero ocupado. You are a waiter at a restaurant and everyone wants something from you. Answer the questions you hear affirmatively. Then listen and repeat as the speaker gives the correct answer.

Modelo: You hear: Camarero, ¿me trae un cóctel de camarones?
You say and write: *Sí, se lo traigo en seguida.*

1. Sí, ________ ________ ______________ (conseguir) en seguida.
2. Sí, ________ ________ ______________ (pedir) en seguida.
3. Sí, ________ ________ ______________ (decir) en seguida.
4. Sí, ________ ________ ______________ (traer) en seguida.
5. Sí, ________ ________ ______________ (servir) en seguida.
6. Sí, ________ ________ ______________ (dar) en seguida.

Nombre: ______________________ Fecha: ______________________

SEGUNDA PARTE

¡Así es la vida!

6-40 Mamá, Papá y Lola cenan en el comedor. Listen to the following conversation and indicate whether the statements are **cierto (C)** or **falso (F)**, according to what you hear. Listen to the conversation as many times as is necessary to find the correct answers.

C F 1. La mamá prepara el desayuno.

C F 2. Lola y sus padres comen pollo.

C F 3. Comen también arroz y frijoles.

C F 4. El café está en el congelador.

C F 5. La tostadora está en la mesa.

C F 6. Tienen un kilo de pan.

C F 7. Hay flan para mañana.

C F 8. Los frijoles se calientan a fuego lento.

C F 9. La torta está en el horno.

C F 10. Papá tapó el arroz.

Nombre: ______________________ Fecha: ______________________

¡Así lo decimos! Vocabulario

6-41 Una receta. Listen to the description of how the chef prepared **el picadillo criollo** and fill in the blanks with the words you hear. Check your answers in the Answer Key.

CÓMO PREPARÉ EL PICADILLO CRIOLLO PARA EMPANADAS

(1) ______________ en rodajas cuatro cebollas y un (2) ______________. Corté en cuatro partes dos (3) ______________ medianos. En una (4) ______________ calenté a (5) ______________ ______________ dos (6) ______________ de aceite. Freí las (7) ______________, el ají y un diente de ajo (8) ______________. Lo (9) ______________ ______________ a fuego (10) ______________ por cinco minutos. (11) ______________ los tomates picados, una (12) ______________ de pimienta, una cucharada de azúcar y medio (13) ______________ de carne picada, mojada antes en leche. (14) ______________ todos los (15) ______________ y añadí un cuarto de (16) ______________ de pimentón, una cucharada de salsa picante, una (17) ______________ de aceitunas y tres huevos duros cortados. (18) ______________ todo por diez minutos, mezclando todo con una (19) ______________ de madera. Lo dejé enfriar en un (20) ______________ en el (21) ______________. Saqué la masa de las empanadas del (22) ______________ dos horas antes de hacer el picadillo. Preparé las empanadas y las (23) ______________ a 375° por 40 minutos.

Pronunciación

Sounds of *ch* and *h*

The **ch** is pronounced much like the initial sound in the English word *chop*.

chica	**chocolate**	**cacho**	**pecho**
chino	**Chile**	**mucho**	**leche**

The Spanish **h** is silent.

habla	**hora**	**Hernán**	**Héctor**
Hola	**hacer**	**alcohol**	**hielo**

Nombre: ______________________ Fecha: ______________________

6-42 Pronunciemos. You will hear a series of words that contain the Spanish **ch** sound. Repeat each word or phrase after the speaker.

1. el chico
2. cacho
3. China
4. las chicas
5. chisme
6. chofer
7. charro
8. che
9. Chile
10. chocolate

6-43 Pronunciemos más. Now you will hear a series of words and phrases that contain the letter **h.** Repeat each word or phrase after the speaker. Remember that the **h** is not pronounced.

1. hotel
2. hemisferio
3. hacer
4. los hombres
5. el hospital
6. ¡Hola!
7. la hacienda
8. La Habana
9. ¿Qué hora es?
10. la historia

¡Así lo hacemos! Estructuras

3. The preterit of regular verbs

6-44 ¿Qué pasó? Use the preterit tense of the verbs in parentheses to complete the following sentences. Then listen and repeat as the speaker gives the correct answer.

1. Yo (cocinar) ______________ mucho la semana pasada.
2. ¿Tú (comprar) ______________ el azafrán en el mercado?
3. El dependiente (vender) ______________ dos kilos de cebollas.
4. Nosotros (pelar) ______________ las papas en la cocina.
5. Yo (leer) ______________ la receta esta mañana.
6. Ella (trabajar) ______________ en un restaurante famoso.

Nombre: ______________________ Fecha: ______________________

6-45 ¿Qué hicieron? Using the cues provided, answer the following questions in complete sentences. Then listen and repeat as the speaker gives the correct answer.

MODELO: You hear: ¿A qué hora nadaste?
You see: las nueve y media
You say: *Nadé a las nueve y media.*

1. cereal y frutas
2. comer con nuestros abuelos
3. el parque
4. todos los ingredientes para la cena
5. un microondas

6-46 Preguntas de los padres. Answer the questions you hear affirmatively. Be sure to include the direct object pronoun. Then listen and repeat as the speaker gives the correct answer.

MODELO: You hear: ¿Compró tu mamá los recipientes?
You say and write: *Sí, ella los compró.*

1. Sí, ______________________.
2. Sí, ______________________.
3. Sí, ______________________.
4. Sí, ______________________.
5. Sí, ______________________.
6. Sí, ______________________.

6-47 Preguntas de mi mamá. Answer the questions you hear negatively. Then listen and repeat as the speaker gives the correct answer. Check the spelling of the verbs in the Answer Key.

MODELO: You hear: ¿Llegaste tarde a la farmacia?
You say and write: *No, no llegué tarde a la farmacia.*

1. No, no ______________________.
2. No, no ______________________.
3. No, no ______________________.
4. No, no ______________________.
5. No, no ______________________.
6. No, no ______________________.
7. No, no ______________________.

4. Verbs with irregular forms in the preterit (I)

6-48 ¿Qué pasó? Form sentences using the verbs you hear, according to the subjects provided. Then listen and repeat as the speaker gives the correct answer.

1. Yo ______________ crema para el café.
2. Paco ______________ el pan francés.
3. Usted ______________ mucho después del almuerzo.

Nombre: ______________________ Fecha: ______________________

4. Los abuelos de Raúl ______________ en septiembre.

5. Yo ______________ el ejercicio.

6. Tú ______________ estudiando por la noche.

7. Ella ______________ hambre.

8. Los camareros ______________ los calamares.

9. Yo ______________ ocho horas.

6-49 Preguntas durante el almuerzo. Answer the questions you hear using the cues provided. Then listen and repeat as the speaker gives the correct answer.

MODELO: You hear: ¿Quién murió en el accidente?
You see: Nadie
You say: *Nadie murió en el accidente.*

1. tú
2. solamente seis horas
3. la torta de chocolate
4. José y María
5. el cocinero

6-50 Preguntas. Complete the following sentences with the preterit form of the verbs you hear. Then listen and repeat as the speaker gives the correct answer. Check the spelling of the verbs in the Answer Key.

1. Susana ______________ el menú rápidamente.

2. Tú ______________ las papas.

3. Los niños no ______________ el menú.

4. ¿Quiénes ______________ cuando cantaron "Feliz cumpleaños"?

5. Yo ______________ que ______________ música en la cocina.

6. Marcos ______________ que ______________ el teléfono.

Nombre: ______________________ Fecha: ______________________

¿Cuánto sabes tú?

6-51 En el mercado. Look at the following picture and select whether the statements are **cierto (C)** or **falso (F).**

1. C F
2. C F
3. C F
4. C F
5. C F
6. C F
7. C F
8. C F

6-52 El mejor restaurante. Listen to the advertisement and answer the following questions. Then listen and repeat as the speaker gives the correct answer. You may need to listen to the advertisement more than once.

1. ¿Qué les gusta a las personas que comen en "Los Antojitos"?
2. ¿Cómo es el restaurante "Los Antojitos"?
3. ¿Los precios de "Los Antojitos" son más altos o más bajos que los de los otros restaurantes?
4. ¿Cuál es la especialidad del restaurante "Los Antojitos"?
5. ¿Qué plato está muy rico?

6-53 Preguntas en el restaurante. Write a response to the questions you hear. Answers will vary.

1. ______________________________
2. ______________________________
3. ______________________________
4. ______________________________
5. ______________________________
6. ______________________________

Nombre: ______________________ Fecha: ______________________

7 ¡A divertirnos!

Workbook

PRIMERA PARTE

¡Así es la vida!

7-1 El fin de semana. Reread the conversations in **¡Así es la vida!** on page 224 of your textbook and choose the most appropriate answer.

Escena 1

1. El problema de Susana, Ricardo, Julia y Eduardo es que no saben...

   a. qué día es. b. qué van a hacer. c. qué tiempo hace.

2. Una actividad posible es...

   a. hacer ejercicio en el gimnasio. b. hacer un pícnic. c. ir al partido de básquetbol.

3. Susana no quiere ir al partido porque...

   a. hace frío. b. hace buen tiempo. c. hace mal tiempo.

4. Otra actividad posible es...

   a. ir a un concierto. b. hacer una excursión. c. ir a la feria internacional.

5. Finalmente deciden...

   a. ir al partido de básquetbol. b. ir a la playa. c. ir a la feria internacional.

Escena 2

6. Al llegar a la playa, los chicos no encuentran...

   a. el mar. b. el carro. c. la bolsa con las toallas.

Nombre: ______________________ Fecha: ______________________

7. Eduardo olvidó la bolsa en...

   a. el carro. b. la residencia de estudiantes. c. la playa.

8. Los chicos no van a poder...

   a. nadar en el mar. b. secarse. c. hacer un pícnic en la playa.

¡Así lo decimos! Vocabulario

7-2 ¡A completar! Complete each statement with the most appropriate word from the word bank.

bolsa hacer un pícnic heladera sombrilla traje de baño

1. Hace mucho sol, necesito una ______________________.
2. Paco quiere nadar en la playa, necesita un ______________________.
3. El hielo está en la ______________________.
4. Tenemos sándwiches y bebidas para ______________________.
5. Las toallas están en la ______________________.

Nombre: ______________________ Fecha: ______________________

7-3 En el teatro. A friend has invited you to the theater tonight. Read the ticket carefully. Then answer the following questions in complete sentences in Spanish.

TEATRO HISPANIOLA

"DIATRIBA DE AMOR CONTRA UN HOMBRE SENTADO"
TEATRO LIBRE DEL CARIBE

JUEVES, 25 DE OCTUBRE, 2004
HORA: 21:00
PRECIO: 600 PESOS
BUTACA
FILA: 3 ASIENTO: 10

TEATRO HISPANIOLA
C/ DE ALBATROS 42
CABARETE, REPÚBLICA DOMINICANA
(809) 571-0290
201303549 REF: 1222546051

CAJA DE CABARETE CAJA DE CABARETE CAJA DE CABARETE CAJA DE

1. ¿Cómo se llama el teatro? ______________________
2. ¿Cómo se llama la obra teatral (*play*)? ______________________
3. ¿Cuál es la dirección del teatro? ______________________
4. ¿Qué día es la obra teatral? ______________________
5. ¿A qué hora es? ______________________
6. ¿Cuánto cuesta el boleto (*ticket*)? ______________________
7. ¿Cuál es el asiento (*seat*)? ______________________
8. ¿Hay un número de teléfono para el teatro? Si lo hay, ¿cuál es? ______________________

7-4 ¿Qué tiempo hace? Complete the sentences by choosing the most logical option. The first sentence has been done for you.

hace buen tiempo	hace frío	hace mucho frío	uso un paraguas (*umbrella*)
hace fresco	hace mucho calor	nado en el mar	voy a esquiar

1. En diciembre *hace frío*.
2. En otoño ______________________.
3. Cuando voy a la playa, ______________________.
4. Necesito otro suéter cuando ______________________.
5. En la primavera ______________________.

6. Cuando nieva, yo ______________________.

7. En el verano ______________________.

8. Cuando llueve, yo ______________________.

7-5 Preguntas y respuestas. Answer the following questions with complete sentences in Spanish.

1. ¿Qué tiempo hace hoy?

____

2. ¿Para qué está ideal el día?

____

3. ¿Qué haces si el día está despejado y de pronto (suddenly) empieza a llover?

____

4. ¿Qué bebes cuando hace mucho frío?

____

5. ¿Qué haces cuando hace calor en la playa?

____

6. ¿Nieva o llueve en tu ciudad?

____

7. ¿En qué estación hace mucho frío?

____

8. ¿En qué estación hace mucho calor?

____

Nombre: ______________________ Fecha: ______________________

¡Así lo hacemos! Estructuras

1. Irregular verbs in the preterit (II)

7-6 ¿Adónde fuiste ayer? Complete the following dialog with the appropriate preterit form of the verbs in parentheses. Use the **yo** and **tú** forms only.

1. ¿Adónde (ir) ______________ tú ayer?

   (Salir) ______________ con mis amigos.

2. ¿Adónde (ir) ______________ con tus amigos?

   (Ir) ______________ a una fiesta.

3. ¿(Tener) ______________ que comprar refrescos?

   Sí, (tener) ______________ que comprar refrescos.

4. ¿(Estar) ______________ en la playa?

   Sí, (estar) ______________ en la playa y (dar) ______________ un paseo

5. ¿Con quién (dar) ______________ un paseo?

   (Dar) ______________ un paseo con mis amigos.

7-7 ¿Qué pasó? To find out what happened last week, yesterday, and last night, complete each paragraph with the preterit form of the indicated verb.

ir

1. La semana pasada yo ______________ a un concierto. Mi novia no ______________, pero mis amigos ______________ conmigo. Después, nosotros ______________ a un restaurante a comer.

tener

2. Ayer nosotros ______________ que ir a la playa. Yo ______________ que comprar refrescos y mis hermanas ______________ que hacer sándwiches. Nosotros ______________ que comprar bolsas, y papá también ______________ que comprar una sombrilla.

Nombre: ______________________ Fecha: ______________________

dar

3. Yo le ______________ la sombrilla a mi novia, y mis amigos le ______________ la bolsa. Mi hermano le ______________ un cesto (*basket*) que compró anoche. Todos nosotros le ______________ más cosas para llevar a la playa.

estar

4. Anoche yo ______________ con mis amigos en un restaurante. Nosotros ______________ allí por dos horas. La comida ______________ muy buena y nuestros profesores también ______________ con nosotros en el restaurante. Luego, mis amigos y yo ______________ en casa de mi hermano. ¿Dónde ______________ tú anoche?

7-8 Nuestra fiesta. Find out about our party last night. Complete the following paragraph with the correct preterit form of the verbs in parentheses.

Anoche mi hermano y yo (1. dar) ______________ una fiesta y muchos de nuestros amigos (2. ir) ______________ a la fiesta. Mi hermano (3. tener) ______________ que prepara la comida y yo (4. tener) ______________ que limpiar la casa. Nuestros amigos Pepe y Paco (5. estar) ______________ en la fiesta con sus novias Adela y Anita. Paco (6. tener) ______________ que bailar con Adela toda la noche. Nosotros (7. dar) ______________ mucha comida en la fiesta. La fiesta (8. estar) ______________ muy buena. ¿(9. Ir) ______________ tú a una fiesta anoche?

Nombre: ______________________ Fecha: ______________

2. Indefinite and negative expressions

7-9 Conversaciones. Complete each conversation with the appropriate affirmative and negative expressions from the word bank. You will have to use some words twice.

algo algún nada ni... ni ninguno

1. ¿Quieres refrescos o agua mineral para el pícnic?

   No quiero ______________ refrescos ______________ agua mineral para el pícnic.

2. ¿Deseas tú ______________ para llevar al pícnic?

   No, gracias no deseo ______________ para llevar al pícnic.

3. ¿Tienes ______________ sándwich en el cesto (*basket*)?

   No, no tengo ______________.

algo alguien algún nadie ningún nunca siempre

4. ¿Te preparo ______________ de postre para el pícnic?

   No, chico. ¿Por qué no compras ______________ pastel.

5. ¿Hay ______________ tomando el sol en la playa?

   No, no hay ______________ tomando el sol en la playa.

6. ¿Vamos al cine esta noche?

   No chico, ¿por qué no hacemos ______________ diferente? ______________ vamos al cine por la noche.

7. Bueno, ¿qué quieres hacer?

   No sé. ¿Vamos a un concierto? ______________ vamos a ______________ concierto.

7-10 Ana y Paco riñen. Ana and Paco are quarreling. Ana has a number of complaints against Paco. Play the role of Paco, and change Ana's statements from affirmative to negative or vice versa.

Ana: Tú no me llevas a la playa nunca.

Paco: (1) ____

Ana: Tú nunca me das ningún regalo.

Paco: (2) ____

Ana: Tú no me llevas ni a la discoteca ni al cine.

Paco: (3) ____

Ana: Tú tampoco me invitas a dar un paseo.

Paco: (4) ____

Ana: Tú quieres a alguien más que a mí.

Paco: (5) ____

Ana: Tú no me quieres.

Paco: (6) ____

Segunda parte

¡Así es la vida!

7-11 Hablando de deportes. Reread the passages in **¡Así es la vida!** on page 236 of your textbook and indicate whether each statement is **cierto (C)** or **falso (F).**

C F 1. María Elena Salazar juega al fútbol en el invierno.

C F 2. Ella nunca nada en el invierno.

C F 3. Daniel Sánchez es entrenador de un equipo de béisbol.

C F 4. Daniel les enseña a sus jugadores a ser agresivos.

C F 5. A Daniel le caen bien los árbitros.

C F 6. Daniel va a participar en las Olimpíadas de Beijing.

C F 7. Alejandra Jiménez practica el atletismo.

C F 8. No le gusta ver deportes.

C F 9. A Alejandra le gusta el tenis.

C F 10. A Alejandra le fascina el boxeo.

Nombre: ______________________ Fecha: ______________________

¡Así lo decimos! Vocabulario

7-12 Los deportes. Explain the following sports to someone who is unfamiliar with them by completing each statement with words or expressions from the word bank.

aficionados	balón	cancha	entrenador	ganar	pelota
árbitro	bate	empatan	equipo	guante	raqueta

1. Para jugar al tenis, necesitas una ______________ y una ______________.
2. Para jugar al béisbol, necesitas un ______________ y un ______________.
3. Para jugar al baloncesto, necesito un ______________.
4. Juego al fútbol en una ______________.
5. Cuando hay errores en un partido el ______________ del equipo se enoja.
6. Los ______________ gritan mucho durante un campeonato.
7. Cuando juegan, todas los equipos quieren ______________.
8. El ______________ toma las decisiones.
9. Todos los jugadores forman un ______________.
10. Cuando dos equipos ______________, ni ganan y ni pierden.

7-13 Asociaciones. Match the word or expression in the right column to the word in the left column.

1. ____ correr
2. ____ empatar
3. ____ gritar
4. ____ esquiar
5. ____ nadar
6. ____ el bate
7. ____ ganar
8. ____ el ciclismo
9. ____ patinar
10. ____ el tenista

a. no ganar ni perder
b. la natación
c. una bicicleta
d. el béisbol
e. el atletismo
f. el hockey
g. el/la campeón/ona
h. el/la aficionado/a
i. la raqueta
j. los esquís

Nombre: ______________________ Fecha: ______________________

7-14 Crucigrama. Read each description or definition and write the correct word in the corresponding squares.

Horizontales

1. los dos equipos tienen el mismo número de puntos
3. una cosa redonda (*round*) y blanca que se usa para el béisbol
5. la persona que enseña y ayuda a los jugadores
7. las cosas que los beisbolistas se ponen en las manos
10. los Chicago Cubs, los New York Nets, los Green Bay Packers...
12. expresarse en voz muy alta
13. cosas grandes y redondas que se usan para el básquetbol
14. palos de madera o de aluminio para el béisbol
15. tener más puntos que el competidor al final del partido

Verticales

2. darle a una pelota con el pie
3. zapatos especiales que se usan para patinar
4. ir muy rápido a pie
5. las cosas necesarias para jugar un deporte
6. un deporte entre dos personas que llevan guantes grandes y pantalones cortos
8. una persona muy famosa y popular
9. una serie de acciones en un partido para ganar puntos
11. darle a una pelota con un bate

Nombre: ____________________ Fecha: ____________________

7-15 ¿Te gustan los deportes? Describe your attitude toward the following sports. Begin each sentence with **Me gusta** or **No me gusta** and give a reason why, using one of the adjectives from the word bank.

MODELO: el tennis
Me gusta el tenis porque es muy activo.

aburrido	agresivo	divertido	interesante	rápido
activo	disciplinado	emocionante	lento	violento

1. el básquetbol

   ____

2. la natación

   ____

3. el ciclismo

   ____

4. el hockey

   ____

5. el tenis de mesa

   ____

6. el esquí

   ____

Nombre: ______________________ Fecha: ______________________

7-16 La liga americana. Look at the standings that follow. Then answer the questions in complete sentences in Spanish.

LIGA AMERICANA				
División Este				
EQUIPOS	**PG**	**PP**	**PROM**	**JV**
x-Toronto Azulejos	95	67	.586	--
Nueva York Yanquis	88	74	.543	7
Baltimore Orioles	88	77	.525	10
Detroit Tigres	85	77	.525	10
Boston Medias Rojas	80	82	.494	15
División Central				
x Chicago Medias Blancas	94	68	.580	--
Kansas City Reales	84	78	.519	10
Cleveland Indios	76	86	.469	18
Minnesota Mellizos	71	91	.438	23
Milwaukee Cerveceros	69	93	.426	25
División Oeste				
x Tejas Rancheros	86	76	.531	--
Seattle Marineros	82	80	.506	4
California Angelinos	71	91	.438	15
Oakland Atléticos	68	94	.420	18
x Campeón de división				

PG = Partidos ganados; PP = Partidos perdidos;
PROM = Promedio (*average*); JV = Juegos vueltos

1. ¿Cuántas divisiones hay en la liga?

____

2. ¿De dónde son los Mellizos?

____

3. ¿Qué equipos tienen el mismo promedio (*average*)?

____

4. ¿Cuántos juegos han ganado los Azulejos?

____

5. ¿Cuál es el promedio de los Atléticos?

____

6. ¿Cuál de estos equipos es tu favorito? ¿Por qué?

____

Nombre: ______________________________ Fecha: ______________________

¡Así lo hacemos! Estructuras

3. Irregular verbs in the preterit (III)

7-17 El partido de anoche. Complete the paragraph with the correct preterit form of the verbs in parentheses.

Anoche yo (1. poder) ________________ ver jugar a mi equipo favorito, Los Medias Rojas de Boston, y (2. ponerse) ________________ muy contento de verlos. Mis amigos (3. venir) ________________ de otra ciudad para ir al estadio conmigo, y ellos (4. traer) ________________ sus guantes. En el partido, nosotros (5. saber) ________________ la nacionalidad de la estrella del equipo, Pedro Martínez. Es dominicano. Un aficionado nos lo (6. decir) ________________. Yo (7. ponerse) ________________ muy contento porque Los Medias Rojas ganaron el partido. ¿(8. Poder) ________________ tú ver el partido también?

7-18 Una carta. Find out what Luis Alberto says in a letter to his friend by using the correct form of the verbs in parentheses.

20 de enero
Querido Rafael:

El mes pasado yo (1. ir) ________________ de vacaciones a casa de Manuel Vargas en la República Dominicana. Allí nosotros (2. tener) ________________ la oportunidad de visitar muchos lugares de interés. Nosotros (3. andar) ________________ por la capital, donde yo (4. poder) ________________ comprar regalos para mi familia. Luego, Manuel y yo (5. ir) ________________ a visitar el interior de la isla. Nosotros (6. estar) ________________ en la playa de Sosúa. Allí Manuel (7. buscar) ________________ a varios de sus amigos, y yo los (8. conocer) ________________. Al día siguiente, nosotros (9. estar) ________________ en la ciudad de Santiago de los Caballeros. Por la noche, los amigos de Manuel (10. venir) ________________ a buscarnos para ver un partido de béisbol. El partido (11. ser) ________________ muy emocionante y Sammy Sosa, la estrella del equipo dominicano, (12. jugar) ________________ y (13. batear) ________________ muy bien.

Los aficionados (14. gritar) ________________ mucho y (15. animar) ________________ mucho a su equipo. Yo (16. querer) ________________ conocer a Sammy Sosa, pero no (17. poder) ________________. Después de estar una semana en Santo Domingo, yo (18. venir) ________________ para los EE.UU. Ayer le (19. escribir) ________________ a Manuel y le (20. dar) ________________ las gracias por todo.

Un saludo de
Luis Alberto

4. Impersonal and passive *se*

7-19 El/La experto/a. Let's see how much you know about sports. Answer the following questions with complete sentences in Spanish.

1. ¿Qué se necesita para jugar al béisbol?

   ____

2. ¿Para qué se usa una raqueta?

   ____

3. En el baloncesto, ¿dónde se pone el balón?

   ____

4. ¿Con qué se juega al vólibol?

   ____

5. ¿Qué se usa para boxear?

   ____

6. ¿Qué se tiene que hacer para ganar un partido?

   ____

7. ¿Qué se puede hacer cuando el árbitro toma una mala decisión?

   ____

8. ¿Qué se debe hacer para ser una estrella?

   ____

Nombre: ______________________ Fecha: ______________________

7-20 El entrenador. You are one of the best baseball managers in the league and you want to give tips to your players. Complete the paragraph with the pronoun **se** and the correct form of the verbs in parentheses.

(1. decir) ______________ que cuando (2. jugar) ______________ al béisbol, (3. tener) ______________ que escuchar muy bien al entrenador. Antes de comenzar a batear (4. mirar) ______________ bien al lanzador y (5. estudiar) ______________ sus movimientos. Luego, (6. necesitar) ______________ un bate bueno, (7. tomar) ______________ el bate bien y uno se para enfrente del lanzador. Cuando (8. lanzar) ______________ la pelota, (9. dar) ______________ un golpe (*blow*) fuerte con el bate y adiós pelota.

7-21 El Batazo. You go to your favorite restaurant El Batazo because you can practice Spanish there. Complete the description of the restaurant with the passive **se** and the correct form of the verbs from the word bank.

abrir	cerrar	hablar	saber
atender	decir	poder	traer

Me gusta mucho el restaurante El Batazo. (1) ______________ que es muy bueno y (2) ______________ que es barato. En El Batazo, (3) ______________ español y (4) ______________ bien al cliente. Allí (5) ______________ ver a los jugadores cuando van a comer y (6) ______________ guantes y bates. El Batazo (7) ______________ a las doce del día, y (8) ______________ a las doce de la noche.

NUESTRO MUNDO

Panoramas

7-22 ¡A informarse! Based on the information from **Nuestro mundo** on pages 250–251 of your textbook, choose the most appropriate answer for each of the following questions.

1. La isla de Cuba...

   a. no recibe turismo. b. es la más grande de las Antillas. c. está industrializada.

2. Un medio de transporte típico en La Habana es...

   a. el coco-taxi. b. el tren. c. el metro.

3. El merengue es...

   a. un baile típico de la República Dominicana.

   b. una playa en Cuba.

   c. la moneda de la República Dominicana.

4. La economía dominicana es importante por...

   a. la industria.
   b. la tecnología.
   c. el turismo.

5. El ámbar, que se encuentra en la República Dominicana, es...

   a. un insecto.
   b. un escorpión.
   c. una joya.

6. El Morro en San Juan de Puerto Rico es...

   a. un tipo de comida.
   b. una fortaleza.
   c. una famosa playa puertorriqueña.

7. Puerto Rico es...

   a. un estado libre asociado.
   b. independiente.
   c. un estado más de los EE.UU.

7-23 Tu propia experiencia. Choose one of the three islands (Cuba, the Dominican Republic, or Puerto Rico) and use the Internet and library sources to research what sports are popular with the island's population. In your own words, talk about their main sports events and their star players.

____

____

____

____

____

____

____

____

____

____

Nombre: ______________________ Fecha: ______________________

Taller

7-24 El fin de semana pasado

Primera fase. Interview four students to find out how they spent last weekend. Fill in the following chart, based on your interviews. Remember to ask if they ate out, saw a movie, went shopping, and so forth. Fill out part of the chart for yourself as well.

ESTUDIANTE	ACTIVIDADES	¿CON QUIÉN?	¿DÓNDE?

Segunda fase. Use the information from the **Primera fase** to write a brief paragraph comparing what you and the other students did last weekend.

MODELO: *Ana, Esteban y Elia fueron a ver una película. Yo no fui al cine, pero salí a cenar en un restaurante muy bueno con unos amigos...*

____

____

____

____

____

Nombre: ______________________ Fecha: ______________________

7-25 Los hispanos y los deportes

Primera fase. Many professional athletes in the U.S. are of Hispanic origin, especially in the sport of baseball. Select two Hispanic professional athletes and look up information by using the Internet and library resources. **¿Dónde nació? ¿Dónde aprendió a jugar su deporte? ¿Dónde vive ahora?** and so forth. Make a list in Spanish of the information that you find.

Nombre: ______________________

Lugar de nacimiento: ______________________

Su deporte: ______________________

El equipo (los equipos): ______________________

Entrenamiento (*training*): ______________________

Información misceláнea: ______________________

Nombre: ______________________

Lugar de nacimiento: ______________________

Su deporte: ______________________

El equipo (los equipos): ______________________

Entrenamiento (*training*): ______________________

Información miscelánea: ______________________

Segunda fase. Now choose one of the athletes you researched in the **Primera fase** and write a brief paragraph, describing the athlete in Spanish.

____

____

____

____

Nombre: ______________________ Fecha: ______________________

7-26 Más allá de las páginas: La herencia indígena y africana. Nicolás Guillén was a mulatto (person of mixed Black and White ancestry). The current population of the Caribbean islands still reflects strong indigenous and African heritages that have influenced language, music, religion, and politics. Select one of the following topics to research on the Internet or in the library. Organize the information you find in an outline or in a brief summary in Spanish.

- La herencia africana en las islas del Caribe
- Los taínos (grupo indígena)
- Los siboneyes (grupo indígena)
- Los caribes (grupo indígena)

____

____

____

____

¿Cuánto sabes tú?

7-27 ¿Sabes usar el pretérito irregular (II)? Fill in the blanks with the most appropriate preterit form of the verbs from the word bank.

decir hacer ir poder traer venir

1. Intentamos ganar el partido de fútbol, pero el otro equipo jugó muy bien y nosotros no ______________ ganar.
2. Ayer Juan ______________ a mi casa y me ______________ la raqueta de tenis que le pedí.
3. Yo ______________ al estadio para ver a mi equipo, pero perdieron el partido.
4. Antonio me ______________ la verdad; no hay boletos para el próximo partido.
5. Mis amigos ______________ toda su tarea y después fuimos a nadar a la piscina.

Nombre: ______________________ Fecha: ______________________

7-28 ¿Sabes usar las expresiones indefinidas y negativas? Fill in the blanks by choosing the most appropriate indefinite or negative expression.

1. No me gusta ______________ de los deportes violentos.

   a. algo b. nadie c. ninguno d. siempre

2. ______________ voy a la playa cuando llueve.

   a. nunca b. nada c. alguien d. algo

3. Me gusta ir de excursión y ______________ me gusta ir a conciertos.

   a. tampoco b. ni... ni c. algún d. también

4. No vino ______________ a mi casa el viernes pasado.

   a. alguien b. tampoco c. nadie d. siempre

5. ¿Tienes ______________ guante de béisbol?

   a. algún b. alguno c. alguna d. ningún

7-29 ¿Sabes usar el pretérito irregular (III)? Fill in the blanks with the most appropriate preterit form of the verbs from the word bank.

conocer estar haber poner saber ser

1. Ayer Jorge______________ que su padre ______________ boxeador profesional.
2. Teresa, ¿dónde ______________ la toalla? Tengo que ir a nadar y no la encuentro.
3. ______________ una excursión a las montañas el fin de semana pasado y no pude ir.
4. Fernando y Raúl ______________ a Sammy Sosa cuando (ellos) ______________ en Chicago. ¡Fue una experiencia inolvidable para ellos!

7-30 ¿Sabes usar el se pasivo e impersonal? Fill in the blanks with the pronoun **se** and the correct form of the verbs in parentheses.

1. En los estadios de fútbol (prohibir) ______________ beber alcohol.
2. (Decir) ______________ que el fútbol es el rey de todos los deportes.
3. No (vender) ______________ entradas para el próximo partido.
4. (Escuchar) ______________ buena música en los conciertos.
5. Cuando hace buen tiempo, (dar) ______________ paseos por el parque.

Nombre: ______________________________ Fecha: ______________________

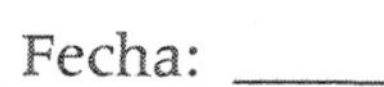

Lab Manual

PRIMERA PARTE

¡Así es la vida!

7-31 Cuatro amigos. As you listen to the following conversation, select the letters that correspond to all correct statements, according to what you hear. Listen to the conversation as many times as is necessary to find all the correct answers.

1. Los chicos quieren...
   a. salir mañana.
   b. pasear por el centro.
   c. hacer un pícnic.
2. Andrea...
   a. quiere dar un paseo.
   b. quiere ir a un partido.
   c. es estudiante.
3. Cristina...
   a. piensa que un partido es una buena idea.
   b. prefiere hacer un pícnic un día de la primavera.
   c. piensa que el plan de Ricardo es estupendo.
4. Esteban...
   a. dice que prefiere ir al cine.
   b. prefiere un pícnic.
   c. lleva las bebidas.
5. Ricardo...
   a. lleva la sombrilla y la heladera.
   b. prepara el almuerzo.
   c. piensa que puede hacer mal tiempo.

Nombre: ______________________________ Fecha: ______________________

¡Así lo decimos! Vocabulario

7-32 ¿Lógico o ilógico? Listen to the following conversations. Based on your knowledge of the vocabulary in **¡Así lo decimos!**, indicate whether each conversation is **lógico (L)** or **ilógico (I)**.

1.	L	I	6.	L	I
2.	L	I	7.	L	I
3.	L	I	8.	L	I
4.	L	I	9.	L	I
5.	L	I	10.	L	I

7-33 ¿Qué tiempo hace? Complete the following sentences with the most logical weather expression. Then listen and repeat as the speaker gives the correct answer.

1. En general, solamente __________ aquí en invierno.

   a. hace calor   b. nieva   c. hace buen tiempo

2. Salgo a tomar sol en la playa porque __________.

   a. llueve   b. hace calor   c. hace frío

3. Hace mal tiempo hoy. Hace mucho viento y __________.

   a. hace sol   b. llueve   c. hace calor

4. Llevamos suéteres porque __________.

   a. hace fresco   b. nieva   c. hace mucho calor

5. Hace sólo diez grados. __________.

   a. Hace mucho calor   b. Hace viento   c. Hace mucho frío

Nombre: ______________________ Fecha: ______________________

¡Así lo hacemos! Estructuras

1. Irregular verbs in the preterit (II)

7-34 Tú y yo. Answer the questions you hear, following the model and using the cues provided. Then listen and repeat as the speaker gives the correct answer.

MODELO: You hear: ¿Fueron ustedes al gimnasio?
You see: nosotros sí / Paco no
You say: *Nosotros fuimos al gimnasio, pero Paco no fue al gimnasio.*

1. yo sí / Raúl no
2. Daniela y yo sí / Carmen no
3. Luisa y yo sí / Margarita no
4. nosotros sí / Jaime y Rosa no
5. yo sí / ellas no

7-35 Preguntas personales. Answer the questions you hear, based on your own experience. Compare the verb forms in your answers with those in the Answer Key.

MODELO: You hear: ¿Llegaste tarde a la farmacia?
You say: *No, no llegué tarde a la farmacia.*

1. ...
2. ...
3. ...
4. ...
5. ...
6. ...
7. ...
8. ...

2. Indefinite and negative expressions

7-36 Antes de ver la película. Change each sentence you hear to its opposite, following the model. Then listen and repeat as the speaker gives the correct answer.

MODELO: You hear: ¿Alguien está cocinando?
You say: *Nadie está cocinando.*

1. ...
2. ...
3. ...
4. ...
5. ...
6. ...

Nombre: ______________________ Fecha: ______________________

7-37 El pícnic que nadie quiere. Answer the questions you hear negatively, using negative and indefinite expressions and informal commands. Then listen and repeat as the speaker gives the correct answer.

Modelo: You hear: ¿Traigo algunos tomates?
You say: *No, no traigas ninguno.*

1. No, no ______________________.
2. No, no ______________________.
3. No, no ______________________.
4. No, no ______________________.
5. No, no ______________________.
6. No, no ______________________.

Segunda parte

¡Así es la vida!

7-38 ¡El campeonato! Eduardo and Silvia are watching the final game of the national championship in Lima, Peru, on television. Listen to the conversation and select the letters corresponding to all statements that are correct, according to what you hear. Listen to the conversation as many times as is necessary to find all the correct statements.

1. Eduardo y Silvia miran un partido de...
   a. béisbol.
   b. fútbol.
   c. tenis.
2. Eduardo es fanático...
   a. de los Rojos.
   b. del Independiente.
   c. del Boca.
3. El campeón es...
   a. el equipo de Silvia.
   b. el equipo de Eduardo.
   c. el equipo Rojo.
4. El entrenador...
   a. es una estrella.
   b. es un fanático.
   c. está tranquilo.
5. Arturito es...
   a. la estrella de la noche.
   b. un jugador de fútbol.
   c. el árbitro.
6. Boca...
   a. pierde.
   b. empata.
   c. gana.

Nombre: ______________________ Fecha: ______________________

¡Así lo decimos! Vocabulario

7-39 Los deportes. Write down the name of the sport that corresponds to the following pictures. Then listen to the descriptions and write the letter of the description you hear that corresponds to the picture.

1. ______________

3. ______________

5. ______________

2. ______________

4. ______________

¡Así lo hacemos! Estructuras

3. Irregular verbs in the preterit (III)

7-40 ¡Absolutamente no! Answer the questions you hear negatively, following the model. Then listen and repeat as the speaker gives the correct answer.

MODELO: You hear: ¿Pusiste los libros en la mochila?
You say: *No, no los puse.*

1. No, no ______________________.
2. No, no ______________________.
3. No, no ______________________.
4. No, no ______________________.
5. No, no ______________________.
6. No, no ______________________.
7. No, no ______________________.
8. No, no ______________________.

7-41 ¿Qué pasó ayer? Form complete sentences, using the cues provided. Then listen and repeat as the speaker gives the correct answer.

Modelo: You see: nosotros / saber / las repuestas
You say: *Nostros supimos las repuestas.*

1. yo / no / poder / dormir en toda la noche
2. tú / no / poner / las bebidas en la heladera
3. ¿usted / venir / ayer?
4. nosotros / hacer / el ejercicio
5. ellas / decir / la verdad
6. Federico / no / poner / las toallas en la bolsa
7. ¿ustedes / traer / los trajes de baño?
8. yo / decir / la verdad
9. tú / venir / a visitarnos
10. Carlos y Abel / saber / la fecha del concierto
11. nosotros / estar / en la playa
12. yo / querer / nadar mucha distancia en poco tiempo

4. Impersonal and passive *se*

7-42 En el restaurante. Form complete sentences, using the cues provided, to describe a typical restaurant. Then listen and repeat as the speaker gives the correct answer.

Modelo: You see: decir / que tienen los mejores precios
You say: *Se dice que tienen los mejores precios.*

1. hacer / ensaladas frescas
2. servir / papas fritas
3. servir / este pollo con una salsa picante
4. lavar / los platos sucios
5. preparar / el salmón con arroz
6. dar / el veinte por ciento
7. comer / la hamburguesa con cebolla
8. poner / el azúcar en el recipiente pequeño

Nombre: ______________________________ Fecha: ______________________

7-43 Lo que se hace... Transform the following sentences into impersonal expressions, using the impersonal **se.** Then listen and repeat as the speaker gives the correct answer.

MODELO: You see: Prepararon sándwiches para llevar al partido.
You say: *Se prepararon sándwiches para llevar al partido.*

1. Este equipo perdió el campeonato.

2. Los aficionados animaron a las jugadoras.

3. La temporada terminó ayer.

4. Nombraron el hockey como un deporte rápido. (nombrar = *to name*)

5. Cancelaron el partido.

6. Encontraron las raquetas de tenis.

¿Cuánto sabes tú?

7-44 Ignacio y Mónica. Listen to the conversation as often as necessary to answer the following questions. Then listen and repeat as the speaker gives the correct answer.

1. ¿Qué deporte practica la hermana de Enrique?

2. ¿Qué hace ella hoy?

3. ¿Le gusta a Ignacio el vólibol?

4. ¿Y a Fernanda?

5. ¿A qué hora es el partido?

6. ¿Lleva Fernanda los refrescos?

7. ¿Quién prefiere llevar la heladera?

8. ¿Quién lleva la música?

7-45 Los gustos. Listen to the description of the things Alberto, David, Carolina, and Graciela like and dislike. Then indicate whether the following statements are **cierto (C)** or **falso (F).** You may need to listen to the description more than once.

C F 1. A Alberto le cae bien Carolina.

C F 2. Graciela le cae bien a Alberto.

C F 3. A Alberto le molesta David.

C F 4. A David le gusta Carolina.

C F 5. A Carolina le gusta la natación.

C F 6. A Carolina le cae mal David.

C F 7. A Graciela no le cae bien Carolina.

C F 8. Los deportes le interesan a Graciela.

7-46 Haces una invitación. When you speak to a friend on the telephone, what do you say to invite him to go out this weekend? Write your answers to the questions you hear. Answers will vary.

1. ____

2. ____

3. ____

4. ____

5. ____

Nombre: ______________________ Fecha: ______________

8 ¿En qué puedo servirle?

Workbook

PRIMERA PARTE

¡Así es la vida!

8-1 De compras. Reread the conversations in **¡Así e la vida!** on page 260 of your textbook. Then choose the correct answer for each of the following questions.

1. ¿Qué hacen Victoria y Manuel en el centro de Lima?

   a. comen en un restaurante b. van de compras c. visitan un museo

2. ¿Dónde se encuentra la sección de ropa de mujeres?

   a. en el tercer piso b. en el segundo piso c. en el primer piso

3. ¿A quién le pidió Victoria la tarjeta de crédito?

   a. a Manuel b. a su madre c. a su padre

4. ¿Cuál fue el favor que el padre les pidió a sus hijos?

   a. pagar los libros c. no usar las tarjetas de crédito

   b. comprarle una camisa

5. Según Manuel, ¿cómo pagó sus libros?

   a. con tarjeta de crédito b. al contado c. con un cheque

6. ¿Por qué va Manuel al almacén Saga Falabella?

   a. para comprar libros b. para acompañar a Victoria c. para comprar camisas

7. ¿Dónde están las chaquetas?

   a. en el segundo piso b. en el tercer piso c. en el cuarto piso

Nombre: ______________________ Fecha: ______________________

8. ¿Cuál es la talla de Manuel?

   a. cuarenta b. ganga c. probador

9. ¿Dónde se prueba la camisa?

   a. es una ganga b. en el probador c. en la sección de mujeres

10. ¿Por qué es una ganga la camisa?

    a. porque es bonita b. porque le queda bien c. porque es barata

¡Así lo decimos! Vocabulario

8-2 En el almacén. Read the following paragraph about a shopping excursion and fill in the blanks with the appropriate word or phrase from the word bank.

abrigo	corbata	pantalones	venta-liquidación
billetera	de manga corta	probador	vestido
bolso	gangas	tarjeta de crédito	zapatillas de tenis
centro comercial	ir de compras		

Este fin de semana voy al (1) ______________ para (2) ______________. Voy a comprar un (3) ______________ azul y un (4) ______________ negro. En el almacén voy a ir al (5) ______________ para ver si me queda bien o mal la ropa. También necesito comprar una (6) ______________ para mi padre. Tiene una camisa nueva (7) ______________ y (8) ______________ nuevos. También tiene una (9) ______________ de cuero. Ahora solamente necesita unas (10) ______________ para hacer deporte. El almacén tiene una (11) ______________ maravillosa, y hoy hay muchas (12) ______________. Tengo mi (13) ______________ preparada en mi (14) ______________. ¡Adiós!

Nombre: ______________________ Fecha: ______________________

8-3 ¿Qué ropa llevas? What do you wear in the following situations? Begin each statement with **llevo** and use colors or other adjectives that describe your clothing.

MODELO: *A clase, llevo vaqueros y una blusa azul. También llevo sandalias marrones.*

1. A una celebración familiar, ____

____.

2. Al centro estudiantil, ____

____.

3. A un partido de básquetbol, ____

____.

4. Cuando hace mucho frío, ____

____.

5. Cuando hace mucho calor, ____

____.

8-4 El/La cliente/a responde. Imagine that you are shopping in a department store and a salesperson asks you the following questions. How do you respond? Write your answers with complete sentences in Spanish.

Dependiente: Buenas tardes. ¿En qué puedo servirle?

Tú: (1) ____

Dependiente: ¿Cuál es su talla?

Tú: (2) ____

Dependiente: ¿Quiere probárselo en el probador?

Tú: (3) ____

Dependiente: ¿Qué más necesita?

Tú: (4) ____

Dependiente: ¿Cómo desea pagar?

Tú: (5) ____

Nombre: ______________________ Fecha: ______________________

8-5 El/La cliente/a pregunta. Now imagine that the salesperson answers you. What did you ask? Write the questions.

Tú: (1) ______________________

Dependiente: La sección de mujeres está a la derecha.

Tú: (2) ______________________

Dependiente: Las blusas en rebajas están aquí.

Tú: (3) ______________________

Dependiente: Sí, claro. El probador está aquí.

Tú: (4) ______________________

Dependiente: Le queda muy bien.

Tú: (5) ______________________

Dependiente: No, no le queda grande. Está perfecta.

8-6 La ropa. Complete each statement with a logical word from the word bank.

abrigo	caja	ganga	pagar al contado	talla
botas	camiseta	manga corta	rebaja	tela

1. Cuando hace mucho frío, necesito un ______________.
2. Cuando hace sol, me pongo la ______________ de los Medias Rojas de Boston.
3. No me gusta usar tarjetas de crédito; me gusta ______________.
4. La dependienta pone el dinero en la ______________.
5. Si los pantalones le quedan muy grandes a alguien, necesita una ______________ más pequeña.
6. Cuando algo está muy barato, es una ______________.
7. Cuando hace mucho frío y nieva, no llevas sandalias; llevas ______________.
8. Cuando hace mucho calor, no llevas una camisa de manga larga; llevas una camisa de ______________.
9. El algodón es una ______________.
10. Cuando da un descuento, la tienda pone los precios en ______________.

Nombre: ______________________ Fecha: ______________________

¡Así lo hacemos! Estructuras

1. The imperfect of regular and irregular verbs

8-7 ¿Qué hacían cuando iban de compras? Describe what the following people used to do whenever they went shopping. Complete each sentence with the correct imperfect form of the verbs in parentheses.

1. Cuando Ana iba de compras, (comprar) ______________ la ropa en unos grandes almacenes.
2. Mis padres (pedir) ______________ el recibo (*receipt*) de la compra.
3. Juan nunca (saber) ______________ cuál era su talla.
4. Antes de llegar a la tienda, nosotros (contar) ______________ el dinero.
5. Los niños (jugar) ______________ en el tercer piso de los almacenes.
6. Mucha gente (leer) ______________ el anuncio de las rebajas en el periódico.
7. Andrea les (escribir) ______________ a sus amigos para contarles sobre las rebajas.
8. La dependienta nos (atender) ______________ muy amablemente.
9. La gente no (dormirse) ______________ en los grandes almacenes.
10. Nosotros (reírse) ______________ de alegría cuando encontrábamos gangas.

8-8 Los recuerdos de mi abuela. Describe how things used to be by changing each of the following statements from the present indicative to the imperfect.

Modelo: Ahora, bailamos rock.
Antes, bailábamos vals.

1. Ahora, trabajamos cincuenta horas a la semana.

   Antes, ______________ cuarenta horas a la semana.

2. Ahora, vemos mucha televisión.

   Antes, no ______________ mucha televisión.

3. Ahora, viajamos en avión a todas partes.

   Antes, ______________ en carro a todas partes.

4. Ahora, compramos y gastamos mucho.

   Antes, ni ______________ ni ______________ mucho.

5. Ahora, comemos en restaurantes.

   Antes, ______________ en casa.

8-9 Los recuerdos de la dependienta. Complete the store clerk's reminiscences with the correct imperfect form of the verbs in parentheses.

Cuando yo (1. trabajar) ______________ de dependienta, nosotras (2. llegar) ______________ a la tienda temprano, (3. conversar) ______________ con las otras dependientas y luego (4. entrar) ______________ a la tienda. Nuestra tienda siempre (5. abrir) ______________ a las nueve de la manaña. Después de abrir, mientras la supervisora nos (6. anunciar) ______________ las ofertas especiales del día, mis compañeras y yo (7. atender) ______________ a los primeros clientes y les (8. mostrar) ______________ la mercancía en rebaja. Los clientes siempre (9. ser) ______________ amables y, a veces, algunos de ellos (10. ponerse) ______________ nerviosos si no (11. encontrar) ______________ gangas. Generalmente, nosotras (12. ayudar) ______________ a todos los clientes. Todas nosotras (13. llevar) ______________ el mismo uniforme en la tienda y, después del trabajo, nosotras (14. ponerse) ______________ otra ropa. A nosotras nos (15. gustar) ______________ mucho trabajar en la tienda, porque (16. divertirse) ______________ todos los días.

8-10 Recuerdos de nuestras profesiones. Complete the following paragraphs with the correct imperfect forms of the indicated verbs.

ser

1. Cuando yo _______________ dependiente, _______________ muy amable con los clientes. Mis compañeros también _______________ muy amables. Nuestra supervisora _______________ muy paciente con los clientes. Nosotros _______________ un equipo muy unido.

ir

2. Cuando mi familia y yo _______________ de vacaciones, yo _______________ a los museos. Mis hermanos _______________ de excursión por la mañana y, por la noche, ellos _______________ a las discotecas. Los domingos todos nosotros _______________ de compras al centro.

ver

3. En mi profesión de depediente de unos grandes almacenes, yo _______________ a muchos clientes. Los otros dependientes _______________ a muchos clientes también. En los grandes almacenes, mientras un cliente _______________ la ropa de rebaja, el otro _______________ la venta-liquidación. Bueno, nosotros _______________ muchas cosas en los grandes almacenes.

8-11 Cuestionario. What were things like when you were a child? Answer the following questions with complete sentences in Spanish.

1. ¿Cómo eras tú cuando eras niño/a?

____

2. ¿A dónde ibas a menudo con tus amigos?

____

3. ¿Dónde vivías?

____

Nombre: ______________________ Fecha: ______________________

4. ¿Qué hacías en la escuela?

____

5. ¿Veías mucho a tus parientes?

____

2. Ordinal numbers

8-12 Números, números. Complete each statement with the ordinal number corresponding to the number in parentheses. Remember to use agreement.

1. Ana prefiere la (5) ______________ chaqueta, la verde.
2. La loción de afeitar está en el (4) ______________ mostrador (*counter*).
3. La sección de ropa para hombres está en el (8) ______________ piso.
4. ¡Es la (9) ______________ tienda en la que entramos hoy!
5. El (2) ______________ dependiente es al que necesitamos buscar.
6. El (7) ______________ probador no está ocupado.
7. Es el (6) ______________ par (*pair*) de zapatos que compro hoy.
8. Es la (3) ______________ rebaja del año.
9. Los abrigos están en el (10) ______________ piso de la tienda.
10. Hoy es el (1) ______________ día de rebaja.

Nombre: ______________________________ Fecha: ______________________

8-13 ¿Dónde está? On which floor of the department store will you find the following items? Fill in the blanks to complete each statement with the correct information.

P
Servicios: Aparcamiento.

3-2

P-1
Servicios: Aparcamiento. Carta de compra. Taller de Montaje de accesorios de automóvil. Oficina postal.

1.er SÓTANO
Departamentos: Librería. Papelería. Juegos. Fumador. Mercería. Supermercado de Alimentación. Limpieza.
Servicios: Estanco. Patrones de moda.

PLANTA BAJA
Departamentos: **Complementos de Moda.** Bolsos. Marroquinería. Medias. Pañuelos. Sombreros. Bisutería. Relojería. Joyería. Perfumería y Cosmética. Turismo.
Servicios: Reparación de relojes y joyas. Quiosco de prensa. Óptica 2.000. Información. Servicio de intérpretes. Objetos perdidos. Empaquetado de regalos.

1.a PLANTA
Departamentos: **Hogar Menaje.** Artesanía. Cerámica. Cristalería. Cubertería. Accesorios automóvil. Bricolaje. Loza. Orfebrería. Porcelanas. (Lladró. Capodimonte). Platería. Regalos. Vajillas. Saneamiento. Electrodomésticos.
Servicios: Listas de boda. Reparación de calzado. Plastificación de carnés. Duplicado de llaves. Grabación de objetos.

2.a PLANTA
Departamentos: **Niños/as.** (4 a 10 años). Confección. Boutiques. Complementos. Juguetería. **Chicos/as.** (11 a 14 años) Confección. Boutiques. **Bebés.** Confección. Carrocería. Canastillas. Regalos bebé. Zapatería de bebé. **Zapatería.** Señoras, caballeros y niños. **Futura Mamá.**
Servicios: Estudio fotográfico y realización de retratos.

3.a PLANTA
Departamentos: **Confección de Caballeros.** Confección ante y piel. Boutiques. Ropa interior. Sastrería a medida. Artículos de viajes. Complementos de Moda. Zapatería. Tallas especiales.
Servicios: **Servicio al Cliente.** Venta a plazos. Solicitudes de tarjetas. Devolución de I.V.A. Peluquería de caballeros. Agencia de viajes y Centro de Seguros.

4.a PLANTA
Departamentos: **Señoras.** Confección. Punto. Peletería. Boutiques Internacionales. Lencería y Corsetería. Tallas Especiales. Complementos de Moda. Zapatería. Pronovias.
Servicios: Peluquería de señoras. Conservación de pieles. Cambio de moneda extranjera.

5.a PLANTA
Departamentos: **Juventud.** Confección. Territorio Vaquero. Punto. Boutiques. Complementos de moda. Marcas Internacionales. **Deportes.** Prendas deportivas. Zapatería deportiva. Armería. Complementos.

6.a PLANTA
Departamentos: **Muebles y Decoración.** Dormitorios. Salones. Lámparas. Cuadros. **Hogar textil.** Mantelerías. Toallas. Visillos. Tejidos. Muebles de cocina.
Servicios: **Creamos Hogar.** Post-Venta. Enmarque de cuadros. Realización de retratos.

7.a PLANTA
Departamentos: **Oportunidades** y Promociones.
Servicios: **Cafetería. Autoservicio** "La Rotonda". **Restaurante** "Las Trébedes".

ANEXOS

Preciados, 1. Tienda de la Electrónica: Imagen y Sonido. Hi-Fi. Radio. Televisión. Ordenadores. Fotografía. **Servicios:** Revelado rápido.

Preciados, 2 y 4. Discotienda: Compact Disc. Casetes. Discos. Películas de vídeo. **Servicios:** Venta de localidades.

MODELO: *Busco una blusa para mi hermana. Voy a la cuarta planta (floor).*

1. Necesito comprar un regalo para el bebé de mi hermana. Voy a la ____________________ planta.
2. Quiero comprar una lámpara. Voy a la ____________________ planta.
3. Mi reloj no funciona. Lo llevo a la ____________________.
4. Deseo una corbata para mi papá. Voy a la ____________________ planta.
5. Necesito unos zapatos de tenis nuevos. Voy a la ____________________ planta.

6. Me gusta leer y quiero comprar un libro nuevo. Voy al ______________________.
7. Mi madre quiere comprar toallas. Ella va a la ______________________ planta.
8. Tengo hambre. Voy a la cafetería en la ______________________ planta.
9. Necesito unas faldas. Voy a la ______________________ planta.
10. Quiero una tarjeta de crédito. Voy a la ______________________ planta.

Nombre: ______________________ Fecha: ______________________

Segunda parte

¡Así es la vida!

8-14 ¿Qué compraste? Reread the conversations in **¡Así es la vida!** on page 272 of your textbook. Then choose the correct answer for each of the following questions.

1. ¿Qué está haciendo Victoria?

   a. está estudiando b. está conversando con su hermano c. está comprando

2. ¿Quién llama por teléfono a Victoria?

   a. Lucía b. su hermano Manuel c. su madre

3. ¿Cuántas veces llamó Lucía a Victoria?

   a. cuatro b. una c. tres

4. ¿Adónde fue Victoria?

   a. de excursión b. de compras c. a la universidad a estudiar

5. ¿Qué compró Victoria primero?

   a. un llavero de plata b. un frasco de perfume c. un vestido rojo

6. ¿Qué compró en la joyería?

   a. un llavero de plata b. un frasco de perfume c. un vestido rojo

7. ¿Por qué fue a la perfumería?

   a. a comprar colonia para su novio Gustavo c. a comprar colonia para su hermano Manuel

   b. a comprar colonia para su padre

8. ¿Qué compró para su madre?

   a. un frasco de perfume b. un frasco de colonia c. un llavero de plata

9. ¿Cómo pagó Victoria?

   a. con tarjeta de crédito b. al contado c. con un cheque

10. ¿Por qué necesita Victoria un vestido elegante?

    a. para regalárselo a su madre b. para ir a la universidad c. para ir a una fiesta

Nombre: ______________________ Fecha: ______________________

¡Así lo decimos! Vocabulario

8-15 ¿Qué compras en estas tiendas? What can you buy in these stores? Match each store with a product.

1. ____ en la droguería	a. botas
2. ____ en la joyería	b. rosas
3. ____ en la papelería	c. un frasco de colonia
4. ____ en la zapatería	d. aspirinas
5. ____ en la perfumería	e. un llavero de plata
6. ____ en la farmacia	f. cuadernos
7. ____ en la florería	g. champú

8-16 Unos regalos. Everyone has a birthday this month. Use words or expressions from the vocabulary in **¡Así lo decimos!** on page 273 of your textbook to write what you will buy for each person.

MODELO: *A mi mamá, le compro un frasco de perfume.*

1. A mis hermanas, ______________________.
2. A mi novio, ______________________.
3. A mi papá, ______________________.
4. A mi mejor amigo/a ______________________.
5. A mi profesor/a de español, ______________________.
6. A mi hermano menor, ______________________.

Nombre: ______________________ Fecha: ______________________

¡Así lo hacemos! Estructuras

3. Preterit versus imperfect

8-17 Ayer fue un día diferente. To find out how yesterday was different from all other days, fill in the blanks with the correct preterit or imperfect form of the verbs in parentheses.

1. David siempre ______________ sandalias, pero ayer ______________ botas. (usar)
2. Mercedes y Víctor siempre ______________ joyas, pero ayer no ______________ joyas. (ponerse)
3. Todas las mañanas nosotros ______________ de compras, pero ayer no ______________ de compras. (ir)
4. Roberto y Alicia ______________ mucho dinero, pero ayer no ______________ nada. (gastar)
5. Generalmente, a mí no me ______________ bien el color azul, pero ayer me ______________ bien la camisa azul. (quedar)
6. A veces, yo ______________ la ropa que compraba, pero ayer no ______________ nada. (devolver)
7. Las botas que me gustan siempre ______________ mucho, pero ayer no ______________ tanto. (valer)
8. Normalmente, yo ______________ con tarjeta de crédito, pero ayer ______________ al contado. (pagar)

8-18 En el mercado. Every Saturday, my roommates and I used to go to the market. Complete the statements with the correct preterit or imperfect form of the verbs in parentheses.

1. María y Elena siempre (iban/fueron) ______________ a la carnicería.
2. Paco siempre (encontraba/encontró) ______________ los mejores precios del mercado.
3. Nosotros nunca (encontramos/encontrábamos) ______________ estacionamiento.
4. Mientras Jorge (compró/compraba) ______________ las bebidas, Margarita (tomó/tomaba) ______________ café en la cafetería del mercado.

5. Un sábado por la mañana, nosotros (nos despertamos/nos despertábamos) ______________ tarde, y no (pudimos/podíamos) ______________ hacer las compras.
6. Frecuentemente, todos (gastamos/gastábamos) ______________ bastante dinero, mientras que Paco (gastó/gastaba) ______________ poco dinero.
7. El domingo, después de las compras, nosotros (hicimos/hacíamos) ______________ un gran pícnic.
8. Después de tres años, nosotros (nos mudamos/nos mudábamos) ______________ a casas diferentes. (Era/Fue) ______________ maravilloso vivir con María, Elena, Paco y Jorge.

8-19 El verano. Describe what happened to you and your relatives during the summer. Complete the following paragraph with the correct preterit or imperfect form of the verbs in parentheses.

Todos los veranos, yo (1. ir) ______________ a casa de mis tíos en el campo. Mis primos y yo (2. hacer) ______________ muchas cosas. Durante el día, (3. ir) ______________ a la ciudad. Por las tardes, mientras Benito (4. tocar) ______________ la guitarra, nosotros (5. cantar) ______________. Todos los sábados, (6. salir) ______________ de excursión a las montañas. Allí siempre (7. jugar) ______________ y (8. nadar) ______________ en el río. Un día, mi prima Isabel (9. oír) ______________ un ruido que (10. venir) ______________ de una montaña. De pronto, todos (11. correr) ______________ para ver qué (12. haber) ______________ allá. Al llegar al lugar (13. descubrir) ______________ un salto. Nosotros (14. tomar) ______________ muchas fotos y luego (15. regresar) ______________ a la casa. Todos nosotros (16. estar) ______________ contentos. Yo nunca voy a olvidar ese verano.

Nombre: ______________________ Fecha: ______________________

8-20 Una historia amorosa. Complete the following story by filling in the blanks with the correct preterit or imperfect form of the verbs in parentheses.

(1. Haber) ______________ una vez un chico que (2. llamarse) ______________ Clodoveo, pero sus amigos le (3. decir) ______________ "Clodoveo el feo", porque (4. ser) ______________ muy feo. Todos los veranos, Clodoveo (5. ir) ______________ con su familia a Lima, que (6. quedar) ______________ lejos de su casa. Un día, la familia de Clodoveo (7. conocer) ______________ a la familia Bello en un parque de la ciudad. Los Bello (8. tener) ______________ una hija que (9. llamarse) ______________ Florinda. Ella (10. ser) ______________ tan linda que sus amigos; le (11. decir) ______________ "Florinda la linda". Clodoveo y Florinda (12. comenzar) ______________ a salir, y (13. empezar) ______________ a hacer muchas cosas juntos. A menudo, ellos (14. caminar) ______________ () por el centro de la ciudad, (15. ver) ______________ una película o (16. ir) ______________ al teatro. Florinda le (17. gustar) ______________ mucho a Clodoveo, pero él no (18. atreverse) ______________ a decírselo. Un día, mientras los dos (19. caminar) ______________ por el parque, Clodoveo le (20. cantar) ______________ una canción romántica a Florinda. Después, le (21. decir) ______________ que la (22. querer) ______________ mucho, y le (23. dar) ______________ unas flores que (24. ser) ______________ muy bellas. Florinda (25. emocionarse) ______________ tanto que le (26. dar) ______________ un beso a Clodoveo y (27. enamorarse) ______________ de él. Dos años más tarde, Clodoveo y Florinda (28. casarse) ______________. (29. Tener) ______________ muchos hijos y (30. vivir) ______________ muy felices.

Nombre: ______________________ Fecha: ______________________

NUESTRO MUNDO

Panoramas

8-21 ¡A informarse! Based on the information from **Nuestro mundo** on pages 282–283 of your textbook, decide if the following statements are **cierto (C)** or **falso (F).**

1. En las islas Galápagos no existe vida animal.
2. El Centro de Investigación Charles Darwin está en las Galápagos.
3. Charles Darwin formuló su teoría de la evolución de las especies en las Galápagos.
4. El galápago y la iguana marina no son especies protegidas.
5. El Ecuador no es una zona volcánica.
6. La alpaca tenía importancia religiosa para los incas.
7. La lana de la oveja es más fuerte que la lana de la alpaca.
8. Inti Tayta creó la civilización incaica.
9. Las tradiciones incas han desaparecido.
10. El camino Inca está a una altura de 2.380 metros.

8-22 Tu propia experiencia. Use the Internet and library sources to research what products originate from Peru or Ecuador. Make a list of the products, find out what currency these two countries use, and estimate how much it would cost in U.S. dollars to buy a sample of each product listed.

____

____

____

____

____

____

____

____

Nombre: ______________________ Fecha: ______________________

Taller

8-23 De compras

Primera fase. Interview four to five students in your class to find out about their last trip to a department store or supermarket. Ask for information that will help you complete the following chart. Fill in information about your last shopping trip as well.

ESTUDIANTE	¿ADÓNDE?	¿CON QUIÉN?	¿CUÁNDO?	¿QUÉ?	¿DINERO?
TÚ					

Segunda fase. Now write a paragraph to describe and compare the different shopping trips, using the information from the chart you completed in the **Primera fase.**

____

____

____

____

____

____

8-24 En el Perú y el Ecuador. The shopping experience in other countries can seem very different for tourists from the U.S. and Canada. Look up advice for tourists shopping in Peru or Ecuador on the Internet or through library sources. You should be able to find tour guides in both places. Make a list, in Spanish, of things that tourists should or should not do when shopping in the country you select. Then make a similar list in Spanish for foreigners shopping in your area.

Nombre: ____________________ Fecha: ____________________

EN EL PERÚ / EL ECUADOR

EN ____________

8-25 Más allá de las páginas: Las leyendas incas. The Incas had many legends that were passed down orally. Some of these legends have survived. For many people, their "real" history is equally fascinating. Select one of the following topics, and research the topic on the Internet or in the library. Organize the information you find in an outline or in a brief summary in Spanish.

- Leyendas de la creación: Los dioses (Viracocha, Inti, Mamá Kilya, Ilyapa)
- El derrumbamiento de los incas: Huayna Capa, Atahualpa, Huáscar y Pizarro
- Los quipu: Sistema de registrar información
- Las carreteras de los incas (no tenían ruedas [*wheels*] o caballos)
- El quechua: Idioma de los incas
- La arquitectura: Las ruinas de los incas

Nombre: ______________________ Fecha: ______________________

¿Cuánto sabes tú?

8-26 ¿Sabes usar el imperfecto? Fill in the blanks with the appropriate imperfect form of the verbs in parentheses.

1. Mientras Julio (pagar) ______________ la camisa, nosotros (comprar) ______________ zapatos.
2. Nosotros siempre (leer) ______________ el periódico por la mañana.
3. Cuando ellos (ir) ______________ de compras, (gastar) ______________ mucho dinero.
4. Tú siempre (estar) ______________ atento a las rebajas.
5. Marina (ponerse) ______________ joyas para asistir a las bodas.

8-27 ¿Sabes los números ordinales? Read the list of sentences and establish a logical order by matching them with an ordinal number.

1. ____ Me pruebo los pantalones.	a. primero
2. ____ Salgo de los grandes almacenes.	b. segundo
3. ____ Busco el departamento de ropa de hombres.	c. tercero
4. ____ Pago los pantalones al contado.	d. cuarto
5. ____ Entro en los grandes almacenes.	e. quinto
6. ____ Voy al mostrador.	f. sexto
7. ____ Encuentro los pantalones que estoy buscando.	g. séptimo

Nombre: ______________________________ Fecha: ______________________

8-28 ¿Sabes diferenciar el pretérito del imperfecto? Fill in the blanks with the appropriate preterit or imperfect form of the verbs in parentheses.

Cuando yo (1. ser) ________________ pequeño, me (2. gustar) ________________ mucho ir de compras con mis padres. Ellos siempre me (3. comprar) ________________ lo que yo (4. querer) ________________. Un día, nosotros (5. ir) ________________ al centro comercial, y yo (6. ver) ________________ un abrigo. El abrigo (7. ser) ________________ muy caro, pero yo se lo (8. pedir) ________________ a mis padres. Ellos me (9. decir) ________________ que no, por ser el abrigo tan caro. Ese día (yo) (10. aprender) ________________ una lección: No se puede tener todo lo que se quiere.

Nombre: ______________________ Fecha: ______________

Lab Manual

PRIMERA PARTE

¡Así es la vida!

8-29 De compras. Listen to the following conversation. Then select the letters for all statements that are correct, according to what you hear. Listen to the conversation as many times as is necessary to find all the correct answers.

1. Luisa y su amiga Rita van a una tienda...
   a. por la mañana.
   b. por la tarde.
   c. a comprar ropa.
2. Rita quiere ver...
   a. unos pantalones de cuero.
   b. un cinturón de cuero.
   c. una blusa.
3. La blusa de seda es...
   a. blanca.
   b. azul.
   c. de manga corta.
4. Hoy están de rebaja...
   a. las blusas.
   b. los pantalones.
   c. los guantes.
5. Rita usa...
   a. talla mediana.
   b. talla estrecha.
   c. talla 44.
6. Los probadores están...
   a. a la derecha.
   b. a la izquierda.
   c. detrás de la caja.
7. Los pantalones...
   a. le quedan estrechos.
   b. tienen un descuento.
   c. le quedan muy bien.
8. La blusa...
   a. es más barata que los pantalones.
   b. le queda estrecha.
   c. es muy cara.

9. Rita compra...
   a. una blusa de seda.
   b. un bolso de cuero.
   c. los pantalones de cuero.

10. Los zapatos y los sombreros...
   a. están cerca de los probadores.
   b. están de rebaja.
   c. están junto a la sección de ropa para hombres.

¡Así lo decimos! Vocabulario

8-30 En la tienda. Complete the following sentences with words and expressions from the vocabulary in **¡Así lo decimos!** on page 261 of your textbook. Then listen and repeat as the speaker gives the correct answer.

1. Buenos días, ¿________________________________?

   ¿Me puede mostrar el vestido de rayas azul y rojo?

   Sí, se lo muestro ahora mismo.

2. ¿________________________________?

   La grande, por favor.

3. ¿________________________________?

   Sí, por supuesto. Los probadores están aquí.

4. ¿Qué tal le queda?

   ________________________________ estrecha.

Nombre: ______________________ Fecha: ______________________

8-31 La vitrina de La Moda. Listen to the sentences and select all the items you hear named in the following picture.

¡Así lo hacemos! Estructuras

1. The imperfect of regular and irregular verbs

8-32 Mi propia experiencia. Write the answers to the questions you hear, based on your own experience as a child. Then compare your answers with the sample replies in the Answer Key.

MODELO: You hear: ¿Dónde vivías cuando tenías diez años?
You write: *Yo vivía en la ciudad de Boston cuando tenía diez años.*

1. ______________________
2. ______________________
3. ______________________
4. ______________________
5. ______________________
6. ______________________
7. ______________________
8. ______________________

Nombre: ______________________ Fecha: ______________________

8-33 Nuestra familia antes. Form sentences, using the cues provided. Then listen and repeat as the speaker gives the correct answer.

Modelo: You see: yo / ir / al supermercado frecuentemente
You say: *Yo iba al supermercado frecuentemente.*

1. tú / ser / muy ordenado
2. Fernando / ver / televisión todas las tardes
3. nosotros / ir / a México todos los años
4. Cecilia y Patricia / ser / buenas amigas
5. yo / ser / buen jugador de fútbol
6. tú / ir / de compras de vez en cuando
7. ella / ser / estudiante de medicina

8-34 Hace diez años... Answer the following questions about your life ten years ago. Then compare your answers with the sample replies in the Answer Key.

Modelo: You hear: ¿Cómo eras tú?
You say: *Yo era pequeña, pero muy fuerte.*

1. ...
2. ...
3. ...
4. ...
5. ...
6. ...
7. ...
8. ...

2. Ordinal numbers

8-35 Muchos números. Answer the questions you hear, according to the cues provided. Then listen and repeat as the speaker gives the correct answer.

Modelo: You hear: ¿En qué piso están los zapatos?
You see: en el / 6 / piso
You say: *Están en el sexto piso.*

1. sí, ésta es la / 4 / tienda que visité hoy
2. trabaja en el piso / 12
3. no, es mi / 1 / reloj de plata
4. quería ir de compras en la / 5 / avenida en Nueva York
5. aquí estoy, en el / 3 / probador a la derecha
6. no, es la / 2 / vez
7. está en el / 10 / piso

Nombre: ______________________ Fecha: ______________________

Segunda parte

¡Así es la vida!

8-36 De compras en el centro comercial. Inés and Marcela are at a shopping center buying Christmas presents. Listen to their conversation and select the letters for all statements that are correct, according to what you hear.

1. Marcela...

   a. va al centro comercial.

   b. va a devolver los aretes.

   c. va a la joyería.

2. Los aretes que Santiago le regaló son...

   a. de plata.

   b. de oro.

   c. lindos.

3. Inés...

   a. compra loción.

   b. está en la tienda con su mamá.

   c. compra un cepillo de dientes.

4. La mamá de Inés...

   a. está enferma.

   b. llegó esta mañana.

   c. es peruana.

5. El apartamento de Inés...

   a. es nuevo.

   b. es grande.

   c. está cerca de la universidad.

6. Marcela necesita comprar...

   a. maquillaje.

   b. desodorante.

   c. jabón.

7. ... va a la droguería.

   a. Marcela

   b. Inés

   c. La mamá de Inés

¡Así lo decimos! Vocabulario

8-37 ¿Lógico o ilógico? Listen to the following incomplete statements and select all the logical words or expressions to complete the statements. Then listen and repeat as the speaker gives the correct answer.

1. a. pulseras.

   b. collares.

   c. guantes.

2. a. está de moda.

   b. tiene una camisa de algodón.

   c. hace juego con el collar.

3. a. hace juego con el vestido.

   b. está de moda.

   c. vas de compras.

4. a. el talco.

   b. el frasco de colonia.

   c. la droguería.

5. a. champú.

   b. pasta de dientes.

   c. talco.

6. a. gasto dinero.

   b. en la farmacia.

   c. en la zapatería.

7. a. la joyería.

   b. un llavero.

   c. un reloj.

8. a. desodorante.

   b. maquillaje.

   c. un cepillo de dientes.

Nombre: ______________________ Fecha: ______________________

¡Así lo hacemos! Estructuras

3. Preterit versus imperfect

8-38 En el pasado. Form sentences using the cues provided. Use each verb in the preterit or the imperfect, as appropriate. Then listen and repeat as the speaker gives the correct answer.

MODELO: You see: Marcela / decir / que / ir de compras ayer
You say: *Marcela dijo que fue de compras ayer.*

1. Pablo / trabajar / cuando / (yo) / llamarlo / por teléfono
2. mis abuelos / siempre / visitarnos / en ese hotel / cuando / (nosotros) / tener / vacaciones
3. ser / una noche fría / y / nevar / mucho
4. generalmente, / (nosotros) / estudiar / en la biblioteca / cuando / haber / un examen
5. ayer / (yo) / encontrar / un restaurante fantástico / mientras / caminar / por el centro
6. anoche / (nosotros) / salir / a las diez, / ir / al centro comercial / y / buscar / el regalo perfecto para el cumpleaños de Rodrigo
7. ser / las cinco de la tarde / y / hacer / mucho calor
8. nosotros / no saber / que / tú / estar / tan triste
9. ¿cuántos años / tener (tú) / cuando / ir (tú) a Bolivia?

8-39 El pasado reciente. Listen to the following two descriptions and complete the sentences by filling in the blanks, according to what you hear. Refer to the verbs provided. Then check your answers in the Answer Key.

1. Qué día interesante (1. tener) ______________ hoy. Primero, (2. levantarse) ______________ temprano, porque (3. querer) ______________ ir al centro comercial. (4. Ir) ______________ a tener la venta-liquidación más grande de todo el año. Normalmente, no (5. salir) ______________ de mi casa a tan temprano, pero este año (6. decidir) ______________ que (7. ir) ______________ a comprar muchos regalos para mis amigos y para mi familia.

Nombre: ______________________________ Fecha: ______________________

2. —Hola, Marcos, ¿(8. ir, tú) ________________ a trabajar anoche?

—Yo no (9. trabajar) ________________, porque (10. estar) ________________ muy enfermo. (11. Llamar) ________________ a mi supervisora para decírselo, y ella me (12. decir) ________________ que yo (13. poder) ________________ tener el fin de semana libre.

8-40 El reportero. You will hear two different stories. As you are listening, refer to the verbs in parentheses. Fill in the blanks, using the present tense forms of the verbs. Then check your answers in the Answer Key.

Mientras yo (1. buscar) ________________ unos zapatos que (2. estar) ________________ de rebaja, (3. hablar) ________________ por teléfono. Yo le (4. preguntar) ________________ a mi mejor amiga si (5. deber) ________________ comprar los zapatos para hacer juego con mi vestido nuevo. Cuando le (6. decir) ________________ el precio, ella (7. contestar) ________________ que (8. ser) ________________ una ganga. (9. Ir) ________________ al mostrador inmediatamente para comprarlos.

Me (10. gustar) ________________ muchísimo la película que yo (11. ver) ________________. Esteban (12. pasar) ________________ por mí temprano, y nosotros (13. comer) ________________ en un restaurante cerca del cine. Como (14. hacer) ________________ buen tiempo, él y yo (15. caminar) ________________ al cine. La película que (16. ver) ________________ (17. ser) ________________ de España, y nos (18. hacer) ________________ reír mucho.

Nombre: ______________________________ Fecha: ______________________

8-41 En el almacén. Fill in the blanks to complete the story, using the preterit and the imperfect forms of the verbs in parentheses. Then listen and repeat as the speaker gives the correct answer.

(1. Ser) ________________ las ocho y media de la noche cuando yo (2. llegar) ________________ al almacén e (3. hacer) ________________ mis compras en sólo quince minutos. (4. Haber) ________________ mucha gente comprando regalos y, por eso, (5. esperar) ________________ quince minutos más para pagar. ¡No (6. saber) ________________ por qué la gente (7. estar) ________________ comprando tanto! Cuando (8. salir) ________________ del almacén, yo (9. ver) ________________ que ellos (10. poner) ________________ toda la mercancía a un increíble 75% de descuento. Ahora, entiendo por qué yo no (11. gastar) ________________ mucho dinero.

¿Cuánto sabes tú?

8-42 Anuncio del radio. Listen to the radio advertisement. Then answer the following questions as the speaker asks them. Finally, listen and repeat as the speaker gives the correct answer.

1. ¿Adónde piensa ir la amiga de Soraya?
2. ¿Qué es Cursiri?
3. ¿Qué cosas venden ahí?
4. ¿Venden ropa para hombres?
5. ¿Cómo son los precios?
6. ¿Acompaña Soraya a su amiga?
7. ¿En qué ciudad está Cursiri?
8. ¿Cuál es el número de teléfono de la tienda?

Nombre: ______________________ Fecha: ______________________

8-43 Una conversación en el centro comercial. Carmen went shopping, but Lucía stayed home because she was sick. Complete their conversation by filling in the blanks, according to what you hear. Then check your answers in the Answer Key.

Lucía: Hola, Carmen, ¿cómo te (1) __________ con las compras?

Carmen: Muy bien, pero (2) __________ mucho dinero.

Lucía: ¿Qué (3) __________?

Carmen: (4) __________ por varias tiendas. (5) __________, fui a la (6) __________ y (7) __________ un (8) __________ para mi hermano. ¿Sabes a quiénes (9) __________ allí?

Lucía: No tengo ni idea. ¿A quiénes?

Carmen: A Marcos y a Estela. Me (10) __________ que la boda es en enero. No sabes qué mal lo (11) __________ ellos.

Lucía: ¿Por qué? ¿Qué pasó?

Carmen: Ellos (12) __________ unos anillos para la boda que (13) __________ de plata mexicana, pero no los (14) __________ porque no (15) __________ suficiente dinero. Creen que van a estar en (16) __________ pronto.

Lucía: Bueno, ¿qué más (17) __________?

Carmen: (18) __________ de la joyería con Marcos y Estela. Ellos (19) __________ almorzar, pero yo (20) __________ comprando.

Lucía: ¿Y después?

Carmen: Después, (21) __________ a La Moda.

Lucía: ¿Qué (22) __________ allí?

Carmen: Como tenían una (23) __________-__________, miré las rebajas, y (24) __________ unos (25) __________ azules muy elegantes y dos camisas. Una de (26) __________ y la otra de (27) __________. También (28) __________ unos (29) __________ italianos por sólo 80 pesos. Después, compré unas cosas en la (30) __________.

Lucía: ¿A qué hora (31) __________?

Carmen: A las siete y media (32) __________ del centro commercial, y (33) __________ las ocho cuando (34) __________ a casa.

Nombre: ______________________ Fecha: ______________________

9 Vamos de viaje

Workbook

PRIMERA PARTE

¡Así es la vida!

9-1 Un viaje. Reread the conversations in **¡Así es la vida!** on page 292 of your textbook. Then complete the statements with the most appropriate answer.

1. La nacionalidad de Mauricio y Susana es...

   a. mexicana. b. venezolana. c. colombiana.

2. Ellos quieren...

   a. trabajar en una agencia de viajes. c. tomarse unas vacaciones.

   b. estudiar en la universidad.

3. Rosario Díaz es...

   a. la agente de viajes. b. la profesora. c. la novia de Mauricio.

4. Susana dice que ellos están...

   a. en Venezuela. b. de vacaciones. c. corriendo de un lado a otro.

5. Mauricio quiere...

   a. ir a Cancún. b. conocer a Susana. c. un folleto.

6. A Susana no le gusta la idea porque...

   a. se conocieron allí. b. hay demasiados turistas. c. es muy caro.

7. Rosario les muestra...

   a. un folleto. b. una fotografía. c. una guía.

8. El viaje incluye...

   a. pasaje de ida y hotel.

   b. pasaje de ida y vuelta y comida por ocho días.

   c. pasaje de ida y vuelta, comidas y seis noches de hotel.

9. El viaje cuesta...

   a. 800 dólares por dos personas.

   b. 1.600 dólares por dos personas.

   c. 400 dólares por persona.

10. Después de leer el folleto, ellos...

    a. deciden ir a Cancún.

    b. deciden ir a Colombia.

    c. deciden no ir de vacaciones.

¡Así lo decimos! Vocabulario

9-2 Asociaciones. Match each word or expression in the left column with the most logical word or expression from the right column.

1. ____ el aduanero
2. ____ el pasaje
3. ____ el guía
4. ____ el equipaje
5. ____ facturar
6. ____ el asiento
7. ____ el avión
8. ____ la agencia de viajes

a. ida y vuelta
b. despegar
c. la sala de reclamación
d. el equipaje
e. el folleto
f. la aduana
g. la ventanilla
h. la excursión

Nombre: ____________________ Fecha: ____________________

9-3 ¡A escribir! Write original sentences using the paired words from activity **9-2.**

1. ____________________
2. ____________________
3. ____________________
4. ____________________
5. ____________________
6. ____________________
7. ____________________
8. ____________________

9-4 De viaje. Choose the word or expression that best completes each sentence.

1. Quiero ir de viaje. Voy a hablar con...

   a. un aduanero.

   b. un aeromozo.

   c. un agente de viajes.

2. El agente de viajes hace...

   a. el avión.

   b. el pasillo.

   c. la reserva.

3. Soy estudiante y no tengo mucho dinero. Compro un boleto de...

   a. clase turista.

   b. aduana.

   c. ida y vuelta.

4. Puse mi loción y mi máquina de afeitar dentro de...

   a. la maleta.

   b. asiento.

   c. folleto.

5. Voy al mostrador para facturar...

   a. la reserva.

   b. el equipaje.

   c. el pasaje.

6. Hay mucha gente abordando el avión. Tenemos que...

   a. cancelar el vuelo.

   b. hacer cola.

   c. facturar el equipaje.

7. Antes de comprar una excursión, es bueno leer el...

   a. aterrizaje.

   b. folleto de información.

   c. pasaje.

8. En un hotel, el precio incluye...

   a. folleto.

   b. pasaje de ida y vuelta.

   c. hospedaje.

Nombre: ______________________ Fecha: ______________

9-5 Cuestionario. How do you like to do things when you travel? Answer the following questions with complete sentences in Spanish.

1. Cuando viajas en avión, ¿dónde prefieres sentarte? ¿Por qué?

   ____

2. Tú no fumas. ¿En qué sección te sientas?

   ____

3. ¿Qué haces si hay una demora con tu vuelo?

   ____

4. ¿Qué pones en tu maleta?

   ____

5. ¿Qué facturas y qué llevas en el avión? ¿Por qué?

   ____

¡Así lo hacemos! Estructuras

1. *Por* or *para*

9-6 ¡A completar! Complete the following sentences by filling in the blanks with **por** or **para.**

1. Emilio caminaba ____________ el aeropuerto buscando la puerta de su salida.
2. ____________ mí, viajar en avión es más interesante que viajar en coche.
3. Julio llegó al aeropuerto ____________ la tarde.
4. Estuvimos en la sala de espera ____________ dos horas.
5. Necesito la tarjeta de embarque ____________ el vuelo.
6. ¿Compraste los billetes ____________ mil dólares?
7. Carlos fue a la agencia de viajes ____________ los boletos.
8. Busqué el folleto ____________ ti.
9. Nosotros salimos ____________ San Andrés.
10. Mañana ____________ la noche, te llamo desde Caracas.

9-7 Decisiones. Decide whether to use **por** or **para,** and fill in the blanks in the following sentences.

1. El avión salió ______________ Colombia.
2. Nuestro viaje es ______________ el martes.
3. El vuelo 79 es dos veces ______________ semana.
4. El avión vuela a 600 millas ______________ hora.
5. ______________ mí, es la mejor aerolínea del mundo.
6. ______________ ser tan joven, el piloto vuela muy bien.
7. ______________ fin, salió el avión.
8. ¡______________ Dios que me vuelvo loca con tantos pasajeros!
9. ______________ ir a Colombia, hay que tener un pasaporte.
10. La luz entraba ______________ la ventanilla del avión.
11. El boleto es ______________ viajar.
12. Este folleto es ______________ ti.
13. Tú estudias ______________ ser piloto.

9-8 Actividades durante las vacaciones. Describe your plans for an upcoming vacation. Fill in the blanks to complete the paragraph using **por** or **para.**

El sábado salimos (1) ______________ Venezuela. Fuimos (2) ______________ los boletos ayer. Vamos (3) ______________ avión, y vamos a quedarnos allí (4) ______________ dos semanas. El agente de viajes planeó muchas excursiones (5) ______________ nosotros. (6) ______________ las mañanas, vamos a hacer excursiones (7) ______________ muchos lugares y, (8) ______________ las tardes, vamos a participar en varias actividades. Podemos dar un paseo (9) ______________ el parque nacional, montar a caballo (10) ______________ la playa o tomar sol (11) ______________ una hora. (12) ______________ el sol de Venezuela, el agente nos recomendó una loción bronceadora (*suntan lotion*). Vamos a Venezuela (13) ______________ descansar un poco y (14) ______________ divertirnos.

Nombre: ______________________ Fecha: ______________________

9-9 Pequeña composición. Write a short description (eight sentences) to one of your friends about a trip you took, your weekend, or your school. Use **por** and **para** in your sentences.

____

____

____

____

____

2. Adverbs ending in *-mente*

9-10 ¿Cómo lo hacen tus amigos? Indicate how the following people do each activity, using an adverb formed from the adjectives in parentheses.

1. Jorge y Juan trabajan (cuidadoso) ______________________.
2. Sofía camina (lento) ______________________.
3. Teresa siempre se viste (elegante) ______________________.
4. Tú hablas español (fácil) ______________________.
5. Carlitos molesta a su hermano (frecuente) ______________________.
6. Pedro, el jugador de béisbol, corre (rápido) ______________________.
7. Yo aprendo ciencias físicas (difícil) ______________________.
8. Esteban juega al fútbol (maravilloso) ______________________.

9-11 ¿Cómo hacen su trabajo estas personas? Describe how these airline employees behave on the job by completing each sentence with the adverbial form of the words from the word bank.

alegre	cuidadoso	general	rápido
claro	elegante	lento	sólo

1. La aeromoza (*flight attendant*) es muy simpática y está contenta. Nos habla

   ______________________.

2. El empleado nos prepara el boleto ______________________, porque no quiere cometer errores.
3. Estas aeromozas llevan ropa muy bonita y cara. Se visten ______________________.

4. ______________, los pilotos vuelan ______________ dos o tres veces a la semana. No se les permite volar más veces por semana.
5. La aeromoza ayudó a mi abuelo que caminaba ______________ hacia la puerta de salida.
6. El agente de viajes nos explicó el itinerario de los dos viajes muy ______________, con todos los detalles.
7. Los aeromozos estudian mucho para aprender a reaccionar ______________ en una emergencia, cuando no tienen mucho tiempo para pensar.

Nombre: ______________________ Fecha: ______________________

Segunda parte

¡Así es la vida!

9-12 Una carta. Reread the e-mail letter in **¡Así es la vida!** on page 305 of your textbook, and answer the following questions by choosing the most appropriate response.

1. ¿De dónde acaban de llegar Susana y Mauricio?

   a. de Cartagena, Colombia   b. de la isla de San Andrés   c. de Venezuela

2. ¿Cuánto tiempo estuvieron en San Andrés?

   a. un día   b. cuatro días   c. tres días

3. ¿Cómo era el hotel en San Andrés?

   a. grande y hermoso   b. grande y viejo   c. pequeño y hermoso

4. ¿Cómo era el cuarto del hotel en San Andrés?

   a. oscuro   b. pequeño   c. muy grande

5. ¿Qué hacían ellos durante el día en San Andrés?

   a. se levantaban temprano y exploraban la isla

   b. se levantaban tarde y desayunaban en la habitación

   c. se levantaban tarde y desayunaban en el comedor

6. ¿Qué hicieron ellos el último día en San Andrés?

   a. recorrer la isla en bicicleta   b. esquí acuático   c. bucear

7. ¿Cómo comparas el hotel de Cartagena con el hotel de San Andrés?

   a. más grande   b. más antiguo   c. más lujoso

8. ¿Qué sitios van a visitar ellos en Cartagena?

   a. la playa   b. sitios de la época colonial   c. un jardín tropical

9. ¿Qué van a hacer esta noche en Cartagena?

   a. visitar un jardín tropical   c. visitar sitios de la época colonial

   b. pasear en un coche con caballo

Nombre: ______________________ Fecha: ______________________

10. ¿Cuándo regresan?

    a. el domingo   b. el lunes   c. esta noche

¡Así lo decimos! Vocabulario

9-13 ¡A completar! Complete each statement with an appropriate word or expression from the word bank.

bosque	flores	isla	montar	piscina	rollo de película
estadía	gafas de sol	mapa	pescar	río	vista

1. Cuando hace mucho sol, tengo que ponerme las ______________ para ver bien.
2. Para no perderme en la ciudad, consulto el ______________.
3. En el jardín hay muchas ______________.
4. Nuestra ______________ en el hotel fue por cuatro noches.
5. Quiero sacar más fotos. Necesito comprar un ______________.
6. En el ______________ hay muchos árboles.
7. La ______________ desde mi balcón es impresionante.
8. En el hotel hay una ______________ para poder nadar.
9. Me gusta ______________ en el lago.
10. No sé ______________ a caballo.
11. San Andrés es una ______________.
12. El Amazonas es un ______________.

Nombre: ______________________________ Fecha: ______________________

¡Así lo hacemos! Estructuras

3. The Spanish subjunctive: An introduction and the subjunctive in noun clauses

9-14 ¡A practicar! Give the present subjunctive form of the following verbs.

1. Nosotros: caminar ______________ beber ______________ escribir ______________
2. Ellos: hacer ______________ oír ______________ traer ______________
3. Yo: conocer ______________ dormir ______________ sentarse ______________
4. Ustedes: llegar ______________ seguir ______________ sacar ______________
5. Tú: sentirse ______________ buscar ______________ ser ______________
6. Él: dar ______________ venir ______________ estar ______________
7. Usted: leer ______________ levantarse ______________ salir ______________
8. Ella: devolver ______________ ir ______________ decir ______________

9-15 Las vacaciones de mamá. Our mother wants to go on a vacation, and our brother Felipe is in charge. Write out the things Felipe wants us to do.

Modelo: Julio / comprar una guía turística
Felipe quiere que Julio compre una guía turística.

1. Romelio / llamar a la agencia de viajes

   Felipe quiere que Romelio ______________ a la agencia de viajes.

2. Ernesto y Carlota / leer el folleto

   Felipe quiere que Ernesto y Carlota ______________ el folleto.

3. nosotros / hablar con el guía del viaje

   Felipe quiere que nosotros ______________ con el guía del viaje.

4. yo / encargarme del hospedaje

   Felipe quiere que yo ______________ del hospedaje.

5. tú / hacer la reserva

   Felipe quiere que tú ______________ la reserva.

6. Rosa / pedir dos semanas de vacaciones

   Felipe quiere que Rosa ______________ dos semanas de vacaciones.

Nombre: ______________________ Fecha: ______________________

7. Paula y yo / preparar las maletas

   Felipe quiere que Paula y yo ______________ las maletas.

8. papá / comprar cheques de viajero

   Felipe quiere que papá ______________ cheques de viajero.

9-16 Unas recomendaciones. Complete the following recommendations by filling in the blanks with the present subjunctive form of the verbs in parentheses.

1. El agente de viajes quiere que usted...

   (reservar) ______________ el pasaje de ida y vuelta.

   (cambiar) ______________ dólares por la moneda local.

   (tener) ______________ el pasaporte en regla (*valid passport*).

   (pagar) ______________ con tarjeta de crédito.

2. Los aduaneros quieren que tú...

   (hacer) ______________ cola.

   (mostrar) ______________ el pasaporte.

   (abrir) ______________ el equipaje de mano.

   (esperar) ______________ en la sala de espera.

3. La aeromoza quiere que nosotros...

   (abordar) ______________ el avión.

   (abrocharse) ______________ el cinturón de seguridad.

   (sentarse) ______________ en nuestros asientos.

   (darle) ______________ la tarjeta de embarque.

4. Nosotros queremos que...

   el avión (despegar) ______________ a tiempo.

   el avión no (tener) ______________ sección de fumar.

   el piloto (ser) ______________ experto.

   el avión (aterrizar) ______________ sin problemas.

Nombre: ______________________ Fecha: ______________________

4. The subjunctive to express volition

9-17 En el hotel. Complete the following paragraphs about what the personnel recommends and prefers with the correct present subjunctive form of the verbs in parentheses.

El recepcionista recomienda que los huéspedes (1. dormir) ______________ mucho por noche y que (2. hacer) ______________ muchas actividades durante el día. También recomienda que (3. sacar) ______________ muchas fotos de los alrededores. Insiste en que no (4. quedarse) ______________ todo el día en el hotel y que (5. recorrer) ______________ las playas.

La recepcionista prefiere que yo (6. hablar) ______________ con ella y que (7. pagar) ______________ la cuenta inmediatamente. Quiere que le (8. dar) ______________ la tarjeta de crédito. También quiere que la (9. llamar) ______________ si necesito una reserva para el próximo año.

El guía recomienda que nosotros no (10. levantarse) ______________ tarde y que (11. acostarse) ______________ temprano. Sugiere que (12. ir) ______________ a la playa por dos o tres días y que (13. empezar) ______________ a descansar más. También sugiere que nosotros (14. montar) ______________ a caballo y que lo (15. pasar) ______________ de maravilla.

9-18 Una viaje con los amigos. Pablo and his friends have decided to go on a vacation. Complete Juan's, one of Pablo's friends, explanation about how they're going to go about this. Write the correct subjunctive, indicative, or infinitive form of the verbs in parentheses.

Uno de nuestros amigos, Pablo, participa en un viaje a la isla de San Andrés. Ahora insiste en que nosotros (1. participar) ______________ con él. Desea que todos nosotros (2. ir) ______________ de vacaciones y que (3. pedir) ______________ vacaciones. Pablo dice que la isla (4. ser) ______________ maravillosa y que nosotros (5. poder) ______________ pasarlo muy bien, pero también nos recomienda que (6. hacer) ______________ una reserva antes de (7. empezar) ______________ a preparar las maletas. Nos sugiere que (8. llamar) ______________ al agente de viajes y que (9. comprar) ______________ cheques de viajero. Es necesario (10. hacer) ______________ la reserva dos meses antes, según Pablo. Durante el viaje, desea que (nosotros) (11. ir) ______________ de excursión. También, nos aconseja que (12. pescar) ______________ en el lago y que (13. montar) ______________ a caballo. Es necesario (14. explorar) ______________ toda la isla durante el viaje. Nos pide que (15. sacar) ______________ muchas fotos y que (16. comprar) ______________ recuerdos de la isla durante el viaje. ¡Vamos a (17. pasarlo) ______________ maravillosamente bien muy pronto!

9-19 Recomendaciones. Imagine that a friend wants some advice about going on a vacation. Give your recommendations by completing the following sentences. Use a different verb in each sentence.

1. Te recomiendo que ______________________________.
2. Quiero que no ______________________________.
3. Te aconsejo que ______________________________.
4. Te pido que ______________________________.
5. Te prohíbo que ______________________________.
6. Te digo que tú y tus amigos ______________________________.
7. También les sugiero que ustedes ______________________________.
8. Deseo que ustedes ______________________________.

Nombre: ______________________________ Fecha: ______________________

NUESTRO MUNDO

Panoramas

9-20 ¡A informarse! Based on the information from **Nuestro mundo** on pages 320–321 of your textbook, decide if the following statements are **cierto (C)** or **falso (F).**

1. Cartagena de Indias era importante para los españoles por su puerto.
2. Hoy en día nadie visita Cartagena de Indias.
3. En Colombia no hay depósitos de piedras preciosas.
4. Según la leyenda, los caciques indios llevaban piedras preciosas en sus prendas durante las ceremonias religiosas.
5. Las obras de Gabriel García Márquez son un ejemplo del realismo mágico.
6. Gabriel García Márquez ganó el Premio Nóbel de Literatura en 1982.
7. La isla Margarita es una reserva natural donde no se pueden practicar deportes acuáticos.
8. La isla Margarita está en el mar Caribe.
9. En algunos festivales se puede ver la mezcla de tradiciones indígenas y cristianas.
10. Venezuela es importante por sus reservas de petróleo.

9-21 Tu propia experiencia. Use the Internet and library sources to research possible tourist destinations in Colombia or Venezuela. Describe the tourist sites, and make a list of activities that you can do while vacationing there.

____

____

____

____

____

____

____

Nombre: ______________________ Fecha: ______________________

Taller

9-22 Un viaje desastroso

Primera fase. Imagine that you took a trip that turned out to be a disaster. List the following information, using the preterit and the imperfect in your narration.

¿Dónde? ______________________

¿Cuándo? ______________________

¿Cómo? (el transporte) ______________________

¿Con quién? ______________________

¿Actividades? ______________________

¿Problemas? ______________________

____

____

____

____

Segunda fase. Now use the information you listed in the **Primera fase** to organize a narration that describes the disastrous trip.

____

____

____

____

____

____

____

Nombre: ______________________ Fecha: ______________________

9-23 Las vacaciones y los viajes. Colombia and Venezuela have many attractive vacation opportunities. Whether you want lazy days on the beach, an ecotourist adventure in a rain forest, or a mountain biking expedition through the Andes, you'll find a place in Colombia or Venezuela. Decide what kind of vacation you would like to take if you could travel to Colombia or Venezuela. Use the Internet or library resources to investigate vacation travel packages. Do some comparison shopping as you explore the opportunities. Then input the information you find in the chart below in Spanish.

PAÍS/CIUDAD	TRANSPORTE	HOTEL	AMENIDADES	ACTIVIDADES	COSTO	MISCELÁNEA
TÚ						

9-24 Más allá de las páginas: Restricciones

Primera fase. The narrator of ***Relato de una vida equivocada*** gives an account of the restrictions that she endured. Very possibly, children she might have would not have the same restrictions. Make a list of the restrictions you had as a young child. Then make a list of the restrictions you think your parents may have had as children. Finally, list the restrictions your children have or will have.

DE NIÑO/A, YO

____

____

____

____

____

____

Nombre: ______________________ Fecha: ______________________

DE NIÑOS, MIS PADRES

MIS HIJOS

Segunda fase. Now write a brief narrative describing a restriction that you had as a child that bothered you. Compare your situation to that of your parents' and to how you restrict or will restrict your own children. Use the imperfect to describe general situations, but use the preterit to narrate specific incidences in the past.

Nombre: ______________________________ Fecha: ______________________

¿Cuánto sabes tú?

9-25 ¿Sabes usar *por* y *para*? Fill in the blanks with **por** or **para** to complete the paragraph.

Hoy (1) _______________ la mañana fui a la agencia de viajes (2) _______________ preguntar el precio de un viaje a la isla Margarita. Quiero ir de vacaciones (3) _______________ una semana y salgo (4) _______________ la isla Margarita la semana que viene. Necesito tener el viaje pagado (5) _______________ el lunes y, (6) _______________ supuesto, espero pasarlo muy bien.

9-26 ¿Sabes usar los adverbios acabados en *-mente*? Complete the following statements, using an adverb formed from the adjectives in parentheses.

1. Pagué el pasaje (inmediato) _______________.
2. Abordé el avión (tranquilo) _______________.
3. Me abroché el cinturón (rápido) _______________.
4. La azafata nos trató (amable) _______________.
5. El piloto aterrizó el avión (cuidadoso) _______________.
6. Los pasajeros salieron del avión (lento) _______________.

9-27 ¿Sabes usar el presente de subjuntivo? Fill in the blanks with the appropriate forms of the present subjunctive of the verbs in parentheses, when necessary.

¡Me encanta ir de vacaciones! En mis próximas vacaciones, espero que todos mis amigos (1. poder) _______________ ir conmigo. Deseo que el hotel (2. ser) _______________ grande y lujoso y que (3. estar) _______________ cerca de la playa. Mis amigos quieren (4. montar) _______________ a caballo, (5. ir) _______________ a la playa y (6. sacar) _______________ muchas fotografías. Ellos quieren que yo (7. buscar) _______________ información sobre un posible destino y que (8. preguntar) _______________ los precios en la agencia de viajes. Espero que nosotros lo (9. pasar) _______________ estupendamente y que (10. hacer) _______________ todas las actividades planeadas.

Nombre: ______________________ Fecha: ______________________

9-28 Más subjuntivo. Fill in the blanks with the appropriate indicative, subjunctive, or infinitive form of the verbs in parentheses.

1. Necesitamos (encontrar) ______________ boletos baratos para ir de vacaciones.
2. María insiste en que nosotros (ir) ______________ a un lugar cerca de la playa.
3. Yo le sugiero que ella (buscar) ______________ en la Red (*Internet*).
4. Ella me pide que yo la (ayudar) ______________ a buscar un lugar para ir de vacaciones.
5. Quiero que el lugar (tener) ______________ piscina y que (estar) ______________ al lado del mar.

Nombre: ______________________ Fecha: ______________________

Lab Manual

Primera parte

¡Así es la vida!

9-29 La luna de miel. Listen to the following conversation between Silvia and Marcelo as they make plans for their honeymoon. Then select the letters for all statements that are correct, according to what you hear.

1. Silvia y Marcelo quieren...
   a. ir a la Argentina.
   b. un viaje feliz.
   c. ir de viaje.
2. Silvia describe...
   a. dos viajes interesantes.
   b. un viaje a México.
   c. un viaje a España.
3. El viaje a México...
   a. es tan largo como el viaje a España.
   b. es menos largo que el viaje a España.
   c. es más largo que el viaje a España.
4. El viaje a España...
   a. es de dos semanas.
   b. incluye un pasaje de primera clase.
   c. ofrece excursiones a otras ciudades.
5. Las excursiones desde Madrid incluyen...
   a. Barcelona, Sevilla o Santander.
   b. Toledo y Ávila.
   c. Ávila y Valencia.
6. El viaje a...
   a. México es tan caro como el viaje a España.
   b. España es más caro que el viaje a México.
   c. España cuesta menos que el viaje a México.
7. Marcelo prefiere...
   a. la sección de no fumar.
   b. un asiento de ventanilla.
   c. el viaje a España.
8. Marcelo y Silvia van a tomar un vuelo...
   a. de ida solamente.
   b. con escala en Miami.
   c. sin escala.

Nombre: ____________________ Fecha: ____________________

¡Así lo decimos! Vocabulario

9-30 Los Colón están de viaje. Listen to the dialog and answer the following questions. Then listen and repeat as the speaker gives the correct answer.

1. ¿Adónde van los Colón?
2. ¿Están en la lista de espera de Avianca?
3. ¿En cuál aerolínea van ahora?
4. ¿Dónde hace escala el vuelo de los Colón?
5. ¿Hay cola en el mostrador de Avianca?
6. ¿Qué va a hacer Virginia?
7. ¿Tienen ellos las tarjetas de embarque?
8. ¿Cuántas maletas llevan?

¡Así lo hacemos! Estructuras

1. *Por* or *para*

9-31 Respuestas breves. Answer each question you hear, using one of the following idiomatic expressions with **por.** Then listen and repeat as the speaker gives the correct answer.

por aquí	por eso	por fin	por supuesto
por ejemplo	por favor	por lo general	por último

9-32 De viaje en Suramérica. Complete the following sentences with **por** or **para.** Then listen and repeat as the speaker gives the correct answer.

1. Mañana salimos __________ Bogotá.
2. Paseamos __________ el centro __________ visitar los monumentos y museos.
3. Los pasaportes son __________ ustedes y van a estar listos __________ mañana.
4. Pagamos diez mil soles __________ los dos pasajes.
5. Los pasajeros fueron __________ las maletas.
6. ¿Van a viajar __________ avión __________ la tarde o __________ la mañana?
7. ¿Necesitaron mucho dinero __________ el viaje?
8. Estuvimos en Suramérica __________ un mes.

2. Adverbs ending in *-mente*

9-33 Después del viaje. Complete the following sentences, using the adverb derived from the adjectives in parentheses. Then listen and repeat as the speaker gives the correct answer.

1. Carmen y Jorge hablaban (alegre) ______________.
2. El avión llegaba (lento) ______________ a la puerta de salida.
3. La aeromoza pasó (rápido) ______________ por el avión.
4. (Final) ______________, los pasajeros salieron del avión.
5. Pasamos por la aduana (fácil) ______________.
6. (Único) ______________ los agentes de aduana pueden entrar aquí.
7. El piloto aterrizó (correcto) ______________.
8. Carmen está (verdadero) ______________ contenta porque va a ver la ciudad.

9-34 ¿Cómo lo hacen? Answer the questions that you hear in complete sentences, using the adverb derived from each of the following adjectives. Then listen and repeat as the speaker gives the correct answer.

1. tranquilo
2. frecuente
3. correcto
4. claro
5. lento
6. fácil

SEGUNDA PARTE

¡Así es la vida!

9-35 Después de las vacaciones. Listen to the conversation between Gabriela and her mother after Gabriela's vacation in Argentina. Then select the letters for all statements that are correct, according to what you hear. (*Note:* **los pájaros** means *birds.*)

1. Gabriela y Jorge...
   a. estuvieron una semana en un parque nacional.
   b. lo pasaron regular.
   c. llegaron anoche.

Nombre: ______________________ Fecha: ______________________

2. Jorge...

   a. estaba muy contento porque escaló unas montañas.

   b. escaló dos montañas y le gustó.

   c. nadaba en el lago a menudo.

3. Gabriela...

   a. escaló dos montañas.

   b. pescaba en el lago frecuentemente.

   c. estuvo junto al río Verde, montando a caballo.

4. Desde su habitación, tenían una vista...

   a. de la piscina.

   b. del volcán.

   c. de las montañas.

5. A Gabriela...

   a. le gustó recorrer el país.

   b. le gustaron los bosques y las montañas.

   c. le gustó montar en bicicleta.

6. Gabriela y Jorge...

   a. tuvieron un problema cuando perdieron el mapa.

   b. la pasaron maravillosamente cuando perdieron el mapa.

   c. recibieron ayuda de otro auto cuando perdieron el mapa.

7. La mamá de Gabriela...

   a. manda besos a Jorge y saludos a su hija.

   b. espera ver a Jorge y a su hija el sábado.

   c. no tiene ganas de ver a Jorge.

Nombre: ______________________ Fecha: ______________________

¡Así lo decimos! Vocabulario

9-36 Cosas de las vacaciones. Listen to the following definitions. Then match the number of each definition with one of the following words. Check your answers in the Answer Key.

____ el bosque

____ la cocinita

____ comprar recuerdos

____ la estadía

____ el fuerte

____ las gafas de sol

____ el hotel

____ ir de excursión

____ la isla

____ el lago

____ el mapa

____ montar a caballo

____ el monumento

____ el museo

____ el palacio

____ pescar

____ la vista

____ el volcán

Nombre: ______________________ Fecha: ______________________

¡Así lo hacemos! Estructuras

3. The Spanish subjunctive: An introduction and the subjunctive in noun clauses

9-37 La aeromoza. The flight attendant has advice for the passengers. Using the cues provided, tell what she wants each passenger to do. Then listen and repeat as the speaker gives the correct answer.

MODELO: You see: los niños / no / correr / por el pasillo del avión
You say: *La aeromoza quiere que los niños no corran por el pasillo del avión.*

La aeromoza quiere que…

1. yo / caminar / por el pasillo del avión
2. tú / venir / al frente
3. usted / comer / toda la comida
4. nosotros / hacer / nuestro trabajo durante el vuelo
5. los niños / hablar / mucho
6. tú / ver / el volcán en la distancia
7. yo / traer / mi computadora
8. nosotros / escuchar / al piloto

9-38 La aeromoza insiste en... The flight attendant insists that the passengers do certain things. Form sentences, using the cues provided. Then listen and repeat as the speaker gives the correct answer.

MODELO: You see: tú / tomar / un asiento rápidamente
You say: *La aeromoza insiste en que tú tomes un asiento rápidamente.*

La aeromoza insiste en que…

1. yo / pensar / en las vacaciones
2. tú / jugar / con los niños
3. nosotras / dormir / tranquilamente
4. ustedes / no / llegar / tarde al vuelo
5. el pasajero / empezar / a comer ahora

Nombre: ______________________________ Fecha: ______________________

9-39 Más sugerencias de la aeromoza... Form sentences, using the cues provided. Then listen and repeat as the speaker gives the correct answer.

Modelo: You see: usted / poner / el abrigo allí
You say: *La aeromoza quiere que usted ponga el abrigo allí.*

La aeromoza quiere que...

1. el piloto / ser / simpático con los pasajeros
2. yo / darle / la información a la agente del mostrador
3. nosotros / estar / preparados para aterrizar
4. tú / ir / a la sala de reclamación de equipaje
5. ellos / saber / la hora de la llegada

9-40 Durante las vacaciones. Complete the following sentences, using the cues provided. Then listen and repeat as the speaker gives the correct answer.

Modelo: You see: yo / querer / que / tú / ir / de vacaciones
You say: *Yo quiero que tú vayas de vacaciones.*

1. el señor Ureña / desear / que / ustedes / poner / las maletas aquí
2. tu madre / te / recomendar / que / venir / pronto
3. nosotros / preferir / que / ella /montar/ a caballo
4. yo / querer / que / nosotros / salir / de aquí
5. el guía turístico / me / prohibir / que / escalar / esa montaña

4. The subjunctive to express volition

9-41 El guía. Form complete sentences, using the cues provided. Then listen and repeat as the speaker gives the correct answer.

Modelo: You see: el guía / insistir en / los Pérez venir inmediatamente
You say: *El guía insiste en que los Pérez vengan inmediatamente.*

1. el guía / recomendar / tú / dejar / de fumar
2. los guías / desear / usted / hacer / una cola
3. el guía / querer / yo / tomar / un folleto
4. el guía / preferir / nosotros / darle / unas fotos
5. el guía / necesitar / el turista / tomar / un asiento

Nombre: ______________________ Fecha: ______________________

9-42 Preguntas del guía. Answer the questions you hear, using the cues provided. Then listen and repeat as the speaker gives the correct answer.

1. ir al museo por la tarde
2. volver en dos semanas
3. Marcos / escalar montañas
4. comprar recuerdos
5. los turistas / visitar al palacio

¿Cuánto sabes tú?

9-43 ¿Quién está en el aeropuerto? Listen to the descriptions of some of the people in the picture that follows. Then decide who is who, based on the information you hear. Label the picture accordingly with the names provided.

Josefina Pereda
Federico Ruiz
la familia Peña
Pablo
Dolores Gutiérrez
Rosa Romero
Ema Flores
Pedro
el señor Ramírez
Ricardo Bello

9-44 Preguntas personales. Write an appropriate response to the following questions or statements. Because answers will vary, compare your answer to the answers that are provided. Then read your response to practice communication and pronunciation.

1. ____
2. ____
3. ____
4. ____
5. ____

Nombre: ______________________ Fecha: ______________________

10 ¡Tu salud es lo primero!

Workbook

PRIMERA PARTE

¡Así es la vida!

10-1 ¡Qué mal me siento! Reread the conversations in **¡Así es la vida!** on page 330 of your textbook and answer the questions below.

1. ¿Qué le pasa a don Rafael?

   a. está enojado　　b. se siente mal　　c. tiene sueño

2. ¿Qué quiere doña Carmen?

   a. ir al médico　　b. darle medicamento　　c. ir a la farmacia

3. ¿Cómo se llama el médico?

   a. don Rafael　　b. doña Carmen　　c. doctor Estrada

4. ¿Qué parte del cuerpo le duele a don Rafael?

   a. la cabeza　　b. la garganta　　c. el brazo

5. Según don Rafael, ¿a qué no es alérgico?

   a. a las pastillas　　b. a los jarabes　　c. a los antibióticos

6. Según el médico, ¿qué tiene don Rafael?

   a. una bronquitis　　b. una infección　　c. una pulmonía

7. ¿Qué le receta el doctor Estrada a don Rafael?

   a. unas inyecciones　　b. un jarabe　　c. unas pastillas

8. ¿Por qué desea el doctor Estrada que don Rafael vaya a verlo la próxima semana?

   a. para pagarle　　b. para un examen físico　　c. para recetarle más pastillas

Nombre: ________________________ Fecha: ____________________

9. ¿Qué odia don Rafael?

   a. las pastillas b. los antibióticos c. visitar al médico

10. ¿Qué es lo primero para el doctor Estrada?

   a. el dinero b. la salud de sus pacientes c. los antibióticos

¡Así lo decimos! Vocabulario

10-2 ¡A completar! Complete each statement by filling in the blanks with a word or expression from the word bank.

boca	dolor de cabeza	radiografía	sangre	tenía náuseas
diagnóstico	los pulmones	receta	se rompió un hueso	tomarse la temperatura

1. Si alguien cree que tiene fiebre, debe ____________.
2. Después de examinarte, el médico te da el ____________.
3. Cuando nos rompemos un hueso, debemos ir a radiología para una ____________.
4. Cuando alguien está enfermo, a veces el médico le ____________ unas pastillas.
5. Si uno tiene ____________, debe tomarse dos aspirinas.
6. Cuando era niño, Antonio siempre ____________ cuando viajaba en el coche de sus padres. Le dolía mucho el estómago y vomitaba.
7. Esta semana Jorge no puede hacer ejercicio con nosotros porque la semana pasada, ____________ cuando corríamos.
8. Los dientes y la lengua están dentro de la ____________.
9. La ____________ es un líquido rojo que pasa por todo el cuerpo.
10. Los órganos que usamos para respirar son ____________.

Nombre: ______________________ Fecha: ______________

10-3 ¿Qué me recomienda usted? You are a doctor and you need to recommend various courses of action to your patients. Match each complaint with the most appropriate answer.

1. ____ Me duele mucho la garganta.
2. ____ Toso tanto que no puedo dormir.
3. ____ Creo que me rompí el dedo del pie.
4. ____ Comí demasiado y ahora me duele el estómago.
5. ____ Me duele mucho la cabeza.
6. ____ Creo que tengo un resfriado.
7. ____ No puedo respirar bien cuando hago ejercicio.

a. ir al hospital para una radiografía
b. tomarse un jarabe para la tos
c. tomarse un antiácido
d. guardar cama por dos días
e. dejar de fumar
f. tomarse dos aspirinas
g. tomar un antibiótico durante diez días

10-4 El cuerpo. Identify the numbered parts of the body in the following illustration.

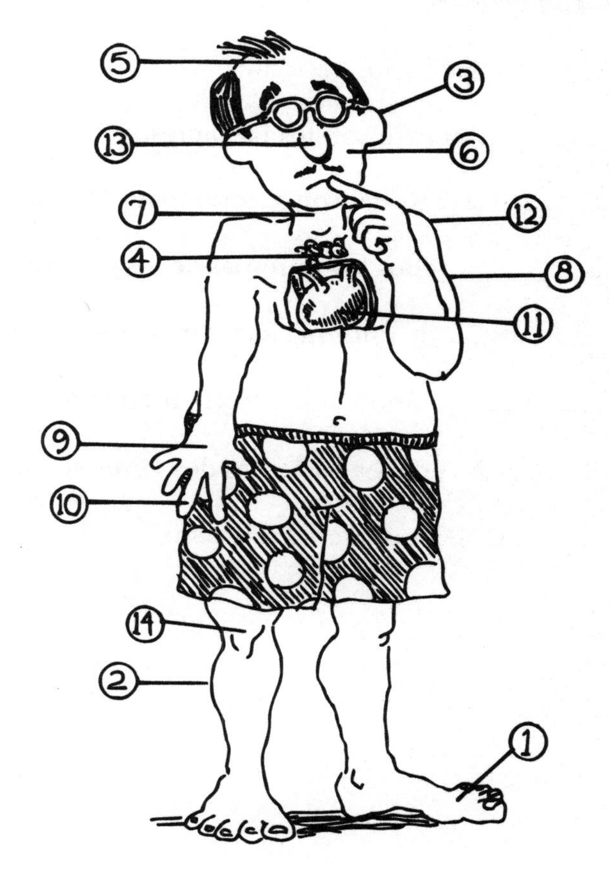

1. ______________________
2. ______________________
3. ______________________
4. ______________________
5. ______________________
6. ______________________

7. ______________________
8. ______________________
9. ______________________
10. ______________________
11. ______________________
12. ______________________
13. ______________________
14. ______________________

¡Así lo hacemos! Estructuras

1. The *nosotros* commands

10-5 El profesor de medicina. You are teaching at a university hospital and this is what you tell your students. Complete the statements with the **nosotros** command of the verbs in parentheses.

MODELO: (Levantarse) ______________ a las cinco.
Levantémonos a las cinco.

1. (Tratar) ______________ bien a los pacientes.
2. (Hablar) ______________ mucho con los pacientes.
3. (Irse) ______________ a las seis del consultorio todos los días.
4. (Estudiar) ______________ todos los síntomas de los pacientes.
5. (Consultar) ______________ la información con la enfermera.
6. No (recetar) ______________ antibióticos frecuentemente.
7. (Venir) ______________ a ver a los pacientes dos veces al día.
8. (Poner) ______________ siempre atención a todo.

Nombre: ______________________ Fecha: ______________________

10-6 En el hospital. Your new colleague in the hospital is always asking your opinion about what task you should both do next. Answer each of your colleague's questions affirmatively. Use object pronouns to avoid repetition.

Modelo: ¿Empezamos la operación?
Sí, empecémosla.

1. ¿Nos preparamos para hacer el examen físico?

   Sí, ______________________.

2. ¿Estudiamos los síntomas?

   Sí, ______________________.

3. ¿Escribimos la receta?

   Sí, ______________________.

4. ¿Leemos el diagnóstico?

   Sí, ______________________.

5. ¿Buscamos el jarabe?

   Sí, ______________________.

10-7 El médico interno. You are an intern in a hospital and you ask your medical professors for advice. One professor agrees with you and the other doesn't. Use the **nosotros** command to express their responses, and use object pronouns to avoid repetition.

Modelo: preparar el horario de trabajo
Tú: ¿Preparamos el horario de trabajo?
Profesor 1: *Sí, preparémoslo.*
Profesora 2: *No, no lo preparemos.*

leer la radiografía

1. Tú: ¿Leemos la radiografía?

   Profesor 1: ______________________

   Profesora 2: ______________________

hablar con la especialista

2. Tú: ¿Hablamos con la especialista?

   Profesor 1: ______________________

   Profesora 2: ______________________

Nombre: ______________________ Fecha: ______________________

recetar más pastillas

3. Tú: ¿Recetamos más pastillas?

   Profesor 1: ______________________

   Profesora 2: ______________________

pedirle la información al enfermero

4. Tú: ¿Le pedimos la información al enfermero?

   Profesor 1: ______________________

   Profesora 2: ______________________

recetar más antibióticos

5. Tú: ¿Recetamos más antibióticos?

   Profesor 1: ______________________

   Profesora 2: ______________________

ponerles inyecciones a los pacientes

6. Tú: ¿Les ponemos inyecciones a los pacientes?

   Profesor 1: ______________________

   Profesora 2: ______________________

repetirle el examen físico a don Rafael

7. Tú: ¿Le repetimos el examen físico a don Rafael?

   Profesor 1: ______________________

   Profesora 2: ______________________

operar al niño

8. Tú: ¿Operamos al niño?

   Profesor 1: ______________________

   Profesora 2: ______________________

Nombre: ______________________ Fecha: ______________

2. Indirect commands

10-8 ¡Que todo vaya bien! Imagine that you are a doctor and the nurse is listing the health issues of several patients. Give advice, using the expression in parentheses as an indirect command.

Modelo: El señor García cree que tiene fiebre. (tomarse la temperatura)
¡Que se tome la temperatura!

1. Juan José se rompió el brazo. (hacerse una radiografía)

   ¡Que ______________ una radiografía!

2. La señora Ramona tose mucho. (tomarse un jarabe para la tos)

   ¡Que ______________ un jarabe para la tos!

3. Don Rafael está resfriado. (guardar cama por dos días)

   ¡Que ______________ cama por dos días!

4. Al señor Ramírez le duele el pecho. (dejar de fumar)

   ¡Que ______________ de fumar!

5. Doña María dice que le duele la garganta. (hacer una cita conmigo)

   ¡Que ______________ una cita conmigo!

10-9 Consejitos. Imagine that your children are planning to do the following activities. Ask someone to give them advice, using indirect commands.

Modelo: Van a nadar en el río.
¡Que tengan mucho cuidado!

1. Van a ver televisión.

   ____

2. Van a la fiesta de Antonio.

   ____

3. Van a almorzar.

   ____

4. Van a estudiar para el examen.

   ____

5. Van a llamar a la tía Isabel.

   ____

Nombre: ______________________ Fecha: ______________________

Segunda parte

¡Así es la vida!

10-10 Mejora tu salud. Answer the following questions, based on the spa advertisement on page 341 of your textbook.

1. ¿Dónde está situada la Hacienda La Fortuna?

   a. en La Fortuna b. cerca de sitios arqueológicos c. cerca de la playa

2. ¿Qué actividad en el spa puede ayudar a adelgazar?

   a. baño con esencias botánicas b. reflexología c. dieta de baja grasa

3. ¿Qué actividad en el spa ayuda a aliviar el estrés?

   a. dieta de baja grasa b. masajes c. acupuntura

4. ¿Qué actividad en el spa ayuda con las enfermedades crónicas?

   a. masajes b. acupuntura c. sauna

5. ¿En qué lugar geográfico se encuentra el spa?

   a. cerca del río Amazonas b. cerca del río de la Plata c. cerca del lago Titicaca

6. ¿De que tipo (*kind*) de agua es el spa?

   a. termal b. medicinal c. fría

Nombre: ______________________ Fecha: ______________________

¡Así lo decimos! Vocabulario

10-11 ¡A escoger! Select the most appropriate word or phrase to complete each statement. Then write the word or phrase in the space provided.

1. Si alguien desea adelgazar, necesita eliminar de su dieta...

   a. las frutas.

   b. la grasa.

   c. las legumbres.

2. Para controlar el peso se necesita...

   a. fumar.

   b. subir de peso.

   c. estar a dieta.

3. Para subir de peso, se necesita...

   a. estar a dieta.

   b. adelgazar.

   c. comer muchos carbohidratos.

4. Nosotros necesitamos tener bajo...

   a. el cigarrillo.

   b. el colesterol.

   c. estar a dieta.

5. La escuela y el trabajo causan mucho...

   a. estrés.

   b. sobrepeso.

   c. diabetes.

6. Para ponernos en forma, tenemos que...
   a. comer más.
   b. hacer jogging.
   c. subir de peso.
7. Un alimento rico en proteínas es...
   a. el pescado.
   b. el azúcar.
   c. el aceite.
8. Un tipo de ejercicio es...
   a. guardar la línea.
   b. levantar pesas.
   c. el reposo.

10-12 Cuestionario. Answer the following questions with complete sentences in Spanish.

1. ¿Cómo guardas la línea?

   ____

2. ¿Quieres adelgazar o subir de peso?

   ____

3. ¿Necesitas ponerte en forma?

   ____

4. Cuando haces ejercicio, ¿qué haces?

   ____

5. ¿Te cuidas bien? ¿Qué haces para cuidarte?

   ____

6. ¿Qué tipo de alimentos comes?

   ____

Nombre: ______________________ Fecha: ______________________

¡Así lo hacemos! Estructuras

3. The subjunctive to express feelings and emotions

10-13 En el gimnasio. Fill in the blanks with the appropriate present subjunctive form of the verbs in parentheses.

MODELO: (yo) / esperar / (tú) / hacer ejercicio
Espero que hagas ejercicio.

1. Me enoja que tú no (cuidarse) ______________________ mejor.
2. ¿Temes que (haber) ______________________ mucha grasa en el chocolate?
3. Nosotros sentimos que tú no (poder) ______________________ levantar pesas esta tarde.
4. ¿Ustedes lamentan que el club no (estar) ______________________ abierto?
5. Mis amigos esperan que yo (hacer) ______________________ ejercicio con ellos.
6. Pablo está contento de que nosotros (ir) ______________________ al gimnasio hoy.
7. El atleta se sorprende de que ellos (fumar) ______________________ después de correr.
8. Los equipos insisten en que todos nosotros (participar) ______________________.
9. ¿Usted se alegra de que yo (mantenerse) ______________________ en forma?
10. Me sorprende que tú (estar) ______________________ a dieta.

10-14 La vida de Luis. Complete the paragraph about Luis's career plans with the correct form of the present subjunctive, present indicative, or infinitive of the verbs in parentheses.

Los padres de Luis desean que él (1. estudiar) ______________________ para (2. ser) ______________________ abogado, pero él quiere (3. estudiar) ______________________ medicina. Todos los días les dice a sus padres que (4. querer) ______________________ ser médico, pero ellos prefieren que (5. ser) ______________________ abogado. Prefieren la profesión de abogado, porque creen que los médicos nunca (6. tener) ______________________ tiempo para nada. Esperan que su hijo (7. divertirse) ______________________ y que no (8. trabajar) ______________________ todo el tiempo. Luis dice que sus padres no (9. tener) ______________________ razón, pero comprende también que ellos (10. querer) ______________________ que él (11. estar) ______________________ contento. Finalmente, los padres le dicen que la decisión (12. ser) ______________________ suya y que no les

Nombre: ______________________ Fecha: ______________________

molesta que (13. ir) ______________ a ser médico. Él se alegra mucho de que sus padres (14. comprender) ______________ y (15. respetar) ______________ su decisión. Ojalá Luis (16. conseguir) ______________ cumplir sus sueños.

10-15 Tu familia y tu salud. What are the things that you fear, you hope for, and you are happy about regarding your family and your health. Write at least five sentences, using the expressions from the word bank.

Modelo: *Me alegro de que mis hijos estén bien. Temo que se enferme mi abuela.*

Espero que	Me enoja que
Estoy triste de que	Me preocupa que
Lamento que	Ojalá
Me alegro de que	Temo que

1. ______________________________
2. ______________________________
3. ______________________________
4. ______________________________
5. ______________________________

10-16 ¿Qué esperas? Write six things that you hope will occur this year. Begin your sentences with **Ojalá.**

Modelo: *¡Ojalá que tengamos más vacaciones!*

1. ______________________________
2. ______________________________
3. ______________________________
4. ______________________________
5. ______________________________
6. ______________________________

Nombre: ______________________ Fecha: ______________________

4. The subjunctive to express doubt and denial

10-17 Unas opiniones. María disagrees with everything Carlos says. Play the part of María, and change Carlos's statements from affirmative to negative or vice versa.

Modelo: Carlos: Creo que hacer ejercicio es muy bueno.
María: *No creo que hacer ejercicio sea muy bueno.*

Carlos: Estoy seguro de que el estrés se puede remediar.

María: (1) ______________________.

Carlos: No niego que ponerse en forma requiere esfuerzo.

María: (2) ______________________.

Carlos: Creo que él consigue adelgazar.

María: (3) ______________________.

Carlos: No dudo que ustedes se mantienen en forma.

María: (4) ______________________.

Carlos: Pienso que el entrenador personal sabe mucho.

María: (5) ______________________.

Carlos: No niego que los atletas están a dieta.

María: (6) ______________________.

Carlos: Estoy seguro de que Esteban y Rocío guardan la línea.

María: (7) ______________________.

Carlos: Creo que Ramiro hace ejercicio también.

María: (8) ______________________.

10-18 Tu opinión. Guillermo makes many unfounded statements. Set him straight by using a verb or expression from the word bank, making any necessary changes.

Modelo: Nosotros siempre vigilamos nuestro nivel de colesterol.
No es cierto que nosotros vigilemos nuestro nivel de colesterol.

Dudar	No creer	No estar seguro/a de
Negar	No es cierto	

1. A él le gusta hacer ejercicios aeróbicos.

____

2. Tengo que subir de peso.

____

3. Nosotros nos cuidamos mucho.

____

4. Hay mucha grasa en la carne.

____

5. Es muy difícil ponerse en forma.

____

6. Pedro Manuel es el mejor entrenador personal de la ciudad.

____

7. Comer carbohidratos engorda mucho.

____

8. Todos nosotros siempre hacemos footing por la mañana.

____

9. Los médicos recomiendan comer mucha carne.

____

10. Fumar no tiene ningún riesgo.

____

Nombre: ______________________________ Fecha: ______________________

10-19 El estado de salud ideal. Fill in the blanks to make statements about the ideal health. Follow the model.

MODELO: Tal vez este mes (hacer) *haga* más ejercicio.

1. Tal vez no (comer) ________________ tanta grasa.
2. Quizás (controlar) ________________ mi nivel de estrés.
3. Quizás (adelgazar) ________________.
4. Tal vez (cuidarse) ________________ más.
5. Quizás (ir) ________________ al gimnasio todas las mañanas.
6. Tal vez (levantar) ________________ pesas en el gimnasio.
7. Tal vez (mantenerse) ________________ en forma.
8. Tal vez (consumir) ________________ menos calorías todos los días.
9. Quizás (dejar) ________________ de fumar.
10. Quizás (tener) ________________ en cuenta la cantidad de bebidas alcohólicas que tomo.

NUESTRO MUNDO

Panoramas

10-20 ¡A informarse! Identify if the following statements are true for Paraguay, for Bolivia, or for both countries.

1. El país no tiene salida al mar.

   a. Paraguay b. Bolivia c. Paraguay y Bolivia

2. El país tiene frontera con Brasil.

   a. Paraguay b. Bolivia c. Paraguay y Bolivia

3. El cultivo de ganado es económicamente muy importante.

   a. Paraguay b. Bolivia c. Paraguay y Bolivia

4. La Santísima Trinidad de Paraná está en este país.

   a. Paraguay b. Bolivia c. Paraguay y Bolivia

5. La minería es de mucha importancia para la economía del país.

   a. Paraguay   b. Bolivia   c. Paraguay y Bolivia

6. La capital del país está situada a una altura considerable.

   a. Paraguay   b. Bolivia   c. Paraguay y Bolivia

7. El río Paraná cruza este país.

   a. Paraguay   b. Bolivia   c. Paraguay y Bolivia

8. Este país produce electricidad consumida en Brasil.

   a. Paraguay   b. Bolivia   c. Paraguay y Bolivia

9. Este país andino tiene el lago navegable más alto del mundo.

   a. Paraguay   b. Bolivia   c. Paraguay y Bolivia

10. El español es idioma oficial en este país.

   a. Paraguay   b. Bolivia   c. Paraguay y Bolivia

10-21 Tu propia experiencia. Use the Internet and the library to investigate **las misiones.** Write a paragraph explaining what they are, who built them, and why. Focus on the missions in Bolivia and Paraguay, and compare them with the missions in the U.S.

____

____

____

____

____

____

Nombre: ______________________ Fecha: ______________________

Taller

10-22 Nuestra salud este mes

Primera fase. Interview three classmates to find out what health problems they have had in the last thirty days. Use the following chart to record the information. Fill in the chart with information about yourself, as well.

ESTUDIANTE				TÚ
VECES ENFERMO/A				
RESFRIADO				
GRIPE				
FIEBRE				
DOLOR DE ESTÓMAGO				
DOLOR DE CABEZA				
CLÍNICA / HOSPITAL				
¿...?				

Segunda fase. Now use the information from the chart in the **Primera fase** to write a brief report on the health of the students in your class. Try to make some general assessments, as well as provide some specific cases.

MODELO: *Este mes, varios estudiantes tuvieron dolor de estómago. Ana tuvo que ir al hospital porque...*

____

____

____

____

____

____

Nombre: ______________________ Fecha: ______________________

10-23 La medicina en el altiplano. For years, medical doctors would treat patients in high altitude areas such as La Paz, Bolivia, based on their sea-level training. Today, medical researchers are trying to find out more about health in high altitudes. Using the Internet or library resources, look up information about the effects of high altitude on health. What are some of the remedies for ill effects? Organize the information you find in a list or on a chart in Spanish.

____

____

____

____

____

____

Nombre: ______________________ Fecha: ______________________

10-24 Más allá de las páginas: Los guaraníes. Ibotí, the girl who helped Manuela in **"El ñandutí"** was Guaraní, an indigenous group that lived in central South America before the Europeans arrived. The language and many aspects of the culture of the Guaraní still survive. Use the Internet or library resources to find the following information.

CINCO EXPRESIONES EN EL IDIOMA GUARANÍ

____

____

____

DOS RECETAS TRADICIONALES DE LOS GUARANÍES

____

____

____

DOS CANCIONES EN GUARANÍ

____

____

____

UN INSTRUMENTO MUSICAL GUARANÍ

____

____

____

UNA DESCRIPCIÓN DE UNA PERSONA TÍPICA GUARANÍ

____

____

____

Nombre: ______________________ Fecha: ______________________

¿Cuánto sabes tú?

10-25 ¿Sabes usar los mandatos? Fill in the blanks with the **nosotros** command form of the verbs in parentheses.

1. Este paciente está muy mal. (Operar) ______________ al paciente hoy.
2. Fumar no es bueno para la salud. (Dejar) ______________ de fumar.
3. Hay que ir al médico, por lo menos, una vez al año. (Hacer) ______________ una cita.
4. Estar en forma es muy importante. (Cuidarse) ______________.
5. Hay que controlar el nivel de estrés. (Descansar) ______________ un poco más.

10-26 ¿Sabes usar los mandatos indirectos? You are talking to your teacher about your friend Roberto, who has not been able to make it to class in the last week due to illness. Complete the following conversation with the indirect command form of the verbs in parentheses.

Usted: Profesor, Roberto está enfermo, pero quiere hacer su tarea. ¿Qué debe hacer?

Profesor: Primero, que (1. cuidarse) ______________.

Usted: ¿Qué puede hacer para estar al día?

Profesor: Que (2. leer) ______________ los capítulos 6 y 7 del libro y que (3. hacer) ______________ las actividades del cuaderno.

Usted: ¿Algo más?

Profesor: Sí. Que (4. repasar) ______________ el capítulo 5 y que (5. escribir) ______________ un ensayo sobre el contenido del capítulo. Esto es todo.

Usted: Muchas gracias profesor. Se lo voy a decir.

10-27 ¿Sabes usar el presente de subjuntivo? Fill in the blanks with the present subjunctive form of the verbs in parentheses, when necessary.

Lamento que Roberto (1. estar) ______________ enfermo. Le recomiendo que (2. guardar) ______________ cama durante dos días y que (3. tomar) ______________ el jarabe que le recetó el médico. Es importante (4. seguir) ______________ las instrucciones del médico. Quizás yo (5. hacer) ______________ una cita con el médico para un examen físico. Ojalá Roberto (6. mejorarse) ______________ pronto y (7. poder) ______________ volver a la universidad.

Nombre: ______________________ Fecha: ______________

Lab Manual

Primera parte

¡Así es la vida!

10-28 Hablando con la farmacéutica. As you listen to the following conversations, select the letters for all statements that are correct, according to what you hear. Listen to the conversations as many times as necessary to find all the correct answers.

1. A Paula...
   a. le duelen los oídos.
   b. le duele la garganta.
   c. le duelen los músculos.
2. La farmacéutica...
   a. le pregunta a Paula si tiene gripe.
   b. le pregunta si tose.
   c. le dice a Paula que vea a un médico.
3. A Paula...
   a. no le gusta ir al médico.
   b. le da un jarabe para la tos.
   c. le duele el pecho.
4. Marcos...
   a. se siente mejor.
   b. quiere un antiácido.
   c. tiene dolor de estómago.
5. Don Felipe...
   a. se siente mal.
   b. necesita tomarse la presión.
   c. quiere que le pongan una inyección.
6. Alejandro...
   a. se rompió un brazo.
   b. necesitó sacarse una radiografía.
   c. es un muchacho muy enfermo.
7. Don Felipe...
   a. es el esposo de doña Ester.
   b. tiene gripe.
   c. tiene un nieto que se llama Marcos.

¡Así lo decimos! Vocabulario

10-29 Prueba de la salud. Select the letter of the word or expression that best completes each sentence you hear. Then listen and repeat as the speaker gives the correct answer.

1. a. el estómago
   b. el brazo
   c. la sangre
2. a. te duele el tobillo
   b. haces ejercicio
   c. guardas cama
3. a. operó
   b. sacó la lengua
   c. tosió
4. a. hizo una cita
   b. tomó la temperatura
   c. recetó el jarabe
5. a. la oreja
   b. el corazón
   c. el cuello
6. a. tengo un resfriado
   b. me ponen una inyección
   c. me hacen una prueba de sangre

¡Así lo hacemos! Estructuras

1. The *nosotros* commands

10-30 ¿Qué van a hacer? Form **nosotros** commands using the cues provided. Then listen and repeat as the speaker gives the correct answer.

1. ir / al consultorio
2. buscar / la radiografía
3. escribir / el diagnóstico
4. hacer / una cita enseguida
5. dejar / de fumar
6. pedir / el antibiótico

10-31 Estamos enfermos. You and your roommate think you have food poisoning and plan to go to the doctor tomorrow. What should you do? Respond with **nosotros** commands, using the verbs you hear and the cues provided. Then listen and repeat as the speaker gives the correct answer.

MODELO: You hear: hablar
You see: ______________ con el médico mañana.
You write and say: *Hablemos con el médico mañana.*

1. ______________ para el consultorio médico.
2. ______________ temprano para no llegar tarde a la cita.
3. No ______________ tarde.
4. ______________ cama y ______________ toda la noche.
5. ______________ qué nos duele.
6. ______________ el antiácido.

2. Indirect commands

10-32 Situaciones médicas. Answer the questions you hear, using an indirect command and the cues provided. Include object pronouns when indicated. Then listen and repeat as the speaker gives the correct answer.

1. verlo / Eduardo
2. tomármela / la enfermera
3. sacar / tú
4. dárselo / la doctora Iglesias
5. ir / mi esposo conmigo

10-33 ¡No quiero! Based on what the speaker does not want to do, use the cues provided to indicate who should do each activity. Use object pronouns when indicated. Then listen and repeat as the speaker gives the correct answer.

1. llamar / Eduardo
2. comprarlas / ellos
3. ponértela / ellos / a ti
4. hacerla / Rosalía
5. dejar de fumar / tú

Nombre: ______________________ Fecha: ______________________

Segunda parte

¡Así es la vida!

10-34 "Me duele la espalda..." As you listen to the following conversations, select the letters for all statements that are correct, according to what you hear. Listen to the conversations as many times as necessary to find all the correct answers.

1. La doctora Roca...
   a. dice que los resultados son negativos.
   b. recomienda pastillas para el dolor de espalda.
   c. insiste en que el problema es el peso.
2. Carlos...
   a. tiene mucho dolor de espalda.
   b. se siente bien.
   c. prefiere comer frutas y beber agua mineral.
3. La doctora...
   a. quiere que Carlos pierda peso lentamente.
   b. prefiere que Carlos haga una dieta muy complicada.
   c. piensa que el plan no va a ser tan horrible.
4. A Carlos...
   a. le sugiere que consuma bebidas alcohólicas.
   b. le aconseja que coma comida con muchas proteínas.
   c. le recomienda que haga ejercicio.
5. La doctora dice que hacer el jogging...
   a. va a ayudar a Carlos a bajar de peso.
   b. ayuda a mantenerse en forma.
   c. no es necesario.
6. Carlos tiene que...
   a. controlar su peso todas las noches.
   b. hacer una lista de lo que come.
   c. ver a la doctora en dos semanas.

Nombre: ______________________ Fecha: ______________________

¡Así lo decimos! Vocabulario

10-35 ¿Lógico o ilógico? Choose the most logical word or expression to complete each sentence that you hear. Then listen and repeat as the speaker gives the correct answer.

1. a. padecer de diabetes
   b. una bebida alcohólica
   c. levantar pesas.
2. a. la gimnasia
   b. la grasa
   c. la diabetes
3. a. más grasas en la dieta
   b. bajar de peso
   c. hacer reposo
4. a. productos lácteos
   b. proteínas
   c. ejercicios aeróbicos
5. a. hacer jogging
   b. adelgazar
   c. subir de peso
6. a. sobrepeso
   b. cigarrillo
   c. peso

¡Así lo hacemos! Estructuras

3. The subjunctive to express feelings and emotions

10-36 ¿Cómo reaccionan? Answer the following questions using the cues provided. Then listen and repeat as the speaker gives the correct answer.

MODELO: You hear: ¿Qué espera la doctora Roca?
You see: su paciente / cuidarse
You say: *La doctora Roca espera que su paciente se cuide.*

1. las clases de ejercicio / ser / tan caras
2. tú / adelgazar / tanto
3. la dieta / terminar / pronto
4. el profesor / padecer / de diabetes
5. tú / tener / menos estrés

Nombre: ______________________ Fecha: ______________________

10-37 ¿Cómo se siente cuando...? Listen to the following sentences and combine them with the cues provided to form new sentences. Then listen and repeat as the speaker gives the correct answer.

1. Nos molesta...
2. Me enoja...
3. Siento...
4. Esperamos...
5. Me sorprende...

10-38 Posibilidades. Form sentences using the cues provided. Then listen and repeat as the speaker gives the correct answer.

1. ojalá / no / dolerle / la garganta
2. ojalá / Ud. / no / tener / alergias a los productos lácteos
3. ojalá / ellas / poder / ir al gimnasio luego
4. ojalá / nosotros / poder / bajar de peso
5. ojalá / tú / no / necesitar / una inyección

4. The subjunctive to express doubt and denial

10-39 ¿Dudamos mucho? Form sentences using the cues provided. Then listen and repeat as the speaker gives the correct answer.

1. no creer (tú) / que / ellos / mantenerse / en forma
2. dudar (ellos) / que / María / estar / a dieta
3. pensar (nosotros) / que / los niños / necesitar / jarabe
4. estar (tú) / seguro de / que / Felipe / hacer / ejercicio
5. no dudar (ellas) / que / los antiácidos / ayudar / con el dolor de estómago
6. creer (yo) / que / él / cuidarse
7. no pensar (usted) / que / el diagnóstico / ser / bueno
8. no negar (yo) / que / la doctora / saber / cuáles son mis síntomas

Nombre: ______________________ Fecha: ______________________

10-40 ¿Qué piensan? Based on the comments you hear, state opinions by writing the appropriate verb forms. Then listen and repeat as the speaker gives the correct answer.

1. Yo no (creer) ______________ que tú (comenzar) ______________ a hacer ejercicio mañana.
2. Ellos (negar) ______________ que yo (sentirse) ______________ mejor.
3. Nosotros no (dudar) ______________ que ellos (subir) ______________ de peso.
4. Tú (dudar) ______________ que nosotros (salir) ______________ para el gimnasio ahora.
5. Mario no (pensar) ______________ que tú (llegar) ______________ a tiempo para la cita.
6. Tú (creer) ______________ que el doctor generalmente (operar) ______________ por la mañana.

10-41 Una vida saludable. Answer the questions you hear using the cues provided. Then listen and repeat as the speaker gives the correct answer.

MODELO: You hear: ¿Crees que muchos pacientes vienen hoy?
You see: tal vez...
You say: *Tal vez muchos pacientes vengan hoy.*

1. tal vez...
2. quizás...
3. tal vez...
4. quizás...
5. tal vez...

Nombre: ______________________ Fecha: ______________________

¿Cuánto sabes tú?

10-42 ¿Qué se dice del cuerpo? The following Spanish sayings refer to at least one part of the body. As you listen, complete the following picture by labeling the parts of the body you hear mentioned.

Nombre: ______________________ Fecha: ______________________

10-43 ¿Cuáles son sus síntomas? Using the pictures that follow, answer the questions you hear about the people depicted. Then listen and repeat as the speaker gives the correct answer.

1.

2.

3.

4.

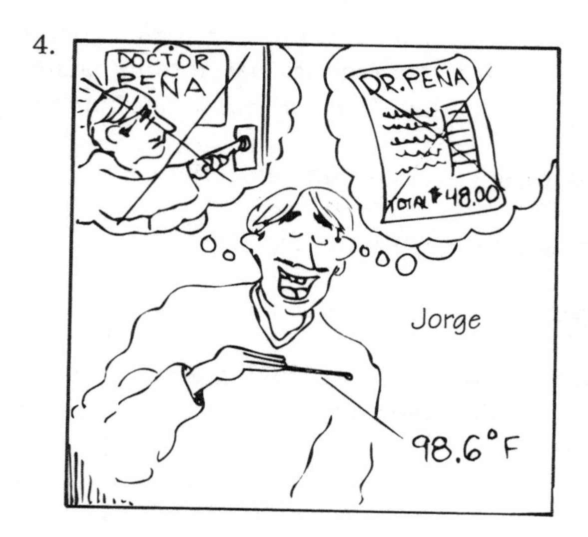

5.

6.

Nombre: ______________________________ Fecha: ______________________

10-44 Doctor, ¿qué puedo hacer? Listen to the medical problems of the following people and respond using the cues provided. Then listen and repeat as the speaker gives the correct answer.

MODELO: You hear: Doctora, me duele el pecho.
You see: sugerir / hacerse una radiografía de los pulmones
You say: *Le sugiero que se haga una radiografía de los pulmones.*

1. dudar / ir a necesitar una inyección
2. pensar / necesitar hacer ejercicio
3. esperar / volver en dos semanas
4. alegrarse de / sentirse mejor
5. molestarme / no mantenerse en forma

10-45 Preguntas personales. Answer the questions you hear, based on your personal experience. Compare your responses with the sample answers in the Answer Key.

1. ____
2. ____
3. ____
4. ____
5. ____
6. ____
7. ____
8. ____

Nombre: ______________________ Fecha: ______________________

11 ¿Para qué profesión te preparas?

Workbook

Primera parte

¡Así es la vida!

11-1 Los trabajadores. Reread the business cards in **¡Así es la vida!** on page 362 of your textbook and complete the following statements by choosing the most appropriate answer.

1. Margarita Alfonsín Sandini es...

   a. psicóloga clínica. b. abogada. c. analista de sistemas.

2. Trabaja en...

   a. el Centro Comercial Houssay. b. la calle Torrogo. c. el hospital.

3. Su número de teléfono es el...

   a. dos, seis, nueve, nueve. c. dos, siete, siete, cuatro, dos, seis, ocho.

   b. dos, siete, siete, cinco, cinco, seis, uno.

4. Rafael Betancourt Rosas es...

   a. ingeniero industrial. b. psicólogo clínico. c. abogado.

5. Su oficina está en el...

   a. centro comercial. b. hospital. c. edificio Díaz de Solís.

6. La doctora Mercedes Fernández de Robles es...

   a. abogada. b. psicóloga clínica. c. ingeniera industrial.

7. Su oficina está en el...

   a. hospital. b. centro comercial. c. edificio Díaz de Solís.

8. Ramón Gutiérrez Sergil es...

   a. abogado. b. analista de sistemas. c. ingeniero industrial.

9. La calle donde se encuentra su oficina se llama...

   a. Torre las Brisas. b. San Juan. c. la avenida Fernández Juncos.

10. Trabaja en...

   a. San Juan. b. Montevideo. c. Buenos Aires.

¡Así lo decimos! Vocabulario

11-2 ¡A completar! Choose a word or expression from the word bank to complete each of the following statements.

a comisión	entrenamiento	meta	secretario
arquitecta	intérprete	peluquero	veterinaria

1. Esa ____________________ nos va a diseñar una casa nueva.
2. Este ____________________ es magnífico. Puede escribir a máquina sesenta palabras por minuto sin errores.
3. El ____________________ me recomienda que use más champú.
4. Mariluz sabe muchos idiomas; ella es la ____________________ de su compañía.
5. La supervisora de los nuevos empleados ha preparado un buen programa de ____________________. Ellos van a aprender mucho sobre sus responsabilidades durante esta semana.
6. Los vendedores no reciben un salario fijo. Ellos trabajan ____________________.
7. Mi ____________________ es obtener ese puesto.
8. La ____________________ curó a mi perro.

Nombre: ______________________ Fecha: ______________

11-3 Palabras relacionadas. What words do you remember from previous lessons that are related to these new vocabulary words? Match the new words with the most appropriate word.

____ 1. el/la dentista	a. la cuenta
____ 2. el/la contador/a	b. la receta
____ 3. el/la cocinero/a	c. la pastilla
____ 4. el/la vendedor/a	d. la comisión
____ 5. el/la viajante	e. pasta de dientes
____ 6. el/la doctor/a	f. el viaje

11-4 Combinación. Use corresponding elements in the two columns to form eight logical sentences.

un gerente	apagar un fuego
una veterinaria	atender a los clientes
un mecánico	contratar más empleados
un peluquero	cortar el pelo
una carpintera	curar a mi perro
una bombera	hacer muebles
un cartero	reparar el coche
un vendedor	repartir las cartas

1. ______________________________
2. ______________________________
3. ______________________________
4. ______________________________
5. ______________________________
6. ______________________________
7. ______________________________
8. ______________________________

Nombre: ______________________ Fecha: ______________________

11-5 Los anuncios clasificados. Read the following **VideoMúsica** want ad and answer the questions by choosing the most appropriate answer.

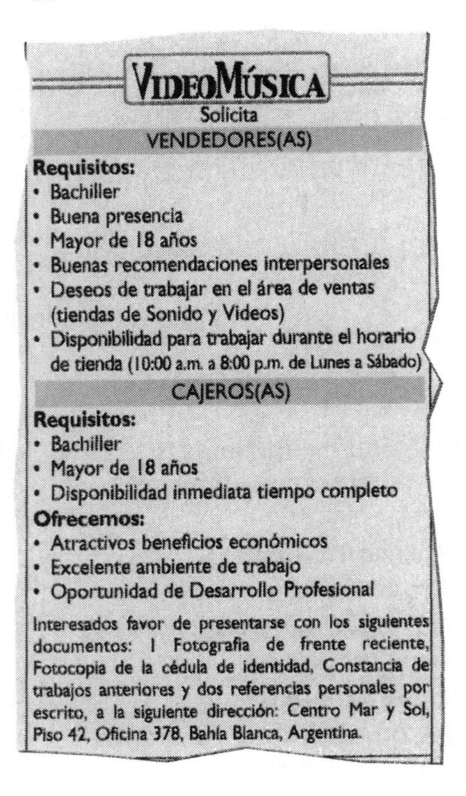

VIDEOMÚSICA
Solicita
VENDEDORES(AS)
Requisitos:
- Bachiller
- Buena presencia
- Mayor de 18 años
- Buenas recomendaciones interpersonales
- Deseos de trabajar en el área de ventas (tiendas de Sonido y Videos)
- Disponibilidad para trabajar durante el horario de tienda (10:00 a.m. a 8:00 p.m. de Lunes a Sábado)

CAJEROS(AS)
Requisitos:
- Bachiller
- Mayor de 18 años
- Disponibilidad inmediata tiempo completo

Ofrecemos:
- Atractivos beneficios económicos
- Excelente ambiente de trabajo
- Oportunidad de Desarrollo Profesional

Interesados favor de presentarse con los siguientes documentos: 1 Fotografía de frente reciente, Fotocopia de la cédula de identidad, Constancia de trabajos anteriores y dos referencias personales por escrito, a la siguiente dirección: Centro Mar y Sol, Piso 42, Oficina 378, Bahía Blanca, Argentina.

1. ¿Qué solicita VideoMúsica?

   a. actores/actrices y bailarines/as   b. vendedores/as y cajeros/as   c. contador/a e intérprete

2. ¿Qué requisitos deben satisfacer los/as vendedores/as?

   a. mayor de 21 años   c. mayor de 18 años

   b. disponibilidad inmediata tiempo completo

3. ¿Qué documento no tienen que traer los solicitantes?

   a. cédula de identidad   b. pasaporte   c. referencias personales

4. ¿Qué no ofrece VideoMúsica?

   a. largas vacaciones   b. buen ambiente   c. desarrollo profesional

Nombre: ______________________________ Fecha: ______________________

¡Así lo hacemos! Estructuras

1. The subjunctive with impersonal expressions

11-6 El/la jefe/a de personal. You are the personnel director of a large firm, and you are describing how you and your staff should conduct yourselves. Fill in the blanks with the correct form of the verbs in parentheses.

1. No es malo (hablar) ______________________ con los supervisores.
2. Es necesario que tú (mirar) ______________________ el horario de trabajo.
3. Es indispensable que tú (conseguir) ______________________ clientes.
4. Es importante que ustedes (leer) ______________________ algo sobre la empresa.
5. Es mejor que todos nosotros (saber) ______________________ cuáles son nuestras responsabilidades.
6. Siempre es bueno que usted (conocer) ______________________ al gerente.
7. Es urgente que ustedes (ser) ______________________ siempre puntuales.
8. Es preciso que yo les (dar) ______________________ entrenamiento a todos los empleados.
9. Es bueno que ustedes siempre (decir) ______________________ la verdad.
10. Es importante que nosotros (trabajar) ______________________ bien.

11-7 ¡A completar! Complete the following sentences with the correct form of the verbs in parentheses.

1. Es cierto que nuestra compañía (tener) ______________________ muchas metas.
2. Es dudoso que los puestos de esa compañía (ser) ______________________ mejores que los nuestros.
3. Es urgente que los bomberos (apagar) ______________________ el fuego en ese almacén.
4. Es extraño que allí no (haber) ______________________ buenos carpinteros.
5. Es obvio que un arquitecto (diseñar) ______________________ edificios.
6. Es importante que la supervisora siempre (estar) ______________________ temprano en el trabajo.
7. Es mejor que el gerente me (subir) ______________________ el sueldo.
8. No es preciso que la cartera (venir) ______________________ temprano hoy.

9. Es difícil (hacer) ______________________ dos trabajos diariamente.

10. Es una lástima que tu hermana y tú no (conseguir) ______________________ ese puesto.

11. Es fácil (trabajar) ______________________ a comisión.

12. Es bueno que los empleados (conocer) ______________________ a los supervisores.

13. En una compañía internacional, es indispensable (saber) ______________________ dos idiomas.

14. Es posible que nos (dar) ______________________ un buen sueldo.

15. Es malo que los empleados (conversar) ______________________ mucho en el trabajo.

16. Es necesario (llegar) ______________________ a tiempo al trabajo.

17. Es cierto que yo (reparar) ______________________ computadoras.

18. Es increíble que ese vendedor no (vender) ______________________ más.

19. Es imposible que los peluqueros (sacar) ______________________ muelas.

20. No es dudoso que ellas (estudiar) ______________________ para ser psicólogas.

11-8 Entrevista. Imagine that you are the president of an important corporation, and you are being interviewed by a group of students. Answer their questions with complete sentences in Spanish.

1. ¿Qué es importante para conseguir un buen puesto?

____

2. ¿Qué es indispensable en su compañía?

____

3. ¿Qué es necesario para ser un buen gerente?

____

4. ¿Qué es evidente en un buen empleado?

____

5. ¿Es cierto que las personas bilingües están mejor preparadas?

____

Nombre: ______________________ Fecha: ______________________

11-9 La despedida de Miguel. The company is about to fire Miguel. His friend Ricardo wants to help him; however, his friend José is reluctant. Find out what happens by completing the dialog with the correct form of the verbs in parentheses.

Ricardo: ¿Oíste lo que le (1. pasar) ______________________ a Miguel Griffin?

José: No, ¿qué es lo que le (2. ocurrir) ______________________?

Ricardo: Es evidente que el gerente no lo (3. querer) ______________________ más.

José: Bueno, pero es verdad que Miguel (4. ser) ______________________ muy perezoso y muy arrogante.

Ricardo: Es increíble que tú (5. decir) ______________________ eso de Miguel.

José: ¡Cómo es posible que tú (6. ser) ______________________ tan tonto!

Ricardo: Mira, es mejor que nosotros (7. llamar) ______________________ a la supervisora.

José: Sí, pero es probable que ella no nos (8. escuchar) ______________________.

Ricardo: Entonces, es indispensable que tú (9. hablar) ______________________ con el gerente. Tú lo (10. conocer) ______________________ a él, y (11. ser) ______________________ su amigo.

José: Sí, pero es posible que él (12. estar) ______________________ de vacaciones.

Ricardo: Es obvio que tú (13. ser) ______________________ un mal amigo, y no (14. querer) ______________________ ayudar a Miguel.

José: Es una lástima que tú (15. hablar) ______________________ tan mal de mí.

Ricardo: Mira, es mejor que tú no (16. decir) ______________________ esas cosas.

José: Bueno, es verdad que tú y yo (17. tener) ______________________ muchas diferencias. ¡Hasta luego!

Nombre: ______________________ Fecha: ______________________

SEGUNDA PARTE

¡Así es la vida!

11-10 En busca de empleo. Reread the letter and interview in **¡Así es la vida!** on page 371 of your textbook, and answer the following questions by choosing the most appropriate answer.

1. ¿Quién es Isabel Urquiza Duarte?

   a. una estudiante universitaria b. una analista programadora c. una chica puertorriqueña

2. ¿Por qué lee ella los avisos clasificados?

   a. para divertirse b. quiere conseguir trabajo c. quiere estudiar en la universidad

3. ¿En qué se especializa Isabel?

   a. programación b. finanzas c. informática y contabilidad

4. ¿Cómo se considera ella?

   a. responsable b. poco profesional c. experta

5. ¿Qué incluye ella con su carta de presentación?

   a. su foto b. las notas de la universidad c. el *currículum vitae*

6. ¿Quién es la señora Posada?

   a. la madre de Isabel b. la gerente de Centro de Cómputo S.A. c. una amiga de Isabel

7. ¿Por qué quiere trabajar Isabel para esta empresa?

   a. por el sueldo b. porque es una buena empresa c. por el horario

8. ¿Qué le pregunta Isabel a la señora Posada?

   a. el horario b. los beneficios c. el sueldo

9. ¿Por qué consiguió Isabel el puesto?

   a. por ser bilingüe b. por ser experta en informática c. por su experiencia

Nombre: ______________________ Fecha: ______________

¡Así lo decimos! Vocabulario

11-11 La carta de presentación. Complete the following letter with words and expressions from the word bank.

calificaciones	experiencia práctica	referencia
capaz	honrado	solicitud de empleo
currículum vitae	la saluda atentamente	vacante
estimada	recomendación	

(1) ______________ señora:

Le escribo esta carta para presentarme y para solicitar la (2) ______________ de contador que se anunció en *El Mundo*. Yo tengo mucha (3) ______________ y mis (4) ______________ son numerosas, como usted puede ver en el (5) ______________ que adjunto. He incluído tres cartas de (6) ______________ y la (7) ______________ que me envió su secretaria. También incluyo el nombre de mi supervisor que sirve de (8) ______________. Espero tener la oportunidad de entrevistarme con usted. Soy muy (9) ______________ y (10) ______________. Esperando su respuesta a la presente.

(11) ______________,

Rodrigo Rodríguez

11-12 ¿Qué haces? Tell what you do in the following situations, using complete sentences in Spanish.

Modelo: Tu jefe no te da un aumento de sueldo.
Busco otro puesto.

1. Tienes una entrevista muy importante.

____

2. Recibes una mala evaluación de tu supervisor.

____

3. Tu jefe no te quiere ascender.

____

4. Tu mejor amiga recibió el puesto que tu querías.

____

5. Recibiste una bonificación anual muy grande.

____

6. Tu jefa despide a tu mejor amigo.

____

7. No recibiste el aumento que esperabas.

____

8. La empresa te va a enviar (*to send*) a un país hispano.

____

Nombre: ______________________ Fecha: ______________________

¡Así lo hacemos! Estructuras

2. Formal commands

11-13 El jefe sargento. You have a boss who likes to give commands. Complete the orders your boss gives you by using the correct singular formal command of the verbs in parentheses.

1. No (dormir) ______________________ en el trabajo.
2. (Sacar) ______________________ la basura de mi oficina.
3. (Leer) ______________________ los nuevos contratos.
4. (Rellenar) ______________________ los formularios.
5. (Empezar) ______________________ a hacer su trabajo.
6. No (poner) ______________________ los papeles sobre la mesa.
7. No (almorzar) ______________________ en la cafetería.
8. (Preparar) ______________________ su almuerzo en casa.
9. (Firmar) ______________________ los documentos antes de almorzar.
10. (Escribirles) ______________________ las cartas comerciales a los clientes.
11. No (hablar) ______________________ por teléfono con sus amigos.
12. (Contratar) ______________________ a los nuevos empleados.
13. No (beber) ______________________ bebidas alcohólicas en el trabajo.
14. (Cerrar) ______________________ la puerta antes de salir.
15. (Llegar) ______________________ temprano al trabajo.
16. (Ir) ______________________ al banco después del almuerzo.
17. (Estar) ______________________ aquí a las ocho.
18. (Hablar) ______________________ con el jefe de personal.
19. No (salir) ______________________ de la oficina temprano.
20. (Seguir) ______________________ todas mis instrucciones.

Nombre: ______________________ Fecha: ______________________

11-14 En el laboratorio. You work in the biochemistry laboratory as an assistant, and your professor is giving you instructions about what to do. Use the **usted** command form of the verbs in parentheses.

1. (Estar) ______________ a las ocho en el laboratorio.
2. (Traer) ______________ el microscopio.
3. (Abrir) ______________ el libro.
4. (Leer) ______________ las instrucciones.
5. (Seguir) ______________ las instrucciones.
6. (Mirar) ______________ por el microscopio.
7. (Hacer) ______________ la fórmula.
8. (Ir) ______________ a la pizarra.
9. (Escribir) ______________ el resultado en la pizarra.
10. (Terminar) ______________ el experimento.
11. (Salir) ______________ del laboratorio.
12. (Volver) ______________ mañana por la mañana.

11-15 Rosalía y Felipe. Rosalía and Felipe are about to get married. Rosalía's grandfather provides the following advice to them for a successful marriage. Use the **ustedes** command form of the verbs in parentheses.

1. (Vivir) ______________ el presente, pero (pensar) ______________ en el futuro.
2. (Hablar) ______________ de deportes, pero no (conversar)______________ de política.
3. (Comer) ______________ poco y (dormir) ______________ ocho horas todos los días.
4. (Trabajar) ______________ mucho y (comprar) ______________ poco.
5. (Discutir) ______________, pero no (reñir) ______________.
6. (Querer) ______________ a sus suegros, pero no (vivir) ______________ con ellos.
7. (Recordar) ______________ y (seguir) ______________ mis consejos.

Nombre: ______________________________ Fecha: ______________________

11-16 Recomendaciones para una entrevista. Your friends Fernando and Jorge have opposite recommendations for your job interview. You ask them questions, and they cannot agree about the instructions they give you. Fill in the blanks, following the model.

Modelo: ¿Llevo vaqueros?
Sí, lleve vaqueros.
No, no lleve vaqueros.

1. ¿Me quito el sombrero?

   Sí, ____________________ el sombrero.

   No, no ____________________ el sombrero.

2. ¿Llamo a la empresa para confirmar la entrevista?

   Sí, ____________________ a la empresa.

   No, no ____________________ a la empresa.

3. ¿Llevo un currículum vitae conmigo?

   Sí, ____________________ un currículum vitae.

   No, no ____________________ un currículum vitae.

4. ¿Le doy la mano al gerente?

   Sí, ____________________ la mano.

   No, no ____________________ la mano.

5. ¿Muestro mis cartas de recomendación?

   Sí, ____________________ las cartas.

   No, no ____________________ las cartas.

6. ¿Relleno el formulario antes de ir?

   Sí, ____________________ el formulario.

   No, no ____________________ el formulario.

7. ¿Pregunto el sueldo?

   Sí, ____________________ el sueldo.

   No, no ____________________ el sueldo.

8. ¿Hablo con confianza?

   Sí, ______________________ con confianza.

   No, no ______________________ con confianza.

3. The subjunctive and the indicative with adverbial conjunctions

11-17 Una jefa exigente. You and your friends work as interns at a computer firm, and you have a demanding supervisor. Complete what she says with the correct form of the verbs in parentheses.

1. Guillermo, encienda la computadora antes de que nosotros (empezar) ______________________ a trabajar.
2. Pedro Arturo, ponga los datos en la hoja electrónica a fin de que la compañía (tener) ______________________ la información.
3. Amalia y Zenaida, calculen las cuentas a menos de que el gerente les (decir) ______________________ que no.
4. Martín y Catalina, impriman bien los números en caso que ustedes los (necesitar) ______________________.
5. Ramón y tú, lean bien las instrucciones para que no (haber) ______________________ errores.
6. No hagas nada sin que yo lo (saber) ______________________.
7. Ustedes, no comiencen el trabajo a menos que yo (buscar) ______________________ la información.
8. Yo los voy a ayudar con tal que todos ustedes (querer) ______________________ aprender.

Nombre: ______________________ Fecha: ______________________

11-18 La rutina del trabajo. Using the conjunctions in parentheses, combine each pair of statements to discover the routine that Miguel follows at work and how he feels about it. Use the present indicative, present subjunctive, or infinitive. Follow the model.

MODELO: Miguel va a ir al banco. Sale del trabajo. (después de)
Miguel va a ir al banco después de que salga del trabajo.

1. Normalmente, él llega a la oficina. Su jefe todavía no está. (cuando)

____

2. Él va a hablar con el gerente. Llega a la oficina. (tan pronto como)

____

3. Él va a firmar los cheques. Va al banco. (antes de)

____

4. Él entrevista a los candidatos. La empresa tiene los mejores empleados. (para que)

____

5. Miguel va a ascender. La supervisora se jubila. (en cuanto)

____

6. Miguel trabaja horas extra. Puede ir de vacaciones. (a fin de que)

____

7. Él no se quiere ir de la empresa. Lo contratan en otra empresa. (sin que)

____

8. Él va a trabajar. Él tiene sesenta y cinco años. (hasta que)

____

9. No va a contratar a nadie. Un empleado renuncia. (a menos que)

____

10. Miguel está contento en la empresa. Le aumentan el sueldo todos los años. (con tal que)

____

Nombre: ______________________________ Fecha: ______________________

11-19 La contratación de personal. Who does the hiring in the office? Rewrite each statement by changing the first verb to the future and making any other necessary changes.

MODELO: Hablé con él cuando pude.
Voy a hablar con él cuando pueda.

1. Yo entrevisté a los candidatos mientras ella revisó los expedientes.

   Yo ______________ a los candidatos mientras ella ______________ los expedientes.

2. Establecimos las cualificaciones necesarias hasta que el jefe llegó.

   ______________ las cualificaciones necesarias hasta que el jefe ______________.

3. El jefe nos ayudó cuando tuvo tiempo.

   El jefe nos ______________ cuando ______________ tiempo.

4. Contratamos a dos personas aunque el jefe no quiso.

   ______________ a dos personas aunque el jefe no ______________.

5. Les hablamos del plan de retiro luego que empezaron a trabajar.

   Les ______________ del plan de retiro luego que ______________ a trabajar.

6. Les dimos un aumento de sueldo tan pronto como mostraron su potencial.

   Les ______________ un aumento de sueldo tan pronto como ______________ su potencial.

Nombre: ______________________________ Fecha: ______________________

11-20 ¡A completar! Complete the following statements with the subjunctive or infinitive form of the verbs in parentheses.

1. Voy a mandar una solicitud para (conseguir) _______________ empleo.
2. Voy a ir a la entrevista a menos que no (sentirse) _______________ bien.
3. Mis amigos dicen que hable con confianza para que ellos me (contratar) _______________.
4. La empresa despidió a dos trabajadores después de (evaluar) _______________ su trabajo.
5. Aunque yo (estar) _______________ nerviosa, voy a conseguir el puesto de trabajo.
6. Voy a empezar a trabajar tan pronto como (recibir) _______________ la confirmación de la empresa.
7. Voy a esperar su respuesta hasta que yo (encontrar) _______________ nuevos avisos de empleo en los anuncios clasificados.
8. Voy a mandar mi currículum vitae en cuanto el gerente de la empresa lo (pedir) _______________.
9. Voy a conseguir experiencia práctica mientras (trabajar) _______________ en esta empresa.
10. Voy a jubilarme después de (trabajar) _______________ muchos años en el trabajo de mis sueños.

11-21 Mis ideales. Complete the following paragraph, using the correct form of the verbs in parentheses.

Yo (1. ser) _______________ un/a idealista y mi plan (2. ser) _______________ el de encontrar mi trabajo ideal tan pronto como (3. ser) _______________ posible. Primero, voy a llamar a muchas empresas para que nadie me (4. quitar) _______________ la oportunidad cuando (5. haber) _______________ vacantes. Luego, voy a mandar mi currículum vitae a todas las grandes empresas, a menos que éstas no (6. contratar) _______________ a nuevos empleados. Después de que mi plan (7. tener) _______________ éxito, voy a tratar que la

Nombre: ______________________ Fecha: ______________________

empresa me (8. ofrecer) ______________ desarrollo profesional. Voy a trabajar siempre para (9. aprender) ______________ y (10. poder) ______________ tener éxito en mi profesión.

NUESTRO MUNDO

Panoramas

11-22 ¡A informarse! Based on the information from **Nuestro mundo** on pages 386–387 of your textbook, decide if the following statements are **cierto (C)** or **falso (F).**

1. El tango es un baile popular de la Argentina.
2. El tango se originó en la Patagonia.
3. En la Argentina no se puede esquiar.
4. Bariloche es una famosa playa argentina.
5. El Aconcagua es el punto más alto de los Andes.
6. La Argentina y el Uruguay son países conocidos por la pesca.
7. Los argentinos consumen más carne que cualquier otro país del mundo.
8. El gaucho vive en las pampas de la Argentina y del Uruguay.
9. Punta del Este es famoso por sus playas.
10. El béisbol es más popular que el fútbol en la Argentina y el Uruguay.

11-23 Tu propia experiencia. Use the Internet, library resources, documentaries, and movies to find out about Evita Perón. Write a paragraph explaining who she was and her importance in Argentinean history. Then compare her to a public figure that you have knowledge of who may have played a similar role in history.

____

____

____

____

____

____

Nombre: ______________________ Fecha: ______________________

Taller

11-24 Las carreras

Primera fase. Make a list, in Spanish, of the expectations that you have about your career or profession. (The two columns on the right will be used for the **Tercera fase.**)

	YO	ESTUDIANTE	ESTUDIANTE
TIPO DE CARRERA QUE BUSCAS			
TRES (TIPOS DE) COMPAÑÍAS QUE TE INTERESAN			
UNA ALTERNATIVA (POR EJ., AUTO EMPLEO)			
AMBIENTE (*ENVIRONMENT*) DE TRABAJO QUE ESPERAS (POR EJ., OFICINA GRANDE)			
SUELDO QUE QUIERES PARA EMPEZAR			
SUELDO DESPUÉS DE DIEZ AÑOS			
BENEFICIOS QUE QUIERES (POR EJ., MÉDICO)			
ELEMENTOS ABSOLUTAMENTE NECESARIOS			
ELEMENTOS PREFERIBLES			
ELEMENTOS NO ACEPTABLES			
¿...?			

Segunda fase. Now imagine that you are working with an employment agency that will conduct interviews with college students to build candidate profiles. Based on the categories in the **Primera fase,** write eight questions you might use in the interviews.

MODELO: *¿Para qué profesión te preparas?*

1. ______________________________

2. ______________________________

3. ______________________________

Nombre: ______________________ Fecha: ______________________

4. ______________________

5. ______________________

6. ______________________

7. ______________________

8. ______________________

Tercera fase. Now interview two classmates, using the questions you wrote in the **Segunda fase.** Then fill in the information about your classmates in the chart from the **Primera fase.**

11-25 Acuerdos

Primera fase. The establishment of trade agreements, such as NAFTA, is changing the nature of international business. Several agreements have been established in the Spanish-speaking countries, as well. Use the Internet or library resources to look up information on **Mercosur** and on one of the following groups. Then complete the chart with the information that you gathered.

ALADI

MCCA

CARICOM

Pacto Andino

	MERCOSUR	
PAÍSES EN EL ACUERDO		
FECHA DEL ACUERDO INICIAL		
ELEMENTOS BÁSICOS DEL ACUERDO		
VENTAJAS		
DESVENTAJAS		
¿...?		

Nombre: ______________________ Fecha: ______________________

Segunda fase. How are the two agreements you researched similar? How are they different? How do they compare to NAFTA? Write at least four comparisons (two similarities, two differences), answering these questions in Spanish.

1. ____
____

2. ____
____

3. ____
____

4. ____
____

11-26 El gaucho: Un oficio temprano. The gaucho is an Argentine tradition that has inspired many poets, artists, and historians. Read the following passage about the origin of the gaucho. Then answer the questions.

Los conquistadores españoles trajeron millares de animales domésticos al Nuevo Mundo. Hacia el año 1650, muchos de estos animales escaparon del control de las ciudades coloniales. Se escaparon al desierto, o sea el territorio salvaje, habitado por los grupos aborígenes prehispánicos.

Muchas personas urbanas tenían grandes intereses económicos en esas vacas y caballos del desierto, por el precio de su cuero (*hide*). Pero, ¿quién podía atraparlos y sacarles el cuero en medio del territorio aborigen?

De allí nació una tradición argentina—el gaucho. Los gauchos eran de origen diverso: criollos, portugueses, mestizos y negros. Salían al desierto en busca del cuero de las bestias en grupos de aproximadamente diez gauchos. Un buen flete (caballo), un recado o una montura (*saddle*) y un avío (provisiones) le eran indispensables al gaucho para sobrevivir en las pampas.

Estas expediciones se llamaban vaquerías. En el siglo XVII, se convirtieron en un sólido ingreso económico para las colonias, cuando los cueros se empezaron a exportar a Europa. El negocio de la exportación de cueros creció de una manera asombrosa: En 1605, se exportaron 50 cueros; en 1625, se exportaron 27.000 y en 1670, 380.000.

El primer eslabón de esta cadena comercial eran los gauchos. Los jinetes (*riders*) del desierto perseguían los animales dentro de las tierras de los aborígenes. Atrapaban los animales y rápido se bajaban de su flete para apoderarse del cuero, desechando el resto del animal.

El rasgo que los distinguía como grupo era su habilidad de jinetes y el cuidado y respeto que sentían por sus caballos. Estas destrezas y actitudes nacieron con las primeras vaquerías, pero aún podemos verlas en la actualidad.

Nombre: ______________________ Fecha: ______________________

1. ¿Qué situación dio paso a (*gave way to*) la profesión del gaucho?

____

2. ¿Qué llevaba siempre el gaucho en sus expediciones?

____

3. En tu opinión, ¿quién se beneficiaba más del trabajo del gaucho?

____

4. ¿Qué aspectos del trabajo del gaucho serían muy criticados hoy en día?

____

5. ¿Con qué tradición estadounidense podemos comparar la de los gauchos y las vaquerías? Explica algunas semejanzas y diferencias.

____

____

11-27 Más allá de las páginas. Marco Denevi's story has an open ending. Taking into consideration the social and humanistic view of the author, finish the story in your own words.

____

____

____

____

____

____

Nombre: ______________________ Fecha: ______________________

¿Cuánto sabes tú?

11-28 ¿Sabes usar el presente de subjuntivo con expresiones impersonales? Fill in the blanks with the appropriate present subjunctive form of the verbs in parentheses.

1. En el trabajo, es importante que el sueldo (ser) ______________ bueno.
2. En el trabajo, es necesario que (haber) ______________ buen ambiente.
3. En el trabajo, es indispensable que (tú) (tener) ______________ vacaciones.
4. En el trabajo, es preciso que la empresa (ofrecer) ______________ buenos beneficios.
5. En el trabajo, es malo que los empleados (estar) ______________ descontentos.
6. En el trabajo, es mejor (trabajar) ______________ en una gran empresa.

11-29 ¿Sabes usar los mandatos formales? Imagine that you are a supervisor, and you have to give commands to your employees. Fill in the blanks with the appropriate formal command of the verbs in parentheses.

1. Ustedes, no (llegar) ______________ tarde al trabajo.
2. Ricardo, (hablar) ______________ con el gerente.
3. Rogelio, (ser) ______________ responsable.
4. Ángeles y Carlos, (asistir) ______________ a las sesiones de entrenamiento.
5. María, (rellenar) ______________ el formulario.
6. Ustedes, (pedir) ______________ ayuda.

Nombre: ______________________ Fecha: ______________________

11-30 ¿Sabes usar el presente de subjuntivo con conjunciones adverbiales? Complete the following paragraph with the present indicative, present subjunctive, or infinitive form of the verbs in parentheses.

Mi jefe es el mejor jefe del mundo. No le importa a qué hora voy al trabajo con tal que (yo) (1. hacer) ______________________ mi trabajo. Cuando (yo) (2. llegar) ______________________ al trabajo, siempre habla conmigo amablemente. Me dice todo lo que tengo que hacer para que (yo) (3. tener) ______________________ tiempo de hacerlo. Siempre me ayuda y me corrige antes de que (yo) (4. cometer) ______________________ algún error. Antes de (5. ir) ______________________ a comer, siempre lo aviso (*let him know*), en caso de que (él) (6. necesitar) ______________________ mi ayuda en algún otro proyecto urgente. De vez en cuando, él me aumenta el sueldo para que (yo) (7. estar) ______________________ contento. Es imposible (8. tener) ______________________ un jefe mejor que el mío.

Nombre: ______________________ Fecha: ______________

Lab Manual

PRIMERA PARTE

¡Así es la vida!

11-31 Una entrevista. As you listen to the following telephone conversation, select the letters for all statements that are correct, according to what you hear. Listen to the conversation as many times as is necessary to find all the correct answers.

1. Jorge...
   a. leyó el anuncio en una revista.
   b. oyó el anuncio por la radio.
   c. vio el anuncio en el periódico.
2. La empresa "Buen Trabajo" publicó...
   a. un solo aviso.
   b. más de un aviso.
   c. tres avisos.
3. Jorge quiere...
   a. un trabajo de secretario.
   b. un trabajo en la construcción.
   c. un trabajo de arquitecto.
4. Jorge es...
   a. contador.
   b. carpintero.
   c. electricista.
5. La dirección de Jorge es...
   a. Valencia 305, tercero, primera.
   b. Valencia 205, tercero, segunda.
   c. Valencia 305, tercero, primero.
6. El horario disponible de Jorge es...
   a. por la tarde.
   b. de 8:30 a 14:00.
   c. por la mañana hasta las doce.
7. La meta de Jorge es...
   a. ser coordinador.
   b. ser jefe de personal.
   c. ser supervisor.
8. Jorge...
   a. quiere ganar 15 euros por hora.
   b. prefiere un sueldo fijo.
   c. está sin trabajo.

9. El jefe de personal...

   a. va a llamar a Jorge.

   b. va a entrevistar a Jorge.

   c. va a darle el puesto de supervisor a Jorge.

¡Así lo decimos! Vocabulario

11-32 ¿A qué profesión corresponde? Listen to the following sentences and choose the letter corresponding to the word or expression that best completes each sentence. Then listen and repeat as the speaker gives the correct answer.

1. a. arquitecto
   b. dentista
   c. peluquero
2. a. analista de sistemas
   b. electricista
   c. cocinera
3. a. plomero
   b. peluquero
   c. viajante
4. a. peluquera
   b. carpintera
   c. secretario
5. a. veterinario
   b. psicólogo
   c. mecánico
6. a. psicóloga
   b. periodista
   c. bombera
7. a. diseñar casas
   b. repartir las cartas y los paquetes
   c. apagar fuegos
8. a. supervisor
   b. electricista
   c. plomero

Nombre: ______________________ Fecha: ______________

¡Así lo hacemos! Estructuras

1. The subjunctive with impersonal expressions

11-33 ¿Cierto o incierto? Listen to the following sentences, and indicate whether they express certainty or uncertainty by placing a check mark in the appropriate column.

	CERTAINTY	UNCERTAINTY
1.		
2.		
3.		
4.		
5.		
6.		

11-34 Responsabilidades del empleado. Form sentences using the cues provided. Then listen and repeat as the speaker gives the correct answer.

Modelo: You see: es importante / el director / saber / la verdad
You say: *Es importante que el director sepa la verdad.*
or
You see: es mejor / hablar / el despacho
You say: *Es mejor hablar en el despacho.*

1. es bueno / los empleados / pedir / los puestos
2. es imposible / el bombero / apagar / todo / los fuegos
3. es dudoso / la secretaria / recibir / la carta
4. no es fácil / leer / las evaluaciones
5. es necesario / la arquitecta / diseñar / la casa / ahora

11-35 ¿Un buen puesto? Answer the following questions using the cues provided. Then listen and repeat as the speaker gives the correct answer.

Modelo: You hear: ¿Qué es necesario?
You see: usted / recibir / mucho entrenamiento
You say: *Es necesario que usted reciba mucho entrenamiento.*

1. (tú) / no / comer / durante la entrevista
2. ustedes / tener / metas claras

3. (nosotros) / cambiar / el horario de trabajo

4. haber / buenas relaciones entre los empleados y los directores

SEGUNDA PARTE

¡Así es la vida!

11-36 Una oferta. As you listen to the following conversation, select the letters for all statements that are correct, according to what you hear. Listen to the conversation as many times as is necessary to find all the correct answers.

1. Carlos Rodríguez...
   a. fue estudiante.
   b. es estudiante.
   c. busca trabajo.
2. La señora Peña...
   a. trabaja en una empresa internacional.
   b. quiere contratar al señor Rodríguez.
   c. entrevista a Carlos.
3. El señor Rodríguez...
   a. no tiene experiencia práctica.
   b. tiene experiencia práctica.
   c. tiene experiencia trabajando en la universidad.
4. El puesto...
   a. es por dos años.
   b. es ofrecido a Carlos.
   c. es aceptado por Carlos.
5. El puesto incluye beneficios de...
   a. plan de retiro para toda la familia.
   b. bonificaciones anuales.
   c. seguro médico.
6. La empresa...
   a. hace una evaluación de los empleados cada dos meses.
   b. decide los aumentos cada seis meses.
   c. asciende a todos sus empleados tres veces al año.

Nombre: ______________________ Fecha: ______________________

¡Así lo decimos! Vocabulario

11-37 ¿Cuál es la mejor respuesta? Listen to the following sentences and choose the letter corresponding to the word or expression that best completes each sentence. Then listen and repeat as the speaker gives the correct answer.

1. a. la despedida de una carta comercial
   b. el saludo de una carta comercial
   c. el título de una empresa popular
2. a. trabaja poco
   b. trabaja mucho
   c. es entusiasta y capaz
3. a. un expediente
   b. una solicitud de empleo
   c. una carta de recomendación
4. a. la renuncia
   b. el seguro
   c. el puesto
5. a. solicitud
   b. agencia
   c. aspirante
6. a. la vacante
   b. la evaluación
   c. la solicitud
7. a. ascender
   b. aumentar
   c. renunciar

¡Así lo hacemos! Estructuras

2. Formal commands

11-38 ¡Bienvenida a nuestra empresa! Use formal commands and the cues provided to give advice to a new employee. Then listen and repeat as the speaker gives the correct answer.

Modelo: You see: no / dormir / en la oficina
You say: *No duerma en la oficina.*

1. llegar / temprano
2. ser / simpático con el director
3. ir / a la oficina de la secretaria para hablar del plan de retiro
4. hacer / todo el trabajo a tiempo
5. rellenar / los papeles correctamente
6. seguir / el horario indicado en el calendario

11-39 En mi primer día de trabajo. Answer the questions that you hear with formal commands using the cues provided. Use pronouns in the proper position when possible. Then listen and repeat as the speaker gives the correct answer. Check the spelling of the verbs in the Answer Key.

Modelo: You hear: ¿Traigo el contrato?
You see: Sí / traer
You say: *Sí, tráigalo.*

1. no / comenzar / con estos expedientes
2. buscar / los nombres de los planes de seguro médico
3. no / venir / a las ocho
4. sí / pedir
5. no / poner / en el despacho del director
6. sí / almorzar / con nosotros
7. sí / leer
8. no / salir / a las 5:00

11-40 Las entrevistas. Respond to each statement or question that you hear with the formal commands for **ustedes** using the cues provided. Fill in any necessary words to complete the sentences. Then listen and repeat as the speaker gives the correct answer.

Modelo: You hear: No sabemos el horario de trabajo.
You see: preguntar / durante / la entrevista
You say: *Pregunten durante la entrevista.*

1. levantarse / 7:00 / mañana
2. vestirse / muy bien
3. hacer / muchas preguntas
4. no / preguntar / hasta / la entrevista final
5. escribir / carta dándoles las gracias por la entrevista

Nombre: ______________________ Fecha: ______________________

3. The subjunctive and the indicative with adverbial conjunctions

11-41 ¡Siempre hay condiciones! Form sentences for each statement that you hear using the cues provided. Then listen and repeat as the speaker gives the correct answer.

MODELO: You hear: Vamos a trabajar para esta empresa.
You see: con tal de que / nos / ofrecer / un plan de retiro
You say: *Vamos a trabajar para esta empresa con tal de que nos ofrezcan un plan de retiro.*

1. a menos que / la compañía / pagar / muy poco
2. porque / ser / los mejores empleados
3. para que / poder / estudiar por la mañana
4. tan pronto como / terminar / las cartas
5. cuando / empezar / la reunión
6. antes de que / llenar / la solicitud
7. aunque / hoy / ser / sábado

11-42 ¿Cuándo? Answer the questions that you hear, based on the cues provided. Include direct object pronouns in your answers when possible. Then listen and repeat as the speaker gives the correct answer.

MODELO: You hear: ¿Cuándo ascienden a los empleados?
You see: ascender / luego que / les / dar / una evaluación positiva
You say: *Los ascienden luego que les den una evaluación positiva.*

1. ir a apagar / cuando / llegar
2. reparar / cuando / tener / problemas
3. ir a ver / si hay / antes de que / llenar / la solicitud
4. llevar / cuando / estar / enfermo
5. no deber dejar / sin que / encontrar / otro trabajo
6. ir a estar / en cuanto / empezar / el año fiscal
7. querer jubilarse / hasta que / tener / 62 años

Nombre: ______________________ Fecha: ______________________

11-43 ¿Cierto o incierto? Listen to the following sentences, and indicate whether the speaker is conveying certainty or uncertainty by placing a check mark in the appropriate column.

	CERTAINTY	UNCERTAINTY
1.		
2.		
3.		
4.		
5.		
6.		

¿Cuánto sabes tú?

11-44 Puestos y beneficios. Complete the following chart as you listen to the descriptions of people and their jobs.

NOMBRE	TRABAJA A COMISIÓN	SUELDO FIJO	PLAN DE RETIRO	SEGURO MÉDICO	BONIFICACIÓN ANUAL
ESTEBAN					
LEONARDO					
CARLOS					
SUSANA					

11-45 Preguntas personales. Write an appropriate response to the questions or statements that you hear. Because answers will vary, compare your answers to the answers that are provided. Then read your response to practice communication and pronunciation.

1. ______________________
2. ______________________
3. ______________________
4. ______________________
5. ______________________
6. ______________________
7. ______________________
8. ______________________

Nombre: ______________________ Fecha: ______________________

12 El futuro es tuyo

Workbook

PRIMERA PARTE

¡Así es la vida!

12-1 El impacto de la tecnología. Reread the discussion in **¡Así es la vida!** on page 398 of your textbook and answer the following questions.

1. ¿Quién es Lorenzo Valdespino?

   a. profesor de tecnología b. estudiante de ingeniería c. analista de sistemas

2. ¿Por qué no podría trabajar él sin la computadora?

   a. porque no sabe b. por su trabajo c. por sus estudios

3. ¿Qué usa Lorenzo en casa?

   a. la Red informática b. el correo electrónico c. una impresora láser

4. ¿Cómo revolucionó la tecnología el trabajo en la oficina de Hortensia?

   a. mejoró la comunicación b. les dio más trabajo c. cambiaron de oficina

5. ¿Qué usan para enviar un mensaje urgente?

   a. un procesador de textos b. el correo electrónico c. la videoconferencia

6. ¿Qué tecnología permite a Hortensia comunicarse en persona?

   a. el fax b. el correo electrónico c. la videoconferencia

7. Según Hortensia, ¿qué les permite la tecnología?

   a. ahorrar tiempo y recursos b. ganar más dinero c. tener más vacaciones

8. ¿Quién es Adolfo Martínez Suárez?

   a. abogado b. ingeniero c. agricultor

9. ¿Para qué usa él un programa de computadora?

   a. para sembrar b. para analizar el suelo c. para regar

10. ¿Qué ha revolucionado la producción agrícola?

   a. el clima b. la ingeniería biotécnica c. los medios de comunicación

¡Así lo decimos! Vocabulario

12-2 Palabras relacionadas. Match each of the following verbs with the most logical noun.

_____ 1. sembrar	a. el contestador automático
_____ 2. fotocopiar	b. la videograbadora
_____ 3. grabar	c. la computadora
_____ 4. programar	d. la pantalla
_____ 5. encender	e. la impresora
_____ 6. transmitir	f. los cultivos
_____ 7. llamar	g. la fotocopiadora
_____ 8. imprimir	h. el fax

Nombre: ______________________ Fecha: ______________________

12-3 ¡A completar! Complete the following statements with words or expressions from the word bank.

antena parabólica	grabar	lector de DVD	procesador de textos
cajero automático	hacer a mano	maquinaria	Red informática
contestador automático	hoja electrónica	pantalla	teléfono inalámbrico
finca	imprimir		

1. El banco está cerrado, pero puedo usar el ______________ para sacar dinero.
2. Hoy no es necesario esperar las llamadas telefónicas, porque el ______________ puede ______________ todos los mensajes.
3. Yo acabo de comprar un ______________ y me gusta mucho. Puedo hablar con mis amigos desde el jardín.
4. A mi esposo le gusta mucho la ______________, porque puede ver muchos partidos que no se transmiten por los canales.
5. La ______________ nos permite conectarnos con todo el mundo.
6. Para escribir mis trabajos universitarios, tengo que usar un______________.
7. A mí me gusta mucho el ______________, porque ahora ya no es necesario ir al cine para ver una película.
8. Mi amigo es agricultor. Trabaja en la ______________ de su padre.
9. Con la imporesora, podemos ______________ documentos.
10. No lo pude ver en la ______________ de mi microcomputadora.

Nombre: ______________________ Fecha: ______________________

12-4 La computadora y sus accesorios. Identify each numbered item in the following picture. Then write sentences, using the words for the items you identified.

1. ____

____

2. ____

____

3. ____

____

4. ____

____

5. ____

____

6. ____

____

Nombre: ______________________ Fecha: ______________________

12-5 El altar de la tecnología. Read the following advertisement. Then answer the questions with complete sentences in Spanish.

1. ¿Qué equipos electrónicos se venden?

   a. computadoras b. televisores c. estéreos

2. ¿Qué se puede hacer por 500 dólares?

   a. montar un altar multimedia

   b. comprar un Pentium III

   c. convertir la computadora con Pentium MMX

3. ¿Cómo se puede recibir un regalo?

   a. gastando 500 dólares

   b. visitando la estación Multimedia

   c. llamando por teléfono

4. Además de un regalo, ¿qué otras cosa ofrece la tienda?

   a. descuentos b. garantía de tres años c. servicio de reparación a domicilio

5. ¿Cómo se llama la tienda?

   a. Pentium III b. Altar de la tecnología c. HP, Epson

Nombre: ______________________ Fecha: ______________________

¡Así lo hacemos! Estructuras

1. The past participle and the present perfect indicative

12-6 ¿Qué han hecho estas personas? Write an affirmative answer that might be given as a response to the following questions. Use object pronouns to avoid repetition, when necessary.

MODELO: ¿Has apagado la computadora?
Sí, la he apagado.

1. ¿Has fotocopiado la carta?

   Sí, ____.

2. ¿Han instalado la antena parabólica?

   Sí, ____.

3. ¿Ha calculado las cuentas el contador?

   Sí, ____.

4. ¿Has archivado los documentos?

   Sí, ____.

5. ¿Han sembrado ustedes tomates este año?

   Sí, ____.

Nombre: ______________________ Fecha: ______________________

12-7 Hay muchas cosas que hacer. Tell what the following people have already done today. Use the subjects and the present perfect of the verbs in the cues provided, and answer in complete sentences.

Modelo: Francisco / conectarse / a la Red informática
Francisco se ha conectado a la Red informácia.

1. nosotros / archivar / los documentos en el disquete

____

2. Fernando / programar / la computadora

____

3. yo / borrar / los archivos del disco duro

____

4. Felipe / imprimir / los documentos

____

5. mis amigos / ir / al despacho

____

6. yo / escuchar / los mensajes del contestador automático

____

7. ¿tú / encender / la impresora?

____

8. nosotros / comprar / el teléfono móvil

____

12-8 En la empresa. Your boss is telling you the things that need to be done. Respond in complete sentences, following the model.

Modelo: Tiene que enviarle un correo electrónico al programador de computadoras.
Se lo he enviado. Ya está enviado.

1. Tiene que darle el disquete a la señorita Muñoz.

____

2. Tiene que guardar el documento en la base de datos.

____

3. Tiene que instalar el nuevo programa de contabilidad (*accounting*) al contador.

____

4. Tiene que pedirme un ratón nuevo para mi computadora.

____

5. Tiene que hacer una búsqueda en la Red informática para el señor Ortiz.

____

12-9 ¡Hecho! Complete the following sentences with the past participle of the verbs in parentheses. Make agreement changes, when necessary.

1. La impresora está (romper) ______________.
2. El cajero automático está (abrir) ______________.
3. El diseño de la página electrónica está (hacer) ______________.
4. Los correos electrónicos están (escribir) ______________.
5. El archivo está (poner) ______________ en el disco duro.
6. El disquete está (llenar) ______________.
7. El fax está (enviar) ______________.
8. La videograbadora está (programar) ______________.
9. José Luis no sabe nada de informática; está (perder) ______________.
10. La hoja electrónica está en blanco; no hay nada (escribir) ______________.

Nombre: ______________________ Fecha: ______________________

2. The future and the future of probability

12-10 En el centro de cómputo. You are the director of the computer center at your institution. Here is what everyone is going to do. Fill in the blanks in the following sentences, using the future tense. Follow the model.

Modelo: Gregorio va a usar el escáner.
Gregorio usará el escáner.

1. Rosalía va a hacer los diseños en la computadora.

   Rosalía ______________ los diseños en la computadora.

2. Manuel Antonio va a imprimir las cartas.

   Manuel Antonio ______________ las cartas.

3. José y Alejandro van a instalar el disco duro.

   José y Alejandro ______________ el disco duro.

4. Tú vas a poner la información en la hoja electrónica.

   Tú ______________ la información el la hoja electrónica.

5. Luisa y yo vamos a mirar la pantalla.

   Luisa y yo ______________ la pantalla.

6. Todos nosotros vamos a leer los mensajes en el correo electrónico.

   Todos nosotros ______________ los mensajes en el correo electrónico.

7. Francisco y Emilio van a venir a ver el procesador de textos.

   Francisco y Emilio ______________ a ver el procesador de textos.

8. Nuestros asistentes les van a dar las instrucciones.

   Nuestros asistentes les ______________ las instrucciones.

9. Carmen y su hermana van a archivar todo.

   Carmen y su hermana ______________ todo.

Nombre: ______________________ Fecha: ______________________

12-11 En la oficina. Imagine that you work at an office. Tell what type of work each person is going to do, using the correct form of the future tense of the verbs in parentheses.

1. Joaquín (escribir) ______________ cartas en el procesador de textos.
2. Ramiro y Arturo (poner) ______________ las cuentas en la hoja electrónica.
3. Ella le (decir) ______________ a la supervisora si hay mensajes de correo electrónico.
4. María Amalia (leer) ______________ un fax.
5. Juan y tú (sacar) ______________ copias en la fotocopiadora.
6. Yo (usar) ______________ el escáner.
7. Ustedes (buscar) ______________ la información en la Red informática.
8. La directora (comunicarse) ______________ con los clientes por teléfono móvil.
9. Enrique y yo (ver) ______________ los diseños en la pantalla.
10. Todos nosotros (preparar) ______________ los trabajos en la computadora.

12-12 Mi amiga y yo. Change the present tense forms of the verbs in parentheses to the future tense to read about two friends and their plans for the future.

Mi amiga Gertrudis y yo (1. asistimos) ______________ a la universidad. Gertrudis (2. toma) ______________ cursos de informática. Yo solamente (3. tomo) ______________ clases de lenguas extranjeras. Ella (4. aprende) ______________ a hacer diseños en la computadora. Yo sólo (5. quiero) ______________ aprender a usar la Red informática. Gertrudis y sus otras amigas (6. van) ______________ a las clases por la mañana. Yo (7. tengo) ______________ que ir por la noche. (8. Nos divertimos) ______________ mucho en la universidad. ¿Qué (9. estudias) ______________ tú en la universidad?

Nombre: ______________________________ Fecha: ______________________

12-13 La nueva jefa. Imagine that the new boss is a very demanding person. Here is what she expects everyone to do by a certain time. Use the future form of the verbs in parentheses.

1. Todos nosotros (llegar) ________________ al trabajo a las ocho de la mañana.
2. La programadora (hacer) ________________ los diseños a las nueve.
3. Tú (traer) ________________ las hojas electrónicas a las diez.
4. Ella (llamar) ________________ a los clientes antes de las diez y media.
5. Ustedes (poner) ________________ el informe sobre el escritorio a las once.
6. La secretaria (imprimir) ________________ las cartas a las doce.
7. Los supervisores (tener) ________________ la información a las doce y media.
8. Todos los empleados (almorzar) ________________ antes de la una.
9. Tú (tener) ________________ la lista de clientes en la pantalla a las tres.
10. Todos los empleados (salir) ________________ del trabajo antes de las cinco.

12-14 Conjeturas. Imagine that you and your friends are going to have a new boss at the office. Answer the following questions, using the future of probability. Be creative.

1. ¿Quién será el nuevo jefe?

   ____

2. ¿Cómo será él/ella?

   ____

3. ¿De dónde vendrá?

   ____

4. ¿Qué planes tendrá?

   ____

5. ¿Qué hará con los empleados?

   ____

Nombre: ______________________ Fecha: ______________________

SEGUNDA PARTE

¡Así es la vida!

12-15 Hablan los jóvenes. Reread the opinions of the people in **¡Así es la vida!** on page 415 of your textbook, and indicate whether the following sentences are **cierto (C)** or **falso (F).**

C F 1. A los jóvenes de Hispanoamérica no les importa el medio ambiente.

C F 2. No hay mucha industria en estos países.

C F 3. Los gobiernos de estos países se han preocupado mucho por proteger los recursos naturales.

Liliana Haya Sandoval

C F 4. La contaminación del aire no es un problema en la Ciudad de México.

C F 5. Los carros y los camiones producen mucha contaminación.

C F 6. Respirar el aire de la Ciudad de México no causa problemas.

C F 7. El gobierno no toma las medidas necesarias para resolver el problema de la contaminación.

María Isabel Cifuentes Betancourt

C F 8. El problema de las enfermedades epidémicas no existe en América del Sur.

C F 9. La contaminación del agua causa el cólera.

C F 10. No hay organizaciones internacionales ayudando a combatir este problema.

Fernanda Sánchez Bustamante

C F 11. Un problema importante en Costa Rica es la pérdida de los árboles.

C F 12. Hoy el 50% del país está cubierto de bosques tropicales.

C F 13. La producción de oxígeno depende de la región tropical.

Nombre: ______________________ Fecha: ______________________

¡Así lo decimos! Vocabulario

12-16 ¡A escribir! Write a complete sentence that shows the meaning of each of the following vocabulary words from the word bank.

atmósfera	desecho	escasez	lluvia ácida
contaminación	energía	fábrica	medio ambiente

1. ______________________________
2. ______________________________
3. ______________________________
4. ______________________________
5. ______________________________
6. ______________________________
7. ______________________________
8. ______________________________

12-17 ¡A completar! Fill in the blanks to complete each of the following statements with a word or expression from the word bank.

conservar	consumir	dispuestos	escasez	medida	multa
naturaleza	radioactividad	reciclaje	reciclar	reforestación	

1. En vez de arrojar todos los desechos, hay que organizar un programa de ______________.
2. Si una fábrica no obedece bien las leyes contra la contaminación, hay que ponerle una ______________.
3. El agua, el aire y las selvas forman parte de la ______________.
4. Si hay muy poco de alguna cosa, se dice que hay ______________ de esa cosa.
5. Según muchos, la gente de los EE.UU. tiene que aprender a ______________ menos y a ______________ más.

6. Si la deforestación es un problema, hay que empezar un programa de ______________.
7. Si se escapa la ______________ de una planta nuclear, puede contaminar el aire.
8. Para ______________ más, la ciudad de Seattle decidió empezar un programa enorme de reciclaje.
9. Los miembros del comité están______________ a escuchar nuevas soluciones.
10. La ______________ para controlar la deforestación es multar a las organizaciones que destruyan los bosques.

12-18 Cuestionario. What are your thoughts about the environment and how it can be improved? Answer the following questions with complete sentences in Spanish.

1. ¿Cuál es el problema más grave que afecta al medio ambiente?

____

2. ¿Qué soluciones puedes ofrecer?

____

3. ¿Cómo se pueden proteger los bosques y las selvas tropicales?

____

4. ¿Qué prefieres, desarrollar la energía solar o continuar con las plantas nucleares? ¿Por qué?

____

5. ¿En qué circunstancias se debe poner una multa a una industria?

____

Nombre: ______________________ Fecha: ______________________

¡Así lo hacemos! Estructuras

3. The conditional and the conditional of probability

12-19 Las promesas del gobierno. Find out what the government promised they would do in the new millenium by writing the conditional form of the verbs in parentheses.

1. El gobierno prometió que (estudiar) ______________ los efectos de la lluvia ácida.
2. El gobierno prometió que (controlar) ______________ la emisión de humo de los carros.
3. El gobierno prometió que (haber) ______________ más medidas contra la contaminación del aire.
4. El gobierno prometió que (multar) ______________ a las industrias contaminantes.
5. El gobierno prometió que (proteger) ______________ las especies animales en peligro de extinción.
6. El gobierno prometió que (establecer) ______________ programas de reciclaje.
7. El gobierno prometió que (plantar) ______________ más árboles en los parques.
8. El gobierno prometió que (poner) ______________ más basureros en las ciudades.
9. El gobierno prometió que (empezar) ______________ la reforestación de los bosques.
10. El gobierno prometió que (administrar) ______________ mejor los recursos naturales.

12-20 La reportera. Mariluz is a television reporter who is concerned about environmental issues. Here is her interview with Roberto, a citizen with the same concerns. Complete the following exchange with the correct conditional form of the verbs in parentheses.

Mariluz: Roberto, ¿qué (1. hacer) ______________ usted para mejorar el medio ambiente en la ciudad?

Roberto: Primero, les (2. informar) ______________ a los ciudadanos de los principales problemas.

Mariluz: ¿De qué problemas (3. hablar) ______________ ?

Roberto: Les (4. explicar) ______________ el problema de la deforestación y la contaminación del aire.

Mariluz: ¿Qué soluciones (5. buscar) ______________ para estos problemas?

Roberto: (6. Promocionar) ______________ un programa de reciclaje en toda la ciudad.

Mariluz: ¿Cómo (7. ser) ______________ este programa?

Roberto: (8. Poner) ______________ basureros para diferentes tipos de basura por toda la ciudad.

Mariluz: ¿Qué (9. sugerir) ______________ usted para solucionar la contaminación del aire?

Roberto: Los ciudadanos (10. deber) ______________ usar más el transporte público.

12-21 Una campaña. Complete the following paragraph with the correct conditional form of the verbs in parentheses.

Roberto y Aurelio, ¿(1. querer) ______________ colaborar conmigo en la campaña "Ciudad Verde"? Nosotros (2. salir) ______________ de mi casa a las ocho y (3. llegar) ______________ al parque a las ocho y media. Nosotros (4. plantar) ______________ tres árboles y (5. ayudar) ______________ a mejorar el aire de la ciudad. Roberto y yo (6. comprar) ______________ los árboles y los (7. llevar) ______________ al parque. (8. Estar) ______________ en el parque por dos horas y luego todos nosotros (9. volver) ______________ a casa a las once.

Nombre: ______________________ Fecha: ______________________

12-22 ¿Qué pasó? The mayor that you were about to interview for your show never arrived for the interview. What happened? Offer excuses to your viewers, using the conditional of probability.

Modelo: olvidarse de la fecha
Él se olvidaría de la fecha.

1. no saber la hora

____

2. tener problemas con su coche

____

3. ir a otra entrevista

____

4. perder la dirección

____

5. entender mal a la secretaria

____

6. estar enfermo

____

12-23 La lotería. Imagine that you have bought a lottery ticket. Write six things you would do with the money if you won the jackpot.

Modelo: *Compraría un carro nuevo.*

1. ____
2. ____
3. ____
4. ____
5. ____
6. ____

4. *Tú* commands

12-24 Mandatos a tu hermano. You are giving your younger brother some tips on how to protect the environment. Complete each of the following statements with the **tú** command form of the verbs in parentheses.

1. (Reciclar) ______________________ todo el papel.
2. (Proteger) ______________________ la naturaleza.
3. (Poner) ______________________ la basura en el basurero.
4. (Comprar) ______________________ productos reciclables.
5. No (arrojar) ______________________ basura al río.
6. (Pedirles) ______________________ a tus amigos que reciclen.
7. No (empeorar) ______________________ la contaminación del aire.
8. No (cortar) ______________________ árboles en el bosque.

12-25 Mandatos informáticos. You are at your new job, and a colleague is teaching you how to use the computer. Fill in the blanks by changing each infinitive in parentheses to the **tú** command form of the verb.

1. (Encender) ______________________ la computadora.
2. (Escribir) ______________________ la contraseña (*password*).
3. (Buscar) ______________________ el documento.
4. No (imprimir) ______________________ el archivo.
5. (Archivar) ______________________ el documento en el disco duro.
6. (Borrar) ______________________ el documento del disquete.
7. No (borrar) ______________________ el documento del disco duro.
8. (Enviarle) ______________________ el documento al jefe por correo electrónico.
9. (Poner) ______________________ una copia del documento en mi escrotorio.
10. No (apagar) ______________________ la computadora.

Nombre: ______________________ Fecha: ______________________

12-26 Mandatos para todos. La señora Rivera is the manager of the office staff. She likes to assign tasks to all employees to keep them busy. Rewrite each command, replacing the direct object noun with a direct object pronoun.

Modelo: Margarita, enciende las computadoras.
Enciéndelas.

1. Pepe, instala los programas. ______________________.
2. Juan, compra más disquetes. ______________________.
3. Pablo, haz las fotocopias. ______________________.
4. Lupe, contesta el teléfono. ______________________.
5. Toño, atiende a los clientes. ______________________.
6. Felipe, busca información en la Red informática. ______________________.
7. Alicia, programa la videograbadora. ______________________.
8. Gabriel, imprime las cuentas del mes. ______________________.
9. Mario, escribe el informe. ______________________.
10. Enriqueta, lleva las cuentas bien. ______________________.

Nuestro mundo

Panoramas

12-27 ¡A informarse! Based on the information from **Nuestro mundo** on pages 426–427 of your textbook, decide if the following statements are **cierto (C)** or **falso (F)**.

1. Hay más de 37 millones de hispanos en los EE.UU.
2. Los EE.UU. es la quinta nación hispanohablante.
3. La televisión en los EE.UU. es sólo en inglés.
4. Los murales méxicoamericanos sirven como conexión entre el pasado y el presente.
5. Juanishi Orosco es un muralista méxicoamericano.
6. No hay representación hispana en los deportes de los EE.UU.
7. Gloria Estefan es de origen cubano.

Nombre: ______________________ Fecha: ______________________

8. Cheech Marín es conocido por su talento musical.

9. Esmeralda Santiago es una actriz puertorriqueña.

10. Ningún atleta de origen hispano ha ganado nunca una medalla para los EE.UU.

12-28 Tu propia experiencia. Think of a traditional Hispanic festivity that is celebrated in your community or of an Hispanic festivity of which you have heard. Describe the celebration, and use the Internet and library to research its origin.

____

____

____

____

____

Taller

12-29 Mis acciones

Primera fase. You may not feel like an activist for the environment, but even the most ordinary citizen does more out of habit to protect the environment than the average citizen did twenty-five to thirty years ago. Make a list, in Spanish, of the environmentally friendly things that you do now. (The **sí** and **no** columns will be used in the **Segunda fase.**)

	SÍ	NO
______________________________	____	____
______________________________	____	____
______________________________	____	____
______________________________	____	____
______________________________	____	____
______________________________	____	____
______________________________	____	____

Segunda fase. Now review each activity from the **Primera fase,** and mark whether or not someone your age would have done those things twenty-five to thirty years ago. If possible, interview someone who could tell you.

Nombre: ______________________ Fecha: ______________________

12-30 Centros de reciclaje. Environmentally friendly movements are catching on in many different parts of the world. Use your Internet search engine to look up **reciclaje.** Make a list, in Spanish, of at least five programs you find in the U.S., Canada, and Spanish-speaking countries. Include information on what the program does or is for in Spanish.

PROGRAMA: ______________________ PAÍS/CIUDAD: ______________________

PRODUCTOS/SERVICIOS: ______________________

____

____

____

PROGRAMA: ______________________ PAÍS/CIUDAD: ______________________

PRODUCTOS/SERVICIOS: ______________________

____

____

____

PROGRAMA: ______________________ PAÍS/CIUDAD: ______________________

PRODUCTOS/SERVICIOS: ______________________

____

____

____

PROGRAMA: ______________________ PAÍS/CIUDAD: ______________________

PRODUCTOS/SERVICIOS: ______________________

____

____

____

Nombre: ______________________ Fecha: ______________________

PROGRAMA: ______________________ PAÍS/CIUDAD: ______________________

PRODUCTOS/SERVICIOS: ______________________

____

____

____

12-31 Más allá de las páginas: Los barrios latinos. Many residents of urban developments work to revitalize neighborhoods, such as the neighborhood in which the narrator of *La casa en Mango Street* lives. They try to instill pride and cultural identity through murals and community projects and through physical improvements to housing, museums, and parks. Look up Hispanic neighborhoods in larger cities by using the Internet or library resources. Many of these barrios have Web sites. Find at least two neighborhoods, and make a list, in Spanish, of things that the residents are doing to revitalize their community.

LA CIUDAD: ______________________ EL BARRIO: ______________________

____

____

____

____

____

LA CIUDAD: ______________________ EL BARRIO: ______________________

____

____

____

____

____

Nombre: ______________________ Fecha: ______________________

¿Cuánto sabes tú?

12-32 ¿Sabes usar el participio pasado? Fill in the blanks with the past participles of the verbs in parentheses to express actions that have already been done.

1. La impresora ya está (encender) ______________.
2. Los documentos ya están (imprimir) ______________.
3. Los nuevos programas ya están (instalar) ______________.
4. El nuevo contestador automático ya está (conectar) ______________.
5. La computadora está (romper) ______________.
6. Los documentos ya están (archivar) ______________ en el disquete.

12-33 ¿Sabes usar el presente perfecto? Fill in the blanks with the present perfect form of the verbs in parentheses.

1. Mariano ya (estudiar) ______________ para el examen.
2. ¿(Ver) tú ______________ la última película de Andy García?
3. Nosotros (acabar) ______________ el trabajo.
4. ¿(Tomar) usted ______________ alguna vez clases de informática?
5. Luciano y Mariana nunca (escribir) ______________ a máquina; siempre lo (hacer) ______________ todo con la computadora.

12-34 ¿Sabes usar el futuro? Fill in the blanks with the appropriate future form of the verbs in parentheses.

La próxima semana Julián y Rosa (1. ir) ______________ a una conferencia sobre el medio ambiente en San Antonio. Ellos (2. reservar) ______________ una habitación en el centro de la ciudad y (3. visitar) ______________ la hermosa ciudad tejana. Yo (4. estar) ______________ en San Antonio también, aunque no (5. asistir) ______________ a la conferencia. Nosotros (6. cenar) ______________ juntos el sábado por la noche y (7. llamar) ______________ a unos amigos nuestros que viven en San Antonio para que cenen con nosotros.

Nombre: ______________________ Fecha: ______________________

12-35 ¿Sabes usar el condicional? Fill in the blanks with the appropriate conditional form of the verbs in parentheses.

Si yo fuera presidente del gobierno, (1. reducir) ______________ los impuestos de los ciudadanos y les (2. poner) ______________ más multas a las industrias más contaminantes. También, (3. controlar) ______________ el proceso de deforestación de los bosques y (4. plantar) ______________ más árboles en las ciudades para mejorar la calidad del aire. Si mi amigo Pedro fuera presidente, él (5. educar) ______________ a la gente sobre el medio ambiente y (6. combatir) ______________ los efectos de la lluvia ácida. Si uno de los dos, Pedro o yo, fuera presidente, el mundo (7. ser) ______________ un lugar mejor para todos.

12-36 ¿Sabes expresar probabilidad? Read the following conversation between Mario and Rubén. Then decide whether to use the conditional or the future form of the verbs in parentheses to express probability.

Mario: ¿Dónde está mi disquete?

Rubén: No sé. (1. Estará/Estaría) ______________ en tu escritorio.

Mario: ¿Qué hora es?

Rubén: (2. Serían/Serán) ______________ las dos.

Rubén: ¿Dónde está hoy la jefa?

Mario: (3. Estará/Estaría) ______________ enferma.

(4.Trabajará/Trabajaría) ______________ hasta tarde anoche.

Rubén: ¿Qué hizo la jefa anoche?

Mario: No sé. (5. Repasará/Repasaría) ______________ las cuentas e

(6. instalará/instalaría) ______________ el nuevo programa en su computadora.

12-37 ¿Sabes usar los mandatos informales? Fill in the blanks with the **tú** command form of the verbs in parentheses.

1. (Escribir) ______________ los informes.
2. (Escuchar) ______________ a tu supervisor.
3. No (jugar) ______________ con la computadora.
4. No (llamar) ______________ con mi teléfono móvil.
5. (Usar) ______________ el teléfono inalámbrico de tu oficina.
6. No (irse) ______________ tarde de la oficina.

Nombre: ______________________ Fecha: ______________

Lab Manual

PRIMERA PARTE

¡Así es la vida!

12-38 ¿Por qué lo necesitas? As you listen to the following conversation, select the letters for all statements that are correct, according to what you hear. Listen to the conversation as many times as is necessary to find all the correct answers.

1. Catalina quiere...
   a. una calculadora.
   b. un procesador de textos.
   c. una computadora y una impresora.
2. La mamá cree que Catalina...
   a. no necesita una computadora.
   b. necesita una pantalla grande.
   c. no necesita una impresora.
3. Catalina...
   a. es estudiante.
   b. programa computadoras.
   c. diseña juegos electrónicos.
4. El precio que sale en la revista es...
   a. diecinueve mil pesos.
   b. veintidós mil pesos.
   c. veinte mil pesos.
5. El precio incluye...
   a. una videograbadora con pantalla grande.
   b. una computadora y una impresora.
   c. suficiente memoria.
6. La madre está enojada porque se rompió...
   a. la videograbadora.
   b. el teléfono inalámbrico.
   c. el contestador automático.
7. Por suerte Santiago puede arreglar...
   a. el fax.
   b. el teléfono.
   c. la videograbadora.

Nombre: ______________________ Fecha: ______________________

¡Así lo decimos! Vocabulario

12-39 Escoge la tecnología. Listen to the following sentences, and select the letter corresponding to the word or phrase that best completes each sentence. Then listen and repeat as the speaker gives the correct answer.

1. a. el contestador automático
   b. el cajero automático
   c. el teclado
2. a. los juegos electrónicos
   b. los faxes
   c. los discos duros
3. a. los télefonos móviles
   b. hipervínculos
   c. DVD
4. a. la finca
   b. la pantalla
   c. la marca
5. a. apagada
   b. instalada
   c. borrada

¡Así lo hacemos! Estructuras

1. The past participle and the present perfect indicative

12-40 ¿Ya lo han hecho? Tell what the following people have done using the cues provided. Then listen and repeat as the speaker gives the correct answer.

MODELO: You see: yo / instalar / el nuevo procesador de palabras
You say: *Yo he instalado el nuevo procesador de palabras.*

1. Camila / programar / el telófono móvil
2. Josefina y Margarita / ir / a la tienda de computadoras
3. nosotros / archivar / los documentos
4. tú / comprar / un ratón nuevo
5. yo / apagar / el escáner
6. ustedes / grabar / la película

Nombre: ______________________ Fecha: ______________________

12-41 ¿Qué hemos hecho hoy? Change the following sentences to the present perfect. Then listen and repeat as the speaker gives the correct answer.

Modelo: You see: Luisa y yo fuimos a fotocopiar los documentos.
You say: *Luisa y yo hemos ido a fotocopiar los documentos.*

1. Yo no dije nada.
2. Tú escribiste el programa.
3. Nosotros fuimos a comprar un juego electrónico.
4. Por fin volvieron sus clientes.
5. Paco y Raúl vieron la hoja electrónica.
6. El abuelo de Isabel murió.
7. Ustedes pusieron la información en el disquete.
8. Pablo y yo hicimos el trabajo.

12-42 ¿Cómo están las cosas? Form sentences using the cues provided. Then listen and repeat as the speaker gives the correct answer.

Modelo: You see: las ventanas / abrir
You say: *Las ventanas están abiertas.*

1. los ratones / instalar / correctamente
2. la videograbadora / programar
3. estos juegos electrónicos / romper
4. el DVD / poner / en el lector
5. las hojas electrónicas / archivar

12-43 Todo ya está hecho. Respond affirmatively to the following questions, using the past participles and **ya** (*already*) to say that these things have already been done. Then listen and repeat as the speaker gives the correct answer.

Modelo: You see: ¿Escribiste las cartas?
You say: *Sí, ya están escritas.*

1. ¿Hiciste las hojas electrónicas?
2. ¿Compraste la pantalla que buscabas?
3. ¿Apagaste el escáner?
4. ¿Cubriste los teclados también?
5. ¿Pusiste los DVD en el lector?

2. The future and the future of probability

12-44 ¿Cúando harán eso? Form sentences using the future tense of the verbs and the cues provided. Then listen and repeat as the speaker gives the correct answer.

Modelo: You see: ustedes / hablar / esta tarde
You say: *Ustedes hablarán esta tarde.*

1. yo / ir / al Perú el año que viene
2. tú / buscar / un escáner nuevo / mañana
3. nosotros / grabar / la película / esta noche
4. ellos / repartir / las cartas / antes del mediodía
5. usted / encender / las computadoras / por la mañana

12-45 En el futuro... Form questions in the future tense using the cues provided. Then listen and repeat as the speaker gives the correct answer.

Modelo: You see: (yo) poner / dinero / en el banco
You say: *¿Pondré el dinero en el banco?*

1. (ellos) querer / manejar / solos
2. venir / mis padres / esta noche
3. cuánto / valer / la pantalla
4. haber / computadoras / allí
5. (tú) tener que comprar / más memoria
6. (nosotros) saber / cómo apagar / la fotocopiadora
7. (yo) poder / instalarlo / mañana
8. (ella) hacer / unos diseños originales
9. (ellos) le decir / la información por teléfono
10. (tú) poner / el escáner

Nombre: ______________________ Fecha: ______________________

12-46 ¿Qué pasará? Answer the questions that you hear using the future tense to express probability. Then listen and repeat as the speaker gives the correct answer.

1. 4:30
2. veinte años
3. ocho euros
4. treinta personas
5. ninguna computadora
6. 9:15

SEGUNDA PARTE

¡Así es la vida!

12-47 Ahora en el programa "Tiempo nuevo"... As you listen to the following interview, select the letters for all statements that are correct, according to what you hear. Listen to the interview as many times as is necessary to find all the correct answers.

1. El tema de la semana es...
   a. "Tiempo nuevo".
   b. el medio ambiente.
   c. la energía.
2. El invitado al programa es...
   a. un especialista en el medio ambiente.
   b. un asesor de energía.
   c. un político de un partido.
3. El doctor Olivares quiere...
   a. consumir los recursos naturales.
   b. gastar dinero en la protección del ambiente.
   c. depositar desechos radioactivos en lugares especiales.
4. El doctor Olivares piensa resolver el problema de energía...
   a. creando parques nacionales.
   b. utilizando la energía nuclear.
   c. con el petróleo.

Nombre: ______________________________ Fecha: ______________________

5. Según el doctor Olivares, la energía nuclear...

   a. produce más contaminación que la energía del petróleo.

   b. es más limpia que la energía que se obtiene del petróleo.

   c. es tan sucia como la energía que se obtiene del petróleo.

6. Las sugerencias del doctor Olivares son...

   a. multar a las fábricas que arrojen desechos a la naturaleza.

   b. aumentar la desforestación.

   c. emprender un programa de uso racional de los recursos.

¡Así lo decimos! Vocabulario

12-48 ¿Cuál es la mejor respuesta? Listen to the following sentences, and select the letter corresponding to the word or phrase that best completes each sentence. Then listen and repeat as the speaker gives the correct answer.

1. a. multa

   b. energía

   c. naturaleza

2. a. la radioactividad

   b. el aire

   c. la atmósfera

3. a. deforestación

   b. medida

   c. reciclaje

4. a. las fábricas

   b. la atmósfera

   c. los recursos naturales

5. a. aumenta la contaminación

   b. protege la planta nuclear

   c. conserva los recursos naturales

Nombre: ______________________ Fecha: ______________________

¡Así lo hacemos! Estructuras

3. The conditional and the conditional of probability

12-49 Las esperanzas para un mundo mejor. Form sentences using the verbs in the conditional tense and the cues provided. Then listen and repeat as the speaker gives the correct answer.

Modelo: You see: nosotros / no contaminar / el agua
You say: *Nosotros no contaminaríamos el agua.*

1 yo / reciclar / los periódicos

2. ustedes / saber / más sobre la lluvia ácida

3. los senadores / estar / dispuestos a ayudar

4. nosotros / mejorar / la protección del medio ambiente

5. tú /no arrojar / basura en la calle

6. mi ciudad / tener / menos contaminación

12-50 No había tiempo... Form complete sentences using the cues provided. Follow the model. Then listen and repeat as the speaker gives the correct answer.

Modelo: You see: Paco / prometernos / él / estudiar / más
You say: *Paco nos prometió que él estudiaría más.*

1. Juan / decirme / ir / a la sierra

2. yo / creer / las fábricas / poder / producir menos humo

3. Ana / decirnos / ella y Raúl / conservar / energía

4. mi esposo y yo / decidir / (nosotros) hacer / todo lo posible

5. Fernando / decirnos / tú / salir / para la planta nuclear

6. tú / decir / (tú) escribir / una carta de protesta

12-51 ¿Qué harían? Answer the questions based on the cues provided. Use the conditional to express probability, and use direct object pronouns when possible. Then listen and repeat as the speaker gives the correct answer.

1. a las 8:00

2. los empleados de la fábrica

3. programas de reciclaje y protección del medio ambiente

4. en un lugar de reciclaje

5. muchas protestas

4. *Tú* commands

12-52 ¿Qué debo hacer? You are a salesperson at an electronics store. Customers ask for your advice on what they need from the store. Tell the customers what they should and should not do using informal commands and the cues provided. Then listen and repeat as the speaker gives the correct answer.

Modelo: You see: comprar / muchos discos compactos
You say: *Compra muchos discos compactos.*

1. ir / departamento / de música
2. instalar / más memoria
3. no pensar / en el costo de los productos
4. poner / los disquetes en una bolsa plástica
5. no salir / sin comprar nada
6. tener / paciencia con la instalación
7. no pagar / ahora porque tenemos un plan de crédito
8. comparar / los precios de los contestadores automáticos

12-53 Consejos para tu mejor amigo. Your best friend has decided to become more aware of environmental conservation issues, and he asks you questions. Tell your friend whether he should or should not do the following things based on the questions that you hear. Use informal commands and direct object pronouns. Then listen and repeat as the speaker gives the correct answer.

Modelo: You hear: ¿Agua?
You see: conservar
You say: *Consérvala.*
or
You hear: ¿El aire?
You see: no contaminar
You say: *No lo contamines.*

1. arrojar
2. no producir
3. observar
4. implementar
5. no usar
6. hacer
7. conservar
8. no buscar

Nombre: ______________________________ Fecha: ______________________

¿Cuánto sabes tú?

12-54 Para el año próximo... Listen to the statements that you hear and predict what will happen next year. Begin your sentences with **Para el año próximo...,** and make all other necessary changes. Then listen and repeat as the speaker gives the correct answer.

Modelo: You hear: Queremos resolver el problema del desempleo.
You say: *Para el año próximo resolveremos el problema del desempleo.*

1. Para el año próximo...
2. Para el año próximo...
3. Para el año próximo...
4. Para el año próximo...
5. Para el año próximo...

12-55 ¿Qué han hecho para el medio ambiente? Answer the questions that you hear using the cues provided. Then listen and repeat as the speaker gives the correct answer.

Modelo: You hear: ¿Llenaste la solicitud?
You see: tener tiempo
You say: *No, no he tenido tiempo. La llenaré pronto.*

1. lavar las botellas todavía
2. recibir notificación
3. estar en el Perú
4. tener problemas con la planta nuclear

12-56 Preguntas personales. Write an appropriate response to the questions that you hear. Because answers will vary, compare your answers to the answers that are provided. Then read your response to practice communication and pronunciation.

1. ______________________________
2. ______________________________
3. ______________________________
4. ______________________________
5. ______________________________
6. ______________________________

Nombre: ______________________ Fecha: ______________

13 ¿Oíste las noticias?

Workbook

PRIMERA PARTE

¡Así es la vida!

13-1 ¿Recuerdas? Decide if the following statements are **cierto (C)** or **falso (F)**, based on the horoscope in **¡Así es la vida!** on page 436 of your textbook.

C F 1. Los leo no van a tener dificultades en sus relaciones personales.

C F 2. Los escorpio pueden ayudar a sus amigos.

C F 3. Los libra se enfrentan a grandes desafíos.

C F 4. Los acuario deben tener prisa para tomar decisiones.

C F 5. Los sagitario no están cumpliendo en el trabajo.

C F 6. Los piscis deben cumplir sus compromisos.

C F 7. Los aries deben recordar el pasado.

C F 8. Los tauro tienen que descansar.

C F 9. Los géminis deben pedir respeto.

C F 10. Los cáncer deben confiar en sí mismos.

¡Así lo decimos! Vocabulario

13-2 Los medios de comunicación. Write ten logical statements about television and newspapers, using one word from the left column and one word from the right. Use each word at least once.

la comentarista	el certamen
el crítico	el concurso
el lector	la crónica social
el meteorólogo	la emisora
el patrocinador	en directo

Nombre: ______________________________ Fecha: ______________________

el radioyente
la reportera
el televidente
las tiras cómicas
el titular
informar
el noticiero
el periódico
la primera plana
la televisión

1. ____
2. ____
3. ____
4. ____
5. ____
6. ____
7. ____
8. ____
9. ____
10. ____

13-3 Las secciones del periódico. Match the name of the newspaper section you would turn to for each of the following situations.

1. ______ Buscas un trabajo.
2. ______ Buscas el resultado del partido de béisbol.
3. ______ Tienes problemas con tu novio.
4. ______ Quieres ir al cine o al teatro.
5. ______ Deseas saber tu futuro.
6. ______ Necesitas saber la fecha del funeral de una persona.
7. ______ Quieres saber quiénes se casan.
8. ______ Deseas saber la opinión del editor.

a. la esquela
b. el horóscopo
c. el editorial
d. el consultorio sentimental
e. la cartelera
f. la crónica social
g. los anuncios
h. la sección deportiva

Nombre: ______________________ Fecha: ______________________

13-4 ¡A escoger! Choose the word that most logically fits in each sentence.

1. A un ______________ le gusta escuchar la radio.
   a. televidente b. radioyente
2. Para enterarse de los acontecimientos del día, se lee ______________.
   a. la televisión por cable b. la primera plana
3. Mi ______________ favorita es WKGB.
   a. estación de radio b. emisora
4. Un ______________ da las noticias a las siete de la noche.
   a. comentarista b. lector
5. La ______________ transmite sus programas todos los días.
   a. emisora b. telenovela
6. El periodista ______________ las noticias del día.
   a. informa sobre b. patrocina
7. ______________ selecciona los programas.
   a. La emisora b. El canal
8. La ______________ del certamen paga los gastos del programa.
   a. patrocinadora b. crítica
9. Me divierto mucho cuando leo ______________.
   a. las esquelas b. las tiras cómicas
10. Voy a leer ______________ esta tarde.
    a. el editorial b. la editorial

Nombre: ______________________ Fecha: ______________________

¡Así lo hacemos! Estructuras

1. The imperfect subjunctive

13-5 Recomendaciones. You just attended a press conference on environmental issues, and you are telling your friends about the conference. Complete each statement with the imperfect subjunctive form of the verbs in parentheses.

1. El señor nos dijo que...

   (conservar) ______________ más energía.

   no (arrojar) ______________ tantos deshechos.

   (consumir) ______________ menos petróleo.

   (proteger) ______________ el planeta.

2. Insistió en que cada ciudad...

   (tener) ______________ un programa de reciclaje.

   (multar) ______________ a algunas fábricas.

   (explicarle) ______________ a la población la importancia del reciclaje.

   no (contribuir) ______________ a la contaminación del medio ambiente.

3. Quería que todos los niños...

   (aprender) ______________ a conservar energía.

   (asistir) ______________ a un programa de reciclaje.

   (estar) ______________ informados sobre la repoblación forestal.

   (hacer) ______________ algo por el medio ambiente.

4. Dudaba que nosotros...

   (poder) ______________ eliminar totalmente la contaminación.

   no (querer) ______________ participar en la conservación.

   no (hablarles) ______________ del programa a nuestros amigos.

   (seguir) ______________ contaminando el planeta.

Nombre: ______________________ Fecha: ______________________

13-6 Un informe. Retell what you heard at the press conference. Change the first verb to the imperfect indicative in sentences 1 through 5 and to the preterit in sentences 6 through 10. Make any other necessary changes.

MODELO: El líder quiere que consumamos menos petróleo.
El líder quería que consumiéramos menos petróleo.

1. Él espera que los gobiernos hagan algo para mejorar el medio ambiente.

____

2. Él quiere que les escribamos a nuestros compañeros.

____

3. También espera que todos aprendan algo de los resultados de la contaminación.

____

4. Duda que se pueda resolver la situación inmediatamente.

____

5. Teme que no haya muchas soluciones disponibles.

____

6. Nos dice que empecemos un programa de reciclaje en el barrio.

____

7. Recomienda que comencemos con un grupo pequeño.

____

8. Insiste en que yo sea el líder del grupo.

____

9. Nos pide que le digamos los resultados.

____

10. Sugiere que todos participen para que tengamos éxito.

____

Nombre: ______________________ Fecha: ______________________

13-7 ¡A completar! Complete each sentence with the present or imperfect subjunctive form of the verbs in parentheses.

1. Es bueno que nosotros (leer) ______________ más periódicos.
2. Me alegré de que tú (ver) ______________ que existía un problema.
3. Los comentaristas reclamaban que les (dar) ______________ la libertad a los presos.
4. Yo prefiero que la prensa (revisar) ______________ las noticias antes de publicarlas.
5. Preferíamos que el gobierno (proteger) ______________ la libertad de prensa.
6. Ella me pidió que le (traer) ______________ las tiras cómicas.
7. Los reporteros temían que (ocurrir) ______________ problemas entre los presos y el mandatario.
8. No creo que (haber) ______________ una mejor revista que ésa.
9. Los televidentes lamentaron que el canal no (transmitir) ______________ la telenovela hoy.
10. Fue indispensable que los radioyentes (darse) ______________ cuenta de la disidencia en el país.
11. El periódico le dijo a los lectores que no (albergar) ______________ esperanzas.
12. Tú esperas que las fotos de tu cumpleaños (estar) ______________ en la página social.
13. Dudábamos que las noticias sobre la cumbre (encontrarse) ______________ en la primera plana.
14. Necesita que nosotros (analizar) ______________ la sección financiera.
15. Esperaba que su esposo (conseguir) ______________ trabajo después de leer los avisos clasificados.

2. Long-form possessive adjectives and pronouns

13-8 ¿Dónde está(n)? No one can find anything at the newsroom today. Answer the questions, following the model.

MODELO: ¿Dónde está tu reseña (*report*)?
¿La mía? No sé.

1. ¿Dónde están mis tiras cómicas?

   ¿________________? No sé.

2. ¿Dónde están tus fotos?

   ¿________________? No sé.

3. ¿Dónde está el editorial de Federico?

   ¿________________? No sé.

4. ¿Dónde están los avisos clasificados de ustedes?

   ¿________________? No sé.

5. ¿Dónde están tus noticias?

   ¿________________? No sé.

6. ¿Dónde está nuestro horóscopo?

   ¿________________? No sé.

7. ¿Dónde está la crónica social del señor Gómez?

   ¿________________? No sé.

8. ¿Dónde están las carteleras de Ana y Paula?

   ¿________________? No sé.

13-9 ¿De quién es? Answer Ramón's questions, using the cues in parentheses. Follow the model.

MODELO: ¿Es tu revista? (ella)
No, no es mía, es suya.

1. ¿Es tu emisora? (Eduardo)

   ____

Nombre: ______________________ Fecha: ______________________

2. ¿Son mis estaciones de radio? (nosotros)

____

3. ¿Son los canales de ustedes? (él)

____

4. ¿Es mi programa radiofónico? (ellos)

____

5. ¿Es el noticiero de Graciela? (tú)

____

6. ¿Son nuestros radioyentes? (nuestros amigos)

____

7. ¿Son mis reseñas? (ellas)

____

8. ¿Es tu concurso? (él)

____

Nombre: ______________________ Fecha: ______________________

13-10 Demasiada repetición. Fill in the blanks in the sentences that follow parts of the dialog, using possessive pronouns to eliminate repetition.

Modelo: Mi horóscopo está interesante hoy. ¿Ya leíste tu horóscopo?
Mi horóscopo está interesante hoy. ¿Ya leíste el tuyo?

Julio: ¿Dónde está mi periódico?

Ernesto: Ni sé. Mi periódico está aquí, pero no he visto tu periódico. ¿Quieres leer una sección de mi periódico?

1. Ni sé. Mi periódico está aquí, pero no he visto ______________. ¿Quieres leer una sección de ______________?

Julio: No, tu periódico no tiene noticias regionales y no lleva mis columnas favoritas.

2. No, ______________ no tiene noticias regionales y no lleva mis columnas favoritas.

Ernesto: ¡Gracias a Dios! Tus columnistas favoritos son extremistas. Mis columnistas favoritos son más razonables y calmados.

3. ¡Gracias a Dios! Tus columnistas favoritos son extremistas. ______________ son más razonables y calmados.

Julio: ¡Tus columnistas favoritos son aburridos! ¡No dicen nada!

4. ¡______________ son aburridos! ¡No dicen nada!

Ernesto: A veces no entiendo tus opiniones.

Julio: Pues, por lo menos mis opiniones son mis opiniones. Tus opiniones son... ¡Tú no tienes opiniones originales! ¿¡Dónde está mi periódico!?

5. Pues, por lo menos ______________ son ______________. ______________ son... ¡Tú no tienes opiniones originales! ¿¡Dónde está mi periódico!?

Ernesto: Pues, no puedo saber dónde está tu periódico; no tengo opiniones.

6. Pues, no puedo saber dónde está ______________; no tengo opiniones.

Nombre: ______________________________ Fecha: ______________________

Segunda parte

¡Así es la vida!

13-11 ¿Cierto o falso? Reread the article in **¡Así es la vida!** on page 451 of your textbook and indicate whether the statements are **cierto (C)** or **falso (F)**.

C F 1. Jorge Ramos ha sido presentador del *Noticiero Univisión* desde los diecisiete años.

C F 2. Jorge es un hispano con mucha influencia en los EE.UU.

C F 3. Su programa sólo se puede ver en Latinoamérica.

C F 4. El trabajo de Jorge ha sido reconocido con varios premios.

C F 5. Jorge es mexicano.

C F 6. Antes de ser periodista, se dedicó al atletismo.

C F 7. Empezó su carrera de periodista en un periódico.

C F 8. El gobierno mexicano dejó que Jorge trabajara libremente.

C F 9. Jorge empezó su carrera televisiva en Los Ángeles.

C F 10. Jorge Ramos no cree que se pueda ser hispano y buen americano a la vez.

Nombre: ______________________ Fecha: ______________________

¡Así lo decimos! Vocabulario

13-12 ¡A completar! Complete each sentence with the appropriate word from the word bank. Make any changes that are necessary.

comedia	filmar	galán	obra	productor
espectador	final	guión	primera actriz	protagonista

1. Los ______________ gastaron mucho dinero en esa filmación.
2. El ______________ de esa película es muy emocionante.
3. El galán y la ______________ se besan al final de la película.
4. Él es muy guapo, es el ______________ de la telenovela.
5. Los ______________ estaban muy emocionados cuando estaban viendo la película.
6. La película se ______________ el año pasado.
7. Las ______________ de Shakespeare son muy interesantes.
8. Me divertí mucho cuando fui a ver esa ______________.
9. ¿Quién escribió el ______________ de la película?
10. Al final de la película, la ______________ se murió.

13-13 Preguntas personales. Answer the following questions in complete sentences.

1. ¿Cuál es tu película favorita? ¿Por qué?

____

____

2. ¿Quién es tu actor/actriz preferido/a y por qué?

____

____

3. ¿Cuáles son las cualidades de una buena película?

____

____

4. ¿Quiénes ganarán el Óscar este año? Explica.

____

____

5. ¿Por qué te gustan o no las telenovelas?

____

____

¡Así lo hacemos! Estructuras

3. *Si* clauses

13-14 Una conversación entre amigos. Complete the conversation between Toño and Sara, filling in the blanks with the correct form of the verbs in parentheses.

Toño: Mira, si tú no me (1. escuchar) ______________________, no podemos hablar.

Sara: Tienes razón, chico. Voy a escucharte ahora mismo, si (2. querer) ______________________.

Toño: Bueno, nosotros no (3. tener) ______________________ tantos problemas si la prensa (4. ser) ______________________ más responsable.

Sara: Sí, pero si nosotros no (5. tener) ______________________ prensa libre, no se (6. saber) ______________________ la verdad.

Toño: No sé, pero si se (7. poder) ______________________ reportar las noticias sin sensacionalismo, nosotros (8. estar) ______________________ mejor informados.

Sara: Es verdad, pero si nosotros no (9. interesar) ______________________ a los televidentes con sensacionalismo, muchos nunca (10. ver) ______________________ ninguna noticia.

Nombre: ______________________ Fecha: ______________

13-15 Si... Fill in the blanks with the appropriate form of the verbs in parentheses to show simple *if* clauses or contrary-to-fact situations.

1. Si ella (tener) ______________ las entradas, la llamaría.
2. Si (ser) ______________ actor, viviré en Hollywood.
3. Si (poder) ______________ ir al teatro, te buscaría a las seis.
4. Si quiero asistir a la obra de teatro, (tener) ______________ que leer la reseña.
5. Si Mariah Carey cantara, yo (ir) ______________ al concierto.
6. Si tú (querer) ______________, nosotros veríamos la película.
7. Si ellas (tener) ______________ amigos, saldrán con ellos al cine.
8. Si hubiera mejores actores, se (filmar) ______________ mejores películas.

13-16 Tus opiniones. Say what you would do in each of the following situations by completing the statements.

1. Si tuviera más tiempo, ______________________________.
2. Si yo llegara más temprano, yo ______________________________.
3. Yo trataré de ser actor/actriz si ______________________________.
4. Yo escribiría guiones de películas si ______________________________.
5. Si puedo ayudar a mis amigos a ser productores de películas, ______________________________

   ______________________________.
6. Yo iría a Hollywood si ______________________________.
7. Si hubiera una compañía de actores aquí, ______________________________.
8. Yo trataría de reseñar esa película si ______________________________.

4. The future perfect and the conditional perfect

13-17 Vamos al cine. Imagine that your friend Cristina, who is a very demanding person, has invited you and your friends to go to the movies. Here is what she expects everyone to have done before the movie starts. Use the future perfect form of the verbs in parentheses.

1. Todos nosotros (llegar) ______________ al cine media hora antes de que la película empiece.

2. Marcos (llamar) ______________ al cine seis horas antes de la hora del comienzo de la película.

3. Tú (traer) ______________ los cupones para las palomitas (*popcorn*) y los refrescos media hora antes de empezar la película.

4. Rosalía (avisar) ______________ a Penélope dos horas antes de ir al cine.

5. Ustedes (comprar) ______________ los boletos.

6. Fernanda (leer) ______________ la crítica de la película.

7. Miguel y Andrés (hacer) ______________ cola en el cine para sentarse en buenas butacas.

8. Todos nosotros (comer) ______________ antes de llegar al cine.

13-18 ¡A completar! Complete the following exchanges with the correct future perfect form of the verbs in parentheses.

1. —¿(Aprender) ______________ ustedes el guión antes de las once de la mañana?

   —Por supuesto, nosotros (memorizar) ______________ el guión antes de esa hora.

2. —¿(Filmar) ______________ las escenas peligrosas antes del martes?

   —Sí, (tener) ______________ tiempo para filmarlas antes del martes.

3. —¿(Escribir) ______________ usted la carta por correo electrónico al productor en una hora?

   —¡Cómo no! La (hacer) ______________ en media hora.

4. —¿(Instalar) ______________ ellos la iluminación antes del almuerzo?

   —No sé si ellos (terminar) ______________ de instalar la iluminación antes del almuerzo.

5. —¿(Poder) ______________ recoger el chófer al galán de la película hoy?

   —Seguro, él (recoger) ______________ al galán antes de las nueve de la mañana.

Nombre: ______________________ Fecha: ______________________

13-19 ¡Un rodaje horrible! The cast has just finished filming a new movie, but they are not pleased. Fill in the blanks with the conditional perfect form of the verbs in parentheses to find out what the cast would have done differently.

El director

1. Teniendo más dinero, (contratar) ______________ a mejores actores.
2. Con un mejor reparto, (grabar) ______________ más escenas dramáticas.
3. Teniendo un buen productor, la cinematografía (ser) ______________ mejor.

El galán

4. Teniendo un director mejor, (nosotros) (actuar) ______________ mejor.
5. Estando en otro estudio, (nosotros) (tener) ______________ más tiempo para filmar.
6. Con otros compañeros de reparto, (yo) (trabajar) ______________ más a gusto (*at ease*).
7. Empezando la grabación antes, (nosotros) (terminar) ______________ la película a tiempo.

La primera actriz

8. Estudiando más el guión, el galán (hacer) ______________ bien su trabajo.
9. Teniendo paciencia, el director (conseguir) ______________ apoyo del productor.
10. Con más dedicación, (nosotros) (ganar) ______________ algún premio.

13-20 Regreso al pasado. Read the following situations and explain what would you have done differently by completing the sentences in the conditional perfect tense.

1. Siendo actor/actriz, ______________________________.
2. Siendo presidente del gobierno, ______________________________.
3. Estudiando en otro país, ______________________________.
4. Con más dinero, ______________________________.
5. Siendo miembro de la Academia de Hollywood, ______________________________.
6. Siendo director/a de cine, ______________________________.
7. Sabiendo hablar español perfectamente, ______________________________.
8. En una universidad diferente, ______________________________.

Nombre: ______________________ Fecha: ______________________

NUESTRO MUNDO

Panoramas

13-21 ¡A informarse! Based on the information from **Nuestro mundo** on pages 462–463 of your textbook, decide if the following statements are **cierto (C)** or **falso (F).**

1. En España hay dieciocho comunidades autónomas.
2. El español es el único idioma oficial de España.
3. Galicia, por su idioma, se compara con Escocia.
4. Hay influencia celta en Galicia.
5. El euskera es un idioma en extinción que no se enseña en las escuelas.
6. El origen del euskera es desconocido.
7. Cataluña es una región muy importante a nivel artístico y político.
8. Andalucía es la región de España donde la influencia árabe es más aparente.
9. El Alcázar es un palacio árabe que se encuentra en Andalucía.
10. El poder de los monarcas Fernando e Isabel dio fuerza al castellano en toda la península.

13-22 Tu propia experiencia. Using the Internet and library sources, research one of the eighteen regions of Spain and explain what makes that region different from the rest of the country. Do you think you can find such differences in your area compared with the rest of the country? Write a brief essay in Spanish explaining why or why not.

____

____

____

____

____

____

Nombre: ______________________ Fecha: ______________________

Taller

13-23 Doctora Corazón

Primera fase. Imagine that you write the advice column **"Doctora Corazón".** Read the following letter your column received, and list in Spanish the problems the writer has. For each problem, list a possible piece of advice.

Doctora Corazón

Dra. Corazón

Viajo mucho por mi trabajo. Paso por Miami por lo menos dos veces al mes. Cuando quiero divertirme y hablar con otras personas, voy a una discoteca muy popular que está cerca de mi hotel. En mi último viaje, conocí a una fabulosa mujer que es modelo. Quedamos en que nos encontraríamos al día siguiente para cenar juntos. Me dio su número de teléfono y yo le di el del hotel, por si algo acaso pasaba y no nos pudiéramos encontrar. Ella nunca apareció ni me llamó. Yo la llamé para saber qué había pasado (*had happened*). Otra vez nos citamos para esa noche, pero otra vez me dejó plantado (*stood me up*). ¡No apareció! Estaba enojado y no quería llamarla, pero un amigo me dijo que quizás algo serio le había pasado y que por lo menos debiera saber si estaba bien. Desde el aeropuerto la llamé. Resultó que no le pasó nada, que solamente no quería verme esa noche y no se había molestado (*had bothered*) en llamarme. Le dije horrores de su manera de comportarse conmigo y lo enojado que yo estaba con ella. Y me fui de Miami. Ahora, acabo de recibir una carta de ella. ¡Parece una carta de amor! Quiere saber cuándo volveré. Quiere recogerme del aeropuerto y pasar todo el tiempo que yo quiera conmigo. ¡No sé qué pensar! ¿Usted entiende esta carta?

Pedro

PROBLEMAS	CONSEJOS
______________________	______________________
______________________	______________________
______________________	______________________
______________________	______________________

Segunda fase. Now use the lists from the **Primera fase** to organize an answer to Pedro's letter in your advice column.

____

____

____

____

____

Nombre: ______________________________ Fecha: ______________________

13-24 Los paradores. If you were to visit Spain, you might want to stay in one of the more than 80 official **paradores.** Use the Internet or library resources to find out what a **parador** is, how the tradition of a **parador** began, and when they were officially established by the government. Try to find at least three that look interesting to you and list in Spanish their names, locations, and the reasons why you like them.

DEFINICIÓN: ____

HISTORIA: ____

____

____

____

TRES PARADORES QUE ME INTERESAN: ______________________________

____

____

____

13-25 Más allá de las páginas: RENFE. In *Solos esta noche,* José and Carmen are locked in a subway station. In the larger Spanish cities, residents have many public transportation options. Use the Internet or library resources to find out what RENFE is and what it provides. Complete the following list in Spanish.

RENFE (DESCRIPCIÓN): ______________________________________

SIGNIFICADO DE LAS LETRAS: ______________________________

____

SERVICIOS: ____

____

____

____

MÁS INFORMACIÓN: ______________________________________

____

____

____

Nombre: ______________________ Fecha: ______________________

¿Cuánto sabes tú?

13-26 ¿Sabes usar el imperfecto de subjuntivo? Fill in the blanks with the appropriate form of the imperfect subjunctive of the verbs in parentheses.

1. El horóscopo me recomendó que (hablar) ______________ más con mis amigos.
2. El comentarista esperaba que la situación política (cambiar) ______________ pronto.
3. El editor quería que el reportero (escribir) ______________ la reseña de nuevo.
4. El periodista quería que el público (saber) ______________ la verdad.
5. Era dudoso que la televisión (decir) ______________ lo que pasó.
6. El gobierno prohibió que los medios de comunicación (publicar) ______________ el escándalo.

13-27 ¿Sabes usar los pronombres y adjetivos posesivos largos? Following the model, complete the conversations with the appropriate long-form possessive adjective or pronoun.

MODELO: —Mi televisor es de treinta y dos pulgadas.
—El mío es de treinta y seis pulgadas.

1. —Mi periódico es muy objetivo en sus reseñas políticas.

   —______________ es muy prestigioso y respetado.

2. —Mi padre siempre lee la prensa deportiva.

   —______________ siempre lee la sección de economía.

3. —A mí no me gusta lo que dice mi horóscopo sobre mi futuro.

   —Pues ______________ dice que voy a tener mucha suerte en el amor.

4. —Mis lectores creen que soy el mejor periodista del país.

   —______________ creen que soy imparcial y objetivo.

5. —Tus lectores no saben lo que dicen.

   —Pues ______________ no entienden nada de periodismo objetivo.

Nombre: ______________________________ Fecha: ______________________

13-28 ¿Sabes completear las cláusulas con *si*? Choose the most appropriate verb form to complete the following sentences.

1. Si Antonio Banderas fuera el galán, (nosotros) ________________ a ver la película.

   a. vamos b. iríamos c. fuéramos

2. Penélope Cruz actúa como si ________________ una actriz veterana; ¡es muy buena actriz!

   a. fuera b. es c. será

3. Me ________________ más la película si el final fuera diferente.

   a. gustará b. gustara c. gustaría

4. Si la televisión muestra la entrega de premios, la ________________ juntos.

   a. viéramos b. veremos c. veríamos

5. Pedro Almodóvar será más famoso en los EE.UU. si ________________ cine más comercial.

   a. hace b. hiciera c. hará

13-29 ¿Sabes usar el futuro perfecto y el condicional perfecto? Fill in the blanks with the appropriate future or conditional perfect form of the verbs in parentheses, according to the context.

1. Con más tiempo, ayer yo (ir) ________________ al cine con mis amigos.
2. La semana que viene nosotros (ver) ________________ la mejor película del año.
3. En diez años, Javier Bardem (tener) ________________ mucho éxito en este país.
4. Con estos avances tecnológicos, los actores y actrices del pasado (ser) ________________ mucho mejores.
5. Con más talento, yo (estudiar) ________________ arte dramático cuando estaba en la escuela secundaria.
6. En pocos años, el cine latino (conseguir) ________________ mucho reconocimiento.

Nombre: ______________________ Fecha: ______________

Lab Manual

PRIMERA PARTE

¡Así es la vida!

13-30 El periódico por la mañana. As you listen to the following conversation, select the letters for all statements that are correct, according to what you hear. Listen to the conversation as many times as is necessary to find all the correct answers.

1. Pablo...
   a. leía los titulares.
   b. leía la cartelera del periódico.
   c. leía la primera plana del periódico.
2. Alejandra...
   a. buscó el periódico.
   b. leía el consultorio sentimental.
   c. quería que Pablo le diera la primera plana.
3. Pablo le dijo a Alejandra que...
   a. viera una telenovela.
   b. mirara la sección financiera del periódico.
   c. leyera la sección deportiva.
4. Pablo y Alejandra leyeron juntos...
   a. la esquela y la crónica social.
   b. el editorial sobre el Perú.
   c. el artículo sobre el Perú.
5. Lucas podía leer...
   a. las tiras cómicas.
   b. la esquela.
   c. el consultorio sentimental.
6. Lucas...
   a. tenía interés en leer la cartelera.
   b. prefería leer los deportes.
   c. eligió leer el horóscopo.
7. Pablo les pidió que...
   a. oyeran las últimas noticias en la televisión.
   b. pusieran noticias en la radio.
   c. escucharan al comentarista de la radio.
8. Lucas...
   a. temía que las emisoras de radio no pasaran noticias.
   b. esperaba ver las noticias de los canales de Latinoamérica.
   c. leyó el horóscopo para él y su mamá.

Nombre: ______________________ Fecha: ______________________

¡Así lo decimos! Vocabulario

13-31 ¿Qué quieres hacer esta noche? Answer the questions that you hear based on the following newspaper clippings. Then listen and repeat as the speaker gives the correct answer.

MUY ESPECIAL

En la televisión

5:30 p.m.

51 **El niño.** Un programa dirigido a los nuevos padres, con Eva y Jorge Villamar.

8:00 p.m.

HIT **Hablando con el Pueblo.** Armando García Sifredo nos trae un programa para Miami tocando temas de interés para toda la ciudadanía. 90 mins.

8:00 p.m.

DIS **Toy Story 2.** Con las voces de Tom Hanks y Tim Allen. Woody descubre que es seguido por un coleccionista. Tiene que decidir si se queda con los otros juguetes o sigue la fama. 1 1/2 hrs.

9:00 p.m.

51 **El Alburero.** Con Rafael Inclán y Rebeca Silva. Un hombre amable habla en rima y trata de conquistar a las mujeres. 100 mins.

En la radio

Mediodía

WWFE-AM (670) Radio Fe. **La mogolla.** Alberto González en un programa de sátira política y social.

10:00 p.m.

WTMI-FM (93.1) Nocturno. Barber: Concierto de violín, Op. 14; Oliveira, violín; Orquesta Sinfónica de St. Louis; Slatkin, director; Thompson: Sinfonía No. 3 en la menor; Orquesta Sinfónica de Nueva Zelandia; Schenk, director. Brahms: Cuarteto de cuerdas No. 2 en la menor, Op. 51; Cuarteto Janacek.

NOCHE

6:00 p.m.

23 51 Noticiero

HIT La bahía 1 hr.

TEL Topacio Repetición

6:30 p.m.

23 Noticiero Univisión

51 Noticiero Telemundo / CNN

GAL ¡Ándale! Paco Stanley. 1 hr.

7:00 p.m.

23 Paulatina

51 Manuela

HIT Chispita

TEL Tele Perú

7:30 p.m.

GAL T.V.O.

HIT Tremenda corte

8:00 p.m.

23 Buscando

51 Película *El sombrero de tres picos*

GAL La bahía

HIT Hablando con el pueblo

TEL Internacional video "Hit 5/10"

8:30 p.m.

GAL Rosa salvaje

9:00 p.m.

23 Al filo de la muerte

51 Película *El Alburero*. Con Rafael Inclán y Rebeca Silva. Un hombre amable habla en rima y trata de conquistar a las mujeres. 100 mins.

GAL Pepita

TEL Topacio Repetición

9:30 p.m.

GAL Madres egoístas

HIT Clásicos del teatro

10:00 p.m.

23 Viña del mar "Festival de Canciones" (Parte 6 de 7). Desde Valparaiso, Chile. 1 hr.

GAL Valeria y Maximiliano

TEL Estudio abierto Luis Conte

10:30 p.m.

51 Mi vida

GAL La luna

11:00 p.m.

23 51 Noticiero

GAL Vida perdida

HIT Oscar Aguero

TEL Debate Repetición

1. ______________________
2. ______________________
3. ______________________
4. ______________________
5. ______________________
6. ______________________

Nombre: ______________________________ Fecha: ______________________

¡Así lo hacemos! Estructuras

1. The imperfect subjunctive

13-32 ¿Qué quería la prensa? Form sentences using the cues provided. Then listen and repeat as the speaker gives the correct answer.

MODELO: You see: el presidente / hablar / la gente
You say: *La prensa quería que el presidente hablara con la gente.*

1. yo / expresar / mi opinión
2. tú / resolver / el problema
3. los reporteros / ser / exacto
4. nosotros / leer / la crónica

13-33 La estación de radio. Change the sentences that you hear to the imperfect subjunctive. Then listen and repeat as the speaker gives the correct answer.

MODELO: You hear: Es importante que vengas.
You see: venir
You say: *Era importante que vinieras.*

1. salir
2. informarle
3. patrocinar
4. decir

13-34 Durante el noticiero. Answer the questions that you hear using the cues provided. Then listen and repeat as the speaker gives the correct answer.

MODELO: You hear: ¿Qué era importante?
You see: yo / consumir / poco
You say: *Era importante que yo consumiera poco.*

1. (tú) escuchar / al meteorólogo
2. (nosotros) revisar / las notas del acontecimiento
3. solucionarse / el problema
4. poner / más noticias en la primera plana

2. Long-form possessive adjectives and pronouns

13-35 En la oficina de los reporteros. Answer the questions that you hear based on the cues provided. Then listen and repeat as the speaker gives the correct answer.

Modelo: You hear: ¿De quién es el periódico?
You see: Ana y Héctor
You say: *El periódico es suyo.*

1. Alicia
2. yo
3. Vanesa y Julia
4. nosotros
5. tú
6. tú
7. usted
8. yo

13-36 ¿Cómo dividir el periódico? Form sentences using the cues provided. Then listen and repeat as the speaker gives the correct answer.

Modelo: You see: el artículo / ella
You say: *El artículo es suyo.*

1. la primera plana / nosotros
2. las tiras cómicas / tú
3. los anuncios / los padres
4. el horóscopo / yo
5. la sección deportiva / tú
6. la cartelera / yo
7. el consultorio sentimental / nosotros
8. la esquela / los abuelos

Nombre: ______________________ Fecha: ______________________

Segunda parte

¡Así es la vida!

13-37 ¿Te gustó la película? As you listen to the following conversation, select the letters for all statements that are correct, according to what you hear. Listen to the conversation as many times as is necessary to find all the correct answers.

1. Francisca y Alejandro...
   a. fueron al cine.
   b. comieron en un restaurante.
   c. fueron al teatro.
2. A Francisca le gustó...
   a. el rodaje.
   b. la cinematografía.
   c. el galán.
3. Francisca quiere...
   a. regresar al teatro.
   b. regresar al cine.
   c. cambiar el final.
4. Alejandro...
   a. no vio la película.
   b. leyó la novela.
   c. se durmió durante la obra de teatro.
5. A Alejandro...
   a. le gusta el final de la película.
   b. le interesa ser productor.
   c. le encanta el teatro.
6. Alejandro...
   a. prefiere el cine porque cuesta menos que el teatro.
   b. ha actuado en varios dramas.
   c. quiere aplaudir a los actores.

¡Así lo decimos! Vocabulario

13-38 ¿Qué es eso? Select the word or expression from the vocabulary in **¡Así lo decimos!** on page 452 of your textbook that best completes each sentence you hear. Then listen and repeat as the speaker gives the correct answer.

1. a. el filme
   b. el galán
   c. el estudio
2. a. el guión
   b. la telenovela
   c. la productora
3. a. una comedia
   b. protagonista
   c. una cinta
4. a. la ventaja
   b. el protagonista
   c. el espectador

5. a. actuar
   b. grabar
   c. representar

6. a. la escena
   b. la obra
   c. la cinematografía

¡Así lo hacemos! Estructuras

3. *Si* clauses

13-39 ¿Cómo sería diferente? Form sentences using the cues provided to express contrary-to-fact conditions. Then listen and repeat as the speaker gives the correct answer.

MODELO: You see: las compañías teatrales / producir / más obras / el público / ir / más frecuentemente al teatro
You say: *Si las compañías teatrales produjeran más obras, el público iría más frecuentemente al teatro.*

1. el galán / ser / una persona mala / a nadie / gustarle / la película
2. el programa / empezar / a tiempo / (ellos) tener / menos problemas
3. los guiones / estar / en español / ser / más fácil de entender
4. la primera actriz / actuar / mejor / (nosotros) poder / entender su acento
5. (nosotros) querer / ver / una comedia / ir / a esta película

13-40 ¡Éxito en las artes! Change the sentences that you hear to reflect contrary-to-fact conditions. Then listen and repeat as the speaker gives the correct answer.

MODELO: You hear: Si los actores actúan bien, el drama recibe mucho aplauso.
You write and say: *Si los actores actuaran bien, el drama recibiría mucho aplauso.*

1. Si ____.
2. Si ____.
3. Si ____.
4. Si ____.

Nombre: ______________________________ Fecha: ______________________

4. The future perfect and the conditional perfect

13-41 ¿Qué habrá pasado en la telenovela? Your VCR broke and you couldn't tape the last episode of the soap opera. What will have happened? Ask questions using the cues provided. Then listen and repeat as the speaker gives the correct answer. Check the spelling of the participles in the Answer Key.

Modelo: You see: la telenovela / tener / mucha acción
You say: *¿La telenovela habrá tenido mucha acción?*

1. Adriana / saber / la verdad
2. Carina / poner / la evidencia en el auto de Ramón
3. Débora y Jaime / casarse
4. todos / estar / contentos
5. Beatriz / decirle / a Patricio la información confidencial
6. Diego / volver / de Buenos Aires
7. Rosaura / morir
8. Carmen y Rosario / creer / las excusas de sus hijas

13-42 Una visita al futurista. José is visiting a futurist because he wants to know what will have occurred by the year 2020. Answer José's questions as if you were the futurist using the cues provided. Then listen and repeat as the speaker gives the correct answer.

Modelo: You hear: ¿Habitarán los hombres Marte?
You write and say: *No, no habrán habitado Marte.*
or
You write and say: *Sí, habrán habitado Marte.*

1. Sí, ____.
2. No, ____.
3. Sí, ____.
4. No, ____.
5. Sí, ____.
6. Sí, ____.

Nombre: ______________________ Fecha: ______________________

13-43 La primera actriz. Tell what this famous actress would have done if circumstances had been different. Form sentences using the cues provided. Then listen and repeat as the speaker gives the correct answer.

Modelo: You see: yo / filmar / películas en inglés / no hablar bien el idioma
You say: *Yo habría filmado películas en inglés, pero no hablaba bien el idioma.*

1. yo / vivir / Madrid / no / tener / pasaporte
2. yo / estudiar / baile / decidir / estudiar / literatura
3. yo / actuar / Nueva York / cancelarse / el viaje

¿Cuánto sabes tú?

13-44 No tenían mucha esperanza. Change the sentences that you hear to the imperfect subjunctive. Then listen and repeat as the speaker gives the correct answer.

Modelo: You hear: El gobierno aprueba la ley de reciclaje.

You write and say: *No creían que el gobierno aprobara la ley de reciclaje.*

1. No ____.
2. No ____.
3. No ____.

13-45 ¿Quién se entera de qué? Answer the questions that you hear negatively using the cues provided. Then listen and repeat as the speaker gives the correct answer.

Modelo: You hear: ¿El concurso es nuestro?
You see: yo
You say: *No, el concurso no es nuestro, es mío.*

1. ella
2. nosotras
3. yo
4. él

13-46 Si yo fuera directora... Tell your friend what would happen if you became a film director. Form sentences using the cues provided. Then listen and repeat as the speaker gives the correct answer.

1. mi familia y yo / vivir / Hollywood
2. mis productoras / darme / mucho dinero
3. yo / filmar / solamente / lugares exóticos
4. tú / comer / conmigo / restaurantes muy famosos
5. yo / tratar de ayudar / las personas / no tener / casa

13-47 ¡El señor dudoso! Listen to the following questions and fill in the blanks with the correct form, mood, and tense of the verbs in parentheses. Then listen and repeat as the speaker gives the correct answer.

MODELO: You hear: ¿Crees que los anuncios clasificados son inútiles?
You write and say: *Dudo que sean inútiles. Si fueran inútiles, no tendríamos tantos anuncios en los periódicos.*

1. Dudo que el televisor (estar) ______________ encendido. Si (estar) ______________ encendido, no (haber) ______________ tanto silencio.
2. Dudo que (representar) ______________ la verdad. Si la (representar) ______________, no (haber) ______________ tantos periódicos.
3. Dudo que (pagar) ______________ poco. Si (pagar) ______________ poco, (ver) ______________ más anuncios comerciales en la televisión.

Nombre: ______________________________ Fecha: ______________________

14 ¡Seamos cultos!

Workbook

PRIMERA PARTE

¡Así es la vida!

14-1 ¿Recuerdas? Reread the paragraphs in **¡Así es la vida!** on page 472 of your textbook and indicate whether each statement is **cierto (C)** or **falso (F)**.

C F 1. Celedonio Romero es el patriarca de "la familia real de la guitarra española".

C F 2. Los padres de Celedonio fueron grandes músicos.

C F 3. Sus hijos también se han destacado en el mundo de la música.

C F 4. El Cuarteto Romero fue fundado en Málaga, España.

C F 5. La crítica internacional ha apreciado la música de los Romero.

C F 6. Celedonio empezó a tocar la guitarra cuando tenía tres años.

C F 7. Según Celino, las clases de música no son importantes para aprender.

C F 8. Celino aprendió música de su tío y de su abuelo.

C F 9. Celino tocó la guitarra con Pink Floyd y Led Zeppelin.

C F 10. Pepe, miembro de la familia Romero, fabrica guitarras que pueden costar más de $7.000.

¡Así lo decimos! Vocabulario

14-2 ¡A completar! Complete the following statements with a word from the word bank. Make changes when necessary.

aplaudir audición bajo diva ensayar escenario músicos repertorio

1. Si el tenor cantara bien, el público lo ____________________ mucho.

2. El ____________________ musical de Plácido Domingo es muy extenso.

Nombre: ______________________ Fecha: ______________________

3. Yo no tengo miedo de cantar en el ____________ de ese teatro.

4. La solista es una verdadera ____________ de la ópera.

5. Antes de poder cantar en el teatro, necesito tener una ____________.

6. La orquesta tendrá que ____________ por dos semanas antes de que comience la ópera.

7. Un sexteto está compuesto de seis ____________.

8. Un cantanate que tiene la voz grave cuando canta es un ____________.

14-3 Definiciones. Match each definition on the left with its corresponding word.

1. ____ persona que escribe música — a. gira
2. ____ persona que dirige una orquesta — b. banda
3. ____ mujer que canta en una ópera — c. compositor/a
4. ____ conjunto de conciertos en diferentes ciudades — d. director/a
5. ____ grupo musical compuesto por varios músicos — e. soprano

14-4 ¡A escribir! Now write a sentence for each word from the activity **14-3.**

1. ______________________________
2. ______________________________
3. ______________________________
4. ______________________________
5. ______________________________

14-5 ¡Fuera de lugar! Select the word in each group that is out of place.

1. a. viola b. violín c. batería
2. a. trombón b. maracas c. trompeta
3. a. clarinete b. batería c. tambor
4. a. arpa b. acordeón c. guitarra
5. a. sexteto b. gira c. cuarteto

Nombre: ______________________ Fecha: ______________________

¡Así lo hacemos! Estructuras

1. *Hacer* in time expressions

14-6 El tiempo vuela. Write sentences with **hace que** and the cues provided to find out how things happened some time ago.

MODELO: Son las cuatro. El director / llegar / a las dos
Hace dos horas que llegó el director.

1. Hoy es sábado. La orquesta / ensayar / el viernes

____

2. Son las cinco. La ópera / comenzar / a las cuatro

____

3. Son las ocho. El tenor / cantar / a las tres

____

4. Hoy es el 20 de agosto. La audición / terminarse / el 20 de julio

____

5. Hoy es martes. El compositor / componer / la pieza / el sábado

____

6. Hoy es el 3 de mayo de 2004. La banda / tocar / el 3 de mayo de 2003

____

7. Hoy es martes. La comedia / representarse / el viernes

____

8. Son las nueve. El músico / traer / la guitarra / a las ocho y media

____

14-7 ¿Cuánto tiempo hace? Use the cues in parentheses to answer each of the following questions.

1. ¿Cuánto tiempo hace que no vas a un concierto? (un día)

____

2. ¿Hace cuánto que no escuchas una sinfonía? (un mes)

____

Nombre: ______________________ Fecha: ______________________

3. ¿Hace cuánto que buscas boletos para la ópera? (un año)

____

4. ¿Cuánto tiempo hace que no has visto una comedia musical? (dos días)

____

5. ¿Hace cuánto que estás haciendo cola (*standing in line*)? (mucho tiempo)

____

6. ¿Cuánto tiempo hace que compones esta pieza? (dos semanas)

____

7. ¿Cuánto tiempo hace que tocas el piano? (cinco años)

____

8. ¿Hace cuánto tiempo que asistes a las funciones? (tres años)

____

14-8 La enfadada. Complete Mabel's explanation with the verbs in parentheses.

Son las tres y media de la tarde y (1. hacer) ______________ más de una hora que yo (2. esperar) ______________ a Eduardo. (3. hacer) ______________ media hora que (4. peinarse) ______________ en su casa. En quince minutos (5. empezar) ______________ el concierto. (6. hacer) ______________ más de un mes que quiero verlo. Si Eduardo no (7. llegar) ______________ pronto, nosotros (8. ir) ______________ a llegar tarde. Él siempre me (9. decir) ______________ que (10. tener) ______________ que esperar por mí, pero esta vez (11. hacer) ______________ más de una hora que yo lo (12. esperar) ______________.

Nombre: ______________________ Fecha: ______________

2. The pluperfect indicative

14-9 Nunca antes. Fill in the blanks with the pluperfect indicative to complete negative statements that tell what these people had never done before.

Modelo: Andrés / comprar / boletos / para la ópera
Andrés nunca antes había comprado boletos para la ópera.

1. Carlos / visitar / un teatro

   Carlos nunca antes ______________ un teatro.

2. nosotros / conocer / a una diva

   Nosotros nunca antes ______________ a una diva.

3. Herminio / ver / una comedia musical

   Herminio nunca antes ______________ una comedia musical.

4. los músicos / ensayar / esa pieza

   Los músicos nunca antes ______________ esa pieza.

5. la diva / ponerse / un traje feo

   La diva nunca antes ______________ un traje feo.

6. el compositor / componer / una sinfonía

   El compositor nunca antes ______________ una sinfonía.

7. los tenores / enfermarse

   Los tenores nunca antes ______________.

8. el director / abrir / el teatro / por la mañana

   El director nunca antes ______________ el teatro por la mañana.

14-10 ¿Qué pasó? Using the cues provided, write complete sentences in the past tense to describe the problems these people had. Use the preterit in the first half of each sentence and the pluperfect in the second half. Add any necessary words and make any needed changes.

Modelo: cuando / nosotros / recibir / la invitación // ya / empezar / concierto
Cuando nosotros recibimos la invitación, ya había empezado el concierto.

1. cuando / yo / llegar / teatro // mis amigos / ya / sentarse

   ____

   ____

2. cuando / el director / regresar // el coro / ya / cantar

3. cuando / Luis / comprar / entradas // Pedro / ya / conseguir

4. cuando / el tenor / improvisar / pieza // ya / el bajo / ensayar

5. cuando / la soprano / cantar // público / ya / aplaudir

6. cuando / nosotros / volver // la comedia / ya / terminarse

7. cuando / tú / traer / guitarra // ya / sexteto / tocar

8. cuando Ramón y tú / visitar / teatro // yo / ya / hablar / con Plácido

Nombre: ______________________ Fecha: ______________________

Segunda parte

¡Así es la vida!

14-11 ¿Cierto o falso? Reread the article in **¡Así es la vida!** on page 483 of your textbook and indicate whether each statement is **cierto (C)** or **falso (F)**.

C F 1. Carolina Herrera es una importante figura del *jet-set* internacional.

C F 2. Se puede comparar a Carolina Herrera con Donatella Versace.

C F 3. La familia de Carolina era humilde y de la clase trabajadora venezolana.

C F 4. Carolina Herrera sólo diseña para mujeres en Nueva York, India y México.

C F 5. Según Carolina, el estilo latino es recargado.

C F 6. Además de ser un perfume de Carolina Herrera, 212 es el código de teléfono de Nueva York.

C F 7. Hace quince años que Carolina Herrera es diseñadora.

C F 8. Carolina diseña desde trajes para el día hasta trajes de novia.

C F 9. Carolina Herrera sólo es famosa en Latinoamérica.

C F 10. Carolina diseña ropa para la mujer sencilla de todo el mundo.

¡Así lo decimos! Vocabulario

14-12 ¡A completar! Complete the following statements with a word or expression from the word bank. Make changes when necessary.

bien hecha	diseñadora	modelo	sencillez
desfile de modas	disfraces	prenda	tela

1. La ______________________ tenía puesto un vestido diseñado por Carolina Herrera.
2. Carolina Herrera es ______________________.
3. Nuestros ______________________ de Halloween dan miedo.
4. El esmoquin es una ______________________ de vestir.
5. Esta tarde mi novia irá a un ______________________ para ver los nuevos estilos.

6. La ______________________ en el modo de vestir es muy importante.

7. La ropa de Carolina Herrera está muy ______________________.

8. La gabardina es una ______________________.

14-13 ¡A escoger! Choose the adjective that best completes each of the following sentences.

1. Ella tiene mucha gracia y es finísima. Es una persona ______________________.

   a. indispensable   b. fastuoso   c. encantadora

2. Su esmoquin es formal y muy ______________________.

   a. elegante   b. indispensable   c. mundana

3. El baile de disfraces fue muy ______________________.

   a. indispensable   b. fastuoso   c. encantadora

4. Hablar español es ______________________ en el mundo de hoy.

   a. informal   b. indispensable   c. elegante

5. Por favor, no se ponga ropa ______________________ para la boda de mi hermana.

   a. extravagante   b. bien hecho   c. mundano

6. Federico habla cuatro idiomas y le encanta viajar. Es ______________________.

   a. elegante   b. mundano   c. informal

7. Su blusa es de algodón, cuesta poco y es muy ______________________.

   a. encantador   b. mundano   c. extravagante

Nombre: ______________________ Fecha: ______________

14-14 Cuestionario. Answer each of the following questions with a complete sentence in Spanish.

1. Para ti, ¿qué significa estar de moda?

____

____

2. ¿Cuáles son tus telas favoritas? Explica.

____

____

3. ¿Prefieres lo sencillo o lo fastuoso en cuestiones de moda? ¿Por qué?

____

____

4. ¿Qué harías tú si te invitaran a una fiesta formal y no tuvieras la prenda de vestir adecuada?

____

____

5. ¿Te gustaría ser diseñador/a de modas? Da tus razones.

____

____

¡Así lo hacemos! Estructuras

3. The pluperfect subjunctive and the conditional perfect

14-15 ¡A cambiar! Change the following statements from the present to the past. Follow the model.

MODELO: Dudo que haya vuelto la diseñadora.
Dudaba que hubiera vuelto la diseñadora.

1. Es probable que haya tenido un esmoquin.

    ____________ probable que ____________________ un esmoquin.

2. No creo que la modelo haya trabajado allí.

    No ____________ que la modelo ____________________ allí.

Nombre: ______________________________ Fecha: ______________________

3. Dudamos que la costurera haya hecho el vestido.

   ______________ que la costurera ______________________ el vestido.

4. Esperas que no hayan vendido todas las blusas de rayón.

   ______________ que no ______________________ todas las blusas de rayón.

5. Siento que no hayas conseguido un vestido de lentejuelas.

   ______________ que no ______________________ un vestido de lentejuelas.

6. Esperan que tú ya hayas visto el sombrero de pana.

   ______________ que tú ya ______________________ el sombrero de pana.

7. No creo que José y tú hayan abierto un negocio de alta costura.

   No ______________ que José y tú ______________________ un negocio de alta costura.

8. Es probable que hayan traído un disfraz a la fiesta.

   ______________ probable que ______________________ un disfraz a la fiesta.

9. Es imposible que su hermano haya conocido a Carolina.

   ______________ imposible que su hermano ______________________ a Carolina.

10. Tengo miedo que las chicas no se hayan puesto el abrigo.

    ______________ miedo que las chicas no se ______________________ el abrigo.

14-16 ¡Ojalá que! Imagine that you wish that some things that happened would never have occurred. Use the pluperfect subjunctive of the verbs in parentheses.

1. Ojalá que no (morir) ______________ tantos animales para hacer abrigos de piel.
2. Ojalá que los diseñadores no (diseñar) ______________ tantos artículos de piel.
3. Ojalá que muchos diseñadores no (ser) ______________ tan irresponsables.
4. Ojalá que los desfiles de moda no (estar) ______________ tan fastuosos.
5. Ojalá que las tiendas no (vender) ______________ nunca sombreros de piel.
6. Ojalá que nosotros no (vivir) ______________ en un mundo tan superficial.
7. Ojalá que las fábricas de tela no (echar) ______________ deshechos en los ríos.
8. Ojalá que los científicos no (inventar) ______________ artículos de poliéster.

Nombre: ______________________ Fecha: ______________________

14-17 Cambios y más cambios. Change the tenses in the following statements, which show contrary-to-fact situations to the perfect tense. Follow the model.

MODELO: Si me regalaran un abrigo de piel, lo devolvería.
Si me hubieran regalado un abrigo de piel, lo habría devuelto.

1. Si fuera una camisa de algodón, la compraría.

   Si ______________________ una camisa de algodón, la ______________________.

2. Si la modelo quisiera salir conmigo, la invitaría.

   Si la modelo ______________________ salir conmigo, la ______________________.

3. Si tuviera dinero, iría al desfile de moda.

   Si ______________________ dinero, ______________________ al desfile de moda.

4. Si tuviera talento, sería diseñador/a.

   Si ______________________ talento, ______________________ diseñador/a.

5. Si fuera rico/a, tendría un imperio.

   Si ______________________ rico/a, ______________________ un imperio.

6. Si pudiera, haría una campaña en contra de los abrigos de piel.

   Si ______________________, ______________________ una campaña en contra de los abrigos de piel.

14-18 Si yo hubiera sido... Say what you would have done by completing the following statements with the pluperfect subjunctive or the conditional perfect.

1. Si yo hubiera sido modelo, ______________________

   ______________________.

2. Si yo hubiera sido diseñador/a, ______________________

   ______________________.

3. Si yo hubiera sido costurero/a, ______________________

   ______________________.

4. Si yo hubiera sido una persona más divertida, ______________________

   ______________________.

Nombre: ______________________ Fecha: ______________________

5. Si yo hubiera sido una persona más superficial, ______________________

______________________.

NUESTRO MUNDO

Panoramas

14-19 ¡A informarse! Based on the information from **Nuestro mundo** on pages 492–493 of your textbook, decide if the following statements are **cierto (C)** or **falso (F).**

1. El arte moderno hispano no tiene renombre internacional.
2. Santiago Calatrava diseña exclusivamente edificios públicos.
3. Santiago Calatrava es un ejemplo de estilo clásico.
4. Calatrava es uno de los arquitectos seleccionados para el nuevo *World Trade Center.*
5. Salvador Dalí es uno de los artistas más influyentes.
6. La estética es la principal preocupación de Oswaldo Guayasamín en su obra.
7. Fernando Botero se dedica exclusivamente a la escultura.
8. Las figuras de Botero se destacan por su tamaño y voluptuosidad.
9. Las obras de Botero se han exihibido exclusivamente en Colombia.
10. María de Mater O'Neill refleja los colores caribeños en su pintura.

14-20 Tu propia experiencia. Using the Internet and library resources, research a foundation or art exposition dedicated to an Hispanic artist in the U.S. Write about the artist, what is being exhibited, and the public reaction to the foundation or exposition.

____

____

____

____

____

Nombre: ______________________ Fecha: ______________________

Taller

14-21 El arte para mí. Make a list of the one or two art forms that interest you most (paintings, sculpture, architecture, fashion design, literature, etc.). Describe in Spanish the art form and why it interests you. Who are some of your favorite artists (designers, composers, etc.), and what are some of your favorite works?

____

____

____

____

____

14-22 La ropa que llevamos. Who's responsible for the clothing designs that are in style today? Using the Internet or library resources, look up information on today's styles. Are any of the designers Hispanic? Make a list of at least four current styles and describe them in Spanish. List designers, when possible.

____

____

____

____

____

14-23 Más allá de las páginas: Lo real maravilloso. The stories of Enrique Anderson Imbert, like the works by many Latin American authors since the 1940s, have what some call an element of **lo real maravilloso.** The Cuban novelist, Alejo Carpentier, coined the phrase **lo real maravilloso** in an effort to express events of everyday life together with the marvelous nature of Latin American geography and history. Gabriel García Márquez says that it's the way his grandmother used to tell him stories. The real seems to slip into fantasy, often very subtly and matter-of-factly. Write a simple description, in Spanish, of something that happened to you. After you complete the paragraph, alter one sentence or outcome to add a touch of **lo real maravilloso** to the description.

MODELO: *¡Hacía tanto calor que me moría! Mi maestra me había dicho que el color negro atraía el calor y eso me dio una idea. Construí una caja de madera y adentro la pinté de negro. Al día siguiente, salí con mi caja y la abrí, apuntándola hacia el sol. Pero ¡nada! Otro día horrible. Esa noche, entré a la casa enojada con mi caja y la puse en la mesa. Cuando mi hermanito la abrió, gritó y vi, horrorizada, que tenía la cara quemada...*

____

____

Nombre: ______________________ Fecha: ______________________

____

____

____

____

____

____

¿Cuánto sabes tú?

14-24 ¿Sabes usar *hacer* con las expresiones temporales? Fill in the blanks with the appropriate form of verbs in parentheses.

1. ¿Cuánto tiempo hace que no ves a tu primo?

   (Hacer) ______________ dos años que no (ver) ______________ a mi primo.

2. Tu primo es actor, ¿verdad?

   Sí, (hacer) ______________ dos años que (ser) ______________ actor.

3. ¿Cuándo se mudaron tus tíos a Los Ángeles?

   (Hacer) ______________ cinco años que (vivir) ______________ en Los Ángeles.

4. ¿Conoce tu primo a gente importante?

   Sí, (hacer) ______________ tres años, en un estudio de cine, (conocer) ______________ a Antonio Banderas.

5. ¿Cuándo tuvo su primer papel importante?

   (Hacer) ______________ cuatro años que (hacer) ______________ su primera película.

Nombre: ______________________ Fecha: ______________________

14-25 ¿Sabes usar el pluscuamperfecto de indicativo? Fill in the blanks with the appropriate pluperfect form of the verbs in parentheses.

1. Antes de Pedro Almodóvar, nunca me (interesar) ______________ por el cine español.
2. Antes de Almodóvar, nosotros sólo (ver) ______________ cine americano.
3. Antes de *Habla con ella*, Almodóvar ya (hacer) ______________ muchas películas.
4. Antes del Óscar de Almodóvar, el cine español ya (ganar) ______________ otros dos premios de la Academia.
5. Carlos Saura y Fernando Trueba ya (ser) ______________ galardonados con el Óscar a la mejor película extranjera.

14-26 ¿Sabes usar el pluscuamperfecto de subjuntivo y el condicional perfecto? In the following examples, choose the appropriate verb tense to complete the sentences.

1. Si nosotros ______________, no habríamos encontrado boletos.

   a. hubiéramos ido b. habríamos ido c. habíamos ido

2. Si el actor hubiera interpretado mejor su papel, la película ______________ mejor.

   a. había sido b. hubiera sido c. habría sido

3. El público ______________ si el cantante hubiera cantado bien.

   a. hubiera aplaudido b. habría aplaudido c. había aplaudido

4. Juanjo habría coseguido ser parte del coro si él ______________ a la audición.

   a. se hubiera presentado b. se habría presentado c. se había presentado

5. Ojalá la gira del tenor ______________ por mi ciudad.

   a. había pasado b. habría pasado c. hubiera pasado

Nombre: ______________________ Fecha: ______________________

Lab Manual

Primera parte

¡Así es la vida!

14-27 ¡A la ópera! As you listen to the following conversation, select the letters for all statements that are correct, according to what you hear. Listen to the conversation as many times as is necessary to find all the correct answers.

1. Antonio...
   a. cree que Catalina está enferma.
   b. es alto.
   c. tiene un auto.
2. Catalina está...
   a. entusiasmada.
   b. nerviosa.
   c. enfadada.
3. El señor Villamar...
   a. quiere que Antonio y Catalina se diviertan.
   b. quiere que ellos vuelvan muy tarde.
   c. se despide de ellos.
4. Catalina y Antonio...
   a. han llegado tarde.
   b. conversan antes de que empiece la ópera.
   c. se preocupan por el tiempo.
5. Catalina está preocupada...
   a. por la cantidad de luces.
   b. por el vestido que lleva.
   c. por entender las palabras.
6. Durante el intermedio, ellos...
   a. hablan de cuánto les gusta la ópera.
   b. ya quieren irse.
   c. compran refrescos para beber durante el segundo acto.

Nombre: ______________________ Fecha: ______________________

¡Así lo decimos! Vocabulario

14-28 ¿Qué es eso? Choose the word or expression that best completes each sentence that you hear. Then listen and repeat as the speaker gives the correct answer.

1. a. aplaudir
   b. componer
   c. ensayar
2. a. improvisar
   b. representarse
   c. el acto
3. a. sinfonía
   b. gira
   c. bajo
4. a. la solista
   b. el escenario
   c. la batería
5. a. el compositor
   b. el director
   c. el músico
6. a. el saxofón
   b. el violín
   c. la trompeta

¡Así lo hacemos! Estructuras

1. *Hacer* in time expressions

14-29 ¿Habrá espectáculo o no? Describe how long something has been going on using the cues provided and a form of **hacer.** Then listen and repeat as the speaker gives the correct answer.

MODELO: You see: tres días / la diva / no poder / cantar
You say: *Hace tres días que la diva no puede cantar.*

1. dos semestres / (nosotros) componer / la música
2. una semana / la directora / estar / enferma
3. tres horas / peinarte / el pelo
4. más de media hora / Julia y Paco / hablar / por teléfono
5. cuatro días / (yo) no vender / ni un boleto

Nombre: ______________________ Fecha: ______________

14-30 ¿Hace cuánto tiempo que...? Describe how long ago something happened by answering the questions you hear using the cues provided and a form of **hacer.** Then listen and repeat as the speaker gives the correct answer.

Modelo: You hear: ¿Hace cuánto tiempo que compraste los boletos?
You see: dos días
You say: *Hace dos días que compré los boletos.*

1. tres años
2. una hora
3. quince días
4. diez minutos
5. seis horas

2. The pluperfect indicative

14-31 Nunca había hecho eso durante una gira. Form sentences using the pluperfect tense and the cues provided. Then listen and repeat as the speaker gives the correct answer.

Modelo: You see: ella / nunca / cantar / en Nueva York
You say: *Ella nunca había cantado en Nueva York.*

1. ellas / nunca / estar / en este país
2. tú / nunca / arreglar / un clarinete
3. él / nunca / recibir / tanto aplauso
4. nosotras / nunca / hacer / las camas del hotel
5. yo / nunca / cantar / un aria / tan larga

14-32 Antes de la gira. Form sentences using the pluperfect tense and the cues provided. Then listen and repeat as the speaker gives the correct answer.

Modelo: You see: la diva / ya / cantar / el aria
You say: *La diva ya había cantado el aria.*

1. yo / ya / terminar / los ejercicios
2. Ana / ya / escribir / el artículo
3. Paco / nunca / estar / en México
4. tú / solamente / cantar / en comedias musicales
5. antes de este año / mis padres / nunca / viajar / por avión

Nombre: ______________________ Fecha: ______________________

SEGUNDA PARTE

¡Así es la vida!

14-33 La alta costura. As you listen to the following conversation, select the letters for all statements that are correct, according to what you hear. Listen to the conversation as many times as is necessary to find all the correct answers.

1. El desfile de modas es...
   a. dentro de una semana.
   b. a la una y media.
   c. el primero de la estación.
2. El primer conjunto es...
   a. un vestido de tul.
   b. simple.
   c. un vestido de terciopelo.
3. El diseñador quiere...
   a. viajar a Milán.
   b. ver los conjuntos.
   c. añadir una falda.
4. Marguelita quiere...
   a. más dinero.
   b. que el esmoquin sea de cuero.
   c. que Óscar no coma tanto.
5. Óscar...
   a. puede ponerse el esmoquin.
   b. tiene una cita con Calvin Klein.
   c. tuvo problemas en Milán.
6. Pablo...
   a. ha comido demasiado.
   b. querría estar en Milán con Óscar.
   c. no debería haberse puesto el esmoquin.

¡Así lo decimos! Vocabulario

14-34 ¿Qué es eso? Choose the word or expression that best completes each sentence that you hear. Then listen and repeat as the speaker gives the correct answer.

1. a. el conjunto
   b. el disfraz
   c. el esmoquin
2. a. la diseñadora
   b. la modelo
   c. la gabardina
3. a. el poliéster
   b. la piel
   c. la pana
4. a. encantadora
   b. terciopelo
   c. prenda
5. a. estar de moda
   b. el modo
   c. el desfile de moda

Nombre: ______________________ Fecha: ______________________

¡Así lo hacemos! Estructuras

3. The pluperfect subjunctive and the conditional perfect

14-35 Estamos preocupados por el medio ambiente. Change the sentences that you hear to the pluperfect subjunctive. Then listen and repeat as the speaker gives the correct answer.

Modelo: You hear: ¡Ojalá tenga energía!
You write and say: *¡Ojalá hubiera tenido energía!*

1. ¡Ojalá ____!
2. ¡Ojalá ____!
3. ¡Ojalá ____!

14-36 Lo que esperaba la gente. Form sentences using the cues provided. Then listen and repeat as the speaker gives the correct answer.

Modelo: You see: nosotros / empezar / un programa de las artes
You say: *La gente esperaba que nosotros hubiéramos empezado un programa de las artes.*

1. usted / diseñar / más vestidos de boda
2. yo / cantar / mejor / en la ópera
3. tú / solucionar / el problema

14-37 ¿Por qué me enfermé? Tell what would have occurred to the following people if they had not been sick. Then listen and repeat as the speaker gives the correct answers.

Modelo: You see: ellos / empezar / el desfile de moda
You say: *Ellos habrían empezado el desfile de moda.*

1. yo / tocar / la trompeta en el concierto
2. tú / ir a visitar / al diseñador
3. los modelos / controlar / el horario de trabajo
4. nosotros / hacer / más pantalones de cuero
5. usted / ver / más del desfile de moda

Nombre: ________________________ Fecha: ________________________

14-38 La ópera habría sido mejor... Change the sentences that you hear to reflect contrary-to-fact conditions in the past. Then listen and repeat as the speaker gives the correct answer.

Modelo: You hear: Si la diva tiene un nuevo vestido, la ópera es mejor.
You write and say: *Si la diva hubiera tenido un nuevo vestido, la ópera habría sido mejor.*

1. Si ________________________.
2. Si ________________________.
3. Si ________________________.
4. Si ________________________.
5. Si ________________________.

¿Cuánto sabes tú?

14-39 En la oficina del diseñador. Explain why you and your acquaintances did not follow a certain course of action using the cues provided. Then listen and repeat as the speaker gives the correct answer.

Modelo: You see: yo / solicitar el puesto / (yo) / no tener experiencia
You say: *Yo habría solicitado el puesto, pero no tenía experiencia.*

1. (nosotros) / escribir las cartas de recomendación / (nosotros) / no tener tiempo.
2. yo / despedir al secretario / él / no cometer el error
3. los Ramírez / contratar a la arquitecta / ella / querer un sueldo fijo
4. yo / pedir un aumento / (yo) / temer perder el puesto
5. ustedes / ascender al nuevo contador / él / marcharse a otra compañía

14-40 Sugerencias de una soprano famosa y vieja. Change the sentences that you hear to reflect contrary-to-fact conditions in the past. Then listen and repeat as the speaker gives the correct answer.

Modelo: You hear: Si enciendo el fax, consumo energía.
You write and say: *Si hubiera encendido el fax, habría consumido energía.*

1. Si ________________________.
2. Si ________________________.
3. Si ________________________.

Nombre: ______________________________ Fecha: ____________________

15 ¿Te gusta la política?

Workbook

PRIMERA PARTE

¡Así es la vida!

15-1 ¿Recuerdas? Reread the interview in **¡Así es la vida!** on page 502 of your textbook, and choose the correct answer for each question.

1. ¿Qué ocurrió en diciembre de 1987?

   a. se acabaron las guerras en América Central

   b. Óscar Arias recibió el Premio Nóbel de la Paz

   c. Óscar Arias fundó la Fundación Arias para la Paz y el Progreso Humano

2. ¿Cómo continúa su labor humanitaria el doctor Arias?

   a. con entrevistas b. con visitas a varios países c. con la Fundación Arias

3. ¿Cuál es el proyecto más importante para el doctor Arias?

   a. conocer a otros Premios Nóbel de la Paz

   b. controlar el tráfico de armas a países en desarrollo

   c. ganar el Premio Nóbel otra vez

4. ¿Para qué hizo el doctor Arias un llamamiento a otros Premios Nóbel de la Paz?

   a. para apoyar un acuerdo internacional

   b. para que conocieran América Central

   c. para hablar de sus premios

5. ¿Cuál el es el objetivo del acuerdo?

   a. la paz mundial b. el control del hambre c. el control del comercio de armas

Nombre: ______________________________ Fecha: ______________________

6. ¿Qué es la Convención Marco?

   a. la reunión de todos los Premios Nóbel de la Paz

   b. un tratado sobre la transferencia de armas a nivel internacional

   c. otro nombre para la Fundación Arias

7. ¿Qué prohíbe la convención?

   a. el uso de armas en lugares públicos

   b. comprar armas a los menores

   c. el tráfico de armas

8. ¿Cómo se puede conseguir más información sobre la convención?

   a. a través de la Red informática b. a través del correo c. a través de correo electrónico

¡Así lo decimos! Vocabulario

15-2 ¡A completar! Complete the following statements with words or expressions from the word bank. Make changes when necessary.

abolir	ciudadano	ejército	firmar	pacifista
armas	conflicto	esfuerzo	fortalecer	pobreza

1. El ________________ de China es muy grande.
2. Óscar Arias es ________________ porque quiere la paz mundial.
3. Hay que ________________ las leyes contra el tráfico de armas.
4. Los EE.UU. tienen muchas ________________ nucleares.
5. Es importante ________________ los gobiernos opresivos.
6. Hay que hacer un mayor ________________ para entender a otros países.
7. Los ________________ tienen el derecho de expresar su opinión.
8. Muchos países invierten en el ejército y los ciudadanos viven en la ________________.
9. Los ________________ armados no ayudan a la paz mundial.
10. Hay que lograr que los países en guerra puedan ________________ la paz.

Nombre: ______________________ Fecha: ______________

15-3 ¡A escribir! Write a complete sentence using each of the following verbs.

1. abolir: ______________________________

____

2. fortalecer: ______________________________

____

3. lograr: ______________________________

____

4. procurar: ______________________________

____

5. promover: ______________________________

____

6. violar: ______________________________

____

15-4 Preguntas personales. Answer each of the following questions with a complete sentence in Spanish.

1. ¿Cómo crees que puede haber paz mundial?

____

____

2. ¿Cuáles son algunos de los derechos humanos?

____

____

3. ¿Qué harías para erradicar la pobreza?

____

____

4. ¿Crees que los países deben abolir los ejércitos? Explica.

____

____

Nombre: ______________________________ Fecha: ______________________

5. ¿Por qué hay conflictos entre los seres humanos?

____

____

¡Así lo hacemos! Estructuras

1. The subjunctive with indefinite and nonexistent antecedents

15-5 ¡A cambiar! Rewrite the following sentences using the subjunctive to describe an indefinite person or object.

Modelo: Quiero hablar con el señor que quiere la paz.
Quiero hablar con un señor que quiera la paz.

1. Busco el editorial que promueve la democratización.

   Busco un editorial que ________________ la democratización.

2. ¿Conoces al político que quiere terminar con la pobreza?

   ¿Conoces un político que ________________ terminar con la pobreza?

3. Hay alguien en la empresa que yo conozco.

   No hay nadie en la empresa que yo ________________.

4. Busco a la comisión que firma los documentos.

   Busco una comisión que ________________ los documentos.

5. Queremos al ejército que no viola los derechos humanos.

   Queremos un ejército que no ________________ los derechos humanos.

6. ¿Buscas al activista que procura la desmilitarización?

   ¿Buscas un activista que ________________ la desmilitarización?

7. Necesito al secretario que entiende la resolución.

   Necesito un secretario que ________________ la resolución.

8. ¿Conoces al activista que logra sus objetivos?

   ¿Conoces un activista que ________________ sus objetivos?

Nombre: ______________________ Fecha: ______________________

15-6 Situaciones. Complete the following statements with the subjunctive or indicative form of the verbs in parentheses.

1. Nuestro país tiene un guerrero (*warrior*) que (ser) ______________ valiente, pero necesitamos unos guerreros que (ser) ______________ más valientes.
2. Conozco al activista que (trabajar) ______________ mucho, pero queremos un activista que (poder) ______________ hacer más.
3. No hay ningún político que (tener) ______________ buenos programas. Hay muchos que no (ser) ______________ muy buenos.
4. Hay muchos ciudadanos que (parecer) ______________ decisivos (*decisive*). Buscamos un ciudadano que (querer) ______________ ser decisivo.
5. Éste es el líder (*leader*) que (respetar) ______________ los derechos humanos. Queremos un líder que no (violar) ______________ los derechos humanos.
6. Conozco al presidente que (eliminar) ______________ la pobreza. Buscamos un presidente que (hacer) ______________ eso.
7. ¿Hay algún país que (querer) ______________ abolir el ejército? No, no hay ningún país que (poder) ______________ hacerlo.
8. ¿Conoces al líder que (estar) ______________ contento con sus esfuerzos? No, no conozco ningún líder que (estar) ______________ contento con sus esfuerzos.
9. Conozco al general que (preferir) ______________ el desarme. No hay ningún general que (lograr) ______________ el desarme.
10. Necesitamos un presidente que (resolver) ______________ los problemas del país. No hay nadie aquí que (lograr) ______________ hacerlo.

Nombre: ______________________ Fecha: ______________________

15-7 Los ciudadanos. Rewrite the following paragraph about the citizens' search for a qualified leader, using the appropriate form of the verbs in parentheses.

Nosotros somos ciudadanos de un país en desarrollo. Buscamos un líder que (1. ser) ______________ honesto, que (2. tener) ______________ buenas ideas y que (3. poder) ______________ resolver nuestros problemas. ¿Sabes dónde hay un líder que (4. tener) ______________ estas calificaciones y que (5. querer) ______________ ayudarnos?

15-8 Anuncios. You are a newspaper publisher and you need to fill some positions. Write ads, using the information given.

MODELO: buscar reportera: hablar español e inglés, saber escribir bien, ser simpático
Se busca una reportera que hable español e inglés, que sepa escribir bien y que sea simpática.

1. necesitar editorialista: ser decisivo, promover el diálogo, lograr nuestros objetivos

   ____

   ____

2. buscar comentarista: tener contacto con los ciudadanos, promover nuestras ideas, procurar llevar nuestro mensaje al pueblo

   ____

   ____

3. solicitar secretaria: hablar bien en público, ser inteligente, llevarse bien con los otros

   ____

   ____

4. necesitar vendedores: poder vender anuncios, creer en nuestro periódico, querer mejorar las ventas

   ____

   ____

5. necesitar artista: poder ilustrar bien, diseñar nuevos diseños, tener nuevas ideas

   ____

   ____

Nombre: ______________________ Fecha: ______________________

2. The relative pronouns *que, quien,* and *lo que*

15-9 Una conversación. Two friends are having a conversation. Complete their conversation, using the relative pronouns **que, quien,** or **lo que.**

Jorge: Allí está el líder con (1) ______________ quiero hablar.

Joaquín: No sabía (2) ______________ lo conocías.

Jorge: No, no lo conozco, pero sé (3) ______________ es honesto.

Joaquín: ¿Sabes (4) ______________ está medio loco?

Jorge: Dicen eso, pero sus ideas son (5) ______________ me gusta.

Joaquín: A mí también me gustan sus ideas, pero (6) ______________ no me gusta es el consejero (7) ______________ está con él.

Jorge: Y ¿quién es?

Joaquín: Es un señor (8) ______________ es muy corrupto.

Jorge: El consejero no me importa; (9) ______________ me importa es el líder.

15-10 El líder tímido. The reluctant leader needs help with his program. Complete the paragraph with the appropriate relative pronoun **que, quien(es),** or **lo que.**

Nuestro líder es muy inteligente. (1) ______________ pasa es (2) ______________ es un poco tímido. (3) ______________ menos le gusta es hablarle al pueblo. Por eso, (4) ______________ tiene que hacer es pedir ayuda. Sus consejeros, en (5) ______________ él confía y (6) ______________ tienen sus mismas ideas, lo ayudan mucho y le dicen (7) ______________ tiene que hacer. Ellos le aconsejan (8) ______________ sea menos tímido y (9) ______________ siempre les diga la verdad. Es muy importante (10) ______________ nuestro líder los escuche y, (11) ______________ (12) ______________ haga, lo haga bien.

SEGUNDA PARTE

¡Así es la vida!

15-11 La política. Reread the speech in **¡Así es la vida!** on page 514 of your textbook. Then decide if the following statements are **cierto (C)** or **falso (F).**

Nombre: ______________________ Fecha: ______________________

C F 1. Ernesto Vidal es candidato a la presidencia de la República de Villamayor.

C F 2. Ernesto Vidal lee su discurso de un papel.

C F 3. La República de Villamayor afronta una reforma de la constitución.

C F 4. Ernesto Vidal duda que Ricardo Murillo sea un buen vicepresidente.

C F 5. Ernesto Vidal hace muchas promesas.

C F 6. Ernesto Vidal promete aumentar los impuestos.

C F 7. Ernesto Vidal promete combatir el crimen.

C F 8. Ernesto Vidal promete un país genial.

¡Así lo decimos! Vocabulario

15-12 ¡A completar! How well can you discuss politics and government? Complete the following statements with a word from the word bank.

alcalde	campañas	deber	discursos	juez	monarquía
asesora	contrincantes	dictador	elecciones	leyes	presidente

1. En una democracia, el ______________________ es el líder del país.
2. Una mujer que le da consejos al presidente es su ______________________.
3. El ______________________ es el líder de una ciudad o de un pueblo.
4. La ______________________ trabaja en una corte (*court*) y decide cuestiones relacionadas con las ______________________.
5. Los candidatos hacen ______________________ elocuentes (*eloquent*) en los que atacan (*attack*) a sus ______________________.
6. Al líder de una dictadura se le llama el ______________________.
7. En los EE.UU. las ______________________ presidenciales son en noviembre.
8. Antes de las elecciones, siempre hay ______________________ políticas.
9. El ______________________ de un gobernador es servir al pueblo.
10. Los países que tienen rey o reina son una ______________________.

Nombre: ______________________ Fecha: ______________________

15-13 Un editorial. What position does Villamayor's leading editorialist take about the upcoming elections? To find out, complete the editorial. Use the present subjunctive, the present indicative, or the infinitive form of each verb, as necessary.

Todos los políticos dicen que van a (1. afrontar) ______________ los problemas del pueblo. También dicen que quieren (2. mejorar) ______________ las condiciones de vida de los ciudadanos. Para mí, es necesario que ellos (3. combatir) ______________ los problemas más graves ahora mismo. Quiero que ellos (4. promover) ______________ unos comités para estudiar estos problemas. También, les sugiero que (5. eliminar) ______________ el desempleo ahora, dándole trabajo a la gente. Así pueden (6. ayudar) ______________ al mismo tiempo en la reconstrucción de las ciudades. No pueden (7. prevenir) ______________ el desempleo totalmente en el futuro, pero hay que hacer algo ahora. El desempleo (8. aumentar) ______________ el número de crímenes y causa otros problemas sociales. Si nosotros (9. apoyar) ______________ a Vidal, es importante que él (10. lograr) ______________ soluciones para algunos de los problemas más graves.

15-14 Las promesas. You are running for an important political office. Write eight campaign promises, using the words or expressions from the word bank.

Modelo: *Si ustedes me eligen, eliminaré la contaminación del aire.*

la corrupción	la honestidad
la defensa	los impuestos
el desempleo	la inflación
la drogadicción	los programas sociales

1. ______________________________
2. ______________________________
3. ______________________________
4. ______________________________
5. ______________________________
6. ______________________________
7. ______________________________
8. ______________________________

Nombre: ______________________ Fecha: ______________________

¡Así lo hacemos! Estructuras

3. *Se* for unplanned occurrences

15-15 Problemas, problemas. Rewrite the following sentences, substituting each of the cues in parentheses to form three new sentences.

MODELO: A Carol se le rompió la silla. (a mí)
A mí se me rompió la silla.

1. A Vidal se le quedó el discurso en casa. (a nosotros, a ti, a mí)

____

____

____

2. Se me perdieron los editoriales. (a Ana, a Pedro y a Rodrigo, a nosotros)

____

____

____

3. Se nos olvidó asistir al foro (*forum*). (a ti, a mí, a mis asesores)

____

____

____

4. A Rodríguez y a Martín se les acabaron los discursos. (a las senadoras, a la representante, al gobernador)

____

____

____

5. A los obreros se les terminó su trabajo. (a nuestros padres, a nosotros, a ti y a tu hermana)

____

____

____

Nombre: ______________________ Fecha: ______________________

15-16 Excusas, excusas. Everyone has excuses. Follow the model and use the cues in parentheses to answer the following questions.

Modelo: ¿Dónde están las estadísticas? (perder/yo)
Se me perdieron.

1. ¿Por qué no oíste el discurso? (olvidarse/yo)

   ______________________ la fecha.

2. ¿Por qué no fueron al foro? (perderse/nosotros)

   ______________________ la dirección.

3. ¿Por qué no fue el dictador a la reunión? (dañarse [*to break*]/él)

   ______________________ el coche.

4. ¿Por qué no siguió Vidal con su programa? (acabarse/él)

   ______________________ el dinero.

5. ¿Por qué no vinieron ellos a almorzar con los representantes? (ocurrirse/ellos)

   ______________________ dormir la siesta.

6. ¿Por qué no llegó la reina? (irse/ella)

   ______________________ el tren.

7. ¿Por qué no escribieron los discursos los candidatos? (olvidarse/sus secretarios)

   ______________________ a sus secretarios.

8. ¿Por qué no hay más programas sociales? (perderse/presidente)

   ______________________ el presupuesto.

Nombre: ______________________ Fecha: ______________________

4. The passive voice

15-17 ¡A cambiar! Rewrite each of the following statements in the passive voice, expressing the agent.

MODELO: El senado aprobó el presupuesto.
El presupuesto fue aprobado por el senado.

1. El dictador eliminó la democracia.

   La democracia ______________ por el dictador.

2. El presidente aumentó el presupuesto.

   El presupuesto ______________ por el presidente.

3. Los ciudadanos eligieron a sus representantes.

   Los representantes ______________ por los ciudadanos.

4. Los candidatos de ese partido ganaron varios escaños (*seats*) en el congreso.

   Varios escaños en el congreso ______________ por los candidatos de ese partido.

5. Yo perdí las elecciones.

   Las elecciones ______________ por mí.

6. La corte suprema resolvió el problema.

   El problema ______________ por la corte.

7. Los representantes hicieron el presupuesto.

   El presupuesto ______________ por los representantes.

8. El congreso abolió el ejército y la compra de armas.

   El ejército y la compra de armas ______________ por el congreso.

9. Los ministros controlaron la inflación.

   La inflación ______________ por los ministros.

10. La reina visitó el Paraguay y el Uruguay.

    El Paraguay y el Uruguay ______________ por la reina.

Nombre: ______________________ Fecha: ______________

15-18 ¿Quién hizo qué? The president wants to know who took care of the following tasks. Answer the questions, based on the model.

MODELO: ¿Se redujo la tasa de desempleo? (el ministro)
Sí, la tasa de desempleo fue reducida por el ministro.

1. ¿Se estableció un programa de reciclaje? (el senado)

____

2. ¿Se le puso la multa a la fábrica? (el juez)

____

3. ¿Se promovieron los derechos humanos? (los representantes)

____

4. ¿Se eliminó la pobreza en esa ciudad? (la alcaldesa)

____

5. ¿Se combatió el crimen en el estado? (la gobernadora)

____

6. ¿Se aumentaron los impuestos? (el congreso)

____

7. ¿Se logró la desmilitarización? (los ciudadanos)

____

8. ¿Se buscaron más fondos para los programas de ayuda social? (los senadores)

____

15-19 Ante la prensa. Imagine that you are a candidate for the U.S. presidency and you are conducting a press conference. Answer the following questions by using complete sentences in Spanish.

1. ¿Cómo será combatido el crimen durante su presidencia?

____

____

2. ¿Qué impuestos se eliminarán?

____

____

Nombre: ______________________________ Fecha: ______________________

3. ¿Qué se hará con el ejército?

____

____

4. ¿Cómo será reducida la tasa de desempleo?

____

____

5. ¿Cómo podrán ser aumentados los programas sociales?

____

____

5. *Pero* or *sino*

15-20 Habla el pueblo. Find out what the people and candidates want by completing each statement with **pero** or **sino.**

1. Los trabajadores no desean más impuestos, ________________ más aumentos.
2. Nosotros queremos elegir a Vidal, ________________ no podemos votar.
3. Antonio y Sebastián no pronuncian un discurso, ________________ que repiten el lema.
4. Mis amigos prefieren más programas sociales, ________________ no quieren pagar por ellos.
5. Él quiere ser senador, ________________ teme pronunciar discursos.
6. Ellos no piensan ser representantes, ________________ gobernadores.
7. No deseamos la dictadura, ________________ la democracia.
8. No prefiero a este candidato, ________________ al otro.
9. Me gusta Vidal, ________________ no me gusta su partido.
10. No voy a votar por él, ________________ por su contrincante.

Nombre: ______________________ Fecha: ______________________

15-21 El discurso de Vidal. Complete Vidal's speech by filling in the blanks with **pero** or **sino.**

Estimados amigos:

Nuestro pueblo busca un nuevo camino, (1) ______________ tenemos que buscarlo con más entusiasmo. Necesitamos tener más programas sociales, (2) ______________ no queremos tener más impuestos. No queremos división, (3) ______________ cooperación. No queremos más crimen, (4) ______________ más ayuda para combatir el crimen. No les pido que voten por mi partido, (5) ______________ por la democracia. Queremos una democracia, (6) ______________ una democracia que sea para el pueblo. Yo quiero que ustedes voten, (7) ______________ voten por mí. Muchas gracias.

NUESTRO MUNDO

Panoramas

15-22 ¡A informarse! Based on the information from **Nuestro mundo** on pages 526–527 of your textbook, decide if the following statements are **cierto (C)** or **falso (F).**

1. Todos los idiomas que se hablaban en las Américas antes de la llegada de Colón han desaparecido.
2. Los mayas dominaban el sur de México y partes de Centroamérica.
3. Los mayas no tenían talento arquitectónico.
4. Los jeroglíficos fueron usados por los mayas para transmitir historias y leyendas.
5. Los aztecas tenían dos calendarios diferentes.
6. No hay restos del náhuatl en el español.
7. Los incas eran expertos en la confección de joyas de oro.
8. El guaraní todavía es idioma oficial en el Paraguay.
9. Las celebraciones hispanas están libres de cualquier influencia indígena.
10. La celebración del día de los muertos representa la fusión de la tradición cristiana e indígena.

Nombre: ______________________ Fecha: ______________________

15-23 Tu propia experiencia. Use the Internet or library resources to further research the indigenous influence in Hispanic celebrations. Choose a traditional celebration in any Hispanic country and explain the origin and meaning of the celebration.

Taller

15-24 Mi programa electoral y mi lema

Primera fase. Imagine that you are running for an elected office. To help you establish your platform, list, in Spanish, your position on ten issues. The issues can be local, national, and/or international.

Segunda fase. Based on the platform you established in the **Primera fase,** create one or more slogans for your campaign.

Nombre: ______________________ Fecha: ______________________

15-25 Partidos políticos. Select a Spanish-speaking country that interests you and use the Internet or library resources to find information on the political parties in that country. Find the names of the more prominent parties and general information on the platform of each party. Then indicate which party you might favor and why.

PAÍS: ______________________

PARTIDOS POLÍTICOS PRINCIPALES: ______________________

____

____

____

PROGRAMAS ELECTORALES

PARTIDOS: ______________________

____

____

____

PARTIDOS: ______________________

____

____

____

PARTIDOS: ______________________

____

____

____

EL PARTIDO POLÍTICO QUE YO PREFIERO: ______________________

____

____

____

____

Nombre: ______________________ Fecha: ______________________

15-26 Más allá de las páginas: La inmigración. "Bajo la alambrada" provides a small glimpse of the dreams and frustrations of immigrants who try to come to the U.S. to work. There are many opinions for and against legislation to restrict immigration and immigrant rights. Make a list of five advantages and disadvantages concerning immigration. Your list should be based on your knowledge of the situation, on interviews with people in your community who are informed on immigration issues, or on information researched on the Internet or in the library.

LA INMIGRACIÓN

VENTAJAS	DESVENTAJAS
______________________	______________________
______________________	______________________
______________________	______________________
______________________	______________________
______________________	______________________

¿Cuánto sabes tú?

15-27 ¿Sabes usar el subjuntivo con antecedentes indefinidos o inexistentes? Fill in the blanks with the appropriate form of the present subjunctive or present indicative, depending on the context.

1. Busco un candidato que (ser) ______________ responsable y honesto.
2. Necesitamos al alcalde que (lograr) ______________ unir al pueblo.
3. No hay nadie que (poder) ______________ acabar con la pobreza.
4. ¿Conoces algún político que (preocuparse) ______________ por el problema de la violencia?
5. Buscamos al juez que (aprobar) ______________ leyes en favor de los derechos humanos.
6. Hay un presidente que (trabajar) ______________ para la democratización de su país.

Nombre: ______________________ Fecha: ______________________

15-28 ¿Sabes usar los pronombres relativos? Fill in the blanks using the appropriate relative pronouns **que, quien,** or **lo que.**

1. La cámara de diputados discutió la ley ______________ soluciona el problema del desempleo.
2. José, ______________ es pacifista, está en contra de una intervención militar.
3. La ley ______________ aprobaron favorece a los más necesitados.
4. No nos gustó ______________ dijo el alcalde sobre los impuestos municipales.
5. El chico con ______________ estudio está interesado en la política.
6. ______________ no entiendo es la violación de los derechos humanos.

15-29 ¿Sabes usar el *se* involuntario? Answer the following questions, using **se** for unplanned occurrences, and fill in the blanks with the missing pronoun and the appropriate preterit form of the verbs in parentheses.

1. ¿Votaste en las últimas elecciones generales?

   No, se (olvidar) ______________.
2. A Eduardo se (caer) ______________ los papeles en la calle.
3. A los políticos se (perder) ______________ el discurso que habían preparado.
4. A ti se (ocurrir) ______________ ideas muy buenas.
5. A mí se (romper) ______________ el disquete que contenía el discurso.

Nombre: ________________________ Fecha: ____________________

15-30 ¿Sabes usar la voz pasiva. Fill in the blanks to give the passive voice of the following sentences.

1. Los ciudadanos votaron por el presidente.

   El presidente ____________ por los ciudadanos.

2. Los diputados discutieron la nueva ley de inmigración.

   La nueva ley de inmigración ____________ por los diputados.

3. El ejército desarmó a los rebeldes.

   Los rebeldes ____________ por el ejército.

4. Los dos países firmaron la paz.

   La paz ____________ por los dos países.

5. El foro (*forum*) de los estudiantes decidió las nuevas medidas.

   Las nuevas medidas ____________ por el foro de los estudiantes.

15-31 ¿Sabes usar *pero* y *sino*? Fill in the blanks to complete the following sentences, using **pero** or **sino.**

1. El gobierno quería subir los impuestos, ____________ no lo hizo.
2. No hablaron de la paz, ____________ de desarme.
3. No quiero votar, ____________ es mi deber como ciudadano.
4. Apoyo las decisiones del gobierno, ____________ algunas no son correctas.
5. No quiero hablar con el senador, ____________ con el diputado.
6. La paz no debe ser un sueño, ____________ una realidad.

Nombre: ______________________ Fecha: ______________

Lab Manual

PRIMERA PARTE

¡Así es la vida!

15-32 Una entrevista con el presidente. As you listen to the following conversation, select the letters for all statements that are correct, according to what you hear. Listen to the conversation as many times as is necessary to find all the correct answers.

1. La reportera Marta quiere...
   a. hablar de su vida social.
   b. que el presidente firme papeles.
   c. entrevistar al presidente.
2. El presidente ofrece...
   a. varias soluciones.
   b. algo de comer.
   c. algo de beber.
3. El presidente se preocupa por...
   a. la economía.
   b. la pobreza.
   c. los impuestos.
4. La entrevista...
   a. es muy chistosa.
   b. tiene varias interrupciones.
   c. termina rápidamente.
5. Marta...
   a. no termina la entrevista.
   b. fija otra cita.
   c. se despide del presidente.
6. Jaime...
   a. es asistente del presidente.
   b. trae el periódico.
   c. trae agua mineral.

Nombre: ______________________________ Fecha: ______________________

¡Así lo decimos! Vocabulario

15-33 ¿Qué es eso? Choose the word or expression that best completes each sentence you hear. Then listen and repeat as the speaker gives the correct answer.

1. a. un arma
   b. un ciudadano
   c. un desarme
2. a. ejército
   b. compra
   c. paz
3. a. la democratización
   b. el esfuerzo
   c. la compra
4. a. pacifista
   b. país en desarrollo
   c. desperdicio
5. a. la democratización
   b. la desmilitarización
   c. la pobreza
6. a. abolir
   b. firmar
   c. lograr
7. a. la compra
   b. el desarme
   c. el desperdicio

Nombre: ______________________________ Fecha: ______________________

¡Así lo hacemos! Estructuras

1. The subjunctive with indefinite and nonexistent antecedents

15-34 El nuevo general del ejército. Form sentences using the cues provided. Then listen and repeat as the speaker gives the correct answer.

Modelo: You see: (yo) buscar / una resolución / promover / el desarme
You say: *Busco una resolución que promueva el desarme.*

1. (nosotros) buscar / un aspirante / ser / capaz
2. (yo) conocer / a un candidato / promover / los derechos humanos
3. (ellos) necesitar / un lema / empezar / con "Presidente..."
4. (ellos) tener / un ejército / fortalecer / su causa
5. haber / un ciudadano / ser / pacifista
6. (nosotros) querer / una resolución / no incluir / violencia

15-35 ¡Quiero ser activista! Change each of the following sentences to the opposite. Follow the model. Then listen and repeat as the speaker gives the correct answer.

Modelo: You see: Tengo un auto que es rojo y blanco.
You say: *Busco un auto que sea rojo y blanco.*

1. Tengo un activista que me informa acerca de la opresión.
2. Tienen unas armas que son del ejército.
3. Tienes un mapa que es del Ecuador.
4. Tengo una resolución que procura inspirar la paz.

15-36 Cuando era más joven. Answer the questions that you hear, which refer to your past using the cues provided. Follow the model. Then listen and repeat as the speaker gives the correct answer.

Modelo: You hear: ¿Qué buscabas?
You see: una vida / no tener / conflictos
You say: *Buscaba una vida que no tuviera conflictos.*

1. unos esfuerzos / abolir / pobreza
2. un padre / fortalecerme
3. un gobierno / no promover / hostilidad
4. un país en desarrollo / sufrir / mucho conflicto

Nombre: ________________________ Fecha: ____________________

2. The relative pronouns *que, quien,* and *lo que*

15-37 El secretario explica todo. Complete the following sentences using the cues provided and the expressions **que, quien(es),** or **lo que.** Then listen and repeat as the speaker gives the correct answer.

1. El señor ____________ llamó ayer es mi padre.
2. Eso es ____________ no me gusta.
3. Ése es el chico con ____________ viajé.
4. Verte contenta es ____________ me importa.
5. La agencia ____________ vende los pasajes es Costamar.
6. Los pasajeros de ____________ hablamos están allí.
7. Aquella señorita es la aeromoza ____________ me atendió.
8. Aquel señor es el piloto a ____________ le dieron el trabajo.
9. Ésa es la chica de ____________ te hablé.
10. ____________ tienes que hacer es estudiar más.
11. La persona con ____________ hablaste es mi hermana.
12. ¿Por qué no me dices ____________ estás pensando?

Nombre: ______________________ Fecha: ______________________

Segunda parte

¡Así es la vida!

15-38 Un debate presidencial. As you listen to the following debate, select the letters for all statements that are correct, according to what you hear. Listen to the debate as many times as is necessary to find all the correct answers.

1. La moderadora quiere...

   a. hablar de su vida social.

   b. que el presidente firme papeles.

   c. hablar con los dos candidatos.

2. El presidente describe...

   a. ideas para mantener el poder en el mundo.

   b. el proceso de las elecciones.

   c. ideas corruptas.

3. El presidente quiere mejorar los problemas con...

   a. la economía.

   b. el desempleo.

   c. el discurso.

4. El debate...

   a. es importantísimo.

   b. mejora nuestro entendimiento de los candidatos.

   c. termina con mucho aplauso.

5. El señor Montañez cree...

   a. que no termina la entrevista.

   b. que es importante controlar el problema de las drogas.

   c. en un gobierno honrado para el pueblo.

Nombre: ______________________ Fecha: ______________________

6. El señor Montañez...

   a. quiere establecer un gobierno que mejore la situación económica nacional.

   b. piensa que los asuntos internacionales deben tener precedencia.

   c. insiste en aumentar los impuestos.

7. El presidente...

   a. subirá los impuestos en el segundo año.

   b. combatirá la drogadicción.

   c. piensa en la visión global.

¡Así lo decimos! Vocabulario

15-39 ¿Qué es eso? Complete the following sentences with words from the vocabulary in **¡Así lo decimos!** on page 515 of your textbook. Then listen and repeat as the speaker gives the correct answer.

1. El ______________________ del ciudadano es votar en las elecciones.
2. El ______________________ es el gobernante de una ciudad.
3. Las ______________________ policía tratan de combatir la corrupción.
4. El ______________________ y la ______________________ son los jefes de una monarquía.
5. La ______________________ es el tipo de gobierno opuesto a la democracia.
6. Algunos gobiernos gastan mucho dinero en ______________________ y armas.
7. Este ______________________ trabaja para la corte federal.
8. Cuando no hay trabajo, hay mucho ______________________.
9. Los ______________________ ______________________ ayudan a mucha gente que tiene poco dinero.
10. La primera ______________________ de Nicaragua fue Violeta Chamorro.

Nombre: ______________________ Fecha: ______________

¡Así lo hacemos! Estructuras

3. *Se* for unplanned occurrences

15-40 Lo que nos pasó durante el día de elecciones. Form sentences using the cues provided. Then listen and repeat as the speaker gives the correct answer.

Modelo: You see: (a él) / ocurrirse / una buena idea
You say: *Se le ocurrió una buena idea.*

1. (a ella) / perderse / las llaves
2. (a ti) / olvidarse / el nombre del candidato
3. (a ellas) / quemarse / la hamburguesa
4. (a nosotros) / olvidarse / las elecciones
5. (a ustedes) / caerse / los papeles
6. (a ti) / quedarse / las llaves
7. (a usted) / perderse / los carteles políticos
8. (a mí) / caerse / el vaso

4. The passive voice

15-41 La campaña. Form sentences using the cues provided. Then listen and repeat as the speaker gives the correct answer.

Modelo: You see: los impuestos / aumentar / el congreso
You say: *Los impuestos fueron aumentados por el congreso.*

1. las cartas / escribir / ti
2. el senado / controlar / los republicanos
3. el presupuesto / preparar / el secretario
4. los cheques / firmar / el representante Álvarez
5. la presidenta / elegir / la gente
6. los candidatos / apoyar / el gobernador

15-42 Después de las elecciones. Change the sentences that you hear to the passive voice. Then listen and repeat as the speaker gives the correct answer.

1. ...
2. ...
3. ...
4. ...
5. ...

5. *Pero* or *sino*

15-43 Los resultados. Form sentences using the cues provided. Then listen and repeat as the speaker gives the correct answer.

Modelo: You see: reducirá la tasa de desempleo / no combatirá la inflación
You say: *Reducirá la tasa de desempleo, pero no combatirá la inflación.*

1. no sería dictadura / democracia
2. ellas querrían ganar las elecciones / no son candidatas

3. Mercedes no eliminó el desempleo / la corrupción

4. él no es el alcalde / el gobernador

5. nosotros no queremos apoyar a la presidenta / a su contrincante

¿Cuánto sabes tú?

15-44 En la oficina del Cuerpo de Paz. Answer the questions that you hear using the cues provided to respond affirmatively or negatively. Then listen and repeat as the speaker gives the correct answer.

Modelo: You hear: ¿Conoces a alguien que sea de Bolivia?
You say: Sí, conozco a alguien que es de Bolivia.
or
You write and say: *No, no conozco a nadie que sea de Bolivia.*

1. No, ______________________.
2. Sí, ______________________.
3. No, ______________________.
4. Sí, ______________________.

15-45 De viaje después de las elecciones. Answer the questions that you hear using the cues provided. Then listen and repeat as the speaker gives the correct answer.

Modelo: You hear: ¿Se te rompieron los libros?
You see: la libreta
You say: *No, se me rompió la libreta.*

1. los periódicos
2. la computadora
3. la maleta
4. los pasaportes
5. la cámara

15-46 Preguntas personales. Write an appropriate response for each question or statement that you hear. Because answers will vary, compare your answers to the answers that are provided. Then read your response aloud to practice communication and pronunciation.

1. ______________________
2. ______________________
3. ______________________
4. ______________________
5. ______________________
6. ______________________
7. ______________________
8. ______________________